MARKETS,
MARKET CONTROL
AND
MARKETING REFORM

MARKETS, MARKET CONTROL AND MARKETING REFORM

Selected papers
by
P. T. Bauer and B. S. Yamey

PROFESSORS OF ECONOMICS
IN THE UNIVERSITY OF LONDON AT THE
LONDON SCHOOL OF ECONOMICS AND POLITICAL SCIENCE

WEIDENFELD AND NICOLSON
5 WINSLEY STREET LONDON W1

SBN 297 76380 6

Made and printed in Great Britain by
The Garden City Press Limited
Letchworth, Hertfordshire

CONTENTS

Part 3 *B. S. Yamey*

PREFACE

Most of the papers reprinted in this volume incorporate some changes in presentation in the interests of clarity and uniformity. In some instances (papers 7, 11 and 16) the changes in presentation are more extensive and involve re-arrangement of sections and minor excisions.

Addenda are appended to most of the papers. These incorporate elaboration of specific issues and points of analysis, and also additional empirical material and bibliographical references.

We are much indebted to Professor F.W.Paish for his permission to include paper 9 of which he is co-author; and to Professor J.Wiseman for his permission to include paper 14 of which he is co-author.

We acknowledge with thanks the permission of the Publishers and Editors of the following journals to reprint articles: *The Business History Review* (paper 8); *Butterworth's South African Law Review* (paper 17); *Economica* (papers 4 and 10); *The Economic Journal* (papers 1, 2, 5, 7, 9 and 13); *The Journal of Development Studies* (paper 12); *The Journal of Political Economy* (paper 3); *The Manchester School of Economics and Social Studies* (paper 15); *Oxford Economic Papers* (papers 6, 14 and 18); and *The Three Banks Review* (paper 16). We are indebted to Dr Philip D. Bradley and the University of Virginia Press for permission to reprint paper 11, and to Kraus Reprint Limited for permission to reprint paper 15.

P.T.B.
B.S.Y.

January 1968

Part 1

P. T. BAUER AND B. S. YAMEY

1

ECONOMIC PROGRESS
AND
OCCUPATIONAL DISTRIBUTION*

The principal purpose of this article is to examine the validity and significance of the widely held view that economic progress is generally associated with certain distinct, necessary and predictable changes in occupational distribution, in particular with a relative increase in the numbers engaged in tertiary activities.[1] Our method is largely analytical; but since a strong empirical basis is claimed for the generalisation we are examining, we have found it necessary to make frequent descriptive reference to the composition of economic activity in economies at different stages of development. Most of the description is concentrated in the first section of the article, which describes and analyses the volume and significance of trading activity in British West Africa. The remaining sections of the article examine the analytical and statistical foundations of the generalisation and suggest that these are defective.

1

The few available occupational statistics of backward economies, especially in the colonies, purport to show that the great bulk of the population is occupied in agriculture. This impression is also often

---

* *Economic Journal*, December 1951, pp. 741–55.

[1] 'For convenience in international comparisons production may be defined as primary, secondary and tertiary. Under the former we include agricultural and pastoral production, fishing, forestry and hunting. Mining is more properly included with secondary production, covering manufacture, building construction and public works, gas and electricity supply. Tertiary production is defined by difference as consisting of all other economic activities, the principal of which are distribution, transport, public administration, domestic service and all other activities producing a non-material output.' Colin Clark, *The Conditions of Economic Progress*, 1940, p. 182.

See also, Professor A.G.B.Fisher, *Economic Progress and Social Security*, 1946, pp. 5 and 6.

conveyed in official statements on economic activity in these territories. An example may be taken from *An African Survey*:

In the Northern Province of Nigeria, at the census of 1931, about 84 per cent of occupied males whose returns permitted them to be classified were shown as engaged in agriculture and fishing, about 9 per cent in manufacture, and under 3 per cent in commerce and finance. ... For Southern Nigeria less detailed information is available. The returns, which are less reliable than those for Northern Nigeria, would suggest that the proportion of males engaged in agriculture is about 82 per cent and that concerned with handicrafts about 4·7 per cent.[2]

Trade and transport are not mentioned. No attempt is made to reconcile this with another statement (on the same page) that almost 30 per cent of the population of Nigeria lived in towns of over 5,000 inhabitants. In the same vein the official *Annual Report on Nigeria* states year after year that the great majority of the population is occupied in agriculture: trade is not among the other occupations listed.

In contrast to these statements and statistics a remarkable multitude of traders, especially of small-scale sellers of both local produce and of imported merchandise, is a most conspicuous feature of West Africa. This is so apparent that it has not escaped attention. It is freely said by responsible administrators that in the southern parts of Nigeria and the Gold Coast everybody is engaged in trade, and this is hardly an exaggeration.

For reasons to be explained it is not possible to give specific quantitative information about the volume of trade or of the numbers engaged in it. Certain sporadic but conservative data, relating, for example, to numbers of market stallholders and hawkers' licences, indicate that the number of selling points, including children hawking very small quantities of goods, is very large in the principal markets. But the figures give an imperfect idea of the multitude of people engaged either part-time or whole-time in selling small quantities of goods or conveying them to dispersed points of sale. In the aggregate there is an enormous amount of activity the quantitative significance of which is obvious to the observer.

The seriously misleading impression created by official statistics and statements derives from the inappropriateness of classification by distinct occupational categories in an economy in which occupational specialisation is imperfect. The economic activity of a large

[2] *An African Survey*, 2nd edition, pp. 1425–6.

4

proportion of the population of West Africa is better described as the performance of a number of different things rather than as the pursuit of a definite occupation. In many of the so-called agricultural households the head of the household trades part-time even during the normally short farming season, and more actively outside the season, whilst members of the family trade intermittently throughout the year. Even if only main activities are considered, it is doubtful whether five-sixths of the population is engaged in agriculture; when it is realised that even the head of the family is likely to have part-time economic activities and that many of his dependants (including children) are engaged at least periodically in trade, it becomes clear that the official statistics in their present form are apt to mislead.

The imperfect specialisation of economic activity is not confined to the agricultural community. Many African doctors and lawyers and almost all the leading chiefs have extensive trading interests. Government employees and servants of the European population trade part-time, either importing merchandise or dealing in merchandise and foodstuffs bought locally. The fluidity of activity extends to personal relations where they bear closely on economic life. A prominent African trader in Lagos whose children are being educated at expensive universities and schools in England includes his wife among his principal retailer customers. Similar commercial relations exist between other prominent Africans and their wives and children.

Even where the conceptual and statistical difficulties arising from imperfect occupational specialisation are fully appreciated[3] it is difficult to collect the required information on subsidiary activities of individuals, particularly on part-time trade. Africans frequently do not regard trade as an occupation, especially when carried on by dependants, and would not refer to it as such when questioned, because they regard it as part of existence and not as a distinct occupation. In many cases it may not be possible to draw the line between the social and commercial activities of, say, a group of women traders in the market. There is, however, no doubt that the commercial element is generally substantial.

Once the level of economic activity has risen from that of a subsistence economy to that of an emerging exchange economy – a process which is encouraged and promoted by the activities of traders

[3] It is not suggested that those responsible for census work in the colonies are unaware of these difficulties. But they are not appreciated by many of those who publish and use the results of their work.

– the task of distribution may require a substantial volume of resources. Much depends upon physical and climatic conditions. But the circumstances of West Africa are certainly not exceptional in requiring a large volume of distributive activity. The large number of dispersed farmers and holdings, poor natural communications and long distances and the difficulties of prolonged storage in the open, together postulate a substantial volume of resources in distribution and transport for raising and maintaining the economy above the subsistence level even at an early stage in economic development. In this type of economy the indispensable tasks of assembly, bulking, transport, breaking of bulk and dispersal may require a large proportion of available resources. Moreover, in an economy which has recently emerged from the subsistence level, some transactions are still likely to be on a barter basis. Barter tends to use more resources, especially labour, than a fully developed money economy to transact a given volume of trade.

There is in West Africa widespread involuntary idleness of unskilled labour, resulting from lack of other co-operant resources, especially capital, to set it to work. This lack of employment is a major feature of comparatively undeveloped economies which in the aggregate comprise probably over half of the population of the world, including India, China, Java, large parts of Eastern and Southern Europe and much of Africa. The dependence of the volume of employment on the amount of the stock of capital used to be a major topic of political economy. The subject gradually receded from economic discussion as economists became preoccupied mainly with unemployment in advanced industrial economies, resulting not so much from lack of co-operant resources as from fluctuations in aggregate demand or various other influences discouraging investment and enterprise. Interest in the subject has revived with the growing realisation of its importance. Very recently unemployment in the 'empty economy'[4] has brought the problem nearer home.

The missing co-operant factor (or factors) of production can be capital, land or technical and administrative skill. The type of scarcity or its incidence varies greatly in different regions and even districts in West Africa as elsewhere. But in many regions the low level of capital and of suitable administrative and technical skills constitutes the principal shortage.

Entry into small-scale trade is easy, as at this level no technical or

[4] J.R.Hicks, 'The Empty Economy', *Lloyds Bank Review*, July 1947.

administrative skill is required and only very little capital. Trade is attractive even for very low rewards in view of the absence of more profitable alternatives.[5] Women and children are also available for trade, partly for social reasons; for example, in some areas the wife is expected to make a contribution to the family's income; also there is little for women to do in the house and there are few schools for children.[6]

The type of resources to be found in trade and transport depends, given the state of technique, upon the relative terms at which different productive resources are available. In an economy such as West Africa, where capital is scarce and expensive and unskilled labour abundant and cheap, the large volume of resources in distribution and transport consists very largely of labour. As compared with more advanced economies there is a mass emphasis on labour rather than on capital. This tendency, which may proceed very far and reveal unsuspected possibilities, permeates West African trading arrangements; a few examples will illustrate it.

In West Africa there is an extensive trade in empty containers such as kerosene, cigarette and soup tins, flour, salt, sugar and cement bags and beer bottles. Some types of container are turned into household articles or other commodities. Small oil-lamps are made from cigarette and soup tins, whilst salt bags are made into shirts or tunics. But more usually the containers are used again in the storage and movement of goods. Those who seek out, purchase, carry and distribute second-hand containers maintain the stock of capital. They prevent the destruction of the containers, usually improve their condition, distribute them to where they can best be used, and so extend their usefulness, the intensity of their use and their effective life. The activities of the traders represent a substitution of labour for capital. Most of the entrepreneurs in the container trade are women or children. The substitution is economic as long as six or eight hours of their time are less valuable (in view of the lack of alternatives)

[5] The relative increase in the numbers engaged in retail distribution in Great Britain and elsewhere during the depression of the early 1930s is a more familiar example which can be largely explained in terms of reduced supply price arising from the absence of suitable alternatives.

[6] It is possible that the numbers attracted into trade in West Africa are increased because of a largely institutional rigidity in money wages. But even if money wages were to fall to the equilibrium level, the number who would find trade attractive would still be very large as long as the underlying economic factors remained broadly unchanged.

7

than the small profit to be made from the sale of a few empty containers. So far from the system being wasteful it is highly economic in substituting superabundant for scarce resources; within the limits of available technical skill nothing is wasted in West Africa.

For various reasons, of which the low level of capital is one, the individual agriculturalist produces on a very small scale. Moreover, the same lack of capital is reflected in the absence of suitable storage facilities and of cash reserves. As a result each producer has to dispose of small quantities of produce at frequent intervals as they become available during and immediately after the harvesting season. This postulates a large number of intermediaries, who, because of the high cost of capital, employ methods of transportation using relatively little capital and much labour. Donkey and bicycle transport are examples, while in some cases there is still head loading and human porterage, especially in the short-distance movement of local crops. The available transport equipment is used continuously with the assistance of large quantities of labour (subject to frequent breakdowns owing to poor roads and low technical skill).

The same phenomenon of the more intensive use of capital, that is its more rapid turnover, can be observed in the breaking of bulk into the minute quantities in which imported merchandise is bought by the ultimate consumer. The purchase of a box of matches is often still a wholesale transaction as the buyer frequently breaks bulk and re-sells the contents to the final consumer in small bundles of ten to fifteen matches. Similarly, at the petty retail stage sugar is sold in lots of three cubes, trade perfume by the drop, salt by the cigarette tin and cheap biscuits by the small heap of three or six. The small purchases are the result of low incomes and low capital, and the activities of the numerous petty retailers represent a substitution of labour for capital.

In Nigeria the small number of telephones and the low rate of literacy render it necessary for the importing firms and the larger distributors to use the services of numerous intermediaries to keep contact with smaller traders and to distribute their goods to them at an economic rate of turnover. The intermediaries reduce the size of stocks which need to be held. This is of particular importance, since the low level of fixed capital tends to enhance the economy's requirements of working capital. The large accumulation of unrailed groundnuts in the producing region of Nigeria is a familiar instance of a general problem.

The narrowness of markets and the backwardness of communications are reflected in inter-regional price differences which provide profitable opportunities for successful arbitrage (particularly in locally produced goods), from region to region. This attracts traders and intermediaries, and also makes it profitable for non-trading travellers to take part in trade, which they frequently do on a casual basis.

The foregoing may be summarised as follows: in West Africa, as in other emerging economies, the indispensable task of commodity distribution is expensive relatively to available resources; of the available resources, capital is scarce and unskilled labour is abundant; the multiplicity of traders is the result of the mass use of unskilled labour instead of capital in the performance of the task of distribution. There is an extensive demand for the services of intermediaries, and there is a large section of the population available to perform these services at a low supply price in terms of daily earnings.

2

The description and analysis of Section 1 show that there are severe limitations and qualifications to the view that a high proportion of labour in tertiary production is both a consequence of and a pointer to a high standard of living. As is well known, this generally held view derives from the statistical investigations and analysis of Mr Colin Clark and Professor A.G.B. Fisher. Thus according to Mr Colin Clark:

Studying economic progress in relation to the economic structure of different countries, we find a very firmly established generalisation that a high average level of real income per head is always associated with a high proportion of the working population engaged in tertiary industries. . . . Low real income per head is always associated with a low proportion of the working population engaged in tertiary production and a high percentage in primary production, culminating in China, where 75–80 per cent of the population are primary producers. High average real income per head compels a large proportion of producers to engage in tertiary production.[7]

Professor Fisher writes:

We may say that in every progressive economy there has been a steady shift of employment and investment from the essential 'primary' activities, without whose products life in even its most primitive forms would be

[7] Clark, op. cit., pp. 6–7.

9

impossible, to secondary activities of all kinds, and to a still greater extent into tertiary production. . . .

The shifts of employment towards secondary and tertiary production revealed by the census are the inescapable reflection of economic progress.[8]

It would appear that the general proposition of Mr Clark and Professor Fisher is based partly on analytical reasoning and partly on statistical evidence. Both types of verification appear to be defective.

The analytical reasoning purporting to sustain the generalisation seems to be based on the view that tertiary production is less essential than primary or secondary production; and that its products are in the nature of luxuries which cannot be afforded in economies with low real incomes. In essence the argument is that the income elasticity of demand for tertiary products is higher than that for the products of primary and secondary activities; and that therefore the demand for tertiary products increases relatively more rapidly with economic progress. Moreover, it is argued that technical progress is relatively slower in tertiary production. For both reasons taken together the proportion of occupied labour in tertiary production is supposed to rise with economic progress. The next section calls into question the validity of this reasoning; in Section 4 it is suggested that the statistical verification claimed for the generalisation is inconclusive.

3

The analytical basis of the generalisation of Mr Clark and Professor Fisher is open to criticism on several independent grounds of which the following are the most important. First, a substantial proportion of tertiary products are not luxuries with a relatively high income elasticity of demand; conversely, some products of primary and secondary production, possibly on a large scale in their aggregate, are such luxuries. Secondly, there may be large-scale substitution of capital for labour in tertiary production in the course of economic progress. Thirdly, the concept of the income elasticity of demand applied to a whole economy raises problems of aggregation which render doubtful any universal proposition about changes in its average value in conditions of change and economic growth; and this is particularly doubtful when relative factor prices and the distribution of incomes change.

For reasons already mentioned in Section 1 the distributive task

[8] Fisher, op. cit., pp. 6–7.

in the early stages of economic development is likely to be expensive in terms of *all* resources. A considerable volume of trading and transport is necessary to develop and sustain an exchange economy at an early stage of its development; it is an essential prerequisite for the development of specialisation and thus for the raising of productivity in primary production. Thus the proportion of resources engaged in tertiary production, notably in trade and transport, is likely to be high. It is possible that this proportion may fall at certain stages because the distributive task becomes relatively easier and less expensive in resources as the economy develops. The task may become lighter with the growth of internal security, the development and improvement of communications and the growth and stabilisation of markets, all of which contribute towards more regular and continuous commercial contacts, more intensive use of available resources in distribution and an increase in the size of trading units. These improvements are likely to have differential effects on productivity in various types of economic activity. It is not unlikely that trade and transport may be particularly favourably affected, and thus that the proportion of resources engaged in them may decline. This decline may continue until the fall is arrested by the possibly increasing volume of other kinds of tertiary products (including more elaborate distributive services) which may be called for at higher levels of real income.

Tertiary production, as it is usually understood, comprises a heterogeneous collection of different services. Some of these are qualitatively indispensable throughout economic development and quantitatively important at an early stage; others are not indispensable at all stages and are quantitatively important only in more advanced economies. The term 'tertiary' carries the misleading suggestion that all these services belong to the latter category of luxuries.

There is no *a priori* reason to believe that as wealth increases a greater proportion of the luxuries consumed must be products of tertiary activities. The durable consumer goods of the North American economies provide numerous examples on a large scale of heavy expenditure on the products of secondary activities with growing wealth. Expensive motor cars, jewellery, works of art, mass produced but high-grade textiles and hand-made bespoke clothes and shoes are products of secondary activities.[9]

[9] Perhaps more fancifully purchases of fur coats, oysters, caviare, lobsters, pheasants and orchids sustain hunting, fishing and farming which are primary activities.

11

The proportion of all resources in tertiary production will not provide an index of economic progress. Moreover, even if it did it would not follow that the proportion of occupied labour engaged in tertiary production must rise with economic progress. This proposition would be valid only if additionally it were legitimate to assume that labour and other productive resources were employed in tertiary production in fixed proportions. This would be true only if substitution were not possible in the whole range of tertiary production, or if the relative terms upon which labour and other factors of production could be obtained remained unchanged throughout the whole course of economic progress. These assumptions are inadmissible. Technical possibilities of substitution between productive resources are obviously possible in tertiary production; and clearly the terms on which labour and capital are available are certain to change in a growing economy.

In Section 1 examples have been given to show the emphasis on the use of labour rather than capital in tertiary production in an under-developed economy. An example has also been given (the trade in used containers) to show how a tertiary activity expands with a lavish use of labour to make good a shortage in the products of secondary production. Conversely, examples abound in more advanced industrialised economies where capital replaces labour in tertiary activities and where secondary production expands to economise on labour-intensive tertiary activities. There are familiar examples on a large scale in domestic services, laundry and repair services, and restaurant and retailing services, where capital equipment is now used instead of labour. The purchase of pre-cooked or prepared canned or processed food, or of paper cups and plates intended for one use only, represents an extension of secondary production to replace the tertiary activities in the kitchen. The mass substitution of capital for labour in tertiary activity in North America is as striking as the reverse substitution in West Africa.[10]

The neglect of the 'substitution effect' destroys the general validity of the quantitative law connecting society's real income and the proportion of occupied population in tertiary production. Technical progress may greatly affect the demand for labour in primary,

[10] Of course in West Africa the time may come when eight hours of a woman's time may be more valuable than the profit margin on the sale of three beer bottles.

secondary and tertiary production, the possibilities of substitution between labour and other resources and the relative supply prices of productive resources.

Changes in relative factor prices and differential rates of technical progress in different branches of production will also affect the relative prices at which different luxuries (that is, goods or services with relatively high income elasticities of demand whether the products of primary, secondary or tertiary production) are available to consumers. This need not necessarily favour the luxuries which are the products of tertiary activities. If it were true, as is sometimes assumed, that productivity increases faster in secondary than in tertiary production, there would be a tendency for consumers to substitute luxuries which are produced by secondary production to those produced by tertiary production.[11]

In any society it is unlikely that all members spend the same proportion of their incomes on tertiary products. Differences may arise either because of differences in incomes or because of differences in tastes and individual circumstances. The share of the total national expenditure on tertiary products is obviously an average for the population as a whole. There is no ground for assuming a unique relationship between changes in this average and changes in national income. Indeed, this average may well fall if the bulk of any increase in the national income accrues to members whose relative expenditure on tertiary products is below the average. In these circumstances the average can be pulled down, even though the income elasticity of demand of each member for tertiary products exceeds unity (which, of course, is by no means necessary). This is a very likely contingency in societies such as India and China, where a large proportion of the population live near starvation levels and where there are great differences in the proportion of individual incomes spent on tertiary products. If in such communities there is a general increase in productivity the proportion of the total national expenditure devoted to the products of primary and secondary activity is almost certain to increase. The same increase in productivity is likely to reduce the superfluity of very cheap labour formerly available for employment in certain types of tertiary activity, notably domestic service, petty

[11] There is no *a priori* reason why technical progress should always be relatively more rapid in primary and secondary production than in tertiary production. But even if it were, it would support Mr Clark's generalisation only if the possibility of substitution mentioned in the text is disregarded.

trade and menial tasks generally, and may thus accentuate the relative decline in tertiary activity.

A reduction in the national average expenditure on tertiary products may also be brought about as a result of other causes not necessarily connected with increasing productivity. Thus graduated taxation and social-security payments may reduce the share of national expenditure on tertiary products through their effects on the pattern of demand and on the supply price of labour.

An important practical conclusion follows from the possibility that there may be a fall in the average proportion of expenditure on products of a relatively high income elasticity of demand with an increase in income, if this proposition is extended internationally. If a large proportion of an increase in world income accrues to countries or to individuals who spend a smaller proportion than the world average on products of a luxury type, it follows that the demand for luxuries would suffer a relative decline. This would tend to turn the terms of trade in favour of the producers of relative necessities and against the producers of relative luxuries. On an international scale the luxuries would be mainly the products of industrialised countries. There is implicit in this possibility a threat to the standard of living of some of these countries. It reinforces the more familiar argument based on population increase, especially in the primary producing countries. The relative demand for the essentials of life can clearly increase either because there are more mouths to feed or because an increase in incomes accrues largely to the relatively poor.[12]

The foregoing analysis may now be summarised. Even if acceptable statistics were found which should show that the proportion of tertiary activities has increased in particular countries with economic progress, the findings would not be evidence of any necessary or predictable tendency. Tertiary production is an aggregation of many dissimilar activities, including domestic service, government service, transport, retail and wholesale distribution, entertainment, education and others. There is no reason why the demand for every one of these should follow a common trend. The only feature common to all tertiary production is that the output is non-material. This does

[12] The two cases differ in their effects. Thus where there is a mere increase in numbers average income per head must fall, and those whose terms of trade are adversely affected are necessarily worse off absolutely. In the other case average income per head must rise, and those whose terms of trade are adversely affected need not necessarily be worse off absolutely.

not appear to provide a logical category of significance in the analysis of demand or of economic progress. Moreover, on the supply side the proportion of the labour force in tertiary production depends upon a number of different forces, the individual and total effect of which is in no way unambiguously determined by secular changes in the national income. Thus any observed correlation between economic progress and occupational distribution should be regarded as more in the nature of a statistical accident than as an indication or proof of a significant economic law.

4

The empirical verification seems to be based upon occupational statistics which generally show both a high proportion of the occupied population in tertiary industries in advanced countries compared with under-developed countries and also an increasing proportion in time series for individual developing countries. These types of comparison seem to be vitiated principally on two counts. First, occupational statistics cannot take into account important difficulties arising out of imperfect economic specialisation. Secondly, the comparability of these statistics is affected by shifts of labour between unpaid and paid activities.

Clear-cut occupational classifications are inappropriate in under-developed countries where specialisation is imperfect. We are not concerned with possible inadequacies in the coverage and the arithmetical accuracy of the statistics but with their significance as a picture of economic activities. As has already been stated in Section 1 above, in these economies statistics convey a false impression of activities by concentrating on one activity of the head of the household to the exclusion of his other activities and of those of the other members of his household.[13] Over a considerable period of development many activities, especially trading, porterage and domestic service, would not be regarded as separate occupations either by official enumerators or by the subjects themselves. This applies particularly where occupations are carried on by part-time workers or dependants. As specialisation becomes more definite and pronounced and as these activities are carried out by specialists, the performers and their performance are more easily identified and recognised and their quantitative extent looms larger, possibly much larger, in

[13] It is not even certain on what criteria the principal activity of the head of the household is chosen for statistical purposes.

occupational statistics, even though in total the volume of these activities may be unchanged or even reduced.

It would seem that the classification of economic activities into three types, while superficially convenient and clear, conceals large arbitrary elements which greatly reduce its value. The activities of the agricultural producer selling his crops can be regarded partly as primary and partly as tertiary; this is particularly evident where he sells to the final consumer. Yet until they are taken over by an intermediary his activities will be regarded as primary. Where the intermediary is a member of the family the activity may continue to be classed as primary. Its tertiary character is likely to be recognised only when the intermediary is an independent middleman. Since the emergence of an intermediary is likely to reduce the total effort in marketing a given volume of produce, tertiary activity may appear to be increasing at a time when it is actually decreasing.

It should not be thought that these difficulties of classification disappear entirely in more advanced economies. On a smaller scale similar difficulties appear in the classification of the activities of different departments of a manufacturing firm or of most forms of large-scale enterprise. Again, the activities of the cobbler and the milliner are likely to be classified as tertiary when these are carried out in establishments (shops) dealing with the public. Yet under factory conditions the activities would be treated as secondary production. A classification of economic activity which is tacitly based on a particular assumed but undefined degree of specialisation and disintegration of functions appears to have little value for economic analysis or statistics. When census material is used it is more than likely that the assumed degree of specialisation differs between countries and periods.

The difficulty of classifying and comparing economic activity where there are differences in the degree of occupational specialisation largely undermines the statistical approach to the study of the relationship between occupational distribution and economic progress. There is much scattered evidence of the importance of some of the main tertiary activities in under-developed societies today,[14] as well as in earlier periods in the history of Great Britain and Western Europe, especially when the services of part-time workers and

[14] In this respect conditions in West Africa are not exceptional. The large number of full-time or part-time domestic and menial servants in India and the Middle East is another obvious example.

dependants are also considered.[15] However, because of the inherent statistical difficulty, meaningful quantification seems to be impossible either in support or in refutation of Mr Clark's generalisation, both with reference to a time series for one country and with reference to international comparisons.

The substitution of unpaid labour, with or without capital, for paid labour (or vice versa) is a form of substitution which affects the proportion of occupied labour in tertiary production and which illustrates and emphasises a conceptual difficulty present in a wide range of problems of economic statistics, particularly of indices of economic welfare. Such substitution takes place at all levels of economic progress, and not necessarily in the same direction at any given level. An obvious example in an advanced economy is the substitution of the activities of the household for those of the paid domestic servant; conversely, the household may frequently purchase the services of restaurants, laundries and repair agencies. Economic progress provides no general indication of the direction in which the shift between paid and unpaid labour will take place. Retail trade provides examples. In a poor economy the poverty of consumers does not allow them to buy in advance of requirements and to store their purchases. The tasks of holding stocks and of breaking bulk into the small quantities required for almost daily consumption devolve upon the paid intermediary. In these instances the activities of middlemen arise in response to the needs of poor consumers, for whom they secure access to commodities which would otherwise be outside their reach. By contrast, in advanced economies today housewives may store substantial quantities of consumer goods, especially of food, and may actually break bulk themselves. This development has gone far in North America. The tertiary activity remains, but unpaid labour of consumers and their own capital are being substituted for the services of the intermediary.

The examples in the preceding paragraph underline the arbitrariness of certain distinctions which are fundamental to national income and employment statistics. The shifting lines of demarcation suggest the advisability of caution in the use of such statistics as indices of economic welfare or as the basis of extrapolation.

[15] Thus there may have been a declining proportion of labour in tertiary activity in the early part of the industrial revolution with a rapid growth in factory production, particularly when allowance is made for paid domestic service performed by dependent members of agricultural households.

2

FURTHER NOTES ON ECONOMIC PROGRESS AND OCCUPATIONAL DISTRIBUTION*

1

In the December 1951 issue of the *Economic Journal* there appeared an article by us which demonstrated that the widely held generalisation linking relative increases in tertiary employment with economic progress was untenable.[1] Two of the published comments on this article, from Professor A. G. B. Fisher[2] and Mr S. G. Triantis[3] respectively, have appeared in the *Economic Journal*. Professor Fisher defends the usefulness for economic analysis of the concept of tertiary production and the validity and significance of the above-mentioned generalisation; Mr Triantis, whilst accepting our comments on the limitations of the usual statistical evidence, produces other statistics which are supposedly free from the objections we have raised.

In this article we discuss the principal points raised in these contributions. In the process we hope that our further observations may be more generally useful for the study of economic growth, particularly in under-developed areas.

2

Professor Fisher argues that the concept of tertiary production provides a 'useful tool of economic analysis'[4] which is particularly valuable 'to facilitate a clearer understanding of the principles according to which the currently significant sectors of a growing economy

* *Economic Journal*, March 1954, pp. 98–106.

[1] 'Economic Progress and Occupational Distribution', *Economic Journal*, December 1951 (reprinted above, pp. 3-17).

[2] A. G. B. Fisher, 'A Note on Tertiary Production', *Economic Journal*, December 1952.

[3] S. G. Triantis, 'Economic Progress, Occupational Redistribution and International Terms of Trade', *Economic Journal*, September 1953. (Reference to these articles will be by authors' names.)

[4] Fisher, p. 820.

can be identified'.[5] We find that this defence of the concept is not convincing. We fail to see how the classification of economic activity into primary, secondary and tertiary elucidates any economic problem which is otherwise beyond the reach of ordinary tools of economic analysis, or throws light on any problem of analysis or of policy. Our scepticism would persist even if it were firmly established that, with rising incomes, labour is redistributed between primary, secondary and tertiary production according to some recognisable and predictable pattern.

The analysis of the problems of economic change and occupational movements in any particular economy requires a search for the causes of the existing distribution of employment (including unpaid employment), and for the forces making for change or obstructing it. When the relevant facts of a particular economy are ascertained, they can usefully be analysed and interpreted, *inter alia*, in terms of relative factor prices, relative product prices, terms of trade, distribution of income, characteristics of demand for different products, opportunities for substitution between capital and different sorts of labour, demand for money income in terms of leisure or the fruits of unpaid effort and institutional rigidities.[6] The tools which are necessary are ones familiar to economists.[7] They help to elucidate the facts of a particular economy; also, they help to explain why the observed phenomena are different from (or the same as) corresponding phenomena in other economies. The fact that a particular economic activity is primary, secondary or tertiary, in the customary senses of those terms, does not seem to be relevant for the necessary process of analysis. The activity becomes no more amenable to analysis by being labelled primary, secondary or tertiary; and, particularly if it is labelled tertiary, the activity merely becomes obscured when it is treated as one of a collection of heterogeneous activities, united only because they possess a characteristic (being services) which is of no analytical interest to the economist. Moreover, while aggregation may be necessary and useful in some branches of economics, aggregation

[5] Fisher, p. 828.

[6] In the analysis of West African conditions in our article we laid too little stress on the effects of institutional rigidities in wage rates. Professor S. Rottenberg has emphasised the importance of wage rigidities in his interesting 'Note on "Economic Progress and Occupational Distribution"', in *Review of Economics and Statistics*, May 1953.

[7] Of course, the study of the changing structure of an economy may require other tools in addition to those of the economist.

19

of economic activities and their division into three broad categories seem to be wholly misplaced in that branch of economics which is concerned with the structure of an economy and changes in the structure.

It should not be inferred from our present and earlier criticisms that we do not agree with some of the main themes which are developed in Professor Fisher's writings. In particular, we recognise the necessity and desirability of occupational shifts in a changing economy, and the importance of institutional impediments to such shifts, both in more-advanced and less-advanced economies. But the validity of his theses does not depend upon a tripartite classification of production; and the concept of tertiary production is not necessary or useful 'for driving home the fundamental truth that there is no invariable natural "balance" between types of production, and that the relations between them require never-ending readjustment to changing circumstances'.[8] The necessity and desirability of occupational shifts are independent of any correlation (or lack of correlation) between tertiary production and economic progress. If anything, the tripartite classification of economic activity, by appearing to neglect changes *within* each of the three categories, would seem to hinder rather than to help in the recognition of the causes, concomitants and consequences of economic change and growth. The formulation of some 'inescapable'[9] relationship between labour in tertiary production and economic progress is apt to lead, however unintentionally, to those very ideas of some desirable or necessary balance between types of production of which Professor Fisher properly disapproves; moreover, the formulation is likely to bring about unfortunate confusion between effects and their causes.

Our earlier misgivings about the usefulness of the classification of economic activities into primary, secondary and tertiary are reinforced by Professor Fisher's recent discussion of tertiary production, notably by his reference to at least three (and possibly four) quite different criteria or approaches for identifying tertiary production, and by his observation that no 'exclusive choice' in favour of any of these is necessary.[10] When, furthermore, the classification of the

[8] Fisher, p. 833.

[9] The adjective is Professor Fisher's in a related context.

[10] Fisher, p. 829. He refers there to two criteria or approaches – income elasticity of demand for products and rates of technical progress. Elsewhere in the article he refers to the customary definition of tertiary products as services.

cultivation of strawberries and mushrooms as tertiary is supported on the grounds that those who 'defend the interests of primary producers' do not have such products in mind,[11] we may doubt whether the concept has any 'identifiable hard core of meaning', let alone usefulness for economic analysis.

Professor Fisher's reluctance to define his concept is not helpful.[12] But though it appears that Professor Fisher does not want to commit himself to a rigorous definition, he nevertheless seems to incline to the view that production should be regarded as tertiary if the product has a high income elasticity of demand (presumably greater than unity). Hence, for example, the claim that the concept of tertiary production is useful as a guide for 'recognising the "growing points" of a progressive economy'.[13] This definition in terms of high income elasticity of demand or of 'growing points' is quite different from the customary definition of tertiary production as the production of services (used, for instance, by both Mr Clark and by Mr Triantis); more important, the customary statistics of labour in tertiary production are presented on the basis of the latter and not of the former definition. Further, a definition in terms of high income elasticities of demand would reduce to a simple tautology the proposition that in a progressive economy there must be a shift towards tertiary *production*. But even then, for reasons given at length in our article, it would not follow that there must necessarily be a relative increase in *employment* in tertiary production.

The income elasticity of demand for a product is not the same in all countries; and it does not remain the same in any one country. A definition of tertiary production in terms of high income elasticity of demand for its products would require the statistician or economist to treat the same activity as tertiary in some countries and as non-tertiary in others, as tertiary in one period and as non-tertiary in another. The difficulties of international and inter-temporal comparisons are obvious. It would be purely coincidental if statistics representing the occupational distribution of labour compiled on customary

He also suggests that the 'services' might be subdivided to differentiate those desired by consumers for their own sake (tertiary) from those (presumably non-tertiary) which are necessary for primary and secondary production.

[11] Fisher, p. 826.

[12] If Professor Fisher could indicate in what ways the different definitions would serve different purposes in economic analysis, his reluctance would be more understandable. In fact, he refers only to one use to which the 'tool' may be put.

[13] Fisher, p. 827. See also his concluding quotation from Cannan on p. 834.

21

lines should at the same time represent the distribution of labour compiled on the required basis of the income elasticity of demand for products. Yet Professor Fisher leans heavily on ordinary occupational census statistics. Indeed, he writes that '. . . census records all over the world afford abundant evidence of the practically universal tendency for rising average income levels to be associated with relatively larger employment in tertiary activities *however defined or described*'.[14] This would seem to involve a degree of boldness in simplification and interpretation which is unusual even in the general field of international economic comparisons.

3

Mr Triantis's article is perhaps the most ambitious published attempt to establish the existence of the connection between economic progress and tertiary production. The main part of the article is devoted to demonstrating that there is acceptable empirical evidence for the widely held view that 'economic development has usually been accompanied by large increases in the percentage of the labour force employed in tertiary activities'.[15] He attempts to demonstrate this indirectly without relying on occupational statistics, because he agrees that 'the use of occupational statistics is subject to several imperfections and qualifications'.[16]

Mr Triantis divides services into three groups: services bought directly by consumers, services which facilitate production and public services. By referring to statistics, to historical experience and (in one important part of the exposition) to what is 'obvious',[17] he

[14] Fisher, p. 832, our italics.   [15] Triantis, p. 628.
[16] Ibid., p. 628.

Nevertheless, after stating this, he refers to Indian and Egyptian occupational statistics in support of his argument that in under-developed countries tertiary activity is unimportant relatively to primary production.

[17] Thus Mr Triantis says, 'It is obvious that activities which facilitate the movement of goods through time and space and the transfer of factors of production expand *pari passu* with the development of specialisation and exchange, which is characteristic of economic advancement' (Triantis, p. 630). This may or may not be obvious; Mr Triantis does not indicate how the rate of expansion of service activities can be compared with (and be found to be the same as) the rate of 'the development of specialisation and exchange'. But the statement, even if it is correct, does not meet the point, indicated and illustrated in our article, that an economy which is developing from a subsistence to an exchange basis may require a volume of services which is higher, in relation to national output, than the volume necessary to sustain a larger national output at a later stage of

deduces that each group of tertiary activities tends to take up a growing share of the national output as the national output increases. Then, by referring generally to statistics of labour productivity, he states that productivity in tertiary industry has been increased less rapidly than productivity in other activities. Putting the two halves together, he infers that the percentage of labour in tertiary production has risen with increasing national income.[18]

Mr Triantis avoids reference, except incidentally, to occupational statistics. Instead he makes use, very largely, of statistics of family budgets and of labour productivity. However, he fails to note that the objections which we levelled against the use of occupational statistics apply equally to family budget statistics and to labour productivity statistics. Changes or differences in the degree of occupational specialisation, and shifts between unpaid and paid employment, create the same difficulties as before.

Mr Triantis uses studies of consumer expenditure to derive the share of services in that part of the national output which enters into personal consumption.[19] According to Mr Triantis 'studies of consumer expenditure strongly suggest that economic development tends

development. The statement ignores the fact that, depending on many factors, a given increment of services to facilitate production may be associated with widely varying increments of final output at different stages of development and in different economies. Neither *a priori* reasoning nor empirical observation suggests that what may be called the 'services-content' of final output rises, falls or remains unchanged with economic progress. We would tentatively suggest that the 'services-content' may be particularly high when the rates of economic growth and of structural change (inter-industry shifts) are rapid. Such changes may be more marked in some poor but developing countries than in richer ones.

[18] The inference may be questioned. The conclusion is sound only in respect of a closed economy in which consumer expenditures on a product directly give rise to production of that product in that country. Mr Triantis recognises the point (Triantis, p. 628, n. 3). It must be stressed that the existence of international trade undermines his approach. This is obviously true for primary and secondary products which can be imported and exported. It is also true, but perhaps less obviously so, of services. It will be purely fortuitous if the 'services-content' of exports is exactly matched by that of imports, particularly (though not only) for countries which do not have their own shipping services or other services which are essential to foreign trade.

Moreover, special difficulties arise, from the point of view of Mr Triantis's approach, in economies where the export of labour is an important generator of income spent domestically.

[19] A point of detail is of interest. Mr Triantis argues (p. 629) as if consumer expenditures on 'trade-union dues and other contributions, and insurance of all kinds (except life insurance, old-age pensions, etc.)' provide an index of activity

23

to be accompanied by a relative increase in the volume of output' of services bought directly by consumers. 'Comparison of family budgets at different income levels in the same country, whether advanced or under-developed', is said to show that the larger the income the greater is the share of expenditure on such services.[20] However there is no need to examine this contention in detail. For the pattern of family *expenditure* gives an inadequate indication of *real consumption* of goods and services, and of the composition of the real national output, to the extent that transactions take place which do not involve money expenditures (that is they occur outside the exchange sector of the economy). Similarly, *money* incomes are not an adequate measure of total income. This in itself would not vitiate comparisons between patterns of expenditure in different countries, or at different times, or for different income groups, if it were true that the excluded items of consumption and output were always the same in composition and in relative importance. But it is known that there are significant shifts between paid and unpaid activities; economic development involves a change from a subsistence to an exchange economy; and it is not likely (and it certainly has not been demonstrated) that incomes and expenditures which do not involve money payments are of equal importance for all income groups. Hence inter-temporal or inter-regional comparisons of family budgets give a seriously distorted picture of changes and differences in real consumption; and this may be true, too, of comparisons between the expenditures of families with different incomes in the same country.[21]

producing services. But such expenditures represent, in large part, transfers of income. Studies of consumer expenditures do not indicate who are the net beneficiaries of such transfers, nor on what the transferred amounts are spent. The bulk of insurance premiums (excluding life insurance) eventually pay for replacement of assets and not for the consumption of services.

Moreover, it must surely be a slip to imply, as Mr Triantis does (at the same place), that expenditures on 'research' figure in family budget studies.

[20] Triantis, p. 628.

[21] The shift of many economic activities from the unpaid to the paid category and the relative growth in importance of the money economy in the course of economic development often exaggerate the growth of national income as conventionally measured. For much the same reason the conventional national income calculations tend to exaggerate the discrepancy in incomes between more-developed and less-developed countries. Attempts to make allowance for the production of services which do not enter the money economy are subject to large errors of estimate.

The shift between the unpaid and paid categories will not always be in the same

The weakness of the method of approach adopted by Mr Triantis is even more striking in respect of his use of statistics of labour productivity. To measure labour productivity in a particular branch of industry it is necessary to have data of output and of the labour force in that branch. Statistics of labour productivity are necessarily based on statistics of the distribution of the labour force in different branches of economic activity, and therefore on the very statistics the use of which Mr Triantis is striving to avoid. Thus a demonstration based on statistics of labour productivity is no more acceptable than the 'proof' provided more directly by statistics of occupational distribution – statistics which Mr Triantis regards as unsatisfactory for his purpose.[22]

Mr Triantis observes that 'in discussions about the importance of tertiary industry in under-developed countries considerable emphasis is usually placed on trade and domestic service. While these occupations might well account for a large part of those engaged in tertiary activity, closer examination might show that they employ relatively small percentages of the total labour force.'[23] This suggests once more that some of the essential points in our article have been missed, namely, that the distinction between tertiary and other activities in relatively unspecialised economies is almost meaningless,[24] and that

direction as national income increases. But in certain phases of development, and particularly in the earlier phases, there tends to be a marked shift of activity (and consumption) from the unpaid to the paid categories. It is highly probable that the inclusion of unpaid activities in the reckoning (a matter involving rough estimates) would reduce the rate of growth of national income, and, even more, the rate of growth of tertiary activity.

[22] There are further criticisms of the use of statistics of labour productivity. Mr Triantis does not discuss the difficulties of calculating and of interpreting labour productivity statistics (quite apart from the basic difficulties set out in the text above). These difficulties are acute when industry produces new products or when the composition of output changes in other ways; such changes are inevitable in growing economies.

Further, the argument of Mr Triantis is based, implicitly, on statistics of labour productivity in *value* terms (e.g. in order to translate consumer expenditures, via labour productivity data, into occupational distribution of labour). The available statistics generally refer to productivity in terms of *physical* products.

[23] Triantis, pp. 631–2. Trade and domestic service are not the only important tertiary activities in poor countries. Transport is obviously important; and this activity should include the time and effort spent in many poor countries by people going to and from work, even if they do not pay (in money) for this transport.

[24] An illuminating discussion of this subject is presented in A. R. Prest and I. G. Stewart, *The National Income of Nigeria 1950–51*, 1953.

25

it is difficult to attach any useful meaning or measurement to the 'total labour force' or subdivisions of it. The significance of these considerations is particularly obvious in the activities of the agricultural population. Many of the so-called farmers spend a large part of their time in small-scale transport, porterage and trade both during the farming season and much more so outside the season. Some members of the cultivator's family are engaged in tertiary activity intermittently throughout the year. It is impracticable to separate the time spent producing crops from that devoted to taking part of the produce to market and to selling it, or to processing it for consumption. But there is no doubt that in so far as any distinction can be drawn, the labour time involved in transport, trade and various forms of domestic service in many of these countries is a significant proportion of labour time devoted to total production, and much more so of that devoted to production for some form of sale.

4

Our article did not attempt to show that labour in tertiary activities is relatively more important or more numerous in less developed than in more developed countries. It drew attention, by way of illustration, to the importance of tertiary activity in countries like West Africa – a phenomenon which comes as a surprise to those of us who have been nurtured on the belief that labour in tertiary activity is correlated directly with national income.[25] Moreover, an analysis of the reasons for the phenomenon, together with the fact that there is nothing in economic growth which necessarily or inescapably causes a relative

[25] Most of our detailed illustrations were drawn from a poor country. Professor Rottenberg, in the article referred to above, has furnished further evidence from another poor country.

It may be useful to point to an example at the other end of the scale. Subject to the limitations inherent in occupational statistics to which we have referred, Canadian data indicate that the proportion of the occupied population in the service industries declined between 1931 and 1941, and again between 1941 and 1948. Cf. statistics presented by Mr A. Maddison, 'Productivity in an Expanding Economy', *Economic Journal*, September 1952, p. 588. The statistics quoted by Mr Maddison are of added significance as they relate to a highly specialised economy.

The declining share of transport in the national income of the United States of America during the last thirty years is suggested by the estimates of Dr H. Barger in *The Transportation Industries 1889–1946*, to which Mr Triantis refers. Dr Barger's estimates also suggest that labour productivity in transportation increased at a faster rate than labour productivity in manufacturing industry.

shift in labour to tertiary production, led us to suspect this law, and, more important, its usefulness in the investigation of economic growth.

The difficulties of statistical measurement need not obstruct the investigation of the economics of less-developed areas or the implications of their economic growth. The inability to submit economic phenomena to quantitative measurement does not mean that the phenomena cannot be understood and analysed. It is not the case that quantitative analysis and measurement are always more precise and significant than qualitative analysis and assessment. There are important problems and topics of which the reverse is true, and in respect of which it may be misleading if discussion and analysis are confined to that part of the data which can conveniently be expressed in quantitative terms. The study of economic progress seems to include many such topics, of which the relationship between economic progress and the distribution of labour is one.

Addendum
(to papers 1 and 2)

The labour-intensity of trading activity in under-developed countries reflects in part the low opportunity costs of the time and effort of large numbers of people. This does not necessarily mean that, but for their participation in trading, many people would be without any work or productive economic activity whatever. It means only that the rewards of trading, meagre though they may be, are relatively attractive to many because of the absence of more satisfactory alternative sources of employment.

The phrase we use in our 1951 paper (p. 6, above) – 'widespread involuntary idleness of unskilled labour' – is misleading. It implies that in the rural areas no economic activity other than trade is available for large numbers of unskilled people, that the marginal product of labour in agriculture is zero, and hence that the opportunity cost of their labour is zero. However, the weight of empirical evidence is to the effect that the marginal product of labour in agriculture in under-developed countries is positive, and not zero (or negative).[26]

[26] A thorough analysis of the hypothesis of zero marginal productivity of labour in agriculture in under-developed economies and a review of empirical evidence are to be found in S. Wellisz, 'Dual Economies, Disguised Unemployment and the Unlimited Supply of Labour', *Economica*, February 1968.

27

The demand for labour in agriculture and agriculture-based activities is generally not steady throughout the year, so that some of those who are engaged in agriculture during some parts of the year are available, at a low supply price, for participation in trading and similar activities at other times. Similarly, year-to-year variations in the size of the main crops may affect the supply of labour for other activities.

Conditions in large cities may give rise to considerable unemployment or under-employment in under-developed countries. Large numbers may be attracted to the cities in search of more attractive work, to escape social controls in the rural areas, or for the excitements of urban life. Many fail to find regular employment. Moreover, the tendency for wages to be set above the market-clearing level in some types of public and private employment (by wage regulation, collective bargaining or 'custom') serves to exacerbate the problem of the urban unskilled 'unemployed': knowledge or rumour of the high wages in these favoured employments adds to the attractions of the city; the number of job-seekers is increased; and, at the same time, the payment of wages above the market-clearing level serves to restrict the number of jobs which are available.[27] The 'unemployed' then swell the ranks of those who crowd the remaining sectors of the

[27] The number of jobs is restricted directly in that those established employers who are constrained to pay above-equilibrium wage rates employ fewer workers than they would do if wage rates were at the lower equilibrium level. The number of jobs in a particular urban centre with a tradition of high wages in certain types of employment may be further restricted indirectly in so far as potential employers avoid establishing enterprises or plants in such a centre.

The following passage from P. Gregory, *Industrial Wages in Chile*, Ithaca, NY, 1967, p. 105, is of interest: 'One should not overlook the further possibility that isolated cases of wage levels far out of line with the opportunity cost of the employed workers may create distortions in the locational distribution of firms and "wage distortion unemployment". The existence of a large and dominant employer in a particular geographic area paying substantially higher wages than those in other firms in the area may dissuade other firms from locating in that area (even though factor supply considerations might otherwise have led to such a location) out of concern for the wage pressures that might arise from the "demonstration effect" of the high wage enterprise. For example, one hears reports in Santiago of metal-working firms that choose not to locate in Concepcion because of a desire to avoid the potential influence of the elevated wage levels of the Huachipato steel mill on the wage demands of their own employees. Conversely, the existence of such high wage islands as Huachipato (and the major copper-mining areas) may serve to attract and retain in an area a large unemployed or underemployed labour force aspiring to eventual absorption in the higher wage employment.'

labour market, including self-employment, where wages and remuneration are not controlled or regulated and are free to find their own low market-clearing levels.

The labour-intensity of trading operations in under-developed countries is a theme of a number of specialist studies, a few of which we list: Sidney W. Mintz: 'The Jamaican Internal Marketing Pattern', *Social and Economic Studies*, March 1955; 'The Role of the Middleman in the Internal Distribution System of a Caribbean Peasant Economy', *Human Organization*, vol. 15, 1957; 'The Employment of Capital by Market Women in Haiti', in Raymond Firth and B.S. Yamey (eds.), *Capital, Saving and Credit in Peasant Societies*, London and Chicago, 1964; Alice G. Dewey, *Peasant Marketing in Java*, New York, 1962; 'Capital, Credit and Saving in Javanese Marketing', in Firth and Yamey, op. cit.; Leon V. Hirsch, *Marketing in an Underdeveloped Economy: The North Indian Sugar Industry*, Englewood Cliffs, NJ, 1961.

Reference should be made to the perceptive discussion of the practical importance of the relationship between the level of wages, the labour-intensity of industrial and commercial activity and the level of urban unemployment in W. Arthur Lewis, *Development Planning*, 1966, ch. II.

3

THE ECONOMICS OF MARKETING REFORM*

1

Statutory measures designed to control or to modify the processes of agricultural marketing or to reshape the structure of trade in agricultural produce are in force in many parts of the world. They are of three broad types. First, there are measures designed primarily to raise the returns of certain classes of producers: monopolistic restriction of supply, differential prices, and subsidies fall in this group. Second, there are various measures designed, at least ostensibly, to stabilise prices or incomes. These two types of measure have received considerable attention in the literature of our subject. In addition, a miscellany of measures designed to improve agricultural marketing have been introduced in recent decades in many countries; these include reduction in the number of intermediaries, control of the channels of marketing, delimitation of the places where transactions may take place, elimination of inferior grades of products, and so forth.[1] Advocates of these miscellaneous measures contend that they are in the interests of producers and of consumers as well. These measures have received little attention in the literature. It is with their implications that this paper is concerned.

Although the discussion is general, illustrative examples are taken principally from the recent history of some of the British colonies in Africa. In some of these territories there is a growing cumulation of official control over agricultural marketing.[2] The arguments

---

* The Journal of Political Economy, June 1954, pp. 210–35.

[1] Some of these measures may be connected with other measures designed to raise returns or to stabilise incomes. Thus elimination of certain inferior grades sometimes serves as a monopolistic device to restrict supplies, while some measures designed to improve marketing methods may facilitate the administration of stabilisation policies. But, on the whole, this miscellaneous group of measures can be distinguished quite easily from the other two classes.

[2] In some of these territories far-reaching control by statutory bodies over the level of prices received by producers is superimposed on these measures. These

advanced in support of the measures and the implications of the measures themselves stand out distinctly in the economic and social context of these territories. Moreover, since agriculture accounts for a very large part of the exports of these territories, the effects of the controls are relatively more important than those of similar ones in more industrialised countries.

There is another reason why our examples have been chosen mainly from poor but developing countries. The activities of traders and the extension of marketing facilities and opportunities have, in the past, promoted the cultivation and harvesting of produce for home consumption and export and have helped in drawing larger numbers of producers into the orbit of the developing money economy. They have extended the area of the exchange economy and have provided increasing numbers of people with the opportunities, means, and incentives to improve their material well-being. The measures under discussion bear upon the activities and numbers of traders and the nature of marketing facilities and opportunities at many points; in particular, they frequently affect the extension and adaptation of trading facilities and the availability of alternative marketing arrangements. The assessment of their desirability must rest heavily upon their effects on the process of economic growth, which are more readily discernible in under-developed territories than elsewhere.

We shall deal with a somewhat mixed group of statutory measures. For convenience of presentation, the regulations are here divided into three broad classes, though no analytical merit or precision is claimed for the classification, as follows: (1) measures which seem to be based on the view that the average farmer or peasant is incapable of making a wise choice among the marketing alternatives which ordinarily are open to him; these are discussed in Sections 2 and 3; (2) measures which reflect dissatisfaction with the effectiveness in practice of competition among traders and other intermediaries;

organisations, by virtue of their statutory monopoly powers over the export of certain crops, are in a position to retain a substantial proportion of sales proceeds. The activities of these bodies reinforce the effects and implications of the measures considered in this paper; but they are not discussed here.

A mimeographed paper by the Colonial Office (dated December 1952) lists the principal measures of statutory control over the marketing of British colonial export produce and the organisations administering them. It runs to over fifty foolscap pages.

these are discussed in Sections 4 to 8; and (3) measures the advocacy of which does not postulate either the commercial incompetence of producers or the ineffectiveness of competition; these are discussed in Sections 10 to 14.

Section 9 deals with a feature of competitive marketing which, although it is not stressed or singled out for special discussion in the literature on marketing reform, may nevertheless be a general cause of discontent with the results of uncontrolled agricultural marketing.

2

It is a common complaint of marketing reformers that unnecessary categories of middlemen are able to interpose themselves between producers, on the one hand, and 'necessary' middlemen and dealers, on the other, and that thereby the costs of marketing are raised.[3] As a corollary, reformers advocate compulsory elimination of the supposedly redundant links in the chain of distribution.

The advocates of such measures generally fail to ask the relevant question concerning why the so-called 'redundant' intermediaries are not by-passed by those with whom they deal. For the services of an intermediary will be used only if the price (margin) he asks is less than the value his customers set on the services he performs for them. They will by-pass him if he provides no services at all (i.e. if he is redundant) or if his charges for his services are excessive in comparison with the costs his customers will incur if they provided these services for themselves. Thus redundant intermediaries and intermediaries charging excessive prices will be eliminated without official intervention. This result must follow unless the parties served by

---

[3] These views are expressed very clearly in the official *Report of Nigerian Livestock Mission*, H.M. Stationery Office, 1950. Thus on p. 95 it is reported that 'the handling of almost the entire trade by a host of redundant dealers and middlemen, the frequent handlings of stock' are among the factors that 'represent for Nigeria economic wastage on a prodigious scale and in large measure accounts for the unjustifiably wide gap between the prices received by the producer and those paid by the consumer'.

Again, on p. 118 it is stated: 'There are, therefore, two, three and sometimes more intermediaries interposed between the seller and ultimate purchaser, with each intermediary in the agency chain retaining for himself as much as may be possible of the sum of money advanced to him, and each, on occasion, trading with part of that money, acquiring textiles and other consumer goods on which a side profit is taken when ultimately these goods go to form part of the price that is paid to the seller.'

them are unaware that it is cheaper to by-pass them or unless institutional arrangements prevent the more economical direct method from being followed.

The agricultural producer rarely sells his output directly to consumers. Usually there are several stages in the marketing process, and it is generally conceded that the middlemen are necessary in some of the stages. The supposedly redundant middleman must stand between another middleman and the producer, between a middleman and the final consumer, or between two middlemen. In each case, at least one of the parties served by an allegedly redundant middleman is a middleman himself. Now, even if it were true that the average farmer or peasant is unaware of other marketing alternatives or is unable to perform simple commercial calculations, a redundant middleman would not be used so long as his middleman-customer was able to see a profit or a saving in direct dealing. It is unlikely that dealers will fail to see an economic opportunity within their field of business or fail to take advantage of it.[4] Hence the knowledge or capacity of the producer is largely irrelevant.

However, it may be doubted whether the general assumption, which underlies so much of the demand for marketing reforms, of the commercial ignorance and lack of wisdom of the average agricultural producer agrees with the facts. Where economic activities are largely specialised, as in Western Europe or North America, the farmer earns the bulk of his income from the sale of farm produce. Hence he has a direct, significant, and continuing interest in opportunities in the market and will try to choose the most suitable channel of distribution. Moreover, in such economies it is usually not difficult for groups of farmers to set up co-operative marketing agencies if they are dissatisfied with the services or margins of the available middlemen.

In the under-developed areas, where economic activities are not generally so specialised, the average producer perhaps does not secure the bulk of his income (cash *and* other) from the sale of one or a few farm products. On the other hand, the low cash incomes and the often very low opportunity costs (which are low because of

---

[4] Official enquiries into marketing in the British colonies in Africa generally stress the ability of the middlemen to look after their interests and to seize any opportunity for increasing their profits. Indeed, it is a frequent complaint that in their zeal for profits many African traders are likely to resort to unscrupulous methods (for a discussion of abuses in marketing, see Section 8, below).

the absence of other profitable opportunities) give the producer a strong incentive to market his output advantageously and keep low the cost to him of discovering and examining available alternative opportunities. This clearly applies in West Africa, where, no doubt as a result of the low level of incomes and the comparative lack of other more productive occupations, Africans will spend much time and effort to secure price advantages in selling their produce or in purchasing merchandise. Sellers of produce are particularly sensitive to price differences. In the Eastern Provinces of Nigeria, for example, women selling palm oil will walk or cycle several miles to secure another penny or twopence on the sale of a beer bottle of palm oil or another shilling on the sale of a four-gallon tin of palm oil.[5] In these circumstances a redundant intermediary (i.e. a dealer whose margin is higher than the value of his services to the parties served by him) would certainly be by-passed.[6]

In these circumstances the compulsory elimination of any class of intermediaries (e.g. itinerant buyers in country districts, market commission agents, or touts) will mean that their services have to be performed on more onerous terms by one or another of the parties between whom they stand. It will involve an otherwise uneconomical measure of vertical integration and, at the same time, a reduction in

[5] The same tendency to spend time and effort in the search for the most satisfactory terms is observable in the behaviour of many African consumers. The desire to make money go further is strong. For example, in Northern Nigeria the salt marketed by a particular merchant firm commands a premium over the same salt marketed by other firms. The salt comes from the same British factory; but the firms supply their own sacks, and those of this particular firm are of slightly heavier quality and therefore ultimately make better shirts.

[6] The ready response of many East African cotton growers to price differences is recognised in the *Report of the Uganda Cotton Industry Commission*, Entebbe, 1948. The commission recommended (pp. 8–9) that a higher price should be paid to the grower if he brought his cotton to a recognised market than if he and his cotton were transported at the expense of a ginner to his ginnery. The commission considered the possibility that the suggested price difference might work to the disadvantage of ginners. It was conceivable that, while growers and their cotton were being transported by ginners, 'growers passing a cotton market might wish to dismount and sell their cotton at the higher price prevailing at the market as compared with their ginnery destination'. But the commission did not think this would be a serious difficulty, 'as the high rails of the . . . lorry would prevent them getting out and the driver who is responsible for getting them to the ginnery would certainly not slow down when passing a store market'. The physical obstacles and hazards were thus thought to be strong enough to thwart the recognised desire for profit maximisation.

the number of marketing alternatives open to the parties concerned. Both these consequences are likely to be particularly serious in under-developed areas.[7]

Institutional arrangements may sometimes deny customers the right to use certain channels or methods of marketing. Restrictive practices may prevent customers from by-passing middlemen whose services are redundant or, more frequently, whose charges are higher than the costs of the prohibited alternatives. The pressure of trade interests has led to such arrangements in the United Kingdom and in North America. There are also examples, though they are less numerous, in under-developed economies.[8] Such practices are against the interests of producers and consumers because they impede the competitive elimination of redundant middlemen and the competitive moderation of excessive charges. But improvement is not to be found either in the compulsory removal of the class of middlemen concerned or in the restriction of their numbers. Both these courses merely reduce the alternatives open to producers and consumers.

It is sometimes contended that the producer in under-developed areas is not always free to use the most advantageous method or

[7] In West Africa the advantages of specialisation of marketing functions between the foreign-owned trading firms and African middlemen are graphically illustrated in some towns. In Eastern Nigeria it is quite usual to see African traders sitting just outside the produce-buying stations of the European firms (or even inside their compounds). They buy produce from smaller traders, who bring in palm oil and palm kernels in small quantities, and, after cleaning and blending, re-sell the produce to the firms. It pays the firms not to buy direct from the small traders but to allow African dealers to carry out the bulking and blending of small parcels, as their margins of profit are less than would be the cost of supervising and maintaining a staff of salaried employees engaged in the same work.

The same principle applies in the sale of imported merchandise. The intermediaries break bulk and save resources at all stages between the first seller and the final buyer. The organisation of retail selling in Ibadan (and elsewhere) exemplifies the services rendered by petty traders both to suppliers and to consumers. Here there is no convenient central market, and it is usual to see petty traders sitting with their wares at the entrances to the stores of the European merchant firms. The petty traders sell largely the same commodities as the stores, but in much smaller quantities. It does not pay the European-owned stores to deal in these smaller quantities on the terms on which the petty traders are prepared to handle this business. On the other hand, consumers find it preferable to deal with the petty traders rather than to buy in less convenient quantities from the adjacent stores.

[8] For example, in some West African towns, market women and their associations are said to have stopped fishermen from retailing their own catches.

channel for marketing his produce because he may be forced to employ the services of a particular intermediary to whom he is financially indebted. But where the producer has a choice among a number of would-be lenders and trader-lenders, he will choose to borrow where the terms are most advantageous to him. The terms of loans from trader-lenders may be a combination of interest payments and the obligation to sell the produce to the lender, possibly on favourable terms to the latter; what in isolation appears to be a forced sale at a low price may simply represent an indirect part of a payment of interest on the loan. Compulsory reduction in the number of trader-lenders is likely to reduce the sources of funds and to make the terms of loans more onerous to borrowers. Any weakness in the position of the borrower flows from his need for a loan; compulsory reduction in the number of would-be lenders would aggravate the borrower's weakness. Moreover, any attempt to prevent traders from lending to producers on condition that the crop is sold to them would not improve the net position of the borrower; the latter might secure an apparently better price on the sale of his produce, but only by being required to make correspondingly higher direct interest payments to the lender.[9]

3

The tacit assumption that producers are so ignorant of their own interests and of the marketing opportunities open to them that they cannot be relied upon to sell their produce as advantageously as possible also underlies occasional proposals that producers be forced to take or to send their produce to specified markets or along specified routes.[10] It is to be inferred from these proposals that, without compulsion, many producers would drive their cattle along unprofitable routes or send their produce to the wrong markets.[11] Again, the

[9] It is often held that much of the borrowing by farmers in West Africa and elsewhere in the colonies is to finance occasional extravagant consumption and that it would be in the interests of the population to restrict the possibility of borrowing for such purposes. This, however, is an entirely different issue from that discussed in the text.

[10] The discussion is not concerned with the regulation of produce routes introduced solely for purposes of veterinary control.

[11] Two examples of proposals for compulsory routing of produce may be mentioned: (i) The Nigerian Livestock Mission, which reported in 1950, recommended that a large abattoir should have the sole right of buying cattle in Kano and an undefined area round it. The purpose is to prevent cattle from being

proposals do not seem to take into account the fact that, even if the producers were ignorant and undiscriminating, better-informed and specialised middlemen would buy up the produce and re-route it. This process insures both that erroneous decisions of producers do not remain effective for long (that is, for no longer than the time necessary to enable middlemen to re-direct the misdirected produce) and that the cost of such decisions is minimised. Further, if compulsory marketing routes are laid down by authority, there is a danger that the route, once chosen (even if correctly chosen in the first place), will not easily be changed even if supply and demand conditions change, with resulting costs (losses) to producers. In under-developed territories the prescription of permitted market places or of marketing routes may seriously retard the opening-up of new areas of production and the spread of the exchange economy, which in the past has often followed the activities of traders pioneering in new regions and along new routes.[12]

4

Critics of agricultural marketing often state or imply that competition among middlemen works against the interests of producers. The argument takes different forms and gives rise to proposals for a variety of remedial measures. Sometimes it is said that there are too few competitors; in other cases it is said that there are too many.

taken on the hoof to the consuming markets in the south. *Report of the Nigerian Livestock Mission*, p. 141. (ii) The Committee Appointed to Review the Working of the Agricultural Marketing Acts in the United Kingdom after the war recommended that there should be a commodity commission for the distribution of horticultural produce. One of its functions was to 'maintain a central market nerve-centre', with the aid of which the commission would give directions to producers 'as to where the goods were to be sent'. Presumably these directions were to be obeyed by the producers. *Report of the Committee Appointed to Review the Working of the Agricultural Marketing Acts*, 1947, pp. 67–8.

[12] There is perhaps one more implication of the measures discussed in Sections 2 and 3 which is worth noting. The arguments in favour of the reform measures imply that producers are unable to make sensible choices between different alternatives and that, left to themselves, many of them are likely to follow courses of action which would be against their own interests to a significant extent. These implied assessments of the lack of discrimination of colonial (and other) producers in matters which affect their activities and incomes directly and fairly continuously are difficult to reconcile with other assessments, frequently (though not necessarily) held by the same observers or officials, of the abilities of these people to decide upon difficult and remote political issues.

In some markets or areas there are only a few buyers of agricultural produce. Almost necessarily, the number of operators declines as the distance from the main assembly, transport, or consuming centres increases. Hence some producers are confronted with only a handful of buyers in the immediate neighbourhood of their farms or holdings. It is argued that such conditions of oligopsony place the producers at the mercy of a few dealers. One type of proposal to improve the position of the producers requires the compulsory centralisation of market transactions. The underlying idea is that the producer will be forced to take his produce to one of a limited number of markets, at each of which there will be a larger number of buyers than would otherwise visit his farm or buy in his locality. In this way competition among buyers is increased for the benefit of the producer.[13]

The essence of this type of proposal is to foster one kind of competition (i.e. the competition of more buyers in one place) by denying to producers access to other opportunities of selling their produce. The idea that competition is stimulated by reducing the alternatives open to producers and consumers is here driven almost to its logical but absurd conclusion.[14]

The proposal for compulsory centralisation of transactions (i.e. for standardisation of one condition of selling) is only one among several suggestions intended to promote competition by compulsory

[13] A proposal along these lines has been put forward by Mr J. Mars in his contribution to a recent study of the Nigerian economy, *Mining, Commerce, and Finance in Nigeria*, ed. Margery Perham, 1948. It is one of his suggestions that the outlying trading stations of the European firms should be compulsorily closed. He argues that there is a large element of local monopoly in their operations and that compulsory centralisation could increase the extent of competition. 'It has been pointed out that the tendency towards oligopsony and eventual monopsony is absolutely inevitable in the produce business of Nigeria if up-country stations of exporting firms remain open. If all such up-country stations were compulsorily closed down, the tendency towards monopsony would be much weakened if not eradicated.'

Somewhat similar reasoning is behind the view, expressed to and by the Canadian Royal Commission on Price Spreads, that it would benefit livestock producers if the practice of selling livestock direct to packers on the farm, instead of at public stockyards, were curtailed. *Report of the Royal Commission on Price Spreads*, Ottawa, 1937, pp. 163–4.

[14] To be consistent, Mr Mars should have advocated compulsory cessation of export produce buying in West Africa so that producers would be forced to take their produce to overseas terminal markets, where the largest numbers of buyers are concentrated.

standardisation, i.e. by reducing the number of alternatives open to customers. Such proposals rest upon a misconception of the nature of competition and of competitive forces. From the narrow definition of perfect competition in static economic analysis, it is inferred that competition prevails only where the customers can choose among a number of *identical* alternatives, that is, among alternatives which are identical as regards quality, place, and time of supply. In fact, where *demand* is not identical or uniform in these respects, competition is not promoted by forcing demand into a common mould by denying to suppliers the opportunity of adapting their product or service to the varying requirements and unstandardised desires of customers. Geographical differences are generally significant in bringing about unstandardised demands. In such circumstances competition tends to take the form of making available to customers a range of alternatives adjusted to individual circumstances. Moreover, the offering of *new* services is a form of competition which may improve the terms upon which the customary services are made available.

Exaggerated emphasis on the dangers of local buying monopolies in any area neglects the fact that such buyers, while appearing to have no competitors, nevertheless have to set their buying prices in competition with other buyers elsewhere; they cannot depress their own buying prices so low that producers (or other intermediaries) would be better off by taking their produce to other more distant buyers. Accordingly, where producers are able to get their produce to other markets without great sacrifice of time, effort, or resources, the prices they receive locally cannot be far below those obtaining in the more important market centres. In West Africa, for example, producers are sensitive to price differences, knowledge of which spreads quickly, and they are generally prepared to cover long distances to secure attractive prices. On the other hand, where producers are not in a position to undertake long journeys or to hold produce so as to reduce the number of journeys, the compulsory closure of local buying would cause otherwise avoidable loss and hardship. This measure would either deprive them of markets altogether or require them to undertake costly journeys to markets, when previously less costly methods of disposing of their produce had been available to them. This reasoning is borne out by the fact that buyers in outlying areas are voluntarily supported by sufficient producers to keep them in business. Even if there is only one buyer in a particular locality, the margin for his services is limited by the ease of entry of competitors into small-scale trading.

The compulsory centralisation of trading may itself promote monopoly practices. Where all dealers and transactions are concentrated, it becomes easier for dealers to form market-sharing or price agreements, provided that they are not too numerous and that entry of new competitors is not easy. It is significant that in some industries effective price agreements require a high degree of standardisation of products and conditions of sale.[15]

The proposal to defeat oligopsony by centralising transactions extols competition and aims at improving it. Other reformers, recognising that there may be few dealers in some areas, incline to the view that effective competition is impossible in the circumstances and propose that local monopolies should be established to operate under strict government control. The view is that if there must be monopoly, it should be a controlled and supervised monopoly. Similar proposals emerge from a quite different chain of reasoning; for a discussion of the economics of these proposals see Section 6, below.

5

The reform of marketing is often urged on the grounds that there are too many competing middlemen and that their competition is not to the best advantage of the producers. This complaint is made not only against the competition of traders but also against that of the first processors of agricultural produce, e.g. the owners of slaughter-houses or of cotton ginneries. The argument takes two forms: first, if there are many competitors, competition is too severe, and this leads to the payment of excessively or uneconomically high prices to producers; second, if there are many competitors, competition is wasteful, and this leads to the payment of unnecessarily low prices to producers.[16] The two forms of the argument are often combined; moreover, each gives rise to the same proposals for reform, namely, that the number of intermediaries (dealers or processors) should be reduced in the interests of producers and that the margins for their services should be controlled.

[15] For example, this seems to be true of the basing-point system. Cf. also P. T. Bauer, 'Concentration in Tropical Trade: Some Aspects and Implications of Oligopoly', pp. 201 to 224, below.

[16] It is often said that excessive competition forces dealers or processors to cheat producers more scandalously and persistently; on this, see below, Section 8.

In recent years it has been frequently and influentially argued that severe competition among intermediaries results, or may result, in bankruptcies among them, with adverse effects on the producers. This argument has been advanced in support of compulsory limitation of the number of intermediaries and/or prescription of *minimum* margins for the performance of their services.[17] Yet producers can only benefit from increased competition for their crop. If some buyers go bankrupt through paying excessively high prices, this cannot harm the producers who have received these prices.[18] Further, as long as entry is free, there is no danger that the surviving merchants or processors will subsequently be able to exploit producers. There is no need to insure a supply of the services of the intermediaries either by protecting a number of them by means of statutory control of numbers or by prescribing *minimum* margins for their services. On the other hand, if the entry of new firms is difficult because of high costs of establishment or similar obstacles, competition is not likely to be severe; and there is no need for official measures to protect the established firms by statutory barriers to new entry.[19]

Compulsory reduction in the number of intermediaries to raise their returns increases the supply prices of their services and thus harms the producers whose services are in joint demand with those of the intermediaries. In contrast, a reduction in the number of intermediaries as a result of competition implies the survival of those who offer the services at a lower supply price, which is to the advantage of producers.

[17] The pre-war agricultural marketing schemes of Great Britain provide examples of such measures, notably in the marketing of milk, potatoes, and pigs, in which the number of middlemen was restricted and/or minimum margins were prescribed by statutory organisations of producers. Some of these measures are reviewed in two articles by P.T.Bauer, 'The Fixing of Retail Milk Prices', *Manchester School*, October 1939 and 'The Failure of the Pigs Marketing Scheme', ibid., April 1941.

Compulsory restriction of the number of intermediaries is a prominent feature in the marketing of cotton in Uganda. Some of these measures are discussed in the *Report of the Uganda Cotton Commission*, Entebbe, 1939.

[18] Unless producers are the creditors of bankrupt intermediaries. But strong competition among buyers means that there will be many buyers willing to pay cash in the struggle for supplies.

[19] It is conceivable that price competition may be severe in oligopolistic markets, even when new entry is difficult. But the competition which, in the past, has given rise to the type of view examined in this section does not resemble the price wars of such oligopolistic markets.

The more common version of the case against so-called 'excessive competition' is that each competitor is unable to obtain sufficient supplies to keep his plant operating at lowest average cost. This, it is argued, means that competitors are forced to pay producers less than the economic price, so that each can have a larger margin per unit of his limited output to meet the higher unit overhead costs brought about by unnecessary multiplication of facilities. It is never quite clear why this situation does not lead to a bidding-up of producer prices in the struggle of each competitor to get closer to his optimum rate or scale of operations, and why this should not lead to the elimination of redundant intermediaries. The events which usually give rise to demands for limiting the number of competitors tend to support the view that excessive competition serves to raise producer prices rather than to depress them.

Generally, if there were significant economies in the operation of fewer and larger buying posts, abattoirs, or ginneries, the interests of traders or processors and the responsiveness of producers to higher prices would promote a market structure comprising a few large establishments, without the need for compulsion. If there were substantial economies, intermediaries operating on a larger scale would be able to offer higher prices for produce. In practice, they would be prepared to pay the higher prices to attract supplies, even though their current rate of purchases might temporarily be below the rate at which the full economies are secured. They would be prepared to absorb the costs of growth if substantial economies were in prospect. The action of intermediaries and producers would tend to bring about a situation in which the possibilities of economies were appropriately balanced with producers' valuations of marketing convenience and the availability of a range of alternatives. Those who advocate the compulsory restriction of numbers in the interests of the economies of operations at optimum rates of output seem to betray some lack of confidence in the premises on which their schemes are based.

6

Where competition is said to work against the interests of producers for the reasons discussed in Section 5, it is usually proposed that the number of competitors should be reduced by state action. The extreme version of such proposals requires the establishment of zonal monopolies.[20] Here the limiting case of the zonal monopoly will be considered. The discussion will throw into clear relief the issues which are involved. The reader will readily be able to allow for the necessary qualifications when numbers are restricted less rigorously.

The establishment and supervision of zonal monopolies raise problems of their own, which tend to negative the superficial attractiveness which such systems present because of their ostensible tidiness, orderliness, and amenability to official control. The absence of the spur of actual or potential competition and the costs and inconvenience of supervision[21] are likely to offset any small economies that may result from compulsory zoning. In under-developed areas a system of zonal purchasing monopolies might also imply either local monopolies in the sale of imported merchandise or a duplication of facilities for the purchase of produce and for the sale of merchandise which would offset or more than offset any theoretical saving in resources. In any event, there would be a reduction in the facilities available to the population which would impose inconvenience and possible hardship on some producers (and consumers). It would also greatly increase the feeling of dependence of customers on whichever firm was selected as the zonal monopolist.[22]

As a corollary of the existence of a zoning system, it would be necessary for government to attempt to control the level of costs and profits of the zonal monopolists. The necessary calculations would

[20] For example, the Nigerian Livestock Mission of 1950 recommended that a proposed body should be endowed with a monopoly in the purchase of livestock in Kano and the surrounding area.

[21] Two kinds of supervision would be involved. The zonal monopolist would have to be regulated by the authorities, in an attempt to prevent the abuse of monopoly power; and the local clerks and employees of the monopolist would have to be supervised much more closely by responsible officers, to prevent their clerks from exploiting the producers who, *ex hypothesi*, cannot remove their custom if they are dissatisfied with their treatment.

[22] A high degree of dependence on one or a few traders may be the source of serious social and political dangers and disadvantages, particularly in under-developed areas, where the traders are frequently members of expatriate or migrant communities. For a detailed discussion see P.T.Bauer, 'Concentration in Tropical Trade: Some Aspects and Implications of Oligopoly', pp. 201 to 224, below.

The *Report of the Uganda Cotton Industry Commission*, 1948, recognises (p. 9) that East African cotton growers do not feel satisfied if they have no choice of buyers: 'Although there is a fixed price for their cotton, they feel that they are more likely to get a square deal if they have the opportunity of going elsewhere if dissatisfied.'

pose difficult problems of assessment and allocation of costs and revenue; for the calculations would often have to refer to a small part of the interrelated activities of large organisations engaged in a great variety of geographically dispersed and dissimilar lines of business. In practice, even in the simplest cases, official allowances for costs and profits tend to be wide of the mark. The allowances are prone to be generous; indeed, they cannot err on the side of under-estimate, since the desired services would then not be provided. Under competitive conditions overgenerous allowances are competed away in favour of the parties between whom the intermediaries operate. With zonal monopolies, however, any additional profits or savings in cost would not be passed on to customers but would be retained by the monopolist.[23]

If the interests of producers are to be protected, it is necessary for the type of service provided by the zonal monopolist to be defined and its supply supervised. If this is not done, the monopolist may reduce his services to cut his costs, even though this action would put a disproportionate burden of costs on the producers. This is more likely to happen if government officials are prone to judge efficiency in terms of the level of costs. Alternatively, the monopolist may tend to improve or elaborate his services and so raise his costs and the price paid by producers for the services. This is likely to happen if there is confusion of technical or operational excellence with economic efficiency. However, if the type of service to be

[23] A West African example is described in our article, 'Competition and Prices: A Study of Groundnut Marketing in Nigeria', pp. 69 to 81, below. It is shown that in recent years intermediaries in the groundnut trade have frequently competed away a substantial part of their allowances for transporting the product which were based on officially calculated transport costs.

Where a licensing system permits several intermediaries to remain in business, it may be thought that their competition would obviate the necessity for official control or profits. But where numbers are limited and new entry is excluded or controlled, it becomes easy for the competitors to conclude price or market-sharing agreements. Hence profit control may remain necessary. In Uganda, where the number of cotton ginneries is controlled and where margins are fixed by the government, *licensed* ginneries command a high market value. This indicates that neither the official control of margins nor the remaining competition is effective in eliminating the monopoly values conferred by licensing. Moreover, where numbers are reduced and controlled, competition frequently raises costs in a manner which would not occur if there were freedom of entry. For example, in Uganda there is a good deal of cross-hauling of cotton by competing ginners. It is difficult to identify and to exclude such costs when the official margins are calculated.

supplied is laid down and controlled, marketing arrangements may become inflexible and fail to be adapted to changing needs – particularly as producers with new or changing needs will not be able to express their requirements in the most effective manner, that is, by removing their custom to more amenable suppliers. The dangers of a rigid system of marketing facilities and the costs of inflexibility are likely to be very high in territories in which the area of cultivation is still extending and in which large areas have not yet been integrated (or fully integrated) with a developing market economy. The cost, in terms of frustrated development, may not be visible or measurable. Finally, detailed official control of the type of service rendered by the zonal monopolists cannot take account of the (possibly widely) divergent needs and requirements of different producers. Those who prefer more (or less) service at higher (or lower) prices are precluded from satisfying their needs or preferences. At best, producers are likely to be offered no more than a few alternatives.

In addition to these effects of the establishment of zonal monopolies on the position of producers as customers of the zonal monopolist, there are also the effects of any organised (especially statutory) restriction of numbers on the potential competitors of the monopolist or protected group of firms. The establishment of a monopoly may bear harshly on those whose entry into the monopolised activity is barred and who may have to content themselves with less preferred alternatives. In many countries, and more particularly in the so-called 'under-developed' world, the potential entrants into trade are frequently agriculturalists. The produce buyer or village trader is quite often the farmer who thinks it worth while to collect and market his neighbours' produce or to cater to their simple requirements. Trading intermediaries are often members or former members of the agricultural community. Thus the establishment of zonal monopolies is likely to harm some producers not only in their capacity as customers of the monopolist but also as potential entrants into trade.

7

It may seem that many of the difficulties enumerated in the preceding section could be avoided if producer-controlled organisations were appointed as the zonal monopolists.[24] When a producers' agency is

[24] Producer-controlled marketing monopolies are frequently advocated for a variety of reasons and not only to secure the alleged economies of zonal purchas-

the zonal monopolist, it may appear as if the interests of the producers and those of the trader or processor (monopolist) are identical. However, in practice, the harmony of interests is not easily established or maintained. Those managing the monopoly are likely to regard their organisation as an end in itself, with interests possibly different from, and even antagonistic to, those of the majority of producers. The divergence of interests and outlook between the administrators of large organisations and their unorganised and often uninformed constituents is a conspicuous feature of modern economic organisation in large-scale public and private enterprise and labour organisation. It is all the more remarkable that this dichotomy of interests is so frequently disregarded in proposals for marketing reform in immature societies, in which the detailed and democratic control by producers over the administrators of the organisations supposed to be acting on their behalf is likely to be feeble and in which a check on the formulation of policy and economy of operations is likely to be absent or weak. Where such organisations are endowed with statutory monopoly powers, a further check is removed, in that dissatisfied constituents cannot transfer their custom elsewhere. At the same time, new entrants cannot expose the possible inefficiency of the organisation or the feasibility of other more attractive price and marketing policies.

Moreover, it is not correct to assume or to imply that the interests of all producers of a particular product are necessarily the same. The producer-constituents of a marketing organisation are likely to have conflicting views on many matters. These include the determination of prices for different grades of the same product; the question of whether each producer should bear his own transport costs or whether these costs should be averaged; the distribution of representation on the governing body; the timing of payments to producers; and the types of marketing service to be provided. The specific policies adopted by an organisation are certain to affect some of its constituents less favourably than others; those who feel that their interests are adversely affected relative to those of their fellow-producers are unable to seek better treatment elsewhere.

ing organisations or of 'rationalised' marketing generally. It is perhaps significant that in the 1930s British farmers did not take advantage of legislation which facilitated the establishment of producer-controlled marketing organisations with statutory powers until the enabling legislation was amended so as to allow for restrictions on the importation of competing supplies.

These considerations suggest that the objections to the establishment of zonal monopolies listed in Section 6 largely apply also to producer-controlled monopolies. These organisations are open to a further objection when they control a large share of the market supply of the product. Here the monopolist-buyer is also a monopolist-seller, and there is an obvious possibility that consumers may be exploited. This danger is often overlooked because the divergence of interests between different sections of the population is not recognised. The danger that the monopoly powers will be used to the detriment of consumers is obvious where the actual producer-constituents are in effective control of their organisation. But it is likely to be present even where the policy of the organisation is effectively directed by its permanent administrators. The latter may wish to justify the organisation to their producer-constituents by selling at high prices; moreover, if costs are inflated as the result of the operation of the monopoly, the administrator will have a direct incentive to take advantage of the selling monopoly.

Proposals for the establishment of zonal monopolies, especially of producer-controlled monopolies, are sometimes advanced to redress alleged inequalities of bargaining power. It is implied that producers, being more numerous and individually less wealthy than merchants, suffer from an inherent selling weakness which causes them to dispose of their produce at lower prices than are warranted by market conditions. It is therefore advocated that their bargaining power should be increased by collective action or, alternatively, that the right to buy should be confined to a single organisation specifically charged with the duty of safeguarding producer interests or to one which is officially supervised and controlled for that purpose.

Such proposals overlook several important considerations. Where several buyers act independently, their competition will insure that producers receive prices in line with market conditions, even though producers are far more numerous than traders and operate on a far smaller individual scale. Under West African conditions even a small number of buyers appears to be sufficient to ensure that producers receive such prices.[25] Even if there are a few buyers, they may still have to pay prices not much out of line with commercial values (as governed by the prices they themselves secure) as long as entry of

[25] This is borne out by the operation of competition in the purchase of groundnuts in Nigeria; see pp. 69 to 81, below.

new buyers is easy; in such conditions any attempt to depress producer prices would be upset by the competing offers of new buyers. In other words, bargaining power – that is, the ability of sellers to secure the full market value for their produce – depends primarily on access to independent alternatives and not on differences in wealth between sellers and buyers. Moreover, even if there are only a few buyers and the possibility of new entry is limited, it does not follow that the position of the actual producers would be improved by the establishment of producer-controlled or other zonal monopolies. As has already been shown, the disadvantages inherent in monopoly buying are not automatically or necessarily removed by changing the organisation of the monopoly or by providing for its official supervision and control.

8

Criticisms of so-called 'excessive competition' among middlemen are often supported by the view that such competition forces middlemen to cheat producers more scandalously. Abuses, such as the use of false weights, feature prominently in discussions of marketing reform, particularly in the under-developed areas; official supervision of transactions or the establishment of producer-controlled statutory marketing monopolies is recommended to protect the producer against such practices.[26] Here both the diagnosis of the effects of abuses and the wisdom of the remedy are questioned. The discussion relates to marketing in under-developed areas.

Where there is competition among middlemen and where new competitors are able to enter the market without difficulty, their gross-profit margins and their earnings are closely determined by the level of rewards obtainable by them in other available occupations, such as small-scale retailing. Earnings, whether from fair trading or improper practices, cannot remain long above this level; competition among the existing traders or from new entrants soon reduces margins. Competition forces buyers to pass on the equivalent of illicit gains to the producers; for example, if debased weights are used, under competitive conditions buyers would be forced to offer

[26] An uncompromising and influential discussion of abuses in marketing and of their effects is in the *Report of the Commission on the Marketing of West African Cocoa*, Cmd. 5845, 1938. The relevant portion of this report was reproduced in the British government White Paper on *The Future Marketing of West African Cocoa*, Cmd. 6950, 1946, which announced the establishment of statutory export monopolies in the West African cocoa trade.

correspondingly higher prices per debased unit in their search for business.[27] From the producer's point of view the result is the same as if he had received payment for the full weight at a lower price per unit.

In general, it does not much matter whether or not producers or consumers themselves are familiar with standard weights and measures. The individual producer is concerned with sales of specific lots of produce, and he will endeavour to obtain price offers for such lots from itinerant traders and/or from traders at one or more trading centres. Even though ignorant of weights, the producer is able to judge which is the most favourable offer. The conclusion is not substantially affected in circumstances in which the producer does not receive several offers simultaneously for the same lot of produce; his knowledge of his trading opportunities is widened by his contact over time with different traders and the treatment and terms offered by each. The ability to make such comparisons and the competition of buyers ensure that producers tend to receive competitive prices for their produce, irrespective of apparent abuses.[28] The ultimate incidence of the alleged abuses tends to be neither on the producers nor on the ultimate buyers of the produce; paradoxically, the illicit gains to middlemen from the use of false weights (for example) are more apparent than real.

On the other hand, the producer is liable to exploitation where he has no choice of buyers and is forced to deal with a sole buyer or a concerted group of buyers, whose monopoly position is protected from competition by barriers in the way of new entry.[29] Here again the question of abuses is largely irrelevant; for, by one means or another, the monopolist will continue to pay an effective price just sufficient to elicit the supply he desires. It is of little consequence

[27] A trader 'inventing' a new type of abuse may secure temporary abnormal gains until his competitors and/or customers become familiar with the new practice. This is unlikely to be significant in an activity such as produce buying.

[28] The protection afforded by experience over time is not available where the buyer or seller enters the market only at long intervals. This situation does not apply to the agricultural producer. Even where dealings are intermittent, the buyer or seller can safeguard himself somewhat by dealing with traders of good repute in the market. However, there is a case for government intervention to make abuses more difficult in such cases. Few economists would deny the wisdom of legislative safeguards against the abuses of share-pushing, for example.

[29] If there is only one buyer but new entry is easy, the buyer will have to pay a price of approximately the same level as would prevail if more buyers were actually operating.

whether this effective price is expressed in terms of standard or of debased weights. In both cases the returns to the producers will be less than the competitive returns.

The discussion suggests that statutory measures to prevent specific abuses are unnecessary under competition and likely to be ineffective under monopoly. In produce buying in under-developed areas the situation is usually a mixture of competitive and monopolistic elements. Accordingly, the statutory measures for the elimination of abuses are partly unnecessary and partly ineffective.

Measures to eliminate specific abuses are likely to be costly and may themselves contain strong possibilities of abuse to the detriment of producers. Most of these measures postulate the establishment and maintenance of expensive control, supervisory, and inspecting staff. The administrative costs can be reduced by requiring all transactions to take place at a limited number of centres, at which the necessary supervisory services are provided. But here the costs are merely transferred to the producer or the smaller trader who has to travel longer distances to market. Moreover, the inspecting staff generally consists of large numbers of petty officials with extensive powers over the activities of traders and producers. They are therefore in a position to abuse their powers for their own profit. Such abuses, however, differ greatly from abuses in competitive markets, in that their fruits will not be competed away in favour of producers. And the backwardness of the producers tends to deprive them of the opportunity of obtaining redress from higher authority.[30]

The foregoing discussion is not meant to deny that it is generally desirable that traders should be honest, that fraud should be punished and that standard weights and measures should be used. It shows that competition among traders safeguards the interests of producers even if traders resort to sharp practices and that in some circumstances the elimination of specific abuses may be ineffective as well as disproportionately costly.[31]

9

In preceding sections the case for a variety of marketing reforms has been questioned on the ground, *inter alia*, that competition among intermediaries protects the interests of producers. It is necessary to

[30] Experience in the operation of compulsory inspection and grading of Nigerian export produce is discussed below in Section 14.

[31] The Uganda Cotton Industry Commission, 1948, reported (p. 15) as follows: 'The buying of seed cotton takes place either at ginneries or at stores situated at

look at this general proposition more closely and to deal with a specific omission.

At any moment of time the activities, offers, and transactions of buyers in a competitive trade may be conceived of as forming part of a process of experimentation and movement leading toward the equilibrium price which is 'justified' by existing supply and demand conditions. Until this equilibrium is reached, competing traders may be offering different prices for the same goods in the same circumstances; or the differences in the prices offered for differing goods in the same or different circumstances may not be the same as the price differentials justified by the given supply and demand conditions. Some price offers may be 'too high', others 'too low'. Discrepancies will tend to be reduced as equilibrium is approached. But as the details of supply and demand change all the time, the scope for the emergence of discrepancies is continuous.

Generally, knowledge of alternatives and luck determine the particular point on the path to equilibrium at which a particular seller disposes of his produce. The producer cannot offer his goods to all buyers at the same time; he cannot know full details of the changing offers of all accessible buyers; and, having taken his produce to one buyer or place, he cannot, without cost, transfer it to some otherwise more advantageous alternative. Thus some producers receive overpayments and others underpayments, as compared with the (theoretically) justified or equilibrium price. The spontaneity of price adjustments in theoretical models and the device of recontracting are absent in workaday agricultural markets. While competition, in the long run, safeguards the average returns to producers as a whole, the returns to individual producers are affected by skill in marketing or by good or bad fortune, even if buying is competitive.

the various buying centres away from the ginneries. We are satisfied by the evidence that cheating takes place both at ginneries and at stores, but, that it is more prevalent at ginneries since there is little or no competition between buyers and also there is more rush and crowding. In fact wherever we have been we have heard bitter complaints by growers of the manner in which buyers deliberately keep them waiting until late in the day, when a huge crowd assembled and in the rush and scramble to get their cotton sold in time to go home before dark the growers are easily swindled.' Clearly, where there are several competing buyers, dissatisfied growers need not put up with delaying tactics of individual buyers. This quotation supports the analysis in the text. The commission went on to note that officers appointed to stop cheating 'are frequently bribed to look the other way', which again bears out the argument in the text.

The significance of the discrepancies between competitive price offers and the (theoretical) equilibrium price is likely to be greatest where short-period fluctuations in supply and demand are frequent, where producers are widely dispersed, and where transport and communications facilities are poor. The discrepancies are therefore likely to be prevalent in agricultural markets generally; in such markets in under-developed areas they are likely to be particularly common.

It may be argued that the overpayments and underpayments (as defined here) of competitive markets constitute a defect and that the workings of such markets are the cause of an additional class of risk.[32] This line of reasoning is likely to appeal to reformers with strong egalitarian leanings; such reformers may feel that all producers in the same situation should be treated alike and that rewards and penalties should not be left to chance or depend upon the possession of particular marketing skills and knowledge.[33] It is not improbable that such sentiments may be shared by many producers as well.

The practical question is, How much weight should be given to the particular point raised in this section? This is a matter of judgment, of weighing advantages against disadvantages. In our view the indicated disadvantage of competition is not significant when compared with the general benefits of competitive trading and with the drawbacks and dangers which attach to alternative systems of controlled or regulated marketing or controlled monopoly buying. This judgment applies with special force to conditions in the under-developed areas. Here the benefits of competitive trading and the drawbacks of regulated marketing are likely to be marked. Thus in conditions in which the price discrepancies are greatest, their significance is, in our opinion, overshadowed by these other more important considerations.

The underpayments and overpayments arising out of the price discrepancies effect a redistribution of a total return among the individual producers. The safeguarding or raising of the total seems to

[32] The individual producer can to some extent reduce his risks by having stable and continuous trading relations with a particular buyer. On the other hand, if the tie is too close or permanent, the beneficent effects of competition may be weakened.

[33] In our discussion of abuses in marketing we showed that in competitive conditions illicit gains are competed away in favour of customers. But those producers who are particularly ignorant or gullible are likely to be losers in the short run as well as in the long run.

be more important than the achievement of what may be thought, by some, to be a more equitable distribution of the total. Even where the price discrepancies are greatest, their effect is cancelled out if the community of agricultural producers is considered as a whole. Moreover, the absolute magnitude of the discrepancies and their effects on individual producers are never likely to be great.[34] To the extent that the incidence of price discrepancies is distributed by chance factors, the returns to the individual producer are little affected over a period of time. To the extent that luck does not enter into the results, the superior marketing knowledge, skill, and effort of some producers give them higher returns than are enjoyed by other producers. There does not seem to be any good reason why such skill, etc., should not be rewarded; in under-developed areas it is one way of encouraging the development of some of the qualities which are necessary if members of the rural population are to become fitted to take a more active part in economic advancement. Moreover, the superior ability and effort of the successful producers indirectly help their fellows; for they improve the effectiveness of competition among traders and tend to reduce the magnitude and duration of the discrepancies.

10

The arguments underlying the measures discussed in preceding sections postulate either a lack of ability on the part of many producers to take advantage of the access to alternatives presented by competitive markets or inadequacies in the working of competition itself. We now turn to a group of measures of intervention in agricultural marketing, the advocacy of which is independent of these alleged shortcomings in competitive markets. In effect, the advocates of this group of measures refuse to accept market prices either as a guide for the decisions of producers or as a basis for their remuneration.

[34] It will be remembered that price discrepancies refer to price differences not 'justified' by supply and demand conditions. As used here, the term does not refer to differences in returns of producers who are in different locations. The presence of these differences, which persist even if equilibrium is reached, has also given rise to demands for specific marketing reforms, which are discussed in the next section. The term 'price discrepancies', as used here, does not refer to differences in prices received by producers who sell their produce at different times in a period in which the market price itself has changed. In practice, the effects of short-term fluctuations in market price are often considered undesirable and lead to demands for measures of price stabilisation. The discussion of these effects and measures is outside the scope of this paper.

A good example is the imposition of a system of control whereby all producers in a zone receive the same price for their produce, irrespective of the distance of the point of first sale from the consuming market(s). It involves a transfer of income from favourably to unfavourably situated producers. Uniform price systems are a common feature of agricultural price and marketing control schemes.[35]

Uniform price systems are superficially attractive because they appear to treat producers equally and equitably. Advocates of such systems claim that it is unfair that certain producers should receive lower prices merely because they happen to be farther away from the markets, and they suggest that the 'burden of transportation' should be borne equally by all producers near or far. It is also contended that uniform prices encourage production by favouring marginal producers. Moreover, uniform price systems sometimes appear to be preferable on administrative grounds; there are fewer prices for the administration to worry about. But these arguments are not convincing.

Production in distant areas requires more transport (i.e. the use of additional scarce resources) to move the crops to the ports or to the markets; it does not seem inequitable, and it certainly promotes the husbanding of scarce resources, to require that the additional costs should be borne by the producers who cause the additional resources to be used and who benefit directly from their use. The suggestion that uniform prices stimulate marginal production overlooks the distinction between the intensive and the extensive margins. Producers near the markets or centres of communication can expand their output of the crops by more intensive effort, by more costly methods of production, or by diversion of effort and resources from other productive activities. Uniform price systems reduce the returns to near-by producers (or prevent the returns from being raised) and so discourage these types of marginal production. Such systems may

[35] In the purchase of Gold Coast cocoa a uniform price payable at all railway stations was introduced in 1942. In Nigeria the railway has for many years had a uniform charge for transporting groundnuts from stations throughout almost the entire northern area. The statutory minimum prices payable at outlying road stations are heavily subsidised by the Nigerian Groundnut Marketing Board. In the purchase of cotton, uniform minimum prices are payable throughout the northern area of Nigeria. In southern Nigeria there has in recent years been increasing pressure for a uniform producer price for cocoa, irrespective of distance from the ports.

54

encourage the extension of cultivation in distant areas, but only by making expansion of cultivation less attractive in more favourable locations.

The enthusiasm for uniform price systems may be less pronounced if it is realised that they result in the use of greater amounts of scarce resources in transportation to yield a given total output of the crop and that they penalise some producers for the benefit of others. These considerations are particularly important in under-developed areas which are poor in capital equipment, especially in transport, and where producers, even those favourably placed near the main markets, are generally poor. If it is intended to develop outlying areas, this can be done much more efficiently by direct subsidy or grant than, covertly and wastefully, by uniform price systems.

The administrative convenience of uniform price is also more apparent than real. If the transportation of the crop to the principal markets is undertaken in the first instance by intermediaries, they naturally have to be reimbursed for transport charges incurred. The marketing authority therefore has to deal with countless claims and to institute burdensome systems of checking, filing, and repayment. These costs of administration are additional to the extra demands on transport resulting from uniform price systems. In the final analysis they amount to reductions in the incomes of producers as a whole. Alternatively, predetermined transport allowances may be given to intermediaries; and, for the reasons given in Section 6, these are likely to err on the side of generosity.

11

In several colonies the government or marketing organisations with statutory powers determine that produce which falls short of stipulated minimum standards or grades may not be exported. Such measures indicate that the authorities concerned do not accept world market valuations as being relevant for production and export decisions; for the minimum exportable qualities which are prescribed are always higher than the lowest qualities that are acceptable and have a price on world markets. Such policies may have serious consequences.

The prohibition of the export of inferior, but commercially marketable, qualities of produce necessarily brings about one or more of three kinds of result which adversely affect the interests of producers and of the economy as a whole. Such measures either (a) frustrate the export of sub-standard output already produced, (2) induce the uneconomic expenditure of additional resources, or (3) deflect production into less valuable activities. These individual effects, to which we now turn, and possible combinations of them exhaust the possible economic consequences of these measures when applied to most export products.[36]

First, the efforts of producers may result in sub-standard output, that is, output which has a commercial value abroad but which falls short of the official minimum exportable quality. Whenever resources (including time and effort) yield a sub-standard output which is not marketed, there is economic loss, both to producers and to the economy, of a kind which could have been avoided if the export of the produce had not been banned. Second, producers may attempt to raise sub-standard output to reach the minimum exportable level. Whenever producers are induced to devote additional resources in an attempt to raise the quality of their output merely because lower qualities may not be exported, the cost of the additional resources must exceed the increase in the commercially realisable value of the output;[37] that is, there is a net loss to the economy. Third, producers who are aware that sub-standard output may not be sold and that

[36] Sometimes the prohibition of the *sale* of poorer qualities of a product may be used as a device to restrict supplies and to raise price. This is a possibility which must be borne in mind, particularly in considering the policies of a statutory organisation with monopoly powers of purchase and sale *within* a country. This inherently restrictive device is the more insidious because it can be spuriously argued that the raising of standards is in the interests of the consumers.

The Nigerian Livestock Mission of 1950 expressed disapproval of the sale of certain kinds of offal, such as guts, hides, and lungs, which in some Western countries are not usually regarded as edible. The sale of these goods in West Africa is deplored as being 'a very unsatisfactory position from the consumer point of view'. *Report of Nigerian Livestock Mission*, p. 109. These remarks ignore the obvious fact that consumers willingly buy these products; their withdrawal from sale would merely force consumers to eat less meat.

It is unlikely that the prohibition of the *export* of poorer qualities will enable the exporting country to influence the world price of any product appreciably. For instance, exports of West African palm oil or East African cotton are a small part of total world supplies; *a fortiori*, the quantities of so-called 'substandard' produce are far smaller still. Even for cocoa, West African supplies of the sub-standard qualities are a negligible part of world cocoa supplies. However, when market prices can be affected, the gains of monopoly have to be set against the adverse effects considered in the text.

[37] If this were not so, producers would voluntarily incur the additional expenditure, even if the export of lower grades were permitted.

56

the improvement of sub-standard produce requires additional re-sources may be deterred from embarking on the cultivation of the product in question. Whenever producers transfer their resources to other activities because of the restrictions on exports, the value of their output in the other activities is less than the commercially realisable value obtainable from the production of the product in question.[38]

The insistence on minimum standards and the obvious pride of some marketing authorities in the improvement of quality of export produce exemplify the confusion of technical and economic efficiency.[39] If economic and technical efficiency were synonymous, it would be in the interests of the motor-car industry and of the British economy to restrict the output of the industry to Rolls Royces or similar high grades of motor-cars. Inferior products would disappear, and the quality of output and exports would be greatly raised. Yet nobody would argue that technically inferior but cheaper cars should not be exported when there is a very large and profitable demand for them in world markets. Similarly, there is no case for refusing to allow the export of inferior grades of colonial produce for which there is a demand at a lower price, simply because they do not conform to certain prescribed technical standards.

12

In some colonies the marketing organisations prescribe different producer prices for different grades of the same commodity; often the grade-price differentials are not the same as the price differentials which prevail in the markets in which the organisations re-sell their produce.[40] For example, the world cocoa market does not generally

[38] Strictly speaking, the decisions are influenced by *expected* returns in alternative activities. But there is no reason to suppose that any *de facto* divergence between expectation and realisation would be more favourable in respect of one activity rather than of another; in particular, there is no reason to suppose that the occurrence of divergences would be biased so as to offset the loss under discussion in the text.

[39] For example, the satisfaction expressed in the annual reports and other official statements of the Nigeria Cocoa Marketing Board is misplaced when the board emphasises that it no longer buys and exports certain lower but commercially exportable grades or when it opposes the establishment of local processing enterprises on the grounds that they would use inferior grades, the production of which the board wishes to discourage.

[40] This section discusses the effects of the prescription of grade differentials divorced from market values. Analytically, such a system is closely analogous

57

distinguish between Grades I and II; very slight premiums of the order of £1 a ton occasionally emerge. The producer prices prescribed by the Nigeria Cocoa Marketing Board for the two grades have in recent years differed by £5 a ton. The Nigeria Oil Palm Produce Marketing Board distinguishes between several grades of palm oil in the producer prices it prescribes. Each grade covers a stipulated range of degrees of free-fatty-acid content. There are differences in the buying prices for different grades far in excess of differences ruling in world markets or stipulated in the contracts of the board with the Ministry of Food. Within each of the grades, however, no allowance is made in producer prices for varying degrees of free-fatty-acid content, though in market contracts (as well as in the contracts between the Ministry of Food and other suppliers) the price paid makes allowance for small differences in free-fatty-acid content. Thus, within each grade, producer-price differentials (which are zero) are smaller than market-price differentials.[41]

The prescription of grade-price differentials in payments to producers which are out of line with market-price differentials either encourages uneconomic expenditures and effort or discourages economic expenditures and effort. On the one hand, where the producer-price differentials exceed the market-value differentials, producers are induced to spend additional effort and resources to raise the grade of some of their output which would not have been profitable (to the producers) if only commercial differences were paid. This means that some producers incur expenditures to raise quality which are in excess of the additional proceeds received by the marketing organisations on the sale of higher grades of produce.[42] If the marketing organisations are considered as the guardians of the collective

to the prohibition of exports falling below some prescribed minimum standards, the effects of which were discussed in the preceding section. But there are various practical differences which are often not unimportant and which seem to justify separate treatment of the prescription of arbitrary price differentials.

The policy of paying grade differentials divorced from market differentials can be carried out only by an organisation which is the sole buyer and exporter of the product in question. In practice, this implies the existence of a statutory marketing monopoly of the kind familiar in British Africa.

[41] If the authority is not prepared to buy produce which is lower in quality than the lowest recognised grade, it follows that the grading system involves the imposition of a minimum exportable standard.

[42] This effect is analogous to the second type of effect produced by the imposition of a minimum exportable standard, discussed in the preceding section.

interests of producers, the results are patently uneconomic; if, however, the organisations are considered by others or by their executives as something apart from the producers, then this policy might nevertheless be favoured, since the extra exertions and expenditures of the producers would not fall upon the marketing organisations, whereas the higher receipts in world markets would obviously raise their sales receipts.

On the other hand, where the producer-price differentials are smaller than market-price differentials, the effect is to inhibit improvement in the quality of output. Some producers are discouraged from improving quality whenever the additional costs are greater than the resulting increase in prescribed producer price, even though they are smaller than the resulting increase in market value. The improvement which is frustrated would be in the interests of producers and of the economy as a whole and also in the interests of the marketing organisations, if these interests require the maximisation of net sales proceeds.

It is conceivable that arbitrarily wide producer-price differentials may result in some loss of production, somewhat analogous to part of the loss brought about by arbitrary minimum exportable standards.[43] Some producers may find that the price paid for the lowest grade is not sufficient to induce them to produce at all and that the extra costs of qualifying for the higher grades (and therefore better producer prices) are beyond their reach for technical or economic reasons. This may affect the distribution of effort between different crops.

Grade differentials in producer prices which are not the same as those obtaining on world markets penalise some producers and favour others. The redistribution that takes place is not likely (save accidentally) to accord with predetermined canons of equity or equality. If redistribution of income according to a given pattern is desired, it is better to achieve it directly; apart from anything else, the uneconomic expenditure of resources and effort, which arbitrary price differentials induce, will be avoided.

13

The policies of imposing minimum standards for export produce and of arbitrarily wide premiums and discounts for different grades of

[43] Compare the analysis in the preceding section of the third type of effect produced by the imposition of minimum exportable standards.

produce are sometimes defended on the grounds that the consequent improvement in the quality of export produce strengthens the position of the exporting country, particularly in unfavourable world market conditions. This view is untenable, for the buyers on world markets judge the produce they buy according to its quality in the light of market requirements. Since the policies under discussion stimulate expenditure of resources and effort in the exporting countries which exceed the additional value in world markets, the result is uneconomic.

It has sometimes been argued that, without restrictions on exports, severe competition among traders forces them to accept all produce offered to them, irrespective of quality, and that, in consequence, competition leads to a constant undermining of the quality of export produce, to the long-run detriment of producers. The argument was used to support the prescription of minimum export standards in Nigeria. The reasoning is not acceptable. If competition is severe, it forces merchants to adjust the prices they pay for different qualities closely in accordance with market valuations. They buy only if they can sell abroad; and the more intense the competition and the finer the margins on which they work, the more closely the shippers have to adjust their buying prices to market requirements. Competition does not cause a constant deterioration in quality; rather, it leads to increasing vigilance in seeking out supplies acceptable in world markets and in linking buying prices with world market values, which is to the advantage of producers.

14

The prescription of minimum export produce standards and of producer-price differentials for different grades requires a system of compulsory inspection of produce to check whether the minimum standard is reached or to determine the particular grade of the produce. The cost of inspection and grading services is an additional disadvantage of the policies in question. The cost is likely to be onerous in poor countries, where administrative talent is scarce. In such countries it is likely that the authorised buying or inspection posts will tend to be curtailed in order to reduce the costs or to raise the technical efficiency of the service. This expedient may be inconvenient and costly to some producers, besides tending to make trading facilities less adaptable to changing and growing needs.

In under-developed areas, where many producers and small-scale traders are illiterate and unaware of their legal rights, a system of compulsory inspection and grading may place them at the mercy of the inspecting officials. Thus in many parts of Nigeria petty tyranny and corruption in the operation of produce inspection have been widespread and oppressive. On extended visits to Nigeria in 1949 and 1950 it was found (by one of the writers) that in many places there was a recognised scale of (illicit) fees payable to produce examiners to have the produce inspected and passed. Those who refused to pay were made to wait for such long periods that their produce deteriorated and fell below standard;[44] or they were forced to sell their produce uninspected to other intermediaries at less than its commercial value; or they were liable to have their produce downgraded by the examiners. Wherever possible, the traders or clerks tried to placate the examiners by paying the recognised tariff; and, indeed, they were likely to complain only when the exaction exceeded the conventional level which was regarded as reasonable. It was universally recognised that complaints to officials would be useless, since formal proof would be difficult to secure. Moreover, a successful denunciation of one examiner followed by his conviction would be noted by his successor, possibly to the serious disadvantage of the protestant.[45] It seems that only very compelling reasons would justify the conferment of such drastic powers under conditions in

[44] A producer or buyer can never compel an examiner to inspect his produce; the examiner can always state that he is engaged elsewhere.

[45] It may be asked how the information in this paragraph has been obtained, since formal proof is admittedly difficult. It was a common subject of discussion throughout southern Nigeria among traders, their commission buyers, and clerks. In many places several individuals interrogated gave identical figures as the scale of bribes current in the area. The prevalence of the practice was admitted as a matter of course by a prominent European official of the Department of Marketing and Exports, who thought that the great majority of the African examiners abused their position. Finally, the following specific piece of evidence is informative. In Benin City a European trader was buying large quantities of rubber in 1950, securing quantities exceeding those bought by well-known large firms active in the area. He explained that he actually paid less than these firms, but, unlike his competitors, he was prepared to buy uninspected rubber at well below the prevailing price for inspected rubber. He then had the rubber inspected; and although part of his purchases were rejected, on balance he obtained his exportable supplies at a very reasonable price. He said that he gained this advantage because he was a European and was thus not liable to the same degree of extortion by the produce examiners as were African traders. Many of the latter were thus anxious to sell to him or to others willing to buy uninspected rubber, in preference to facing the expense and uncertainty of compulsory inspection.

which they are so widely abused. The preceding analysis has failed to reveal any such reason.[46]

The foregoing discussion does not imply that the grading of produce may not be a useful marketing device in appropriate circumstances. Accurate and acceptable grading facilitates commercial communication and reduces marketing costs. It is for this reason that systems of grading (and consequential arbitration of contract) have been developed in world commodity markets voluntarily by those in the markets. However, such systems of grading are voluntary; transactions in ungraded produce or in produce below the standard of the lowest recognised grades take place if it suits the parties concerned. From the point of view of producers and produce exporters, the market recognition of grade specifications may be very convenient, and they may voluntarily submit their produce for inspection and grading.

In export trades in which many shippers are small firms which are not well known or represented in world markets, difficulties arise when supplies on arrival are found to be below contract specification in quantity or in quality. As consignments are normally shipped under a letter of credit, the importer has difficulty in obtaining redress because the exporter has by then received most of the contract price. Moreover, as the exporter is not represented abroad, disputes cannot be referred to arbitration. In these circumstances the additional risks of the importer may seriously retard the development of the export trade. In such cases, however, it is in the interests of both importers and exporters to devise methods to provide safeguards to traders. They are thus likely to support firms of cargo supervisors who can inspect consignments before they are accepted. Where the establishment of such agencies is difficult or delayed, a voluntary inspection scheme by the government may provide the necessary service.[47] Both the problem and the two types of solution are illustrated by recent developments in the Nigerian export trade in logs.

[46] It is sometimes argued that compulsory grading protects the producer against under-payment by middlemen. But, as has been suggested before, when buying is competitive, this protection is unnecessary, and when competition is absent, compulsory grading does not assist the producer. Moreover, even if official inspection, grading, and supervision in markets protect the producer from abuses at the hands of dealers, they may expose him to the risk of possibly more serious abuses at the hands of petty officials.

[47] Government action of this kind could be defended along the lines of the 'infant-industry' argument for protection – but perhaps with more justification.

For many years African traders have exported timber in logs. Recently this has been the only branch of the export trade in which African shippers have been prominent. With the influx of many new shippers after the war, there was a considerable increase in consignments of logs which, on arrival, were seriously below specified weight or quality. Importers were increasingly reluctant to place contracts with the smaller exporters. Eventually, one of the smaller merchant firms undertook to act as cargo superintendent. The services it provided were not regarded as sufficiently extensive; and in 1949 the Nigerian authorities devised a simple and practical scheme which proved an immediate success. It provides for voluntary inspection; the exporter on application can have his consignment inspected during the loading of the timber on to the ship;[48] an official certificate of quality and quantity is issued, which is presented by the exporter to the bank with which the letter of credit is arranged. The actual amount paid out to the shipper under the credit depends on the contents of the certificate, a procedure which effectively safeguards the overseas importer against loss. The scheme has been widely publicised in the principal overseas markets for Nigerian timber, and importers now generally insist on this inspection certificate before arranging a letter of credit.

The scheme is voluntary and serves to protect the interests of the trade without investing the inspectors with compulsory powers and without introducing arbitrary grading or quality standards. Yet it fulfils all the essential requirements, since, unless the overseas importer neglects to take advantage of this simple facility, he is effectively safeguarded against loss and need have no reluctance in placing an order with a shipper unknown to him.[49]

Similarly, there may be a case, in under-developed areas, for government to help in the establishment of brand names for exportable consumer goods such as fruit. But it would not be in the economic interests of producers if the export of un-branded produce of the same kind were debarred. Moreover, if the costs of establishing or promoting the brand are taken out of the proceeds of compulsory levies on producers or out of general taxation, there is a danger of extravagant expenditure. Further, where substantial merchants or producer co-operatives operate in the export trade, the case for government action is weak.

[48] Inspection at this stage is necessary, since timber does not cross a wharf but is either rafted alongside the ship or shipped from lighters. Inspection must thus take place in a form which prevents substitution between the time of inspection and the time of shipment.

[49] Where the inspection and certification of produce raise its marketability, it is possible for the inspectors to charge unauthorised fees for their services. But

15

The effects of a miscellaneous group of measures of marketing reform have been examined in some detail in this paper. There is no need to attempt a summary; moreover, the very diversity of the measures and the differences in the particular effects of each stand in the way of a brief restatement of the implications and consequences of these measures for the producers and the economies affected by them. But, despite their diversity, it is clear that, whatever their sponsors may hope, these measures are prejudicial to the interests of producers[50] and that the adverse effects are particularly serious in under-developed economies. It is sometimes urged that certain measures of economic policy, while uneconomic in the sense of leading to inefficient use of existing resources, may be beneficial in the long run by stimulating growth, especially by acquainting the population with new techniques. However, this argument (whatever its validity in other instances) does not apply to the proposals and measures for marketing reform discussed in this paper, which, as has been shown, are, in fact, likely to inhibit rather than to promote economic growth.

The results and implications of the measures discussed in this paper are so far-reaching and in important respects so contrary to their avowed objectives that the question naturally arises as to how they come to be proposed and adopted in practice. Detailed examination of this question, though of interest, would be inappropriate in the scope for such exactions is limited where use of the services is voluntary. There have been no complaints of unauthorised charges by the users of the service discussed in the text.

[50] Strictly speaking, the measures may be divided into two groups. Some necessarily operate against the interests of producers. The prescription of minimum standards for export produce, the compulsory closing of trading facilities in outlying areas, the compulsory centralisation of transactions, and the prescription of marketing routes are examples falling into this group. Other measures need not necessarily operate against the interests of producers. Official supervision of marketing transactions to check trading abuses and the establishment of officially controlled zonal monopolies are examples in this group. But there is a strong presumption that in practice, and particularly in under-developed territories, the disadvantages of the second type of measure are serious and that they outweigh the possible advantages. It is notable that the sponsors of these measures seem to neglect some of the necessary adverse effects (e.g. the cost of control or the disadvantages of a reduction in the number of alternatives available to producers) and other likely adverse effects of the measures (e.g. the exploitation of producers by minor officials or the failure of marketing facilities to be adapted to meet the expanding and changing needs of a growing economy).

this paper. Whereas our discussion so far has been concerned with description and analysis, examination of the reasons underlying the advocacy of these measures would be speculative and take us outside the sphere of economics. However, we put forward, albeit briefly, a list of what seem to us to be the main influences which bring about widespread and influential support for the measures of marketing reform. It will, of course, be understood that this assessment is incapable of formal proof and is to some extent speculative.

The centuries-old belief in the unproductive nature of trading activities and of traders is still widespread. Even those who do not subscribe to crude notions about the alleged unproductivity of trade are frequently not able clearly to analyse the nature of the services performed by traders. Hence legislators, administrators, and others may start off from the idea that marketing arrangements offer a fruitful field for reform. Moreover, administrators and investigators usually are familiar with marketing arrangements in advanced economies; when they come to examine marketing arrangements in under-developed areas, they may fail to allow for the differences in conditions and in relative factor prices and so make misleading comparisons. They may fail to see the economic rationale of the existing arrangements.

This particular influence may be reinforced by another factor. It may be that when various commissions or committees investigate the marketing problems (or, for that matter, other economic problems) in under-developed territories, they feel that their mission is not justified unless they submit recommendations for extensive changes in existing arrangements. They feel that they are expected to recommend policy rather than to describe and analyse an existing situation. And they see, perhaps subconsciously, a justification for their appointment in a list of recommendations.

Some of the measures examined in this paper stem from a confusion of technical efficiency and economic efficiency. This confusion is present in the prescription of arbitrary price differentials for different grades of produce or the banning of the export of produce below prescribed technical standards. It may also be a factor in the advocacy of limitations on the number of traders or processors so that each may have a larger 'plant'. The technician may be aware of the greater technical efficiency of larger units but less conscious of the additional costs and inconvenience which consumers and/or producers have to bear if there are fewer trading or processing centres. The technician is also often unaware of the varied and important advantages to the population flowing from the presence of independent alternatives and of the stimulating effects on economic growth of the activities of traders. Moreover, the rationale of the price mechanism and the economic functions of prices are not always clearly understood.

The foregoing influences may be reinforced by the confusion, often encountered in discussions on economic policy, of symptom and cause or of result and cause. For instance, a reduction in the number of traders or of stages in the distributive process is likely to be economic if it results from technical changes or other developments inducing customers to dispense voluntarily with the services of some intermediaries. It does not follow, however, that the same result – that is, the reduction in the number of traders or stages – is also economic if it is brought about by compulsion, that is, by the denial of alternatives to customers.

Administrators are likely to have a penchant for tidy and orderly economic arrangements. Marketing conditions which allow a multiplicity of traders, without any rigorous standardisation or division of functions or any clearly defined areas and methods of operation, present an untidy and chaotic appearance; they cannot be satisfactorily illustrated by a simple diagram or flow chart, and they do not remain the same. They may therefore appear to be unnecessarily complicated and confusing. Considerations of administrative convenience may serve to strengthen the view that the uncontrolled system is burdensome, unnecessarily untidy, and without economic justification. An economy in which traders and other intermediaries are subject to official licensing, in which transactions are centralised in recognised markets, and in which all transactions go past at least one official check-post (e.g. for inspection or grading) may seem to be more easily administered than it would otherwise be. But even the apparently greater ease of administration may seem less attractive if the political complications which may arise from the greater dependence of the population on individual traders or protected groups of traders are considered.

Where agriculture provides the main component of the exports of an economy, a cumulation of measures of control over agricultural marketing, each of which may be relatively unimportant in isolation, may provide a practicable basis for a centrally controlled economy. This more far-reaching effect of measures of marketing reform may commend each of these measures more strongly to some administrators and observers.

Lastly, several of the measures discussed in this paper involve control of competition or restriction on the entry of new competitors. Established traders, or some of them, are likely to be strong pressure groups urging the need for the measures in question. Such pressure groups may be influential politically in both advanced and under-developed countries.

Addendum

The preceding discussion and analysis of measures of marketing reform are generally applicable, although the illustrative material, as explained in the opening section, has been taken predominantly from under-developed countries. The emphasis of the discussion would, however, have been rather different in Section 8 had we been considering its subject, marketing abuses, within the context of more advanced rather than of under-developed economies. The difference in emphasis would have reflected certain broad differences (of degree rather than of kind) between more advanced and less advanced economies which bear on the question of marketing abuses and their treatment. Thus in advanced countries, as compared with under-developed economies, there is a greater degree of specialisation in economic activity (including a more specialised role of individuals as consumers); the opportunity cost of time and effort is higher; and official measures of the kind analysed in the paper are likely to be relatively less costly to operate and also more effectively enforced. These differences imply that the enforced use of standard weights and measures has relatively greater advantages and relatively lower costs in advanced than in under-developed countries. The advantages apply especially strongly in respect of transactions in which final consumers are involved. There is less need for officially imposed standards in transactions between commercial producers, traders and manufacturers: experience suggests that it is in the interests of parties voluntarily to develop institutions and practices to regulate such transactions so as to facilitate business (for instance in the introduction of standard contract terms and of provision for arbitration). It should be noted, however, that voluntary arrangements to promote and facilitate business transactions occur also in under-developed economies, especially in contexts where a high degree of trust is required. Certain West African cattle markets provide an interesting example. So-called 'landlords' act essentially as intermediating guarantors in transactions between 'foreign' cattle dealers

67

and local butchers, and in various ways make possible a mutually advantageous trade which involves the extension of credit.[51]

The heterogeneity of units of measure in a market-place in Haiti is described and its implications discussed in a valuable article by an anthropologist, Professor Sidney Mintz.[52] Three separate quotations from this article follow:

Several different kinds of measures, and many unfamiliar units, are in use; for instance, there are two sets of liquids measures, and though most of the solids measures are standard in volume, at least one is not. Some substances are sold without the use of any measure or measuring apparatus. Bargaining is an important part of exchange procedure. Either price, or quantity, or both can change in bargaining.

Underlying the whole of the Haitian economy is a pervasive poverty of all resources but time. This poverty expresses itself, among other things, in the highly diversified agricultural production, leading to a constant but very irregular trickle of widely varying items into the market system. The very small-scale nature of production is matched by the nature of exchange. Trade attracts great numbers of intermediaries each with small stakes. While it requires considerable investment of resources, it is an activity where labour (time) may be readily substituted for capital, such that at least temporary entry is possible to any self-employed woman with large quantities of time and a tiny quantity of capital to invest. Not only traders but also consumers are prepared to invest large quantities of time in the marketing process. It is this plenitude of time which enhances the workability of the system of measures and of trade without measures and reduces the urgency of standardisation. Time is also a central quality of the bargaining process; seller and buyer both can take time to compare shop, to examine stocks, and to discuss prices fully.

Though different sets of measures, and different degrees of precision in estimating quantity, are employed for different goods, buyers and sellers know well what they are getting and have an informed view of the relationship of quantity to price. Perhaps partly because of the lack of standardisation of measures, peasant buyers consider their purchases carefully, and show good judgment in their trading operations.

[51] Abner Cohen, 'The Social Organization of Credit in a West African Cattle Market', *Africa*, January 1965, pp. 8–20.

[52] Sidney W. Mintz, 'Standards of Value and Units of Measure in the Fond-des-Nègres Market Place Haiti', *Journal of the Royal Anthropological Institute*, vol. 91, part 1, 1961, pp. 23–38.

4

COMPETITION AND PRICES:
A STUDY OF GROUNDNUT BUYING
IN NIGERIA*

There are many difficulties in the way of systematic statistical enquiry into the influence of numbers of firms on prices. Most of the difficulties have their origin in the familiar problem of finding situations in which all other factors are constant except the one under investigation.[1] A special difficulty is that of defining and delimiting a particular market and of counting the number of firms operating in it; buyers and sellers located in a geographical area may have (and indeed usually have) access to sellers and buyers outside the area. The numerous obstacles probably explain the apparent paucity of statistical studies of this aspect of price behaviour in spite of its wide relevance for economic theory and policy.

In the course of a general study into the economics of trade in British West Africa it emerged that the organisation and circumstances of the groundnut trade in Nigeria presented an exceptional opportunity for a systematic statistical enquiry into the influence of the number of firms on market prices. This article collates information of the numbers of groundnut buyers and of prices paid for groundnuts in different regions and centres, and analyses the findings.[2]

1

Groundnuts in Nigeria are produced in two geographically distinct regions. Approximately 92 to 95 per cent of the total purchases for

* *Economica*, February 1952, pp. 31–43.

[1] It may sometimes be possible to allow for changes in other factors by means of correlation analysis. However, in the field of price behaviour many of the influences operating in a market cannot be expressed quantitatively.

[2] A comparison of this nature on a small scale has been presented by Professor Hancock in the celebrated chapters on West African trade in his *Survey of British Commonwealth Affairs* (vol. II, part 2, chapter 2). Professor Hancock has compared groundnut prices ruling in the towns of Kano and Baro in Nigeria over a

export is produced in the so-called Northern or Kano area, while the balance is produced in the Rivers area (or Upper Niger–Benue area). The two areas are divided by large and thinly populated stretches of country. In the periods covered by the investigation groundnuts were not moved either by producers or traders from one area to the other. The produce of both areas is exported by the Nigeria Groundnut Marketing Board, a statutory monopoly, and is bought on its behalf by trading firms which act as its licensed buying agents. In the season 1948–9 there were seventeen licensed buyers operating in the Northern area and in 1949–50 there were twenty-one. In the Rivers area there were only two firms buying for the board; both of these firms also operated in the Northern area.

The licensed buying agents make their purchases either through middlemen acting for them on a commission basis or through their own clerks who are employees and are generally remunerated partly by salary and partly by commission. The middlemen have their own network of sub-middlemen. A particular firm may have a clerk employee and also one middleman (or even more) operating on its behalf in the same locality. To some extent the clerk and the middlemen or their sub-middlemen may be in competition with one another although ultimately buying for the same firm. The clerks are generally in charge of retail stores as well; at out-stations produce buying is merely one of their activities. The buying 'establishments' of middlemen are generally very simple and usually temporary. In the Rivers area the two buying agents purchase through clerks only and do not employ middlemen.

Each season the Groundnut Marketing Board prescribes statutory minimum prices to be paid for purchases at a large number of designated markets (gazetted stations) spread throughout the groundnut producing areas. In the Kano area the structure of minimum prices pivots on the uniform price prescribed for all railway stations.[3] In 1949–50 the railway line price was £21 4s. per ton. In the Rivers

number of pre-war years; and from the findings he suggests that the larger number of traders in Kano secured higher prices for producers than in Baro where only two firms operated. Professor Hancock's pioneer effort related to a comparatively small sample and to somewhat fragmentary price statistics. He therefore advanced his conclusions tentatively. The comprehensive comparison set out in the following sections overwhelmingly confirms Professor Hancock's findings.

[3] The Nigerian railway charges a flat rate for the movement of groundnuts throughout the Kano area.

area the structure pivots on two basic prices payable along the rivers; the difference in the two rivers prices (£1 per ton in the period under review) is to allow for the approximate differences in the cost of shipment to the ports. In 1949–50 the two basic rivers prices were £20 and £19 per ton.

At buying stations away from the railway line or the rivers (i.e. at road stations) lower minimum prices are prescribed to allow for the cost of transport to the railway or river stations; the difference is known as the transport differential. In a number of road stations in the Kano area the gazetted minimum prices are fixed at higher levels in relation to the basic price at rail stations than would be warranted by the officially calculated transport differentials. This is designed to encourage production in outlying areas. The licensed buying agents receive for purchases at these stations (subsidy stations) so-called transport subsidies from the board designed to cover what otherwise, on official calculations, would be losses to them.

The buying agents receive from the board no more than the relevant minimum prices[4] for the tonnages bought. They also receive certain tonnage payments known as 'block allowances' to reimburse them for their expenses and to remunerate them for their services. In 1949–50 this block allowance was £4 10s. 6d. per ton for the Kano area and £4 17s. 9d. for the Rivers area. The principal items include the cost of bags, interest, insurance and other finance charges, an allowance for overhead expenses, middlemen's commission and the agents' remuneration. In 1949–50 middlemen's commission was allowed for at 14s. a ton on all purchases in the Kano area. There was naturally no similar item in the Rivers area; but the overhead allowance was raised by over 13s. in recognition of the fact that all purchases were made through the salaried clerks of the trading firms. The licensed agents' remuneration was 8s. 6d. and 7s. 8d. per ton in the Kano and Rivers areas respectively. This was 2 per cent of the basic price. There is no item for transport costs in the block allowance, since the transport differentials and subsidies are deemed to cover the transport expenses of the firms from the road stations to the railway line or the rivers.

The block allowances in the two groundnut areas are settled by negotiation between the marketing board and the licensed buying

---

[4] For purchases at the subsidy stations the buying agents in addition receive payments to compensate them for the officially calculated loss which they are assumed to incur by paying the prescribed subsidised prices.

agents. There is no reason to believe that they are less generous in the Rivers area than in the Kano area. The absolute level is higher in the Rivers area in acceptance of the claims of the buying agents that their costs are higher. Within the total allowance the overhead items are both absolutely and relatively larger in the Rivers area.

2

Although a fair number of buying agents operate in the Kano area the organisation of the trade might suggest that little buying competition would take place there. First, in 1948–9 sixteen of the seventeen agents were members of a confidential market-sharing syndicate; in 1949–50 sixteen out of twenty-one were members of the syndicate. In both 1948–9 and 1949–50 the combined share of members of the syndicate in total purchases was over 90 per cent. The syndicate operates along familiar lines. Members of the syndicate are allotted quotas (shares) and those who purchase more than their quotas make penalty payments to those who are underbought.[5] Secondly, there is a marked degree of concentration in groundnut buying; three of the licensed buying agents handling between one-half and three-fifths of total purchases are financially linked, though their operations locally are largely independent. Thirdly, with quantitatively negligible exceptions all licensed buying agents are European and Levantine (i.e. non-African) firms or traders who operate with substantial capital and who possess a large measure of commercial skill; and their middlemen are in many cases non-African. They buy from customers (producers and small African traders) who in the great majority of instances are illiterate, have little capital and are geographically dispersed.

From these considerations it might well be inferred that price competition, or indeed any form of buying competition, would be negligible in spite of the apparently large number of licensed buyers. In short, it might be expected that the intensity of buying competition in the Kano area would not be materially different from that in the Rivers area, where only two buyers operate.

The broad reasons for the small number of traders in the Rivers area are fairly clear. The area is comparatively poor, undeveloped, sparsely populated and backward. It is therefore not an easy market for traders to enter. However, the comparative backwardness has

---

[5] The penalties approximate to the difference between gross receipts and the short-run avoidable (or escapable or prime) costs of purchase.

not been the only deterrent to entry into a region where it is known that trading is distinctly profitable. One difficulty is that the cheapest method of transport, river shipping, is owned by the two trading firms established in the area. These two firms have developed river shipping and have traded in the area for many years. It would be costly and possibly impracticable for a new trading firm to develop its own river shipping services, while reliance upon the services of the established river lines would increase the risks and inconveniences of trading. Some other firms have recently investigated the possibility of establishing themselves in this region and are likely to start operations in the near future.[6]

3

There has been a substantial measure of buying competition in the Kano area for many years past in spite of confidential buying syndicates and other influences tending to discourage it. Even during the war there was still buying competition in the Kano area despite an officially established and administered system of buying quotas with fines for overpurchases; moreover, new firms were not allowed to buy produce. The statutory minimum producer prices, which from 1942 to 1946 ranged from £6 to £16 per ton at rail stations, were frequently and increasingly exceeded. At first overpayments were of the order of a few shillings per ton, but by 1946 overpayments of 40s. and 50s. per ton were frequent in outlying road stations where the minimum prices were appreciably lower than those fixed for rail stations. These overpayments were particularly large in areas where there were wide transport differentials or where transport subsidies were paid.

Overpayments have been widespread since 1947; and more specific as well as more comprehensive information has become available on this subject, chiefly because, for administrative reasons, more detailed data have been collected of the prices actually paid at a large number of stations. Sufficiently detailed and consistently compiled information

[6] Information on the volume of groundnut purchases at individual markets in the Rivers area seems to suggest that the number of firms operating in them is not limited solely by the extent of the market. In many markets in the Rivers area the volume of groundnut purchases per firm is much greater than the corresponding averages in many markets in the Kano area (including many stations in outlying districts where nevertheless several buyers operate). Moreover, substantial quantities of cotton, benniseed, ginger and shea nuts are also brought to markets in the Rivers area.

is available for thirty-two road stations in the Kano area, at which about two-fifths of all groundnut purchases were made in 1948–9 and 1949–50.[7]

In 1948–9 there was a good harvest and in the following year the crop was short. Wherever the information is available the investigation covers both years to allow for the possible influence of the size of crop on the intensity of competition. In fact this influence appears to have been small.

The principal statistics relevant to the present investigation are presented in Table 1.

TABLE 1

Groundnut purchases and overpayments at thirty-two road stations, Northern Nigeria, 1948–9 and 1949–50

	1948–9	1949–50
Total groundnut purchases in Kano area	315,000 tons	178,000 tons
Groundnut purchases at the 32 road stations	119,000 tons	76,000 tons
Average number of firms represented at the 32 road stations[1]	6	7
Statutory minimum price at railway line	£19 4s. per ton	£21 4s. per ton
Average prescribed minimum price at the 32 road stations[1]	£16 19s. 9d. per ton	£19 3s. per ton
Average price paid at the 32 road stations[1,2]	£18 0s. 1d. per ton	£20 8s. 8d. per ton
Average overpayment at the 32 road stations[1]	£1 0s. 4d. per ton	£1 5s. 8d. per ton
Range of overpayments at the 32 road stations	From 1s. to £3 10s. per ton	From 1s. to £4 5s. per ton

1. Weighted by volumes of purchases at each station.
2. For 1948–9 the prices paid are the averages for the whole season; for 1949–50 they refer to the first half of the season by which time rather more than one-half of the crop had been bought. For various reasons overpayments tend to be larger in the second half of the season, chiefly because greater competition among the owners of transport leaves the buyers with a more generous real allowance on transport differentials. Thus, if anything, the 1949–50 figures tend to understate the extent of overpayments.

[7] The prices were collected partly by the authorities and partly by the licensed buying agents. They were estimated in part. Each price represents a simple arithmetic mean of a more or less continuous series of recorded prices containing a

In both years the gazetted minimum prices were exceeded at every station. The highest overpayments were recorded at road stations where the gazetted minimum prices were lowest and where, therefore, the transport differentials, usually augmented by subsidies, were greatest; in 1948–9 overpayments of £3 10s. were frequent at stations where the minimum prices were slightly over £13 per ton.

4

The presence and the extent of the overpayments are themselves significant; and they gain in significance when contrasted with the position in the Rivers area, where there were only two licensed buying agents. With one interesting but quantitatively negligible exception[8] there has been no record or suggestion of overpayments for groundnuts by licensed buying agents or their representatives in the Rivers area during or since the war. The statutory minima have been observed but have nowhere been exceeded. This is undoubtedly due to the absence of competition and not to the lack of available margins, which, given competition, would have been competed away in favour of sellers. In the Rivers area four-fifths of the tonnage was bought in 1949–50 at buying stations at which only one or other of the two firms was operating. For this large portion of the area informal market sharing by means of zoning was in effect in force.

5

It would have been interesting to investigate the correlation between the extent of overpayments and the numbers of buyers at each road station in the group analysed in the preceding section. Unfortunately the available data cannot be used for this special purpose. The amount of the overpayment depends not only on the extent of

---

large number of successive items. Though the figures are imprecise and in a sense incomplete they are close approximations; they are independently confirmed by trade and official opinion. A personal test check in December 1949 at two stations broadly confirmed that the ruling prices were in accordance with the recorded data.

[8] In one period during the war members of an obscure African tribe, the Kakanda, who engage in canoe trading on the Benue, outbid the licensed buyers at certain up-river stations. They bought groundnuts at these stations above the gazetted minimum prices, took them down the river and sold them either to licensed buyers at the higher gazetted prices prevailing on the lower reaches of the river or sold them at Onitsha for local consumption. These activities were stopped by administrative regulation.

competition but also on the margin available to be competed away in the form of overpayments. This margin is not the same at each road station principally because it is greatly influenced by the difference between the officially recognised transport differential (and subsidy where this applies) and the actual transport costs incurred.[9] Sufficiently detailed information of actual transport costs incurred in the two seasons is not available.

However, there is some information, more limited in scope but of considerable interest, of prices paid in 1949–50 at nine buying stations on the railway line.[10] The figures are tentatively advanced, but it is most unlikely that any errors they may contain would significantly alter the conclusions they suggest.

In 1949–50 24,000 tons were bought at these stations, which was about 15 per cent of total purchases in the Kano area and 45 per cent of total purchases at rail stations. At all these stations the gazetted minimum price was £21 4s. per ton. As there were no transport differentials or subsidies, the prime costs of buying ground-nuts were about the same at each station; hence the margin which could be competed away was also much the same at each station. The major influence vitiating the comparability of overpayments at different road stations was absent.

Information on buying operations at the nine railway stations is shown in Table 2.

There were overpayments at six of the nine markets along the railway line. Moreover, the data suggest very strongly that the extent of overpayments is much influenced by the number of traders present.[11] There were only one or two buying agents represented at the three stations at which no overpayments were recorded. At the other end there were three stations at which six or more

[9] Generally speaking, the margin available to be competed away was greatest at the outlying stations, especially at the subsidy stations where the transport differential and the subsidy together in some cases exceeded £9 per ton. On the other hand, at road stations near the railway line the differential was only a few shillings. Thus even though there might have been a large number of buyers operating under keenly competitive conditions at road stations near the railway line, the overpayments would perforce have been less than at the more remote stations with fewer buyers but larger transport differentials.

[10] This information was kindly collected by the produce department of the United Africa Company in Kano.

[11] The number of clerks and middlemen operating in different localities tends to be proportionate to the number of licensed buying agents. The degree of

TABLE 2

Groundnut purchases and overpayments at nine markets on the railway line, Northern Nigeria, 1949–50

station	number of licensed buying agents	average overpayment in shillings per ton	tonnage bought	average tonnage per buying agent
A	1	0	1,196	1,196
B	2	0	666	333
C	2	0	1,412	706
D	2	10	1,968	984
E	3	11	3,107	1,036
F	4	6	1,975	494
G	6	16	2,885	481
H	7	6	2,756	394
I	10	20	8,967	897

buying agents were represented and two of these had the heaviest overpayments.

But numbers of traders alone do not give a full picture of the degree of buying competition at the different stations. It may be expected that, apart from numbers, the intensity of competition would depend upon various other factors, some of which cannot be expressed quantitatively. These would include the presence of new-comers trying to force their way into the trade generally or into the particular trading centre, and the presence of firms outside the buying syndicate. A further factor may be the presence of firms without extensive organisation in the particular area who might therefore have to a greater extent to rely on price inducements to secure supplies. A racially heterogeneous group of traders comprising Europeans, Levantines and Africans is likely to behave more competitively (even despite agreements) than a homogeneous group of the same size, as the contacts between members are likely to be less continuous and smooth. In addition, Levantine firms tend to be more individualistic in outlook and behaviour.

The influence of competition on prices becomes even clearer when

competition among the clerks and middlemen is largely influenced by the number of licensed buying agents and the market positions of the latter. Cf. also Section 6, below.

the figures in the table, which by themselves are instructive, are subjected to qualitative analysis. Thus station D, which at first sight appears to be an exception, falls into place; for here a newcomer, who was not in the syndicate, had entered the market for the first time in that season and had moreover to contend with the difficulties of a late start in the season. Qualitative analysis also clarifies the position at E. One new firm, again not a member of the syndicate, entered the market here. This firm is a comparatively recently established Levantine firm with no extensive organisation. The comparatively modest overpayments at F and H coincide with the absence of firms outside the syndicate. At F, with one exception, only large established European firms operated; the exception was a Levantine trader financially linked with one of the large European firms operating there. Six of the seven firms which operated at H are the largest members of the syndicate, three of which are linked financially. The situation at I is one of some interest in that all ten firms which operated there were members of the buying syndicate, but four of them were comparatively small firms including three Levantine enterprises. Substantial overpayments occurred here even though all buyers were members of the syndicate.

A study of the entries in the last column of the table (average tonnages per buyer) suggests that differences in overpayments were independent of the scale of operations as measured by average volumes handled. There is evidently no correlation between the average tonnage purchased per firm and the size of overpayment.

The statistics of this section, although on a small scale, suggest several conclusions. They confirm that the emergence of competition under apparently unpropitious circumstances has resulted in substantial overpayments; and they suggest that these overpayments are largely a function of the intensity of competition. They suggest that the number of firms is an important element in the competitive situation; and that even small numbers may result in a substantial measure of price competition. But numbers alone do not provide a full explanation; qualitative assessment is also necessary. Here the role of new entry and of the composition of the group of competitors appear to have been particularly important.

6

It is easier to discover the beneficiaries of the overpayments than it is to determine who bears their cost. The statistics of actual prices in the preceding sections refer to prices paid by middlemen and clerks of licensed buying agents to producers or to those petty middlemen, not affiliated to any licensed buying agent, who bring produce to the buying stations. As the unaffiliated petty middlemen are members of the rural community and in many cases are themselves producers, the overpayments represent additions to the income of the agricultural community.

The heaviest overpayments since 1942–3 (when they were first recorded) have occurred in the comparatively distant Bornu province. In 1949–50 the overpayments at the principal buying stations in that province were of the order of £3 to £4 per ton on a basic minimum road station price of about £16. In this area the officially calculated transport differentials and subsidies are high and have in effect provided the main source from which competition has produced overpayments. The actual transport rates between the principal Bornu buying stations and the railway line tend to be far lower than the figures assumed in the calculation of differentials and subsidies. In 1949–50 the officially calculated transport costs from the principal buying stations to Kano were of the order of £10 per ton, while the actual costs were about £4 per ton. The main reason for the low actual costs was the cheap rate quoted by owners of lorries returning with little cargo from the Lake Chad area to which large consignments of merchandise had been conveyed.[12]

The groundnut producers of Bornu are not only generally illiterate but are among the most backward sections of the peasantry of northern Nigeria. According to the views held in some influential circles the 'bargaining position' of these producers vis-à-vis a handful of generally well financed and organised alien traders, frequently acting in concert, would have been extremely weak. Yet so far from being exploited by the so-called rapacious alien and other middlemen, competition amongst buyers has secured for them prices far in excess of the minima laid down for their protection.

Overpayments represent the surrender by those participating in the

---

[12] This traffic was not peculiar to 1949–50. In recent years groundnuts appear to have been carried from Bornu to Kano or Jos for about 2½ pence per ton-mile, which is remarkably low for an area with a poor road system about a thousand miles from the ports.

trade of part of the incomes and reimbursements provided for in the official structure of prices and block allowances.[13] They are made in order to secure additional supplies and are enforced by competition upon the licensed buyers, and/or their clerks and/or their middlemen.

It is not possible to determine precisely how the burden of any particular overpayment has been shared by the buying agents, their clerks and their middlemen, who are all members of the urban community. However, the magnitude of overpayments at rail stations, where the basic minimum price is payable (i.e. where there are no transport differentials and subsidies) makes it clear that in many cases a share of the burden is carried by the licensed buying agents themselves; some of the overpayments exceed the gross commission payable to middlemen.

7

Although this article is concerned with the influence of the number of traders on the prices received by producers, it would be misleading to neglect other advantages derived by producers and rural middlemen from buying competition among licensed buyers and their employees and middlemen; the benefits of competition are not confined to overpayments.

Local executives of the merchant firms acting as buying agents frequently wish to secure additional tonnage without making overt overpayments, which may meet with displeasure from senior executives. Additional purchases may be secured without actual overpayments by selling equipment and merchandise to favoured middlemen or petty middlemen at prices lower than the prevailing market prices. An important special case of this practice is the favourable allocation of price-controlled (so-called short-supply) equipment and merchandise to these customers. Other concessions take the form of permitting the use of premises at nominal rents or the granting of advances or of trade credits for long periods.

Wherever possible clerks prefer to secure additional tonnage by

[13] It is conceivable that overpayments and out-of-pocket expenses might in some cases together exceed the gross receipts allowed for by the prescribed price structure.

In the multi-product firm some branches of activity might be carried on at a (notional) loss for the benefit of the business as a whole. In groundnut buying there is some evidence that middlemen occasionally 'lost' on groundnut buying but continued in the trade because of market opportunities in the related grain trade.

means of valuable concessions rather than by undisguised over-payments. Such concessions are not at the expense of their own commission or salary, and can be made at the expense of their firm without requiring specific approval from their superiors. As clerks generally sell merchandise as well as buy produce, they are able to favour valued customers on a small scale and so to secure tonnage.

Indirect concessions rather than increased overpayments to secure tonnage competitively may be preferred by the firms for another reason. Some of these concessions can, at least for a short period, be restricted to a limited number of selected customers (who are also suppliers of groundnuts) whereas overpayments must generally be granted to all comers as knowledge of them tends to spread more quickly. Moreover, even where the granting of the concession cannot be concealed, the differential treatment is less likely to cause resentment than differential overpayments since certain concessions (such as the use of premises on favourable terms) in their very nature cannot be made to all customers.

The presence of a number of firms is in itself of value to the producer by reducing his dependence on individual firms or their intermediaries or employees and by providing more buying stations closer to individual producers. This is of some consequence in such vast regions as the groundnut producing area of northern Nigeria.

5

A CASE STUDY OF RESPONSE TO PRICE IN AN UNDER-DEVELOPED COUNTRY*

1

The extent of the response of agricultural producers in under-developed countries to changes in prices and price relationships bears on a wide range of issues of analytical and practical significance, including among the latter problems of public finance and of price and income stabilisation.

There are, however, well-known and serious difficulties in measuring the degree of responsiveness of producers to price changes. There are the familiar problems arising from the usual absence in the real world of anything resembling closely the *ceteris paribus* of the theoretical formulations of functional relationships in economics. There are further difficulties created by the time lags between changes in agricultural capacity and changes in output; and also by the effects of uncertainty about the permanence of absolute and relative price changes. The problems of testing a hypothesis or of measuring the strength of a functional relationship make it difficult to reach objective assessments, and rival hypotheses are likely to flourish side by side, often deriving from opposing policy preconceptions and sometimes giving rise to opposing policy prescriptions.

Though certainly not unknown, situations exhibiting sharply the response of producers to a change in an economic variable are infrequent, and have rarely been described. Situations deliberately induced by the contrivance of changes in the variable, that is, where, in effect, an hypothesis has been postulated and put to the practical test, are even more unusual. There is, therefore, some general interest in the policy of some of the statutory marketing authorities in Nigeria of raising the quality of certain agricultural produce by offering price incentives to peasant producers. This policy was explicitly premised on the hypothesis that peasant producers respond

* *Economic Journal*, December 1959, pp. 800–5.

82

to price differences, and would appropriately adjust their behaviour as producers to the incentives provided by the authorities. The results of this experiment supported the hypothesis in that the average grade produced has risen greatly. The explicitly formulated hypothesis, the introduction of the measures and the consistent results closely resemble the methods of observation and experimentation in the natural sciences. This note describes the measures taken by the authorities, and the response of producers; thus, in effect it reports on the process and the results of a series of contrived experiments.

2

All major agricultural exports of Nigeria are handled by statutory export monopolies (marketing boards) established during and after the Second World War. Two of the marketing boards, the Nigeria Cocoa Marketing Board and the Nigeria Oil Palm Produce Marketing Board, prescribed wide differentials in the prices paid to producers of cocoa and palm oil for various grades of these products in order to encourage the production of higher grades.[1] These differentials in producer prices greatly exceeded the grade differentials in the markets in which the boards sold the produce.[2] The producer prices and grade differentials were announced before the opening of each season, so that there was no price uncertainty; and the agents of the board had to buy all supplies offered to them at not less than

[1] The Nigeria Cocoa Marketing Board was established in 1947 and the Nigeria Oil Palm Produce Marketing Board in 1949. They succeeded the West African Produce Control Board established in 1942, which also had a statutory export monopoly. In 1954 the boards were placed on a regional as distinct from a product basis. The regional boards, each of which handles several crops but only part of the total export of each crop, continued the policy of their predecessors in paying wide price differentials for different grades with the same result as experienced by their predecessors. For convenience of presentation we have confined the discussion to the period before the regionalisation of the boards in 1954. The tables in this paper cover the entire period of operation of the two national boards, spanning the interval between their predecessor, the West African Produce Control Board, and their successors, the various regional boards.

Measures to improve quality by the offer of price inducements were consistently applied only in respect of cocoa and palm oil.

[2] We are not concerned here with the merits of these policies, which are wasteful, since they encourage uneconomic expenditure of effort, discourage economic expenditure of effort and also waste output already produced. This is particularly evident in the refusal to buy so-called sub-standard produce even when this has a positive commercial value. We have analysed the economic implications of these policies in 'The Economics of Marketing Reform', pp. 55 to 60, above.

the announced prices. The producer therefore knew the additional returns for improving his output by more careful tending of the trees, gathering of the produce and preparation for sale to the boards.

The purpose of the prescription of wide grade price differentials and the results of this policy are frequently referred to in the annual reports of the two boards. Here are two extracts from the annual reports of the Nigeria Cocoa Marketing Board:

It is quite certain that, given an adequate cash incentive and the necessary instruction, the Nigerian farmer is capable of producing well-fermented cocoa. That he has not always done so in the past is attributed largely to the fact that the premia offered were too low, for it should be remembered that the fermentation process involves a loss in weight in comparison with beans which are dried only and not fermented (Nigeria Cocoa Marketing Board, *Second Annual Report*, Season 1948–9, p. 22).

That the Board's policy of offering a premium on first grade quality cocoa has resulted in an ever-increasing effort to produce good quality cocoa, is illustrated by the progressively increasing percentage of the total annual tonnage of cocoa marketed in the first grade ... (Nigeria Cocoa Marketing Board, *Fifth Annual Report*, Season 1951–2, p. 10).

The following is a quotation from an annual report of the Nigeria Oil Palm Produce Marketing Board:

Undoubtedly the major factor in the progressive improvement which has taken place in the quality of Nigerian palm oil over the past five years has been the board's producer price policy which has offered considerable financial inducement by way of price differentials in favour of the production of the higher quality grades. Under this incentive, the fruit has been harvested quicker and more care has been taken in its preparation. Higher prices have encouraged the greater use of hand-pressing machines which tend not only to improve quality but also have a more favourable extraction rate than that obtained by traditional methods, and therefore increase production (Nigeria Oil Palm Produce Marketing Board, *Sixth Annual Report*, 1954, p. 14).

3

The results are shown in Tables 1 and 2, which refer to cocoa and palm oil respectively.

The high degree of response of producers to the price incentives clearly emerges from these tables. Thus, the proportion of Grade I cocoa in the purchases of the Cocoa Marketing Board increased from 47 per cent in 1947–8 to 98 per cent in 1953–4; and, after the

TABLE 1
Nigeria Cocoa Marketing Board producer prices for cocoa and composition of purchases by grades, 1947–54

	Grade I		Grade II			Grade III			Grade IV			Total purchases, '000 tons
	A £	C %	A £	B £	C %	A £	B £	C %	A £	B £	C %	
1947–8	62·5	47·0	60·0	− 2·5	24·7	57·0	− 5·5	21·3	47·5	−15·0	7·0	75·0
1948–9	120·0	76·0	115·0	− 5·0	21·2	105·0	−15·0	1·8	90·0	−30·0	1·0	109·0
1949–50	100·0	89·4	95·0	− 5·0	10·5	75·0	−25·0	0·1				99·1
1950–1	120·0	95·1	110·0	−10·0	4·9							110·3
1951–2	170·0	96·0	155·0	−15·0	4·0	Grade no longer purchased			Grade no longer purchased			107·9
1952–3	170·0	95·0	155·0	−15·0	5·0							109·0
1953–4	170·0	98·2	155·0	−15·0	1·8							97·4

Notes

1. Abbreviations:
   A. Producer price of grade, in £ per ton.
   B. Difference between price of grade and price of Grade I, in £ per ton.
   C. Purchases of grade as a percentage of total purchases made by the board.

2. Grade differences: grades were differentiated on the basis of the proportions of unfermented or insufficiently fermented beans and of defective beans.

3. The producer prices in this table refer to those paid for main-crop cocoa which accounted for over 90 per cent of total supplies. The small quantity of light-crop cocoa, harvested later in the season, was subject to a discount of £5 per ton for all grades (somewhat smaller in 1947–8), until parity of treatment was introduced in 1953–4.

85

TABLE 2
Nigeria Oil Palm Produce Marketing Board producer prices for palm oil and composition of purchases by grades, 1949–54

	Special Grade			Grade I		Grade II			Grade III			Grade IV			Grade V			Total purchases, '000 tons
	A £	B £	C %	A £	C %	A £	B £	C %	A £	B £	C %	A £	B £	C %	A £	B £	C %	
1949	No special price			42·75	66·4	37·13	− 5·62	14·5	33·0	− 9·75	12·7	29·63	− 13·12	6·0	26·25	− 16·5	0·4	161·5
1950	53·0	+10·25	0·2	42·75	61·3	37·13	− 5·62	17·8	33·0	− 9·75	14·4	29·63	− 13·12	5·8	26·25	− 16·5	0·5	158·7
1951	71·0	+16·0	6·3	55·0	70·8	43·0	− 12·0	11·4	34·0	− 21·0	7·5	30·0	− 25·0	4·0	Grade no longer purchased			135·2
1952	80·0	+19·0	29·6	61·0	56·3	47·0	− 14·0	7·4	35·0	− 26·0	5·2	30·0	− 31·0	1·5				178·5
1953	75·5	+17·5	50·4	58·0	38·0	45·0	− 13·0	7·2	34·5	− 23·5	4·4	Grade no longer purchased						211·6
1954	65·0	+15·0	60·8	50·0	29·9	38·0	− 12·0	4·4	33·0	− 17·0	4·9							205·0

Notes

1. Abbreviations:

    A. Producer price of grade, in £ per ton.

    B. Difference between price of grade and price of Grade I, in £ per ton.

    C. Purchases of grade as a percentage of total purchases made by the board.

2. Grade differences: the original five grades were based on the free-fatty-acid (f.f.a.) content of the oil, ranging from 0 to 9 per cent f.f.a. content for Grade I by equal steps to 36–45 per cent f.f.a. content for Grade v. This classification was maintained, except that in 1952 the permissible range for Grade IV was narrowed to 27–33 per cent. The Special Grade refers to 'edible' (as distinct from the other 'technical') oil, with a low f.f.a. content (up to 4½ per cent).

3. The table refers only to palm oil produced by smallholders, and not to plantation palm oil.

purchases of the two lowest grades had dwindled to very small quantities, the board discontinued their purchase. Indeed, the increase in the proportion of Grade I cocoa under the stimulus of the price incentive was greater than appears from this series which begins with the year 1947–8. Until 1947, under the West African Produce Control Board, the premium of Grade I over Grade II cocoa was only £2·5 per ton, and in 1946–7 the proportion of Grade I cocoa only 23 per cent of total purchases. It was a deliberate early decision of the Nigeria Cocoa Marketing Board to substitute three new grades for the previous Grade II and to widen the differential between the Grade I price and the prices of the two lowest grades to £5·5 and £15 respectively; the proportion of Grade I cocoa rose to 47 per cent in the 1947–8 season.

From its first year, 1949, the Oil Palm Produce Marketing Board widened the differences in prices paid for the different grades of palm oil. The producer prices paid by the West African Produce Control Board in 1948 ranged from £32·25 per ton for Grade I to £26·25 for Grade V, a spread of £6 per ton. The new board widened the spread of £16·5 in the first two years of its operations. This had little effect on the composition of the board's purchases. The board increased the differentials more markedly in 1951; this was also the first entire year in which the board bought the Special Grade of oil at a special premium price.[3] The extent of the improvement in the produce bought by the board is apparent in the statistics. Thus in 1954 purchases of the Special Grade constituted as much as 60 per cent of all purchases, while, as for cocoa, purchases of the two lowest grades were discontinued after they had fallen to small quantities.

Another experience of the boards' operations, which cannot be presented in the same way, also shows clearly the awareness of producers of economic opportunities and their readiness and eagerness to take advantage of them. Whenever higher prices were announced or even generally anticipated for the following season, producers and intermediaries withheld supplies in the closing months of the previous season, while supplies were rushed forward when a reduction was announced or anticipated. This is reflected in statistics of monthly purchases by the boards, and was sometimes mentioned

[3] Price differentials in favour of the Special Grade were introduced towards the end of the previous year, in which this grade constituted 0·2 per cent of total purchases.

in their annual reports.[4] Yet another example is provided by the decision in 1953–4 of the Nigeria Cocoa Marketing Board to discontinue the payment of higher prices for 'main crop' than for 'light crop' cocoa. The differential had encouraged the mixing of 'light crop' cocoa with the succeeding 'main crop' cocoa, a practice which the board did not like, and sought to discourage by removing that particular price differential.

Addendum

The preceding article was criticised in a published Comment[5] largely on the ground that it ignored changes in economic variables other than the changes in inter-grade price differentials, and that it therefore over-stated the effects of the latter. However, our confidence in the importance of these relative price changes is strengthened by the fact that almost all the other changes or influences mentioned by our critic would have had no differential effect on the output or sales of the various grades. These changes in the economic environment include the control of tree disease, produce inspection, research, the financing arrangements of the purchasing boards and improvement in port facilities. These influences might have affected the terms on which producers could sell palm oil or cocoa relatively to other products, but they would not have affected systematically the relative terms on which they could sell different grades of the same product. Only one or two of the other factors discussed by our critic might conceivably have had a differential effect as among grades – for example, speedier transport made it possible to avoid deterioration in the best quality of palm oil.[6]

The statutory body responsible for the marketing of groundnuts in Nigeria adopted a policy of inter-grade price differentials similar to that described in our paper for palm oil and cocoa. Dr Hogendorn,

---

[4] The willingness of peasants to take risks on anticipated price changes is nothing new in West Africa. Early in this century it was well known that producers withheld supplies of oil nuts when stocks at the processing plants were known to be low. Cf. Charles Wilson, *The History of Unilever*, 1954, vol. 1, p. 182.

[5] V. W. Hogg, 'Response to Price in an Under-developed Economy', *Economic Journal*, December 1960, pp. 852–5.

[6] For a fuller discussion see our 'Response to Price in an Under-developed Economy: A Rejoinder', *Economic Journal*, December 1960, pp. 855–6.

in a recent Note, has traced the effects of this policy, which demonstrate a high degree of responsiveness on the part of producers and traders.[7]

In the situations studied by Dr Hogendorn and ourselves, the changes made by producers in response to changes in relative prices were limited to changes in the quality of their output of a given product. Responsiveness to changes in relative prices involving the substitution of the production of one product for that of others (or for other activites) has been the subject of a number of studies in which a variety of methods of approach has been used. All of these studies known to us support the hypothesis that agricultural producers in under-developed countries shift resources and effort from one product to another according to changes in relative prices, the speed and extent of response being dependent on a variety of other influences and circumstances. A selection of the more recent of these studies follows: R.M.Stern, 'The Price Responsiveness of Egyptian Cotton Producers', *Kyklos*, vol. XII, fasc. 3 (1959); W.O.Jones, 'Economic Man in Africa', *Food Research Institute Studies*, May 1960; R.M.Stern, 'The Price Responsiveness of Primary Producers', *Review of Economics and Statistics*, May 1962; R.Krishna, 'Farm Supply Response in India–Pakistan: A Case Study of the Punjab Region', *Economic Journal*, September 1963; D.E.Welsch, 'Response to Economic Incentive by Abakaliki Rice Farmers in Eastern Nigeria', *Journal of Farm Economics*, November 1965; D.Narain, *The Impact of Price Movements on Areas under Selected Crops in India 1900–39*, Cambridge, 1965; C.H.H.Rao, *Agricultural Production Functions, Costs and Returns in India*, 1965; R.H.Green and S.H.Hymer, 'Cocoa in the Gold Coast: A Study in the Relations between African Farmers and Agricultural Experts', *Journal of Economic History*, September 1966; E.Dean, *The Supply Responses of African Farmers: Theory and Measurement in Malawi*, Amsterdam, 1966; R.E.Baldwin, *Economic Development and Export Growth: A Study of Northern Rhodesia, 1920–60*, Berkeley, 1966.

[7] J.S.Hogendorn, 'Response to Price Change: A Nigerian Example', *Economica*, August 1967, p. 325.

6

ORGANISED COMMODITY STABILISATION WITH VOLUNTARY PARTICIPATION*

In discussions of commodity price stabilisation it is often said that fluctuations in market prices (or proceeds) make it difficult for individual producers to plan their expenditure optimally through time, or for governments to manage their foreign exchange reserves (and hence their development planning) to best advantage. Thus it has been argued that the individual producer who may wish to stabilise or smooth his expenditures through time is unable to do so because he cannot effectively forecast prices or proceeds, and lacks the self-restraint necessary to build up liquid balances in good years, especially when he is under strong social pressures to spend up to the hilt. And individual governments may be in a similar situation, *mutatis mutandis*.

In this article we outline a type of stabilisation scheme adapted to meet the needs of such individuals or governments. The type of scheme has three special characteristics: it is voluntary; it does not require any control over capacity, production, sales, stocks, exports, or imports; and it does not directly affect the price of the commodity in question (and hence relative prices). This combination of characteristics does not seem to be present in stabilisation schemes used in practice or discussed in the literature. Our limited purpose here is to show the feasibility of a voluntary scheme, and the main implications, both analytical and practical, of its mode of operation. The article is concerned neither with the extent of the likely demand for voluntary stabilisation schemes, nor with the advocacy of such schemes as against other schemes (especially since some schemes differ in their objective(s) from that at present under discussion). Moreover, it is not concerned with a set of issues which are common to all commodity stabilisation schemes and not peculiar to the present type of scheme: the determination of the time-span of

* *Oxford Economic Papers*, March 1964, pp. 105–13.

stabilisation, of the extent of stabilisation to be aimed at, and of the detailed decisions (each subject to the possibility of error) in the practical implementation of the chosen policy.

The voluntary smoothing scheme described here will be seen as a voluntary counterpart of compulsory buffer-fund schemes. Buffer-fund stabilisation for individual export commodities is well known from the operations of various statutory marketing boards (as in West Africa and Uganda) and, less frequently, of variable export-duty schemes (as in Malaya).[1] These statutory bodies operate on the exports of a particular commodity, without any direct control over the home market. It has been taken for granted that such schemes must be compulsory, because otherwise producers would opt in when producer prices were being supported and opt out in the reverse situation, in this way destroying the scheme. Our method for voluntary stabilisation would avoid this obstacle.[2]

Section 1 describes voluntary smoothing arrangements for producers of a commodity within a country. Section 2 points up the salient implications of these arrangements. Section 3 notes the implications of the possible application to compulsory buffer-fund schemes of the distinctive operational feature of our voluntary method. Section 4 refers briefly to the application of the voluntary smoothing method at the inter-governmental level.

1

A voluntary smoothing organisation operating strictly in accordance with the methods of compulsory buffer-fund schemes would announce annually its smoothed producer price and pay members for deliveries of the commodity at this rate. It would then export its supplies, accumulating funds when the export price exceeded the

---

[1] To simplify the exposition we make no further reference to variable export-duty schemes, but consider export monopsonies (marketing boards) only, when referring to compulsory buffer-fund schemes.

[2] Our method could be operated so as to attempt to smooth the receipts per unit of product or, by allowing for variations in output, the total receipts of member producers. Compulsory buffer-fund schemes could also pursue either objective, though in practice they have operated on receipts per unit (i.e. producer prices) without attempting to allow for changes in volume. As the pursuit of either objective is possible with our method, we shall refer to the smoothing of receipts generally without specifying it more closely except on one occasion where the context requires it.

producer price, and drawing on them in the opposite situation.[3] But, for the reason already mentioned, such a scheme would be untenable. A method can be devised to overcome this apparently insurmountable obstacle without the conferment on the organisation of the sole right to export. This device is the linking of the individual member's participation in the scheme with a fixed annual quantity of the commodity, referred to henceforth as the 'participation quantity'. Each member would be obliged to deliver annually to the organisation neither more nor less than his stated participation quantity regardless of his actual output. Members would not be able to inflate their claims when the smoothed producer price was favourable relatively to the export price, nor to avoid contributions when it was unfavourable. However, once the device of fixed participation quantities is introduced, it becomes possible to go further and to divorce completely the provision of smoothing facilities from the handling and marketing of the commodity. It is this second variant which we consider throughout the rest of the article.

In this variant members themselves would market their output, and would not sell or deliver anything to the smoothing organisation. The organisation would announce annually the smoothing payment per unit of the commodity it would make to members or receive from them. We call this the 'smoothing adjustment'. Each member would receive or pay the smoothing adjustment in respect of his participation quantity regardless of his actual output or the price obtained by himself. Members therefore would receive the market proceeds on the disposal of their output, and receive or pay the smoothing adjustments specified by the organisation in the pursuit of its smoothing objective. The organisation would do no more than decide the appropriate smoothing adjustments and handle the buffer-fund finances (including the investment of funds) arising from their implementation. The organisation would broadly resemble a savings bank in which participants had individual accounts, with the sole important difference that the organisation and not the depositor would determine the amount of his annual deposit or withdrawal.[4]

---

[3] Throughout this article all prices (producer prices, home market prices, and export prices) are meant to be expressed on a common (strictly comparable) basis, i.e. allowance is made implicitly for differences in transport costs, etc.

[4] The smoothing adjustment per unit in a given year would ordinarily not be the same for all participants, but would differ according to their year of entry into the scheme. This is obvious where, as is likely, the balance (per unit of

Depending on its success in forecasting (i.e. in determining the smoothing adjustments), the organisation would alter favourably the flow of net receipts to its members in respect of their participation quantities. Each member would decide the extent of his participation by his choice of participation quantity, which need not be the same for all members.

The application of our method would be practicable in any situation, the sole requirement being that members must be identifiable. This characteristic is generally present in most parts of the world; moreover, it can be ensured by the issue to members of instruments of membership analogous to savings deposit-books, the use of which is widespread even in largely illiterate societies.

A separate account would be kept for each participant, recording his payments to the organisation and receipts from it. Receipts and payments would be managed so as to ensure that a member did not during his membership receive more from the buffer fund than he paid into it (except for adjustments for interest and expenses).[5] Members could be allowed to change their participation quantities by making or receiving the appropriate *ad hoc* payment. Though some organisations might wish to specify a minimum period of membership, it would be practicable to allow a member to resign at any time with a final settlement of his account.

Where participation is confined to creditworthy producers, a voluntary organisation could be started either at a time when it was to receive payments from members or when it was to make payments to them.[6] Otherwise it would have to be started at a time when the

product) on a member's account with the scheme would be treated as one of the determinants of the smoothing adjustment. The balance would be the same for all members who joined the scheme in the same year, and hence the smoothing adjustment for them would be the same; but, save coincidentally, this balance would not be the same as the balances of members who joined earlier or later. In effect, the organisation would proceed as if there were a separate fund for each year-of-entry cohort of participants, with appropriate levels of smoothing adjustment for each cohort. (Administrative complexities could be reduced by terminating each group after a specified number of years, and by allowing the members to join another group after an initial financial adjustment.) The point raised in this footnote does not affect anything discussed in the rest of this article, and therefore no further reference is made to it.

[5] In compulsory buffer-fund schemes of the kind found in practice the haphazard redistribution of proceeds among producers is unavoidable.

[6] In the latter case it would have to borrow its initial funds; and it could borrow on the security of future claims on its creditworthy members.

appropriate smoothing adjustment involved payments to the organisation, that is when expected market prices were considered favourable in relation to the chosen smoothing objective. In principle, a compulsory buffer-fund scheme could be started at any time, though as far as we know in practice they have all started by the withholding of part of market proceeds from producers.

2

The analytical and operational implications of our smoothing method derive from its central feature, the fixed participation quantities of members.

The smoothing adjustments payable or receivable by a member would not directly affect his output decisions. The amount payable or receivable by him in any year would be given, regardless of his actual output of the commodity or his disposal of it. In this limited sense the smoothing adjustments would be analogous to lump-sum taxes or subsidies. Thus the arrangements would not directly affect the production of the commodity or its domestic or world market prices.[7] A compulsory buffer-fund scheme, on the other hand, directly affects the price of the commodity, and thus the relative prices confronting producers and consumers. Within the country the scheme substitutes its prescribed producer price for the world market price of the commodity. Thus a compulsory scheme affects the total output of the commodity produced (except where the supply has zero price-elasticity); it affects the domestic market price, and hence the absorption of the commodity domestically; and in both these ways it affects the volume of exports and thus export earnings. Where export demand is not perfectly elastic, it also affects the world price of the commodity.[8] Moreover, by altering the relative

[7] Voluntary membership would imply, of course, that the producer had placed himself in a preferred position, and this might influence his economic decisions and thus indirectly affect output and prices. However, as it is shown below, voluntary smoothing facilities could be provided for any product, whether exported or not, in respect of which there was some demand for smoothing facilities. In this way smoothing facilities would be neutral in their indirect effects on the relative attractiveness to producers of different lines of production.

Again, membership of a voluntary scheme would alter the flow of receipts to the producer, and thus might affect his output decisions through time. Or producers might interpret the (implicit) stabilised prices of the scheme as the best available forecast of long-term average price, and act accordingly. These indirect effects on price seem to be common to all stabilisation schemes.

[8] A more detailed analysis of the output and price implications of compulsory

prices confronting producers and consumers, the production and consumption of other commodities are affected. These (probably unintended) consequences of compulsory buffer-fund schemes (and other stabilisation schemes) would be absent in a voluntary scheme.

Two subsidiary points may be noted. First, a constraint on decision-making in compulsory schemes is presented by the influence of the level of its prescribed producer price on sales to the export monopsony. This constraint would be absent in our method since participation quantities are fixed. Thus, unexpectedly perhaps, voluntary arrangements have a greater freedom of manœuvre and therefore a wider range of smoothing possibilities.[9] This difference can be illustrated by means of a simple example. Suppose that in the light of their smoothing objective and forecasts the managers wish to increase the buffer fund by a specific amount in the forthcoming season. This would present no difficulty with our method: the appropriate smoothing adjustment per unit could be announced and the precise amount collected on the known total of fixed participation quantities. In a compulsory scheme, however, the size of the surplus in any year depends in part on the difference between the prescribed producer price and the realised export price, and in part on the amount sold to the monopsony at the prescribed price. There may be no prescribed price which is such that, given the export price, it would elicit sufficient supplies for export to yield the required surplus.[10]

buffer-fund stabilisation is presented by R.H.Snape and B.S.Yamey, 'A Diagrammatic Analysis of Some Effects of Buffer Fund Price Stabilization', *Oxford Economic Papers*, July 1963.

[9] It will be recalled, however, that, except where its members were creditworthy, a voluntary organisation would be less flexible in timing the commencement of its smoothing operations (see p. 93, above). For the same reason smoothing adjustments would have to be made subject to the constraint that at all times the balance of its fund was positive or zero. A compulsory scheme is more flexible, in principle, in that it can go into deficit and subsequently make good its 'losses'.

[10] It is thus fortuitous whether a compulsory scheme can achieve a particular pattern of smoothing. Thus suppose it is desired that a compulsory scheme should equalise annual producer receipts (from home and export sales) over a smoothing period of two years, leaving the buffer fund with no balance (positive or negative) at the end of the period. Let p_1 and p_2 be the prescribed prices, e_1 and e_2 the export prices, and q_1 and q_2 the total output, in the two years; let $e_1 > p_1$ and let $(q_1 - h_1)$ and $(q_2 - h_2)$ be the quantities sold to the export monopsony at prices p_1 and p_2 in the two years. It is therefore necessary that:

(1) $p_1 q_1 = p_2 q_2$;
(2) $(e_1 - p_1)(q_1 - h_1) = (p_2 - e_2)(q_2 - h_2)$;

Second, an additional variable has to be forecast in a compulsory scheme as compared with a voluntary organisation using our method. The voluntary smoothing organisation would know the aggregate volume of the commodity to which the smoothing adjustment would be applied, viz. the sum of the members' participation quantities. The corresponding datum in a compulsory scheme, viz. the volume of sales to the monopsony, has to be forecast.

In Section 1 we saw that the device of fixed participation quantities would enable the smoothing operations to be divorced from the marketing and handling of the commodity. An important corollary is that the scope of our method of smoothing is wider than that of compulsory buffer-fund schemes. In practice compulsory buffer-fund schemes have been confined to commodities which are wholly or partly exported from the countries in question. This is because the flow of exports is readily subject to control, while effective control over disposals of the output of a non-exported commodity would ordinarily have to be extensive and expensive. Our method, on the other hand, would be generally applicable because its implementation would be independent of the disposal of the output or the control of its movements.[11] Moreover our method would have wider potential scope for yet another reason. Because smoothing arrangements would be independent of deliveries of the commodity, smoothing facilities could be made available to those who do not produce the commodity but whose earnings depend on its market price and volume of output. These facilities may be of value to farm workers, traders, and processors.

The central feature of our scheme, the fixed participation quantities of members, enables participation to be voluntary. We note briefly the implications of the voluntary nature of the scheme.

The choice open to producers is widened. Producers would decide whether or not to join the scheme; a compulsory scheme can be avoided only by not producing the controlled commodity. Moreover,

(3) h_1, p_1 is a point on the home demand function in the first year;

(4) h_2, p_2 is a point on the home demand function in the second year.

There may be no pair of prescribed prices, p_1 and p_2, which satisfies all these conditions.

[11] Some compulsory schemes have encountered problems because of smuggling into or out of the country arising from differences between prescribed prices and external prices. These problems would not arise for voluntary organisations.

there could be several different organisations for a particular commodity, with different membership rules, regional affiliations, forms of organisation (private, co-operative, municipal, or state) and smoothing policies. Further, each producer would choose his participation quantity at the time of entry, and could change it at his discretion (by making the appropriate financial adjustment). Where the situation and preferences of producers differ and vary, as is usually the case, the wider choice would lead to a more preferred adjustment of facilities to individual requirements and changes in requirements.[12] Moreover, some (possibly many) producers may prefer to contract out of all organised smoothing, particularly since any attempt at stabilisation is subject to the risk that in error it may in fact destabilise rather than stabilise.

Some compulsory schemes have been transformed into instruments of taxation by diverting part of the buffer funds for purposes other than the maintenance of producer prices or receipts.[13] This could not happen to voluntary arrangements. More generally, the managers or administrators of a voluntary organisation could not deviate from its announced objectives without the approval of members who could and would withdraw if they were dissatisfied. In practice, administrators would be obliged to specify their policy in some detail. The organisers would also have to announce in advance the basis of their remuneration (where relevant, as in a privately organised scheme) and the steps to be taken to safeguard the funds held in trust for the members.

[12] A particular instance of the adaptability of voluntary arrangements may be noted. Crop variations are not necessarily uniform in different parts of a country. A single national compulsory scheme could destabilise the flow of receipts of substantial regional groups of producers even if it reduced the fluctuations in the national total of producers' receipts. It is no solution to have separate regional schemes with different prescribed prices, or a single scheme with different regional prescribed prices; for, wherever possible, producers would deliver their output to the region with the most favourable prescribed price, and thus defeat the purpose of the arrangements. On the other hand, voluntary local or regional organisations could operate to take into account variations in output which diverge from the national pattern.

It would not, however, be practicable to treat each member separately to allow for the individual peculiarities of output variations.

[13] A compulsory buffer-fund scheme could conceivably be used to subsidise producers of a product if the government is prepared to meet its recurrent deficits from general funds. We do not know of any buffer-fund scheme where this has been done.

It is, of course, possible that only few producers would join voluntary smoothing organisations. The decision to participate would depend on individual assessments of the private net benefits of participation. But advocacy of smoothing arrangements for important commodities often does not rest solely on the value of satisfying the needs of producers. It is sometimes argued that the smoothing of the flow of producers' receipts is desirable because it promotes the stability of the economy as a whole; i.e. that smoothing schemes yield social as well as private benefits. Even though they would meet the varying individual needs of producers more closely than compulsory schemes, voluntary smoothing arrangements would not secure the social benefits unless they succeeded in attracting sufficient of those producers who would not otherwise smooth their expenditures. The stabilisation of the economy as a whole may, however, be attempted by government policy measures operating independently of smoothing schemes, although their detailed effects and incidence would be different.

3

We have so far been concerned with the application of the device of fixed participation quantities to *voluntary* stabilisation arrangements. This device could, however, be grafted on to a *compulsory* buffer-fund scheme. The government or its appointed agency could prepare a list of all producers of the commodity and assign to each a fixed (though not necessarily uniform) participation quantity. The list and the individual quantities could presumably be revised from time to time.

It follows that several of the features of the voluntary scheme, discussed in the preceding section, would be shared by such a compulsory scheme. (Thus the authority would not have to handle the commodity nor require monopsony power; and stabilisation could be applied both to exported and to non-exported commodities.) But there would obviously be certain differences between compulsory and voluntary schemes applying the same device of fixed participation quantities. Two points are of interest:

(i) Because the scheme would be compulsory, producers could not withdraw from the scheme and would therefore not be able to exercise control over its policy as in a voluntary scheme. (Even the cessation of production might not automatically release a producer from the scheme.) Thus there would be no effective check on the conversion of the scheme into an instrument of taxation. The incidence of any such taxation would be arbitrary and would depend in part on the necessarily arbitrary determination of individual participation quantities.

(ii) Once an individual had been brought within the scheme – by the assissgnment of a participation quantity – his decisions as to production and disposal of output would not in the short run be affected by the smoothing decisions of the scheme. In this respect it would be like a voluntary scheme, with the particular consequences which have already been noted in Section 2. Thus the use of the scheme as an instrument of taxation (or, alternatively, as an instrument of subsidisation) would not in the short run affect producers' behaviour, since the tax (or subsidy) would be in the nature of a lump-sum imposition (or grant) divorced from actual production or output. Taxation (or subsidisation) through the scheme would not inhibit (or promote) production of the commodity. But in the longer run behaviour would be affected directly in the usual way if it was anticipated that participation quantities would be revised from time to time in the light of changes in capacity and output.

4

Voluntary arrangements would be feasible internationally on the following lines. Governments which lacked confidence in their ability to forecast changes in their export receipts from a commodity, or to cope with the balance-of-payments implications of fluctuations in these receipts, would establish an international organisation. The managers of the organisation would be entrusted with the responsibility for determining a smoothing policy and for implementing it. Each participating government would decide its participation quantity, based, presumably, on the country's normal output or exports of the commodity, the strength of the desire for smoothing cover, the attractiveness to it of the chosen smoothing policy, and its confidence in the management of the organisation. Each participant would make or receive payments to or from the organisation in accordance with its smoothing decisions. If the organisation achieved its objective, the flow of foreign exchange receipts of participating countries would be smoothed to the extent of their participation quantities.

Successful smoothing of the flow of a member country's receipts of foreign exchange would facilitate the management by government of its foreign exchange reserves. It would not, however, by itself smooth the domestic demand for imports, which would be liable to such fluctuations as were associated with fluctuations in producers' receipts from the sale of the product. It would be left to other policy measures to smooth the domestic demand for imports.

A voluntary international organisation of the kind described here would not in any way affect the international marketing of the commodity or trade in it, would not establish any international monopsony or monopoly situations, nor require control of the import or export of the commodity, and would not directly affect the volume of supplies entering international trade.

Part 2

P. T. BAUER

7

THE WORKING OF RUBBER REGULATION*

1

The International Rubber Regulation Scheme operated effectively from June 1934 to the early part of 1942. During this period it controlled 97 per cent of world rubber exports and it applied to over 99 per cent of the area under rubber. It was a quota scheme: basic or territorial quotas were allotted to the participating territories, and exports were restricted in accordance with rates of release prescribed by the International Rubber Regulation Committee (IRRC).[1] The IRRC was composed of delegations from the participating territories. With irrelevant exceptions all the voting members were government officials. Malaya and Netherlands India[2] were much the most important participants, each with about two-fifths of total output; Ceylon was third with about 8 per cent. Most of this

---

Economic Journal, September 1946, pp. 391–414.

[1] Some definition of these terms is necessary. By quota is meant the agreed notional productive capacity under reasonably favourable conditions of each participating territory, calculated largely on the basis of exports in the years 1929–32, with allowances for areas immature during this period. These basic or territorial quotas in effect represented the shares of the participating territories in permitted exports. What mattered, therefore, was not the absolute size of the quotas, but their relationship to each other. In Malaya and Netherlands India, the territorial quotas were divided into two separate parts for estates and small-holdings respectively. Territorial quotas were shared out among individual producers, and the individual shares were known as assessments. As will be noted below, a different method of restriction operated for smallholders in Netherlands India until the end of 1936. Permissible exports in any year were determined by the rates of release prescribed by the IRRC. Production in any one year was usually closely determined by the rates of release because local processing of rubber was over this period negligible in the major producing territories. Stocks within the controlled areas were in effect governed largely by the rates of release; the scheme also placed certain narrow upper limits on stocks which could be held in producing countries.

[2] Netherlands India is the present Indonesia, but as it was Netherlands India throughout the period here reviewed it will be referred to by that name.

103

article will deal with the operation of the scheme in the two principal territories. The scheme covered both estates and smallholdings. The estates are units of several hundred or so acres each operated with substantial capital and employing a large labour force. The small-holdings' acreage is owned by Asians, largely in units of a few acres each, usually worked by the owner and his family, but occasionally employing outside labour, mainly on a share basis. The distinction between estates and smallholdings is broadly clear, although the official line of division differs slightly in the different participating territories.[3]

The scheme was quantitatively among the most important, prob-ably the most important, of the pre-war restriction schemes of primary products. Rubber was in the 1930s much the most important export from the British colonial empire and also the most valuable cash crop of smallholders in the British or Dutch colonies.

The scheme was the second major rubber restriction scheme. It had a predecessor in the Stevenson Restriction Scheme, which operated from 1922 to 1928 in Malaya and Ceylon only. From November 1928 through May 1934 production was unrestricted. Under the Stevenson scheme the assessment per mature acre of Malayan smallholdings was about half of that of estates. After its repeal yields per mature acre on smallholdings regularly exceeded appreciably the yields on estates; some information on this point is presented in Table 4 below. The performance of smallholdings after the repeal of the Stevenson scheme made clear their substantial under-assessment under the scheme.[4]

The division of Malayan territorial quota and its implications are

[3] The smallholders were at the time generally referred to as natives. This usage was inaccurate because in all major producing territories outside Netherlands India much of the smallholding area was owned by Chinese and Indians, who were not natives of the country. These ethnic distinctions have become even clearer now than they were in the 1930s and 40s. In the original version of this paper the terms smallholder and native were used interchangeably. In the present version smallholder is used throughout (except in verbatim quotations from other sources) for reasons of accuracy and consistency. Smallholding and small-holder are used largely interchangeably as adjectives as seems more appropriate in the context.

[4] Throughout this article, under-assessment denotes a situation where produc-tion of one group is compulsorily restricted to a greater extent than that of another group compared to what their production would have been in the absence of restriction at prevailing prices.

TABLE 1

Internal distribution of the Malayan territorial quota,[1] 1934–40

	estates		smallholdings	
	thousand tons	per cent of Malayan quota	thousand tons	per cent of Malayan quota
1934	312·5	61·1	199·1	38·9
1935	334·6	62·5	200·4	37·5
1936	352·6[2]	61·7	219·4	38·3
1937	373·2	61·8	230·9	38·2
1938	377·4	61·7	234·5	38·3
1939	395·9	61·9	244·0	38·1
1940	407·4	62·3	246·4	37·7

1. The total of these quotas slightly exceeded the Malayan territorial quota, and this necessitated the eventual introduction of internal cuts (reductions in rates of release below the internationally agreed rate).

2. For administrative reasons, some properties owned by Indian money-lenders were transferred in 1936 from the estate to the smallholdings quota. Their assessments totalled some 6,000 tons, and to this extent all the tables slightly overstate the true smallholdings quota from 1936 onwards.

shown in the following five tables, of which the first two are formal summaries of the division.[5]

The principal implications of these tables are clear, but some elaboration and clarification may be useful. The sharp reduction in the

In the discussion preceding the introduction of the International Scheme, it was repeatedly stated by official spokesmen in Malaya, Netherlands India and London (including a statement in the House of Commons) that great care would be taken that any regulation scheme should operate fairly between estates and smallholders in that the latter should not be under-assessed and thus bear an unwarranted share of the burden of restriction. In fact, some of these official statements went further and promised that the smallholders would be given the benefit of any doubt in the distribution of quotas.

[5] The tables have been derived from the official *Annual Reports* of the Controller of Rubber, and from the official annual *Malayan Rubber Statistics Handbook*, supplemented in a few instances by reference to the records of the IRRC. The statistics of the age composition of the estate and smallholding acreage required for the statistics presented in Tables 2 and 4 were derived from the records of the IRRC. This information can also be found in various published Malayan agricultural statistics. As the information was conveniently summarised in the records of the IRRC, this source was used for this particular purpose.

TABLE 2[1]

Quotas of Malayan estates and smallholdings expressed in lb per acre, 1934–40
(to the nearest 5 lb)

	estates		smallholdings	
	per acre	per mature acre	per acre	per mature acre
1934	350	385	340	365
1935	375	405	340	355
1936	395	420	375	385
1937	415	440	395	400
1938	425	450	400	405
1939	430	470	405	420
1940	435	500	405	425

1. Mature acreage refers to planted areas five or more years old.

TABLE 3

Shares of estates and smallholdings in Malayan rubber production, 1929–40
(tons, to the nearest 1,000 tons)

	estates		smallholdings	
	tons	as per cent of total Malayan production	tons	as per cent of total Malayan production
1929	246,000	55·2	200,000	44·8
1930	236,000	54·6	197,000	45·4
1931	240,000	55·1	197,000	44·9
1932	240,000	57·6	177,000	42·4
1933	240,000	52·2	221,000	47·8
June–Dec. 1933	149,000	50·9	144,000	49·1
June 1933–May 1934	251,000	49·7	253,000	50·3
Jan.–May 1934	102,000	48·3	107,000	51·7
	regulation introduced			
June–Dec. 1934	160,000	59·7	108,000	40·3
1935	243,000	64·0	137,000	36·0
1936	233,000	63·9	132,000	36·1
1937	314,000	62·4	189,000	37·6
1938	246,000	68·1	115,000	31·9
1939	245,000	67·7	117,000	32·3
1940	334,000	60·8	215,000	39·2

TABLE 4

Annual output of rubber per mature acre of Malayan estates and smallholdings, 1929–40

(lb, to the nearest 5 lb)

	estates	smallholdings	smallholdings as per cent of estates
1929	410	485	118
1930	380	460	121
1931	375	445	119
1932	365	385	106
1933	355	465	131
1934	regulation introduced during the year		
1935	295	240	81
1936	275	230	84
1937	375	330	88
1938	290	200	69
1939	290	200	69
1940	410	370	90

These figures have been calculated by dividing the actual output by the mature area, i.e. by the acreage five or more years old. The relatively wide fluctuations in the last column between 1932 and 1933 reflect the smallholders' reaction to the very low prices of 1932 and to the recovery of 1933. They show the forward rising supply curve of smallholders' rubber. The very low figures in the last column in 1938 and 1939 are explained by sales of rights by smallholders to estates; in 1940 the sales were in the reverse direction. These transactions are discussed in the text.

---

smallholders' share in Malayan production after 1933 reflects the division of the Malayan territorial quota. This can be seen at a glance by comparing Table 1, which shows the division of the quota, with Table 3, which shows the share of the two groups in total Malayan production. From 1934 onwards, estate output was about five-eighths and smallholder output about three-eighths of the total, which corresponded closely to the division of the territorial quota (Table 1). In contrast, the share of smallholders in total production in the last few years before the introduction of regulation was appreciably larger (Tables 3 to 5). This easily accessible information disposes of the suggestion widely canvassed in the 1930s that the reduction of smallholders' production as percentage of total Malayan

107

TABLE 5

Comparison of previous output[1] of Malayan estates and smallholdings with their 1934 quotas

(tons, to the nearest 5,000 tons)

		estates	small-holdings	London price, pence per lb
(a)	Output for calendar year 1933	240,000	220,000	3·2
(b)	Output for twelve months ending May 1934	250,000	250,000	4·5
(c)	Annual rate of production based on seasonally corrected output, March–May 1934	265,000	300,000	5·8
(d)	1934 quotas	310,000	200,000	—
(e)	(d) as per cent of (a)	129	91	—
	(b)	124	80	—
	(c)[2]	117	67	—

1. These are production figures; stock changes are allowed for.
2. In the spring of 1934 the price was nearer to the price visualised under restriction than it had been in 1933. The quotas of different classes of producer may be considered fair (in the sense that neither group is under-assessed) if their ratio is roughly proportionate to approximate unrestricted outputs at the prices envisaged under restriction. This lends special interest to the comparison of (c) with (d).

output was the result of the sales of export rights from smallholders to estates.[6]

Comparison of Tables 1 and 3 sufficiently summarises the principal

[6] In 1938 and 1939 smallholder production was less than the share of small-holders in the quota. In those two years the smallholders were not sellers of export rights to the estates, while in 1940 net sales were in the reverse direction.

Smallholders' export rights were issued to them in the form of coupons; estates were credited with export rights in the ledgers of the control authorities. Many, probably most, smallholders normally sold their coupons immediately to dealers and subsequently produced physical rubber, which the exporting dealers would marry with coupons. Under this system, either group could be net buyers or sellers of export rights via the dealers, depending on whether their output of physical rubber exceeded or fell short of their total export rights. The situation can be seen by comparing the shares of estates and smallholdings in Malayan production with their shares in the quotas which determined their share in export rights.

indication of the division of the Malayan territorial quota. Tables 3 and 5 to a large extent only ring the changes on the same theme. Tables 2 and 4 are, however, useful in forestalling a possible objection to the effect that the division of the quota reflected not so much the under-assessment of the smallholders, but was the result of the relatively larger immature acreage on estates, which was taken into account in determining the territorial quotas, and was thus properly taken into account in dividing the quotas between estates and smallholdings. The information presented in these two tables rebuts this possible objection.[7] If the division of the Malayan territorial quota had been computed on the same basis as was adopted for the calculation of the total Malayan quota, the division would have been about 55–45 per cent, instead of about 62–38 per cent actually adopted.

It was often said before the introduction of rubber regulation that the smallholder output before its introduction could not have been maintained, because the smallholders were overtapping their trees. This assertion was unfounded. An official inquiry on bark consumption and bark reserves on Malayan smallholdings took place in 1931–3, and it found that the rate of bark consumption was far lower than had been believed, and that it was not in excess of the rate of bark renewal; bark reserves on the trees averaged about $7\frac{1}{2}$ years' bark consumption.[8] This is apart from the fact that smallholder acreage relative to the estate area would have been appreciably larger had it not been for the official restriction of the alienation for rubber planting since 1922.[9]

[7] This is apart from the fact that the relatively small immature acreage of smallholders in Malaya was largely the result of official policy since 1922 under which very little land was alienated for new planting of rubber since that date. Planting was largely confined between 1922 and 1934 to producers who owned land alienated to them before 1922, but not yet planted with rubber. Comparatively few smallholders had such unplanted reserve land.

[8] *Bark Consumption and Bark Reserves on Small Rubber Holdings in Malaya,* Kuala Lumpur, Department of Agriculture, SS and FMS, 1934. This report summarised the results of the first systematic enquiry into conditions on Malayan smallholdings. The enquiry was promoted by the obvious need to revise widely publicised views. The results conclusively contradicted oft-repeated statements of the alleged squandering of bark reserves on smallholdings. It also made clear that there were ample reserves for the maintenance for many years at the then current rate of production.

[9] In the autumn of 1933 the application of rubber restriction to Malaya was considered by a committee of the Rubber Growers' Association. Its recommendations were embodied in an unpublished but widely circulated report, intended

It is possible to compute very roughly the monetary equivalent of the under-assessment of the holdings. If the estate and smallholding quotas had been calculated on the same basis as had been adopted internationally for the computation of territorial quotas (including the Malayan quota), the division would have been about 55 per cent for estates and 45 per cent for smallholdings. If the shares of estates and smallholdings had been proportionate to their probable unrestricted outputs and prices envisaged under restriction, the quota would have been divided about equally. If it had been divided on the basis of the actual output of the two classes in the first five months of 1934 before the introduction of regulation (when prices had already risen appreciably from the low levels of 1932 and the early part of 1933, but were still below those envisaged under restriction) the share of the smallholdings would have been about 48 per cent. If the division had been 52–48 per cent, the smallholding quotas for the period June 1934 to December 1941 would have been about 400,000 tons more than they actually were, and some two-thirds of this amount, or about 270,000 tons, would have been exportable. With a conservative valuation of export rights at an average of about 4d. per pound up-country throughout this period, the cost of the under-assessment to smallholders works out at around £10 million.[10] The under-assessment was for holdings which remained under rubber and there was no transfer of land to other uses to be set against this under-assessment. Some labour may have been transferred to leisure, but this would not affect the computation substantially.

The smallholder quota in Netherlands India was also very small in relation both to production on the eve of restriction and even more so in relation to capacity or to supply at prices envisaged under restriction. Indeed, it was so small that its inadequacy almost wrecked the whole regulation scheme in 1935 because for months on

chiefly for the benefit of the Malayan administrations. The suggestions for the division of the territorial quota were much more favourable to smallholders than the division which was actually adopted. Had the proposals of the representatives of large estates been adopted, the smallholders would have fared better than they actually did under the auspices of the local governments.

[10] This figure represents of course a *lucrum cessans*, and not a *damnum emergens*. Smallholder incomes were substantially higher under regulation than they would have been without it. For considerable periods the value of the smallholders' export rights exceeded the incomes they would have earned by tapping their trees in the absence of regulation.

end it proved impossible to restrict smallholder exports to the permitted amounts by the methods of regulation adopted, discussed below. For various reasons, chiefly the absence of acreage statistics, and also because of administrative changes and quota revisions, it is not possible to present a series of tables on Netherlands India similar to Tables 1 to 5 for Malaya. However, there is sufficient information to show the broad picture clearly.

Table 6 is analogous to Table 5 for Malaya.

TABLE 6

Comparison of previous output of Netherlands Indian estates and smallholders with their 1934 quotas

(long tons, to the nearest 5,000 tons)

		estates	small-holders[1]	London price, pence per lb
(a)	Output for calendar year 1933	170,000	115,000	3·2
(b)	Output for twelve months ending May 1934	180,000	185,000	4·5
(c)	Annual rate of production based on seasonally corrected output, March–May 1934	220,000	300,000	5·8
(d)	1934 quotas	205,000	145,000	—
(e)	(d) as per cent of (a)	121	126	—
	(b)	114	78	—
	(c)[2]	93	48	—

1. In this Table, exports have been taken as measuring production for smallholders, because there are no production statistics for Netherlands Indian smallholders over this period. Smallholder exports for March–May probably include some reduction in stocks and this slightly offset actual output. The amount is, however, certain to be very small, as the smallholders kept no stocks and dealers' stocks were also relatively small. Moreover, exports were in accordance with the rapidly rising trend since mid-1933.

2. The considerations summarised in the second note to Table 5 also apply to these figures. Moreover, in Netherlands India very large smallholding areas were reaching maturity in about 1933–4 for which little or no allowance was made in the 1934–5 quotas. The supply of smallholder rubber from Netherlands India was highly elastic, and the 1933 output was at a rate of only about one-third of the officially estimated capacity, an estimate which subsequently turned out to be a very large under-estimate.

111

TABLE 7
The working of the special export tax on smallholder rubber exports in NI
June 1934–December 1936.

	(1) Singapore price of medium blankets expressed in pence per lb	(2) ordinary NI export duty on smallholder rubber at 5% *ad valorem* of f.o.b. values, pence per lb	(3) special NI export duty on smallholder rubber, average rate for month, pence per lb	(4) approx. cost of shipping from NI port to Singapore, processing and marketing, pence per lb	(5) approx. expenses from interior to NI port, pence per lb	(6) approx. average return to smallholder, pence per lb	(7) Singapore price ex export duties, pence per lb
1934							
June	4·8	0·1	—	0·9	0·2	3·6	4·7
July	5·2	0·2	0·7	1·0	0·2	3·1	4·3
August	5·4	0·2	1·9	1·0	0·2	2·1	3·3
September	5·4	0·2	2·7	1·0	0·2	1·3	2·5
October	5·1	0·2	3·0	1·1	0·1	0·7	1·9
November	4·8	0·2	3·0	1·0	0·1	0·5	1·6
December	4·9	0·2	2·7	1·1	0·1	0·8	2·0
Last seven months of year	5·1	0·2	2·0	1·0	0·1	1·8	2·9
1935							
January	5·0	0·2	2·4	1·1	0·1	1·2	2·4
February	4·9	0·2	2·4	1·1	0·1	1·1	2·3
March	4·7	0·2	2·5	1·1	0·2	0·7	2·0
April	4·7	0·2	2·4	1·1	0·1	0·9	2·1
May	5·0	0·2	2·4	1·1	0·1	1·2	2·4
June	5·3	0·2	2·4	1·0	0·1	1·6	2·7
July	5·2	0·2	2·7	1·1	0·2	1·0	2·3
August	5·3	0·2	3·1	1·0	0·2	0·8	2·9
September	5·2	0·2	3·0	1·0	0·2	0·8	2·0
October	5·4	0·2	3·0	1·1	0·1	1·0	2·2
November	5·8	0·2	3·4	1·0	0·2	1·0	2·2
December	5·9	0·2	4·2	1·0	0·2	0·3	1·5
Year 1935	5·2	0·2	2·8	1·0	0·2	1·0	2·2
1936							
January	6·5	0·3	4·3	1·0	0·2	0·7	1·9
February	7·0	0·3	4·3	1·0	0·2	1·2	2·4
March	7·2	0·3	4·6	1·1	0·2	1·0	2·3
April	7·3	0·3	4·9	1·0	0·2	0·9	2·1
May	7·1	0·3	5·1	1·0	0·1	0·6	1·7
June	7·1	0·3	5·0	1·0	0·2	0·6	1·8
July	7·4	0·3	5·0	1·0	0·2	0·9	2·1
August	7·3	0·3	5·4	1·0	0·1	0·5	1·6
September	7·4	0·3	5·4	1·0	0·2	0·5	1·7
October	7·6	0·3	6·1	0·8	0·1	0·3	1·2
November	8·4	0·3	6·4	0·8	0·1	0·8	1·7
December	9·3	0·3	6·7	0·8	0·2	1·3	2·3
Year 1936	7·5	0·3	5·3	0·9	0·2	0·8	1·9

(8)	(9)	(10)		(11)			(12)	(13)
	approx. f.o.b. price ex export duties NI port, pence per lb	ordinary NI export duty as percentage of–		special NI export duty as percentage of–			exports of small-holder rubber– dry weight (long tons)	permis-sible ex-portable amount ex carry-over (long tons)
approx. price f.o.b. NI port, pence per lb		(a) f.o.b. price ex export duties (col. 9)	(b) average return to small-holder (col. 6)	(a) Singapore price (col. 1)	(b) price ex export duties (col. 9)	(c) average return to small-holder (col. 6)		
3·9	3·8	4	4	—	—	—	16,000	12,229
4·2	3·3	5	6	13	23	24	16,200	12,229
4·4	2·3	8	8	35	83	89	12,600	11,006
4·4	1·5	14	16	50	180	200	15,600	11,006
4·0	0·8	24	19	59	345	417	5,600	9,784
3·8	6·6	32	41	62	455	588	4,700	9,784
3·8	0·9	23	27	55	290	346	12,200	8,560
4·1	1·9	9	10	39	103	112	82,900	74,598
3·9	1·3	14	15	48	182	205	9,600	10,423
3·6	1·2	14	16	49	190	216	16,900	10,423
3·6	0·9	21	25	53	276	333	8,900	10,423
3·6	1·0	17	20	51	229	267	13,600	9,728
3·9	1·3	13	15	48	178	200	22,200	9,728
4·3	1·7	11	12	45	140	154	14,300	9,727
4·1	1·2	18	20	53	230	263	8,100	9,033
4·3	1·0	23	27	59	339	404	9,700	9,033
4·2	1·0	23	27	58	323	385	9,600	9,033
4·3	1·1	18	21	55	256	294	17,500	8,339
4·8	1·2	18	20	58	283	323	9,100	8,338
4·9	0·5	53	80	71	927	1,390	2,800	8,338
4·2	1·2	19	22	54	254	294	142,300	112,566
5·5	0·9	29	35	67	518	631	9,200	12,085
6·0	1·4	17	20	62	315	354	16,100	12,084
6·1	1·2	23	26	65	388	443	9,300	12,085
6·3	1·1	29	33	67	471	550	12,500	12,084
6·1	0·7	40	50	71	684	855	10,700	12,085
6·1	0·8	37	45	70	630	773	14,600	12,084
6·4	1·1	29	33	68	489	570	18,100	13,092
6·3	0·6	45	59	73	828	1,071	11,800	13,092
6·4	0·7	48	61	73	813	1,039	9,800	13,091
6·8	0·4	65	92	80	1,494	2,117	12,000	13,092
7·6	0·9	30	34	76	724	838	16,400	13,092
8·5	0·2	24	26	72	479	525	8,800	13,091
6·6	1·0	32	38	72	616	735	149,300	151,057

During the first two and a half years of restriction, from June 1934 to December 1936, there was no individual restriction of smallholders in NI. Smallholder exports were kept in check by means of a special export tax (special as distinct from the ordinary *ad valorem* tax levied on the f.o.b. value of native exports). This tax was designed to depress the price of smallholder rubber in the interior sufficiently to keep exports within the permissible limits, calculated from the total smallholder quota and the international rates of release. It was generally assumed that the absence of land survey and registration in Sumatra and Borneo was the sole reason for the introduction of the special tax as a method for restricting smallholder exports. The main reason, however, was the inadequacy of the smallholder quota, which until 1937 did not permit of individual assessments. The official nineteenth *Report on Native Rubber Cultivation in the Netherlands East Indies*[11] stated explicitly that individual restriction was impossible, first because registration would require too much time, money and labour, 'but more especially because the potential production of native rubber is considered to be so great that a division of the permissible exportable amount, based on productive capacity would result in the individual allotment being very small, and as a result some natives who depend for their existence entirely upon family tapping would be seriously affected, while owners of distant gardens worked with hired labour would benefit, and such owners cannot in the present circumstances be regarded as real producers'. It should be understood that the 'present circumstances' did not mean that the supply price of these producers was too high, but that the quota was too small to go round.

The working of the special export tax is shown in Table 7. The assumptions and data underlying the calculations are summarised in a Note in the Appendix, below. While the table, read together with the Note, largely explains itself, the following points may be emphasised. Had the expenses (columns 4 and 5) been taken as the equivalent of $4\frac{1}{2}$ gilder cents per half kilo (the figure more usually quoted, see Appendix) instead of 4 guilder cents, the average rate of tax would on several occasions have exceeded 6,000 per cent, on our calculations the maximum reached was about 2,100 per cent. The 5 per cent *ad valorem* revenue export tax, which was levied on

[11] Issued by the Division of Agricultural Economics in the NI Department of Agriculture, Batavia, 1934.

the f.o.b. value after payment of the special tax, frequently exceeded 40 per cent of the price ex the special tax.

Although these statistics embody large elements of estimation, the broad picture is clear. For instance, in 1936 exports of smallholders' rubber were 150,000 tons, with an f.o.b. price of about 1d. per lb. Around 1930 several observers put forward estimates of the prospective supply price of NI smallholder rubber for the mid-1930s.[12] These were generally in terms of 10d.–1s. per lb as the minimum necessary to draw out 120,000–150,000 tons of smallholder rubber. Moreover, the estimates were in terms of sterling before devaluation, while, with the exception of the last quarter of 1936, throughout the period covered by Table 7 sterling was devalued substantially in terms of the NI guilder, and a given sterling price in 1934–6 yielded a much lower guilder return to the NI smallholders than in 1929–31.

By 1933–4 it had already become clear that these estimates of the prospective supply price were very large under-estimates. In the early months of 1934 smallholder exports from NI were running at the yearly rate of 300,000 tons, with a London price of 5½d.–6d. per lb in devalued sterling.[13] The substantial exports of 1934–6 revealed that the supply price of NI smallholdings' rubber was a small fraction of the then current estimates.[14]

[12] Some of these are listed by Mr J.W.F.Rowe in London and Cambridge Economic Service, *Special Memorandum* no. 34, 1931, p. 71.

[13] Exports of smallholders' rubber from all producing territories were at an annual rate of about three-quarters of a million tons in the early months of 1934, just before the introduction of restriction. Moreover, very large areas were immature and were due to reach maturity in the late 1930s. Exports in 1934 were very largely the product of family tapping and were harvested from un-selected trees. Thus very large quantities of smallholder rubber would not be affected directly by a rise in money wages; and the long-period supply price may also be reduced if part of the smallholdings area comes to be planted with high yield material. These considerations bear on the competitive position of natural and synthetic rubber.

[14] Mr P.Lamartine Yates' *Commodity Control*, 1943, which purports to give a comprehensive and impartial review of rubber regulation, does not mention the implication of the planting provisions of the scheme, and does not refer to the internal division of the quotas, or to the under-assessment of the smallholders. On the other hand, the book states: 'The native, like peasants everywhere, tends to produce more rather than less when the price begins to fall. . . . In general the reaction to a price fall is quite insignificant; indeed, there is no experience to show how low the price would have to fall before native output was seriously curtailed' (p. 115). These are remarkable propositions. The forward-rising supply curve of smallholders' rubber emerged quite clearly during the slump years. For

Throughout the period of the operation of the special tax the IRRC repeatedly stated that the market price was appreciably below the level which would have yielded a 'reasonable return to efficient producers'.[15] The inadequacy of the market price of those years was also a regular theme of the presidential addresses to the Rubber-growers' Association. Yet close on three-quarters of these prices had to be taxed away to keep NI smallholder exports within permissible limits. According to the official IRRC view, a London price of 8d. was the bare minimum to furnish a 'reasonable return to efficient growers'; the figures in Table 7 are a fair comment on these hackneyed concepts.

When the special export tax was introduced, the NI authorities gave specific and unequivocal guarantees that the receipts would be used solely for the benefit of the native rubber-growing districts, over and above the expenditure allotted to these areas out of the general revenue.[16] The proceeds of the special tax were, however, so large that the authorities were unable to resist the temptation, and a substantial proportion of the proceeds was diverted to the general revenue. The government defended this policy on the grounds that the natives produced at such low cost that even the 1934–6 returns were profitable, while other sections of the NI economy, notably the rubber estates, were in great difficulties.[17]

instance, NI smallholder rubber exports fell from 107,000 tons in 1929 to 61,000 tons in 1932, exports from Sarawak (practically all smallholders' rubber) from 11,000 tons in 1929 to 7,000 tons in 1932. Moreover, in these territories, as elsewhere in the East, there was a steep rise in the area reaching maturity after 1929 (reflecting the Stevenson boom in the mid-1920s), so that in terms of capacity working the supply was much more elastic than would appear from export or production figures. Smallholders' output was substantially curtailed in every important producing territory during the depression. These facts can be ascertained from the most easily accessible sources.

[15] The semi-official *History of Rubber Regulation*, 1944, expresses the same view about the price ruling in 1935–6.

[16] The official nineteenth NI *Report on Native Rubber Cultivation* which we have already quoted, stated in 1934: 'The principle that the proceeds shall be spent for the benefit of the inhabitants of the rubber-producing areas is inseparably bound up with this particular system of restriction. This tax is not a fiscal device, but a means to secure restriction. A proportion of the proceeds is withheld from the exporter, and this is defensible only if the amounts so withheld are spent at once for the benefit of the districts from which the money was derived.'

[17] An official spokesman, addressing the Batavia Volksraad in 1936, argued that the smallholder had no costs, and that the price, even after the heavy export

Only fragmentary information is available on the internal operation of the regulation in other territories. In Ceylon, the assessments per acre of estates also much exceeded those of the smallholdings, and it is probable in that country also that the smallholders were under-assessed, but for various technical reasons this cannot be shown so clearly for that country. Some information on this general subject is available for British North Borneo. There are no official statistics on the division of the territorial quota between the estates and smallholdings in that country before 1939. In that year the average assessment of estates was about 500 lb per mature acre, and that of smallholdings about 215 lb, although the per acre capacity of the latter was unquestionably higher. From fragmentary data it appears that much the same ratio between the assessments of estates and of smallholdings prevailed throughout the operation of restriction. In 1936–7 a series of tapping experiments took place in Sarawak (just across the frontier from British North Borneo) under the auspices of the Malayan Survey Department. The average yield on the smallholdings examined was 489 lb per mature acre. It appears that the smallholders were particularly unfavourably treated in British North Borneo.

2

The planting provisions of the regulation scheme also operated to the disadvantage of the smallholders. Briefly, these prohibited new planting almost completely (with the exception noted in the following paragraph), while permitting at first a very large measure of replanting, and eventually unlimited replanting. To appreciate the effect of these provisions it is necessary to consider some semi-technical aspects of planting practice.

By replanting is meant the uprooting of an existing stand of rubber trees and their replacement by better-yielding material, while new planting is in effect the extension of the planted area. During 1934–8 (the currency of the first regulation period) new planting was completely prohibited, while a maximum of 20 per cent of the planted area could be replanted over this period. In the aggregate this implied virtually unlimited replanting, since it authorised the replanting of about 1·6 million acres (one-fifth of the total 1934 planted area of about eight million acres) within four and a half

tax, was remunerative to them, while the world price (several times the return left to the smallholder) hardly enabled the estates to survive.

years. Each individual owner was, however, also limited to re-planting a maximum of 20 per cent of his acreage under rubber during the whole period, and was only allowed to replant 10 per cent in any given year. In 1939–40 new planting equivalent to 5 per cent of the existing acreage was allowed; for the remaining years of the effective regulation new planting was prohibited; on the other hand, there was no restriction on replanting from 1939 onwards.

These arrangements jeopardised the future of the smallholder rubber industry. Replanting involves a loss of income for six years from the area felled, since it takes about that period for the trees to become tappable.[18] Thus this operation could only be contemplated by producers with ample working capital—i.e. in practice the larger estates, whose managers and owners moreover realised that by cutting out a part of their substantial acreage, they could harvest from the remaining area the crop they would be allowed to export under the scheme. These considerations already ensured that the smallholders would not undertake replanting on any scale. During the first regulation period they could not possibly have replanted to any extent, as each owner was limited to replanting a maximum of 10 per cent of his plantation in any one year, and to 20 per cent over the whole period. It is rarely practicable to replant successfully part of a holding totalling two or three acres or less, since the area to be replanted would be closely surrounded by mature trees which would intercept the sunlight, and whose roots would compete for food with the undeveloped rootlets of the newly planted trees. Moreover, smallholders practise a rough-and-ready rotational system of tapping and resting trees, not entire areas, and they are thus unable to fell part of their areas and harvest the crop from the balance, even if this were technically feasible, which usually it is not. Further, throughout the rubber-planting regions, there are large areas under uncultivated jungle which are suitable for planting of rubber. In these conditions smallholders were baffled by regulations insisting that their holdings should be cut out before they could plant rubber.

Lastly, when applying for permission to replant, much technical information had to be submitted to the authorities in writing, and this again handicapped the smallholder, who never understood the procedure. The planting provisions of rubber regulation enabled

[18] The Rubber Research Institute of Malaya estimated in 1938 that estates required about twelve years to recoup the cash expenses and the loss of income from replanting.

the estates to increase their capacity while effectively prohibiting the smallholders from extending theirs.

The replanting of the estate acreage with high-yielding material, together with the prohibition of new planting, would in the long run have eliminated the smallholders.[19] The physical decay of small-holdings would have been slow, since under smallholding conditions the rubber tree is not so much of a wasting asset as has often been assumed. Nevertheless, in due course there would have been some decline, particularly in areas with a long history of previous cultivation with such food crops as pineapples or tapioca, which make substantial demands on the soil, and unless the smallholders had been allowed some new planting, their share in the total output would have gradually decreased. Much more important in practice was the danger that the smallholders might have been eliminated as effective economic competitors, since without new planting they could not have taken advantage of high-yielding modern planting material.

The insistence on replanting and the prohibition of new planting were not motivated by any real or even by any ostensible apprehensions about the potential shortage of land or a danger of soil erosion. Not only is there unlimited land available in the more important rubber-growing areas, but the rubber tree takes next to nothing out of the soil, and under smallholding conditions actually nothing which would not be put back by the dense cover and the heavy leaf-fall; there is thus no question of soil mining such as has occurred in many countries with apparently unlimited resources of land. An abandoned rubber smallholding reverts to secondary jungle with *hevea* seedlings predominating, and in a few years' time it is as suitable for native rice or rubber-growing as before. In certain areas in the East, especially in NI, a secondary jungle of rubber seedlings is actually beneficial, as it helps to keep out *lalang* (*imperata arundinacea*, a dangerous speargrass), which, when once established over large areas, is difficult to clear up, and also because rubber forests are less liable to burn than most other jungle plants. The need for replanting on estates arose in the past through loss of soil from erosion, loss of stand through root disease and, above all, from

---

[19] During the first regulation period (1934–8) there was comparatively little replanting by estates, and the danger to the smallholder industry was potential rather than actual. There was, however, a gradual increase in the acreage replanted annually and this was much accelerated from 1939 onwards.

rapid development of high-yielding material which rendered obsolete the original stand. There was no case for prohibiting the smallholder to extend his acreage while allowing the estates to increase their capacity.

Under the renewed regulation scheme (1939–43) a total of 5 per cent new planting (5 per cent of the 1938 acreage) was allowed in 1939–40, after which date the International Rubber Regulation Committee was to decide the permissible rate of new planting, and also to declare whether unlimited replanting was to continue for the remaining years of regulation. These matters were decided at two meetings in February and May 1940. At the first, unlimited replanting was permitted until the end of the current scheme. For the second meeting, in view of the important decision which was to be taken, a special statistical annex to the agenda was prepared and circulated by the Secretariat. This annex contained some interesting forward estimates of future consumption and potential capacity.

Two sets of capacity estimates were drawn up, one on the assumption that the estates would replant 70,000 acres annually, while the smallholders would not replant at all, the other on the assumption that estates would replant 70,000 acres and smallholders 40,000 acres a year. The former was rightly stated to be more plausible. No new planting was assumed after 1940. No attempt was made to estimate the price required to call forth the full capacity output. The results are shown in Table 8.

The divergent trends of the capacity of estates and of small-holdings reflected replanting by estates with high-yielding modern material, whilst the capacity of smallholdings declined with their advancing age; on assumption A, one-third of the smallholdings' area would be over thirty years old by 1950, and over six-sevenths by 1960, and thirty years was believed to be the limit of the economic life of the holdings.[20] On assumption B, the rate of decline was not so pronounced, but some reduction was still postulated, as the smallholders were assumed to use unselected seedling material for replanting, and this was not expected to offset the decline in yield from the older areas.

These figures revealed very clearly that the outcome of a policy which prohibited new planting, while permitting a large measure of replanting, would be a large reduction in the smallholders' share of

[20] Holdings, rather than trees, since a prime cause of the decline in yields with age is the loss of stand through disease and windfalls.

TABLE 8

Summary of estimates by the IRRC Secretariat of future physical productivity of plantation rubber
(tons)

year	estates		smallholdings		total capacity
	tons	per cent of total capacity	tons	per cent of total capacity	
Assumption A: annual replanting of 70,000 acres by estates, no replanting by smallholders.					
1939	812,000	53·1	716,000	46·9	1,528,000
1950	992,000	61·1	631,000	38·9	1,623,000
1960	1,037 000	74·2	360,000	25·8	1,397,000
Assumption B: annual replanting of 70,000 acres by estates and of 40,000 acres by smallholders.					
1939	812,000	53·1	716,000	46·9	1,528,000
1950	992,000	61·7	617,000	38·3	1,609,000
1960	1,037,000	71·6	412,000	28·4	1,449,000

total rubber production. The rate of decline of the physical productivity of smallholding assumed for the calculation was almost certainly too sharp, and the estimates of future physical capacity were unduly pessimistic; this was stated in the memorandum, as well as in the course of its discussion by the IRRC. But while it might have been conjectural just how rapidly, and to what extent, the estates would have gained supremacy as a result of the planting provisions, the general trend was both unmistakable and unavoidable. Because of the replanting of estates with high-yielding material, the smallholders would be ousted as economic competitors, even though their physical capacity still remained in existence (or even if it remained intact, which was, however, impossible). This result would follow even if the smallholders were efficient low-cost producers at the beginning of the process.

With these obvious considerations clearly before them, the committee, who had decided on unlimited replanting in February, now resolved on a total prohibition of new planting throughout 1941, the position to be revised again at the end of that year. Disregarding the chronological order, it may be stated that it was then decided to

121

prohibit new planting completely for the remaining period of regulation.

While the threat to the position of the smallholders (the lowest-cost producers) was a notable feature of the planting provisions of rubber regulation, some further points need to be recorded.

As the authorities insisted that replanting should take place on the exact area of the previous stand, improved planting material (chiefly high-yielding budgrafts) was frequently wasted, as it had to be planted on exhausted or unsuitable soil, or on badly sited plantations.

The familiar effects of a restriction scheme of freezing the pattern of an industry and discouraging the expansion of low-cost producers was especially pronounced in the rubber regulation scheme, both because of the wide differences in the supply price of high- and low-cost producers, and also because of the implications of the planting provisions.

Further, replanting expenditure was admitted as a charge against income tax by the revenue authorities, while the assessment for restriction purposes of areas cut out for replanting was maintained. Thus, when in 1940 the British excess profits tax was raised to 100 per cent, companies earning in excess of their standard profits had everything to gain and nothing to lose by replanting on a larger scale. In 1940 there was a great increase in replanting activity, which continued at a rising rate until January 1942, absorbing ever-increasing amounts of scarce resources, and aggravating the deficiency of exports which developed early in 1941. No action was taken by the authorities; in fact, replanting was encouraged by the maintenance of the assessments of the old area. Large-scale replanting continued until the Japanese occupation of the major producing territories.

3

Throughout the regulation period there was fairly free, though not altogether unrestricted, transfer of export rights in the principal producing territories. Table 9 summarises the price of these rights during the second month of each restriction quarter; this month has been chosen to eliminate the often violent fluctuations in the price of these export rights at the beginning and end of the quarter. The qualifications and sources of the data are set out in a Note in the Appendix, at the end of this article. It should be noted that the Malayan prices of estate export rights and smallholders' export coupons are up-country quotations, and 1½–2 cents per lb should be added to these for export duty and transport costs to render them comparable to the Singapore price, which was the world price after payment of duty.

These figures are of particular interest for the first half of 1937, the second half of 1940, and for 1941, as the IRRC stated repeatedly that the releases ruling during these periods represented unrestricted production, and that supplies could not be increased by higher releases. This contention was advanced emphatically during the first nine months of 1941, when the international rate of release was 100 per cent; and it was also repeated in the semi-official *History of Rubber Regulation*. Yet in 1937, 1940 and 1941 output was clearly restricted as the price of export rights was not only positive but generally very high. The relevance of the prices of export rights as evidence of the effectiveness of restriction was consistently ignored in the contemporary discussion.[21]

4

The operation of rubber restriction in Malaya in 1941 offers one of the rare opportunities of measuring quantitatively the effect on output of 100 per cent excess profits tax. During the restriction years the Rubber Growers' Association furnished returns to the IRRC of the costs and outputs of its constituent members. In 1941 the RGA returns for Malaya covered over 90 per cent of the output of the properties owned by sterling companies – i.e. by enterprises liable to the British excess profits tax. By deducting the standard assessments and the production of the RGA estates from the total Malayan estate quota and from the aggregate Malayan estate production, interesting results are obtained which are summarised in the following table. There are no data beyond August.

The divergent production trends cannot be attributed to shortages of labour or of materials, since the locally owned estates and those owned by sterling companies were equally affected. It is possible to ascertain roughly the relative responsibility of over-assessment and

[21] The prices of export rights did, however, give rise to a curious fallacy which found its way into many official publications on the rubber industry. The opinion was frequently expressed that the transferability and the high prices of export rights were responsible for the substantial areas left untapped. These untapped areas were said to reflect sales of export rights. It should be obvious that if one person or group is a net seller of rights and thus taps fewer trees, another person or group must be a net buyer and correspondingly tap more. The areas out of tapping reflected the degree of restriction and the level of prices.

TABLE 9

Prices of exports rights and of coupons and market price of rubber in the second month of each quarter, 1934–41

	Malaya			Netherlands India				Ceylon	
	price of export rights (1)	price of coupons (2)	Singapore price of ribbed smoked sheet (3)	price of export rights (4)	Batavia price of ribbed smoked sheets (5)	price of coupons (6)	Singapore price of medium blankets (7)	price of rights (8)	Colombo price of ribbed smoked sheet (9)
	Straits ¢ per lb			Guilder ¢ per ½ kilo				Rupee ¢ per lb	
1934									
August	—	9	25	—	23	—	—	21	36
November	—	12	21	—	19	—	—	7	30
1935									
February		12	21		19			19	31
May		13	20	No individual restriction (See p. 114)	18	No individual restriction (See p. 114)		19	29
August		11	19		18			20	28
November		16	22		20			23	32
1936									
February	—	20	25	—	22	—	—	29	38
May	—	17	26	—	23	—	—	29	38
August	—	16	27	—	24	—	—	31	39
November	16	16	30	—	34	—	—	34	46

124

1937									
February	17	20	36	19	39	22	40	32	54
May	11	15	36	13	39	13	38	31	53
August	5	7	30	22	32	15	31	29	44
November	6	8	23	18	25	10	24	24	33
1938									
February	15	14	23	20	23	11	24	25	34
May	11	11	19	16	19	13	18	20	27
August	19	19	27	23	27	18	28	31	39
November	20	22	28	24	28	16	30	31	42
1939									
February	20	21	27	23	28	20	29	32	40
May	21	22	28	24	28	20	29	33	41
August	20	20	28	24	30	13	30	32	43
November	24	23	39	22	36	18	35	24	52
1940									
February	23	22	38	22	33	16	34	23	55
May	22	23	37	23	33	16	34	28	55
August	17	18	37	21	32	13	32	19	55
November	16	19	39	20	34	17	34	28	58
1941									
February	13	18	36	13	30	14	32	19	49
May	9	18	41	8	36	19	38	16	61
August	8(July)	4	39	3	33	13	34	10	56
November		not available			33	5(Oct.)	34	1	56

TABLE 10

Rate of production (as per cent aggregate standard production) of Malayan estate producers, January–August 1941

	RGA estates	other estates	all estates	internal rate of release
January	91·5	95·0	93·1	97·5
February	82·3	93·1	87·4	97·5
March	78·0	87·0	82·2	97·5
April	74·7	86·6	80·3	97·5
May	76·6	95·6	85·5	97·5
June	87·4	95·8	91·1	97·5
July	89·4	97·8	93·9	97·5
August	87·9	98·5	92·9	97·5
Total, Jan.–Aug.	83·6	93·7	88·3	97·5

of 100 per cent excess profits tax for the lower rate of production of the sterling companies. During the first half of 1940 (when production is seasonally low owing to wintering) the average internal rate of release in Malaya was 78¾ per cent (the international rate being 80 per cent, with an internal cut of 2½ per cent in the second quarter). Over these six months, when output was not yet affected by 100 per cent excess profits tax, the RGA estates produced at the rate of 72½ per cent of their aggregate standard production, and all other estates at 77½ per cent, which showed that the RGA estates already found it more difficult to produce the permissible amounts than did the other estates. During the first eight months of 1941, when excess profits tax at 100 per cent was in force, the gap between the performance of the RGA estates and that of the locally owned estates was about 10 per cent of standard production, as against 5 per cent in the first half of 1940, and from this it may be inferred that the two factors (over-assessment and 100 per cent excess profits tax) were about equally responsible in 1941 for the lower performance of sterling company-owned estates, compared to other Malayan estates. In addition, the output of all estate producers was adversely affected by the shortages resulting from the lavish use of labour and of materials by the sterling companies, encouraged by the 100 per cent excess profits tax.

Although, as we have seen, output was far from unrestricted in

1941, there developed a substantial shortfall of exports below the permissible levels, which, incidentally, furnished a specious basis for the argument that output was unrestricted. The following table, derived largely from the *Statistical Bulletin* of the IRRC, summarises the export deficits up to the outbreak of the Japanese war.

It will be seen in Table 11 that the NI smallholders alone succeeded in producing the permissible exportable amounts at high rates of release, which again underlines the under-assessment of this group of producers.

The substantial export deficits of 1941 caused much anxiety in official circles, and in the spring and summer a series of meetings was held in London to consider how supplies could be increased. It was eventually decided to appeal to producers and to their governments

TABLE 11

Permissible and actual exports of rubber, January–November 1941

	exports (thousand tons)		deficit	
	per-missible	actual	quantity (thousand tons)	as per cent of permissible exports
Malaya	611	561	50	8
NI estates	312	275	37	12
NI smallholders	301	304	3	+1 (excess)
Ceylon	99	82	17	17
Sarawak	44	35	9	20
British North Borneo	20	18	2	10
India[1]	16	2	16	89
Burma	14	9	5	36
Siam	54	43	11	20
Total	1,473	1,329	144[2]	10

1. India was a special case, as her rubber manufacturing industry was developing so rapidly during 1940–1 that she became a net importer of rubber after mid-1941.

2. The shipping shortage cannot be held responsible for the export deficit. Rubber was a high-priority cargo, and there was no substantial accumulation of port stocks. Moreover, Singapore and Penang were outside the regulated area, and rubber despatched from the Malayan mainland to these shipping ports counted as export under the regulation scheme.

to produce more rubber. As, however, these governments were engaged in operating the restriction machinery, and in enforcing international and internal cuts, this appeal was not successful. The restriction machinery was kept in operation until the outbreak of the Japanese war, and indeed beyond, since in Ceylon it was not abandoned until June 1942, after energetic representations by the Commander-in-Chief, who pointed out that the employees on the staff of the Rubber Controller could be more usefully employed elsewhere. This proposal was unsuccessfully opposed in London. In other territories the machinery operated literally until the arrival of the Japanese. In January 1942 the restriction authorities in British North Borneo were just in time with their formal report to the IRRC that on 31 December 1941 there was no abnormal accumulation of stocks (contrary to the provisions of the regulation scheme) on smallholdings in that territory. That document was posted some two, or possibly three, days before the conquest of North Borneo by the Japanese.

Until the outbreak of the Japanese war restriction was not abandoned, the quotas were not redistributed in favour of under-assessed producers, the employment of labour on replanting was not prohibited, and indeed encouraged, the assessment of producers falling behind with their exports were not reduced, the cost of replanting was not disallowed for taxation purposes, while the assessments on areas cut out for replanting were fully maintained as a bonus for replanting. Very belatedly, towards the end of August 1941, the rate of release was raised to 120 per cent, and this was followed by a sharp fall in the price of export rights; the issue of coupons and rights was, however, still maintained.

5

Some tentative conclusions are suggested by this brief review. It is, for instance, clear that when full weight is given to the importance of smallholdings, ideas of the supply price of natural rubber need drastic downward revision; a point of significance in assessing the measure of assistance which would be necessary to maintain in profitable operation the American synthetic rubber industry in competition with the plantation product.

Wider issues are also raised. As already mentioned, the leaders of the Malayan and of the NI delegation to the IRRC were civil servants; the administration of restriction in the East was also in the hands of civil servants. Yet this method of operation of regulation did not benefit the smallholders. Indeed, they might well have been more favourably treated if the administration of the Scheme had been largely in the hands of the estate representatives.[22] The operation of rubber restriction recalls a passage in Marshall's *Principles of Economics*: 'In many cases the "regulation of competition" is a misleading term, that veils the formation of a privileged class of producers, who often use their combined force to frustrate the attempts of an able man to rise from a lower class than their own.'

The working of rubber regulation does not substantiate the hopes of those who hold that government of industries by trade associations may be made acceptable if they are provided with impartial chairmen. Some aspects of its operation also suggest that when government intervenes in economic affairs the lack of knowledge of economics on the part of civil servants may prove a serious drawback. The inability to see that output cannot be unrestricted when exports rights have a positive value is an instructive example.

APPENDIX

NOTE TO TABLE 7

Although some of the figures in Table 7 contain an element of estimate, they well illustrate the working of the special export tax. The figures in columns 10 and 11 for the last seven months of 1934 and for the years 1935 and 1936 are not the simple averages of the monthly percentage figures, but the averages of the monthly percentages weighted by the corresponding various prices. Conversion of various items from guilder cents to pence, with inevitable rounding off, also involved a few small inaccuracies in calculating the percentages.

Throughout most of the period reviewed, the bulk of NI smallholders' rubber was sold in the form of a grade known as medium blankets; hence the choice of that grade for the prices in column 1.

The cost of processing, transporting and marketing NI smallholders' rubber (including the cost of transport from the principal producing districts to Singapore) was usually estimated in the 1930s at around 4 to 5 guilder cents per half kilo of dry rubber. These figures were usually quoted in the trade press and in the periodic reports on

[22] This possibility is suggested by the episode mentioned in footnote 9.

smallholders' rubber issued by the NI Department of Agriculture. They agree with the estimates in the reports prepared at the time by the late Dr H.N.Whitford, one of the most competent writers on the rubber industry in the 1920s and 1930s, who visited these areas as representative of the Rubber Manufacturers' Association of America. For the calculations in the table a figure of 4 g.c. per half kilo was adopted to ensure that any error was more likely to be on the side of conservatism, that is that it should understate rather than overstate the burden of the special tax. This figure excludes the ordinary *ad valorem* export duty, which was calculated in this table (as it was levied) on the basis of 5 per cent of the export value of smallholders' rubber during the second preceding month.

The average rate of duty in the table refers to the effective rate in force and not to the rates announced during the month; hence the zero rate for June 1934.

The wide fluctuations in the net return to native producers (column 6) indicate the disproportionate effect in the interior of changes in the market price or in the rate of duty. There is room here for an appreciable margin of error in any given month, but the yearly, or even quarterly, averages are unlikely to be seriously affected.

The export figures are reliable; the wide month-to-month fluctuations reflect the reaction of shippers to the announcement of changes in the rate of the special tax, and to a lesser extent their views on the probable course of the market. There was a time-lag between the announcement of changes in the rate of the special tax and the date the new rate applied to dry rubber, and this led exporters to accelerate or withhold shipments in the interim period. These erratic fluctuations cancelled out over a period of a few months.

NOTE TO TABLE 9

In official Malayan and NI terminology, export rights referred to estate export rights, as distinct from smallholders' coupons; in Ceylon there was no distinction. The official usage has been followed in the table. In NI, with negligible exceptions, estate rubber could not be shipped on smallholders' rights or vice versa. In Malaya there was no complete ban, but, for various reasons, rights and coupons were not always fully interchangeable, hence the different sets of prices.

The market in export rights was sometimes narrow, and there were occasional erratic variations (e.g. Ceylon, autumn 1934), but the quotations shown well reflect the general trend. It will be recalled that the Malayan prices of rights and coupons were up-country quotations. Some 1½–2 cents per lb must be added to these for export duty and transport costs to make these quotations comparable to the Singapore price of rubber.

There are no regular quotations of the price of estate export rights before January 1937. Some sporadic figures are available from miscellaneous sources, and these suggest that in 1934 in Malaya the price of these rights was low, as many estates found it difficult to produce their full exportable amount in that year. In 1935 and 1936 the price of estate export rights was fairly high, both in Malaya and the NI; 12–16 Straits cents per lb and 14–16 guilder cents per half kilo indicate the approximate level of prices. Transactions in these rights were, however, on a small scale until the period of high releases in 1937. The purchase in 1935 by the NI Government of 20,000 tons of rights for cancellation to reduce over-exports was an important exception. Some 29 guilder cents per kilo was paid for these rights.

Medium blankets were quoted in Straits cents per lb, and the price has been converted at the average monthly rate of exchange between the Straits dollar and the NI guilder.

The Malayan quotations of estate export rights from 1937 to 1940 are from the *Annual Reports* of the Controller of Rubber, Malaya. No report was issued for 1941, and the figures represent the transactions of a few large companies to whose records I had access. The prices of estate export rights in the NI are from the *Economisch Weekblad*. The Ceylon quotations are from the *Administration Reports* of the Rubber Controller, Ceylon.

The coupon prices are somewhat approximate. For Malaya, the *Malayan Agricultural Journal* frequently published these, but occasionally this information had to be supplemented by reference to various other sources, such as the local press or various administration reports. Moreover, while export rights were transferable between administrations, coupons could be transferred only within each administration (Straits Settlements, Federated Malay States and each Unfederated Malay State), and there was thus one price for rights, but several prices for coupons, and there were often considerable local variations. The prices given here refer principally to Perak and Johore, and occasionally to Selangor; these States contain the great bulk of the smallholdings area in Malaya.

The NI smallholder coupon prices are the quotations in Palembang, and have been taken from the official *Reports on Native Rubber Cultivation* up to May 1940, and thereafter from the *Market Reports* of the Rubber Trade Association of the NI.

It will be noted that at times of high releases (especially 1941) coupons were usually worth more than estate rights, while the reverse ratio held at times of low releases. The former relation reflects the under-assessment of the smallholders; the latter is explained by the comparative ease with which the smallholders could, at times of lower releases, turn to other products such as rice and coconuts.

Addendum

A few weeks after the end of the period covered in this paper the principal rubber growing territories, including both Malaya and Netherlands India, came under Japanese occupation and remained occupied until September 1945. In Malaya rubber regulation was formally maintained until April 1947, when it was repealed. This temporary maintenance of regulations did not affect current output, but somewhat retarded new planting.

There has been no rubber regulation since 1947. But some ideas engendered by its adoption still influence policy in both Malaya and Ceylon. This applies particularly to the extension of capacity, notably to official policy on new planting. New planting is formally permitted both in Malaya and Ceylon, but little land is made available for this purpose. This practice means that producers who had in the past acquired land for rubber planting, but had not used it, can plant it to rubber, but those without alienated but unplanted land cannot do so.[23] Similarly, in both Malaya and Ceylon replanting is heavily subsidised but new planting is not. While it is possible that many producers would prefer replanting to new planting, there are

[23] Alienation is the process by which title to rural land is given out to private individuals by the authorities in Malaysia and Ceylon. The purposes to which land can be used is usually specified when it is alienated. On alienation a capital sum (alienation premium) is usually payable, followed by annual payments known as quit rents, which are subject to periodic revision. Both the premium and the quit rents are charged largely on the basis of the crop cultivated and not on the basis of location or fertility, a practice which leads to an uneconomic use of land. Some effects of this practice are considered in P.T.Bauer and B.S. Yamey, *The Economics of Under-developed Countries*, London and Chicago, 1957, p. 55.

undoubtedly others who would prefer new planting, if land were made available to them on commercial terms. The present policies are almost certainly a partial legacy of the regulation scheme.

The operation of rubber regulation superimposed a virtually complete monopoly on a perfectly competitive situation. Under the scheme the individual producer was confronted by a demand schedule for his output which was horizontal up to the permitted exportable amount, and then dropped vertically to zero, where producers were not permitted to produce more, or to the price of unlicensed rubber, when they were allowed to produce more, but not allowed to export it. The same applies under the various other agricultural restriction schemes in both tropical and temperate countries.

This fairly common arrangement has received less attention in the literature on monopoly than its intellectual and practical importance warrants. The effectiveness of this type of monopoly is closely linked to the standardised nature of the produce. This relationship is a further instance of the connection between the standardised nature of the produce and the effectiveness of market control noted in the paper on concentration in tropical trade in this volume, pp. 201 to 224.

In an earlier article, 'A Note on Monopoly', *Economica*, August 1941, I discussed this arrangement rather briefly, together with certain other forms of monopolistic or quasi-monopolistic arrangements of some practical importance which are also often ignored in the literature.

In the text the monetary value of the under-assessment of Malayan smallholders is estimated in round figures of £10 million for the period 1934–41. This estimate is based on a comparison between the actual division of the Malayan territorial quota and a notional or hypothetical division of 52 per cent (estates) and 48 per cent (smallholdings). On the basis of a hypothetical 55–45 per cent division, the corresponding figure would be about one-third less than on the basis of a 50–50 division, when it would be about a quarter more. Total value of smallholders' output over the period was about £100 million delivered Singapore.

The preferential treatment of estates under rubber regulation is a principal theme of this paper. I wish to note here certain relevant considerations which might be concealed by the critical tone of much of the paper. First, as already noted in the text, the incomes of small-holders in Malaya, and after 1936 in NI also, were much higher under regulation than they would have been otherwise. Second, the rubber industry was very largely the creation of the estates and the small-holders followed some years or decades afterwards, which affected the outlook and attitudes not only of estate representatives but also of administrators. Third, the actions of the restriction authorities, though they may have been misguided, were not the result of bad faith. All the papers of the IRRC, including the most confidential documents, were made available to me without any restriction. I also had free access to all the relevant papers of Guthrie & Company, the agency firm whose then managing director, the late Sir John Hay, was much the most influential figure in the establishment and opera-tion of rubber regulation. There was nowhere even the slightest evidence or suggestion of bad faith. This judgment is supported by the extreme readiness with which documents were made available to me at the time when I was a research student with no official position.

The foregoing considerations do not affect the validity of the analysis of this paper, but they are relevant to an assessment of its implications.

One factor behind the under-assessment of the smallholders was a widespread scepticism of the productive capacity and the long term competitive position of these producers. This scepticism in part reflected wishful thinking and propaganda by estate representatives and European planters who were affected by the competition of smallholders, and who pressed both for the introduction of restric-tions and for favourable treatment under its operation. An early prospective decline in smallholder production was also a recurrent theme of the newsletters of London rubber brokers in the 1930s, with the message that a rise in the price of rubber was to be expected.

But there was also present a genuine and disinterested failure to realise the economic efficiency and competitive strength of a large part of the smallholder industry, a failure which in turn often reflected the misunderstanding of the rationale of certain planning methods and practices of the smallholders. This consideration applied particu-larly to the failure to appreciate the reasons behind the much greater planting density of smallholdings compared to estates. The number of trees per surface unit is usually much higher on smallholdings than on estates. In the 1930s planting density on smallholdings was usually about 200–300 mature trees per acre compared to about 70–90 mature trees on estates. This difference was widely thought to reflect ignorance on the part of smallholders, notably the oversight that a denser stand would result in trees of smaller girth and lower yield. This view was largely mistaken. Within wide limits, planting density is indeed negatively correlated with yield per surface unit. On the other hand, the higher densities and lower yields per tree and per tapper raise tapping costs per pound of rubber. The estates which use substantial capital and employ paid tappers, aim at maximising the return on capital and the profit per acre; and it is held that the higher yields per surface unit from the significantly denser stand would be more than offset by a consequent increase in tapping costs. Smallholders usually employ little capital, and generally incur no cash tapping costs as their trees are tapped by members of the family or by share tappers.[24]

Compared to estates, the smallholders tend to pay greater attention to yields per surface unit, and less to yield per tree which largely explains the difference in densities. Within the smallholdings side of the industry, the smallest holdings are usually the most densely planted.

The higher planting density of smallholdings compared to estates thus reflects largely differences in circumstances especially resource availabilities between estates and smallholdings; and it does not reflect simply incompetence or ignorance of smallholders.[25]

Yet the belief that the dense planting and consequential small girth of trees result in inefficient production played a significant part

[24] Smallholders do of course incur opportunity costs in terms of foregone leisure or alternative crops and activities.

[25] In an article 'The Economics of Planting Density in Rubber Growing', *Economica*, May 1946, I discussed in greater detail the economics of planting density, and also the much higher planting density of smallholdings as a factor in the under-assessment of these producers. The article deals with a number of factors influencing planting density of rubber production. The treatment in that article is over-simplified chiefly because I did not consider sufficiently the costs of smallholder production in terms of foregone leisure, or in terms of alternative products.

In recent years the relation between the size of the agricultural unit and the types and proportions of factor inputs has come to be discussed on a more sophisticated level. One example is an article by Dr D. Mazumdar, 'Size of Farm and Productivity: A Problem of Indian Peasant Agriculture', *Economica*, May 1965, with references to other work in this field.

in the under-assessment of smallholdings. Indeed, certain classes of smallholder received assessments calculated on the basis of the girth of their trees regardless of actual output. Large numbers of small-holdings, especially in Netherlands India received no assessment at all. They were regarded as untappable by the European planters who were often in charge of surveys and assessments in the administration of rubber restriction, although they were fully tappable by the standards of the smallholders.

At several places in this article, it is said or implied that the supply price of smallholders' rubber was lower than that of estate rubber. This formulation is an unwarranted over-simplification. The two groups are not so uniform as is implied by the wording in the text. There are high-cost and low-cost producers in both groups. The aggregate supply schedule at different prices is the sum of the individual supply schedules. It is highly probable that in the 1930s, in the absence of restriction, the estates would have lost much ground to the smallholders, especially to the NI smallholders. But it is certain that an appreciable section of the estate industry would have survived, as the supply price of many estates was lower than that of many smallholders, especially of smallholders in distant areas. The low-cost smallholders alone could not have produced enough rubber to satisfy the demand, and thus to eliminate the estates.

Since the war, the conditions of supply have been much affected by the political developments in Indonesia, which brought about the virtual expropriation of the European estates, and substantial restrictions on the activities of the traders, mainly Chinese dealers, who handled smallholders' rubber. In Malaya, the estates have made much technical progress, especially in the adoption of high yielding planting material and in the production of various types of specialised rubber. On the other hand, they are disadvantaged by substantial restrictions on the employment of expatriate personnel and also by greatly increased taxation, which affect them more than it does smallholders.

It is probable that in the absence of political discrimination against them, the general competitive position of the estates in the main producing areas is perhaps somewhat stronger compared to small-holders than it was before the war. This suggestion is based on the implications of recent technical change in planting and processing which has been of a kind placing a much greater premium on technical know-how than before the war. This judgment is necessarily conjectural. Even if the judgment is correct, the importance of these developments cannot be quantified. The recent technical developments are of much practical significance, but they do not raise issues of much interest either to the economic historian or to the analytical economist.

ORIGINS OF THE STATUTORY
EXPORT MONOPOLIES OF
BRITISH WEST AFRICA*

Government marketing boards have a statutory monopoly over the export from British West Africa (Nigeria, the Gold Coast, Sierra Leone, and the Gambia) of cocoa, groundnuts, palm oil, palm kernels, cotton, and several minor products; these account for practically the whole of the agricultural exports from this area.[1] Recently similar marketing systems, modelled on these organisations in British West Africa, have been introduced throughout British Africa (as well as in other British colonies), so that this type of marketing now covers the bulk of the export crops, and indeed of the cash crops, of most of the population of the British colonies.

This system of marketing is likely to have far-reaching social, economic and political results through a large part of this large area, inhabited by scores of millions of people. The operation of marketing boards has brought about a large measure of socialisation of peasant saving in British Africa, a result of their existence which has attracted little attention. These organisations prescribe the prices payable to the producers for their crops, and the prices, since they are set by a statutory monopoly, can be largely divorced from market values. Thus the marketing boards to a large extent prescribe the level of money incomes and the standard of living of the producers. By setting prices to producers of the major cash crops, the boards greatly influence the direction of production. The boards can decide what grades of produce can be exported and need pay no regard to the acceptability of the product to overseas buyers. They have extensive powers of licensing over intermediaries and processors, who in West Africa, for instance, can operate only on the sufferance of the

---

* *Business History Review*, September 1954, pp. 197–213.

[1] The system of statutory export monopolies is sometimes referred to as statutory marketing. I shall adopt this convenient usage in this article.

marketing boards. Further, the possession of very large funds gives these organisations a dominant strategic place in the economies in which they function.

The present article aims at analysing the historical process that gave birth to the statutory monopolies. Section 1 discusses the pre-1939 system of marketing in British West Africa and the criticisms directed at this system. Section 2 deals with the formation in wartime of various control boards, and with the activities of the Association of West African Merchants. Section 3 shows how, after 1945, these attitudes and influences merged with certain new pressures to promote the establishment of the marketing boards.

1

Until the Second World War West African produce was exported by merchant firms, most of which also handled imported merchandise. The actual buying was done by employed clerks or by various categories of middlemen (local intermediaries). The clerks bought either direct from producers or from middlemen who had collected small parcels from producers or from other smaller intermediaries. The salaried employees of the firms often bought produce from substantial middlemen who had their own organisations of employees and sub-middlemen often running parallel with those of the merchant firms. The middlemen were paid commissions by the firms; moreover, they kept any differences between the prices they paid for produce and those they received from the firms. Clerks also sometimes received small commission payments as well as their salaries.

The pre-war organisation of the marketing of West African exports was subjected to frequent criticism. The multiplicity of intermediaries and the large number of stages in the distributive chain were frequently criticised as being both unnecessarily wasteful and exploitative of the producers. Such complaints were, of course, familiar in discussions of the marketing of primary products. In West Africa the unusually large number of intermediaries lent superficial plausibility to these popular ideas. The criticisms were, however, generally misconceived. They disregarded relevant major aspects of the West African economies, notably the low level of capital and the availability of a large and otherwise unoccupied or partly occupied labour force, and the obvious possibilities open for the population of by-passing redundant traders. They also disregarded the importance of the large number of traders in these territories in widening the market for the produce of remote areas and in stimulating the intensive and extensive expansion of production.

Other criticisms referred to alleged abuses, such as false declarations by middlemen and clerks to their principals (overstating stocks on a falling market and understating them on a rising one), and to the use of incorrect weights. No doubt these practices were prevalent. But the results were not necessarily detrimental to the primary producers. The severe competition among middlemen and clerks generally ensured that any gains from these practices were not retained; the level of earnings and margins secured by these intermediaries were limited (then as now) by the intensity of competition and the ease of entry into the trade.

In general these criticisms were directed against the organisation, practices and methods of the West African export trade, rather than against the high degree of concentration among the merchants. Yet this oligopolistic market situation brought about the frequent market-sharing agreements in the purchase of export crops, which for obvious reasons were very unpopular with the local population. In 1937 the announcement of a market-sharing agreement by the export merchants prompted a strike by the cocoa farmers in the Gold Coast. As a result of this strike, generally known as the cocoa hold-up, a commission of enquiry, the Nowell Commission, was appointed to enquire into the immediate dispute and more generally into the cocoa-marketing system of West Africa.

The Report of the Nowell Commission[2] contained the most important and influential criticisms of the pre-war system of marketing. Parts of the report dealing with alleged abuses were reproduced in a British Government White Paper in 1946[3] in support of the proposals for establishing statutory export monopolies. These passages are still often quoted in criticism of the pre-war organisation of the export trade and of the marketing methods in that sector of West African trade that remains private today.

The Nowell Commission accepted the contention of the export merchants that the unprofitability of their trade had forced them to institute the market-sharing agreement. The commission's report suggested that the export merchants had engaged in competition so intense that their buying prices had frequently been out of parity

[2] *Report of the Commission on the Marketing of West African Cocoa*, Cmd. 5845, 1938.

[3] *Future Marketing of West African Cocoa*, Cmd. 6950, 1946.

with world prices for cocoa. Their fierce rivalry had also led them to pay unduly high commissions to their agents who bought the cocoa from the primary producers. But, although the export merchants paid excessively high prices for cocoa, the primary producers received excessively low prices. The real culprits in the situation were the middlemen (who, like the primary producers, were Africans, whereas the export merchants were Europeans). These clerks, agents, and local intermediaries, the report clearly implied, simultaneously victimised the cocoa growers and cheated the export merchants.

Although the Nowell Commission explicitly stated that its report was based on careful enquiry, its conclusions will not stand examination. The evidence of alleged losses by the export merchants was misleading, largely because it failed to heed the fact that most of these same merchants were also importers of merchandise. The schedules of buying expenses on cocoa submitted by the merchants to the commission, and used to calculate the local parity of world market prices, were debited with a substantial part of the overheads of the firms, and many cost items were rather liberally computed.

If the export trade in cocoa was so unremunerative, why did the firms remain in it? They were free to suspend their cocoa buying whenever they chose to do so; their continued activity in this trade certainly suggests that if offered direct or indirect profits. The principal indirect advantage of produce buying was said to be its beneficial effect on the firms' trade in imported merchandise; many firms claimed that produce buying was essential to promote and support their merchandise trade. But if this contention was valid, part of the profits on merchandise trade should have been credited against the expense of cocoa buying. Without this adjustment it was misleading to assess the profitability of cocoa buying purely on the basis of direct costs and receipts. There was good evidence, moreover, that some firms regarded cocoa buying as a profitable activity in itself, since several important firms both in the Gold Coast and in Nigeria were engaged solely in the export trade. Before the war, these purchased about one-third of all cocoa in the Gold Coast and about one-sixth in Nigeria. In fact, during and shortly after the deliberations of the Nowell Commission, several new firms entered or wished to enter cocoa buying, and one large prospective entrant had no interest in the import trade.

Firms occasionally suffered heavy capital losses as a result of maintaining speculative open positions on falling markets. In some cases these positions were maintained voluntarily and deliberately by the principals of the firm. But the open position was partly enforced upon the largest firm which represented such a large proportion of total cocoa purchases that it could not preserve an effectively covered position by selling forward regularly at the prices at which it bought. But even this firm could have avoided the risk by reducing its commitments, and it showed no inclination to do so.

Finally, even if cocoa buying had been unprofitable, this would not have been evidence of abuses or cause for public concern. It is quite normal, one would suppose, for a business to take losses at times.

The argument that both primary producers and export merchants were exploited by the middlemen was plainly invalid. These middlemen existed by the hundreds; they scrambled vigorously among themselves for business; entry into their ranks was very easy. Any advantage they secured from sharp practice was sure to be competed away in favour of either the producers or the buying firms. Had a middleman's charges for his services been excessive, he would have been by-passed by his customers in favour of another whose charges were not excessive. The Nowell Commission's conclusions can only be counted as expressive of a vague and unanalysed hostility to middlemen.

Several further specific points in the Nowell Report were also rather invalid. The commission counted as an abuse, for instance, the purchase of cocoa crops in advance of the season by African money-lenders and middlemen (using in large part funds advanced to them by the export merchants) at fixed prices which allegedly allowed a large measure of profit. But this was merely a method of financing the harvesting and movement of a seasonal and expensive crop with the help of European capital. So far from being an abuse, it was (and still is) a valuable contribution of expatriate capital to the functioning of economies very short of local capital. Similarly, the multiplicity of middlemen was an inevitable and by no means undesirable feature of economies in which the export crops were produced by tens of thousands of small-scale and dispersed cultivators.

Thus the criticisms of the pre-war marketing system in the Nowell Report disregarded essential features of the local economies and of the market situation. But, in spite of the crucial defects in the commission's argument, it gained considerable currency and influence, partly no doubt because it appealed to attitudes which are widespread in contemporary society. The Nowell Report criticised the (seemingly) chaotic and unorganised system of marketing. It proposed the establishment of collective marketing agencies, and these had the appearance of simplicity, efficiency, and neatness.

The Nowell Report was published late in 1938. Before any action had been taken on it, the outbreak of war in 1939 presented a new situation and gave rise to new arrangements in the West African cocoa trade.

2

There were three principal objectives of the wartime control over West African exports: to deny supplies to the enemy and secure them for the Allies, particularly the United Kingdom; to prevent a collapse of the local price of cocoa; and to increase exports of groundnuts and of oil-palm produce after 1942. There were also three principal elements in the machinery of export control: licensing of exports to direct them to specific destinations; statutory monopoly in the handling of the principal exports; and a system of quotas in the purchase of export produce. Licensing of exports to direct them to specific destinations was an obvious necessity. Neither this aim of policy nor its administration differed substantially from similar arrangements elsewhere, including the United Kingdom. Moreover, this aspect of the controls did not affect permanently the structure of the trade. Accordingly it will not be considered further in this article. On the other hand, the establishment of statutory monopoly in the export of agricultural produce and the operation of a quota system for purchasing, differed greatly from controls over similar commodities elsewhere in the British colonies, and have had far-reaching and lasting effects on the marketing of West African produce. We shall now consider the relation between the objectives of the controls and the machinery introduced to attain them.

At the outbreak of war a collapse of the local price of cocoa was widely feared as the result of difficulties of securing shipping space and of selling the crop in view of the disappearance of some important markets, primlarily Germany. Such a collapse would have had serious social and political results and to avoid it the British government announced in November 1939, that it would purchase through an official organisation at seasonally fixed prices all cocoa offered for sale in the Gold Coast and Nigeria. The organisation in charge was first the Cocoa Control Section of the Ministry of Food. From

143

October 1940 the responsible organisation became the West African Cocoa Control Board operating under the general control of the Colonial Office; and in 1942 this body was enlarged and renamed the West African Produce Control Board. These organisations had a statutory monopoly of export. The export merchants operating in these territories were appointed to act as agents in the purchase of the crop.

Although in the early war years somewhat different arrangements applied to the export of groundnuts and oil-palm produce, after the fall of the Far East in 1942 these products were also taken over by the West African Produce Control Board, again with a statutory monopoly of export.

The wartime establishment of statutory export monopolies in West Africa has come to be taken so much for granted that the grounds for it do not appear to have been examined. Yet it is clear that their introduction was not necessary. Monopoly of export was obviously not required for the support of the local price of cocoa; an official guarantee to act as residual buyer at a seasonally fixed price was all that was necessary.

A statutory export monopoly was equally unnecessary for the expansion of the supplies of groundnuts and oil-palm produce. Indeed the marketing arrangements and price policies of the West African Produce Control Board were not calculated to increase supplies of these products. These products were sold exclusively to the Ministry of Food. The Ministry took over these commodities from the West African Produce Control Board at cost, i.e. the prices paid to producers plus buying expenses and shipping charges to the United Kingdom. Both the prices paid by the Ministry of Food and the local producer prices were exceedingly low. Thus, after the marketing of groundnuts was taken over by the West African Produce Control Board, the prices paid by the Ministry for bulk supplies of West African groundnuts were far lower than were paid by the same organisation for bulk supplies of Indian groundnuts; until August 1942, when the West African Produce Control Board took over this crop (which up to then was handled by export merchants), the prices paid for the supplies from India and West Africa were approximately the same.[4]

[4] Details are given in my paper, 'Statistics of Statutory Marketing in West Africa, 1939–1951', *Journal of Royal Statistical Society*, vol. 117, part 1 (1954), pp. 1–20.

Not only was the establishment of statutory export monopolies unnecessary for the purposes which were stated to be the reason for their introduction, but the policies pursued by these organisations were irrelevant or disadvantageous to the attainment of the officially stated aims of policy. On cocoa transactions the Cocoa Control Board and the West African Produce Control Board began to accumulate profits almost from their inception by paying primary producers less than the sale proceeds received. This policy, although clearly quite irrelevant to the maintenance of the local price of cocoa which was stated to be the reason for the establishment of statutory marketing, was continued throughout the existence of these boards.

A system of quotas was the other principal feature of the wartime control over West African exports. Throughout the war and early post-war years the export merchants, whether acting as shippers or as buying agents on behalf of the government bodies, purchased the crops in accordance with official quotas based on pre-war performances; and those who exceeded their share paid substantial penalties to those who had underbought, the settlement being administered by the government authorities.

It was repeatedly stated in various official publications that the quota system in the West African export trade was essentially analogous to similar arrangements adopted elsewhere.[5] But the analogy fails. Quota systems were indeed widely adopted when it was necessary to share out either a limited market or limited supplies. In West Africa, however, there was an unlimited market for the export crops to which the quota system came to be applied.[6] So, far from being necessary, the system was paradoxical.

In the purchase of cocoa the paradox was evident from the inception of the quotas, since the introduction of the quota system was announced simultaneously with the British guarantee to purchase the entire crop at seasonally fixed prices, which ensured an unlimited market locally. In the purchase of groundnuts and oil-palm produce, the paradox of the quota system was particularly evident after 1942. An acute shortage of these products developed after the loss of Malaya and the Netherlands East Indies, and intensive production

[5] This was stated explicitly in another British Government White Paper, *Report and on Cocoa Control in West Africa*, Cmd. 6554, 1944, para. 24. Both this document Cmd. 6950, already mentioned, drew largely on the Nowell Report.

[6] Similar products in other colonies (e.g. oil-palm produce in Malaya) were not subject to such arrangements.

drives were undertaken in West Africa to stimulate the production of these crops. Extreme measures were also introduced to reduce local consumption, even if only by a few tons, and much hardship was inflicted on the local population and on individual traders to force every ton or donkey load of groundnuts into export. But the quota system was firmly retained, and buyers were fined if they exceeded their quotas. In a sense the paradoxical and unnecessary nature of the quotas was recognised in the system itself. The quotas placed no limit on aggregate purchases or shipments; they were simply shares in unspecified and indeed unlimited totals.

The quota system was in fact a statutory extension and enforcement of the pre-war produce buying pools and syndicates of the West African merchants. These were market-sharing arrangements designed to protect gross and net profit margins of the merchants by restraining buying competition among them.[7] Participants who exceeded their agreed shares were required to make penalty payments to those whose purchases had fallen short of their agreed shares. The penalties were so calculated to deprive the buyer as far as possible of all contributions made by the excess purchases to his overheads and profits.[8] This was precisely the method adopted in the administration of the government-enforced quota system, the provisions of which were practically identical with those of the pre-war syndicates. The system was indeed introduced at the suggestion of the Association of West African Merchants (a trade association of the larger West African merchants with head offices in Europe), and the quotas were calculated and the system administered by those leading members of the association who had participated in the pre-war syndicates.

Quite apart from the paradox of the quota system in the face of

[7] The profit margins were generally formally or informally agreed. In the absence of agreed fixed shares (quotas) among the participants, and of penalty payments for exceeding these, the margins were generally eroded by competitive buying. The agreed shares and the penalty payments were thus both a necessary condition for maintaining or increasing profit margins and a device for sharing out the fruits of the restraint of competition.

[8] The question arises why under such a system individual firms continued to purchase instead of curtailing or even discontinuing their activities and living on premium payments. The answer is complex and would require lengthy discussion which would be inappropriate here. The principal reasons appeared to be the desire of the firms and of their local executives to maintain their position in the market, both for export produce and for imported merchandise; and the fear that producers who consistently failed to reach their agreed shares would have their quotas reduced.

146

an unlimited market, the acceptance by the authorities of this system was surprising for two further reasons. First, in cocoa and groundnut buying there were well-known and substantial competitors of the members of the Association of West African Merchants whose interests were at variance with these firms. Secondly, the syndicates were for obvious reasons unpopular with the local population, and the association of the authorities with such arrangements entailed serious political risks.

This was particularly evident in connection with the cocoa quotas, which were clearly a resumption in a different guise of the 1937 cocoa-buying agreement. This agreement was formally suspended on 28 April 1938, but it was not abandoned until 30 November 1939 on the introduction of the official quota system which had been announced on 17 November. Thus it was withdrawn finally only when official quotas took its place. As the provisions of the 1937 agreement had been made public, there was no difficulty in noticing the connection between the agreement and the quota system, since apart from minor matters of form, the provisions of the quota system were identical with those of the agreement (the calculation of penalties was absolutely identical), save only that these provisions now had statutory force and membership was necessary for participation in cocoa buying.

Neither the danger of a collapse of cocoa prices nor an increase in the exports of oil-palm produce and groundnuts required either a statutory monopoly or the introduction of export quotas; nor does the one system postulate the other. But although both the principal measures were unnecessary for, or indeed rather harmful to, the achievement of the two principal objectives (they could only affect adversely the supply of groundnuts and oil-palm produce, the extension of which was a prime aim of policy), there appears to have been a causal connection between the quota system and the establishment of statutory export monopoly.

The quota system was initiated by the merchants to maintain their profit margins by barring new entry and by restricting competition among themselves. Export quotas (including quotas in the purchase for export) are easier to establish, to enforce, and to administer when there is only a single buyer, especially if that buyer is prepared to arrange a settlement between those who exceed their allotted shares and those who fall short of them. Thus contrary to the more usual attitude of export merchants, the West African merchants were

147

inclined to favour statutory export monopolies, especially for commodities for which there was more than one buyer overseas. Thus the draft scheme for cocoa control submitted by the Association of West African Merchants to the Colonial Office in November 1939, and approved by the authorities, provided both for a statutory export monopoly and for a quota system based on past performance. The merchants may have proposed a statutory monopoly because they did not realise that effective price support was practicable without it. But more probably their proposals were influenced at least partly by a realisation that a statutory monopoly would facilitate the operation of a quota system and increase its effectiveness, particularly in cocoa where there were a number of markets and an even greater number of buyers overseas.[9]

There was also another connection between the quota system and the establishment of statutory marketing. Some senior government officers in West Africa realised, as they could not fail to realise, that the quota system was imposed and ultimately managed by the Association of West African Merchants. This greatly strengthened their desire for radical changes in marketing methods, notably the establishment of statutory export control to restrain the power of the large firms. This attitude was not altogether logical, since it was only the statutory controls enforced by the government authorities which gave the major firms the great powers they possessed; but this inconsistency was not fully perceived. In particular, two successive governors of Nigeria saw in this display of power an important argument for a radical change in marketing methods, without examining too closely what exactly provided the basis of the power.

[9] The desire of the merchants for statutory export quotas to strengthen the operation of the market-sharing agreements was reflected in their evidence before the Nowell Commission. According to the report: 'A principal of one of the Agreement firms proposed the continuance of the system of export control used during the truce [the temporary suspension of the buying agreement during the enquiry into the dispute conducted by the Commission] for a period of, say, ten years. His view was that, under more stable conditions, it would be possible to rationalise the purchase of cocoa on the Coast "by eliminating all forms of redundancy such as overlapping buying stations, as well as reducing supervisory and other costs, there would thus be savings in overheads", the benefits which would be passed on automatically to the producer. He suggested that, with a Buying Agreement unsupported by quotas, there was the risk that shippers not parties to it, or new entrants to the trade, could upset by aggressive competition the member firms' efforts to regularise marketing. Export quotas would give the necessary stability.' Nowell Report, para. 498.

The administrative experience of the West African Produce Control Board and its performance in the marketing of West African exports were repeatedly mentioned in important official publications in support of the decision to continue statutory marketing after the war. The basis for this view is far from clear. On its sales of groundnuts and oil-palm produce to the Ministry of Food, the West African Produce Control Board received far lower prices than were paid by the Ministry for other bulk supplies from sterling areas; and throughout the Control Board's existence its operations provided no foundation for the belief in the advantages of a strong selling position of statutory export monopolies; nor indeed was the board supposed to exploit such a position. Again, it did not (nor was it asked to) reorganise the market structure of the export trade between the producer and the port of shipment.

In discussions and official statements at the time, three kinds of inference were drawn from the experience of the West African Produce Control Board. First, that it was very successful in the marketing of West African produce. Thus in West Africa the substantial surpluses of funds accumulated by the West African Produce Control Board were hailed as evidence of its successful trading operations. In fact these surpluses simply indicated the proportion of sale proceeds it decided to withhold from primary producers (which it was able to do as it enjoyed statutory export monopoly and was thus sole buyer); such surpluses were no indication of the board's success in marketing the crops. Secondly, it was argued that its operations were evidence of the feasibility of organised marketing of peasant crops in backward areas. In fact it merely shows that where there is a statutory export monopoly all exports will necessarily take place through the monopoly. Thirdly, it was inferred that the experience of wartime control demonstrated the feasibility, as well as the beneficial results, of price stabilisation. In fact what it did show was that a statutory export monopoly can prescribe producer prices more or less at any level (below the world level) it thinks desirable, and that it can fix prices at levels which would not be permitted by government if attempted by private organisations. Whatever the merits of the West African Produce Control Board as an instrument of wartime control, its experience cannot be adduced in support of the establishment of permanent statutory export monopolies (except as proof that even in a purely peasant economy a large measure of control is possible).

3

Although the operations of the West African Produce Control Board did not provide substantial arguments in support of statutory monopolies, its presence at the end of the war was a principal factor in the continuation of statutory marketing and the establishment of the marketing boards. Once an organisation such as a statutory export monopoly has been in existence for some years, strong tendencies for self-perpetuation come into play, since the members of the organisation gain an interest in its survival and expansion. They can muster outside support rather readily because they can point to their personal achievements in a way that is rarely possible under conditions of unorganised economic growth. The pressure for continuation of statutory export monopolies becomes practically irresistible when these inclinations and interests reinforce the preference of administrators for tidiness, for large-scale operations, and for administrative convenience (whether apparent or real). These features are deemed advantages of the operation of statutory monopolies, in contrast with a multiplicity of individual firms or traders.

These influences of self-perpetuation were clearly an important factor in the decision to continue statutory marketing in West Africa after the war. They are reflected in several passages in two British Government White Papers on cocoa marketing issued in 1944 and 1946 respectively, referred to earlier in this paper. But they can be seen particularly clearly in a Nigerian Sessional Paper, *Statement of the Policy Proposed for the Future Marketing of Nigerian Oils, Oilseeds and Cotton*,[10] which announced the intention to extend the proposals of the Cocoa White Papers to other products. It stated that the proposals

represent in fact the adaptation of marketing arrangements created and developed by the necessities of war to the purposes of peace. . . . Over a period of years an orderly structure, integrating the pre-war commercial system, has been built up. To take over that structure for maintenance, improvement and extension is, in the opinion of the Government, far wiser than to destroy it and so expose the whole economy and particularly the producers' economy, to the risks, uncertainties and price fluctuations which characterised the inter-war period.

[10] Lagos, Government Printer, 1948.

It added further:

In the event of the abandonment of the present arrangements, the disposal of the considerable sums which have already accumulated would present a problem of no little difficulty. In one way or another, since the return of a contribution made to those funds by each individual farmer is plainly impracticable and, even if practicable, would be of negligible benefit to the individual, these sums would have to be expended for the benefit of the producing communities. That by itself implies the establishment of representative boards to direct the process.

This argument implies that surpluses can never be returned to producers. But the argument would apply with equal force to funds of the marketing boards, the establishment of which was proposed in the Sessional Paper. Indeed, it would apply much more to the marketing boards. The Sessional Paper was issued in 1948. The West African Produce Control Board had accumulated surpluses on oil-palm produce and groundnuts (the Sessional Paper did not deal with cocoa) only since March 1947. Thus a distribution of its funds at the time by subsidising producer prices (a possibility disregarded in the Sessional Paper) would have benefited very largely those primary producers at whose expense the funds had been accumulated. But the operations of the marketing boards would extend over years or decades; and drafts on reserves after years of surpluses would benefit groups of persons very different from those from whom the funds had been collected.

As foreshadowed in the Cocoa White Paper and the Nigerian Sessional Paper, the marketing of West African exports was taken over from the West African Produce Control Board by marketing boards which continued to enjoy their predecessor's statutory monopoly over exports. Cocoa was taken over by marketing boards in 1947, and the other products in 1949 when the West African Produce Control Board was dissolved. The selling arrangements and the Administrative and executive personnel of the West African Produce Control Board in London were left substantially unchanged, as were the buying arrangements in Africa.

The presence of an established export monopoly (the West African Produce Control Board), and the criticisms of the pre-war marketing arrangements were important factors in the establishment of the marketing boards. But they were much reinforced by certain vague attitudes which have been widely current over the last ten or fifteen years. Only brief discussion of these influences and ideas is required here, partly because they are fairly well-known, and partly also because some have already been examined elsewhere.[11]

It was widely but rather vaguely believed in the 1940s that statutory marketing would bring about stabilisation of producer prices, which was regarded as both practicable and desirable. This was the principal theme of the two important Cocoa White Papers which emphasised the undesirable features of the pre-war marketing system of cocoa described in the Nowell Report and insisted particularly on the necessity of avoiding short-term price fluctuations.[12] In neither of the two White Papers, nor in any other official statement, was there any attempt to define stabilisation, or to distinguish between stabilisation of incomes and prices, or to refer to any of the various fundamental conceptual and practical problems and difficulties of stabilisation. Yet without a consideration of these ambiguities and problems, stabilisation becomes a meaningless omnibus term of no value as a guide to policy.

Another characteristic official attitude which runs through the second White Paper is a distinct dislike of traders and intermediaries, to whom the White Paper referred generally as middlemen speculators. Their allegedly nefarious activities were instanced as a major reason for drastic changes in marketing arrangements.[13]

Implicit in the White Papers and in other official statements on West African marketing is a belief in the irrelevance of prices, based on the view that market prices are of little significance and can be disregarded at least with impunity if not with advantage. In particular, it was often suggested in discussions on West African marketing that prices exert little or no influence either on current supply or on the maintenance and extension of capacity.[14] This view, though prevalent

---

[11] See 'The Reduction of Fluctuations in the Incomes of Primary Producers', pp. 156 to 200, below.

[12] Cf. ibid., where several passages from the White Paper are quoted.

[13] The dislike and distrust of middlemen springs from various well-known (one might almost say traditional) motives and opinions, such as the belief that trading in unproductive and traders parasitic. More recently these views have come to be reinforced by administrative antipathy to traders because their activities and their mobility may for various reasons by inconvenient to administrators. Again, the presence of a large number and great variety of traders suggests an economy untidy and unorganised in appearance, and this offends the tidiness complex so widespread in recent years.

[14] Or that in so far as they do affect output the influence is harmful.

at the time of the establishment of the marketing boards, has probably been more important as a factor influencing the policies which came to be pursued.

Lastly, a less obvious but possibly more powerful and persuasive influence than those already mentioned may have also played a part in the establishment of statutory marketing in West Africa; and this influence may have operated through several of the other factors already listed. In recent years there has been widespread and influential advocacy of a large measure of socialisation of saving in under-developed countries and of a closer governmental control over peasant producers, partly as an instrument for the socialisation of saving and partly as an instrument to direct agricultural production. The desire to socialise peasant saving and agricultural investment, and to control and direct the production and distribution of cash crops, has probably been more important as a factor in shaping the policies actually pursued by the boards than as a factor in their establishment. But it was probably significant even at the initial stage. This is suggested by such evidence as the extent of the powers of the boards, amounting to close control over the producers, processors, and traders of the products concerned and going far beyond the powers necessary for any price stabilisation, however defined. The extension of the authority of the boards to all agricultural exports, including products of trivial importance, also points in the same direction.

Although the relative importance of the different influences which brought about the establishment of statutory marketing of West African produce cannot be assessed closely, and may not be a matter of much significance, certain conclusions do emerge from the description and discussion in this paper.

It seems that chance occurrences and the interaction of *prima facie* quite unrelated phenomena were principal factors in the establishment of statutory marketing. There was a clear connecting thread between the desire of the merchants for a quota system in the export trade and the introduction of statutory export monopolies. Again, the presence of an established organisation interacted with largely irrelevant criticisms of the pre-war system, as well as with certain general attitudes and beliefs, to result in an extension and perpetuation of the wartime system of controls. All these factors in turn were reinforced by underlying and unobtrusive but powerful political beliefs.

The failure of the White Papers to discuss the meaning and

153

problems of stabilisation suggests strongly that influences of the kind just listed, not a careful assessment of the possibilities of smoothing incomes of primary producers, have combined to bring about the establishment of comprehensive statutory monopoly over agricultural exports in West Africa.

Addendum

Published information has always been available on the principal themes of this paper, notably on the British government guarantee to purchase total exports at fixed prices; the recognition of the un-limited nature of the market by expressing the buying and shipping quotas as percentages of unspecified totals; the identical nature of the wartime arrangements and of the pre-war market sharing agree-ments in the calculation of the quotas, the expenses and in the penalties for excess purchases. The required information has been available in British government command papers, West African ses-sional papers and the public notices of local governments and of the various control boards. Yet the paradoxical nature of the quota system, and its connection with the pre-war market-sharing agree-ments on one hand and with the establishment of statutory marketing on the other, were overlooked both by academic writers on the war-time and early post-war economic history of West Africa and by civil servants and even by businessmen adversely affected by the quota system. Both the quotas and the export monopolies were simply accepted as wartime necessities.

The circumstances of the establishment of the West African export monopolies present an example of the importance of primary sources for the writing of contemporary history. Reliance on secondary or tertiary sources by writers and observers was probably one reason both for the uncritical acceptance of the quota system and for the failure to see its connection with the introduction of statutory marketing.

The establishment of the statutory export monopolies of West Africa and their subsequent history illustrate well the familiar dis-crepancy between small, almost trivial, proximate causes and their far-reaching repercussions. The desire of the West African merchants to safeguard their margins was behind the establishment of the buying and shipping quotas, and these in turn were a significant factor in the establishment of the statutory export monopolies. The establishment and operation of these latter have had far-reaching and pervasive social, political and economic repercussions, not only in West Africa, but far beyond it because they have served as a model for similar organisations elsewhere. The system has proved not only a potent instrument of taxation, but it has also served as a political and economic power base for the local politician to whom it gave a powerful and easily operated method of control over the livelihood of the producers.

These events also illustrate another important, often ignored phenomenon, namely the difference, discrepancy or even total lack of correspondence between the ostensible and the actual reason for the establishment of an organisation or an institution.

THE REDUCTION OF FLUCTUATIONS IN THE INCOMES OF PRIMARY PRODUCERS*

The principal purpose of this paper is to present proposals for reducing the violence and magnitude of temporary fluctuations in the incomes of primary producers, whether due to variations in prices or in the size of the crop, with as little effect as possible on the rate of adaptation of supply to long-period changes in demand. The proposed method is self-adjusting in the sense that there can be no loss of contact with the trend of prices or of incomes; it explicitly aims at smoothing fluctuations in incomes, rather than in prices; and its adoption would render possible more accurate forecasting of the flow of producers' incomes in the territories concerned for a year or two ahead.

We also show that the measures most widely adopted in recent years have served not only to prolong the difficulties they were intended to solve, but have also tended to restrict supply; and that this applies largely both to measures designed to raise producer incomes and to those designed to constrict them.

Our proposals for a new method of stabilisation, or more precisely for smoothing, are outlined in Section 7; the major implications of these proposals are considered in Sections 8 and 9. Earlier sections review some of the problems of the various methods for raising or stabilising the incomes of primary producers, problems which our proposals are designed to obviate. Section 1 deals with certain general aspects of state action in this sphere; Sections 2 and 3 deal with the operation of price and income supports especially restriction schemes; Section 4 reviews the early years of the operation of the statutory export monopolies of Nigeria and Gold Coast-Ghana, the avowed aim of which was price stabilisation; Sections 5 and 7 examine some basic conceptual problems of stabilisation. Altogether, the second half of the paper from Section 5 onwards, deals with general conceptual and practical issues of stabilisation.

* (With F. W. Paish): *Economic Journal*, December 1952, pp. 750–80.

1

The inelasticities of supply and demand, especially of short-period supply, are the principal factors responsible for the wide price fluctuations of primary products, and particularly of agricultural products. These price fluctuations in turn have often brought about wide fluctuations in incomes.

Price fluctuations are, of course, not the only reason for the instability of incomes of primary producers. Variations in weather conditions or in the incidence of pests frequently cause wide fluctuations in output. When the output of a given area forms a large proportion of the total supply available to a particular market, or to the world as a whole, or where the output of competitive areas is similarly affected, the loss of income due to a smaller output may be partly, wholly or even more than wholly offset by higher prices. Where, however, the area affected is in competition with other areas which have not suffered similarly tthe fall in output will not be compensated by higher prices, and producers' incomes will fall. Nevertheless, it seems that unless they are due to a major natural disaster, variations in producers' incomes caused by crop fluctuations rarely induce governments to take offsetting measures.

When, on the other hand, the fluctuations in producers' incomes are due to changes in prices, governments have frequently and increasingly intervened on the largest scale, both to maintain incomes when prices are low and in recent years to restrict them when prices are high. Unfortunately, in devising measures to reduce fluctuations in incomes governments are confronted with the difficulty that such measures also tend to reduce or prevent the adjustment of supply to changes in demand as expressed through price, and thus to extend the very difficulties which their actions are designed to mitigate.

Moreover, the measures for raising, maintaining or stabilising incomes seem to have a generally restrictive effect owing to an asymmetry in their operations. Measures for the increase of producer prices and incomes often require restriction of output (or at least of supply reaching consumers), as otherwise the assistance to producers might increase supply. But no comparable compensatory action is possible to offset the adverse effects on output of measures taken to restrict producer prices and incomes.[1]

[1] The argument in the text applies largely to measures designed to assist producers of export crops in under-developed countries. It does not apply where

Thus government intervention tends to restrict output of primary products in periods both of low and of high prices, in the former *in order* to raise prices received by producers, and in the latter *as the result* of keeping them down. These results are particularly unfortunate in an epoch which may be one not merely of cyclical fluctuations, but also of a long-term trend in the direction of increasing shortage of primary products, and especially of foodstuffs, in relation both to the growth of population and to the output of manufactures.

2

Since the First World War there have been frequent examples of government action to assist primary producers, especially agricultural producers, by supporting the prices received by them. The following list, which is, of course, not exhaustive, recites the principal types of official action taken between the wars for the maintenance of producer prices and incomes: tariff protection and quotas; levy subsidies (duties, the proceeds of which are used to subsidise home producers); straight subsidies financed out of general revenue (with or without conditions for increasing or restricting production on the home market or for export); the granting of monopoly powers to producers' organisations, with or without the power to restrict production and entry, or to practise price discrimination; stock-holding schemes; statutory restriction schemes (unilateral or international) affecting export products. Although these various measures were often intended to even out temporary fluctuations, they were usually designed to raise more or less permanently the incomes of producers. It was generally impossible to distinguish between measures designed to even out fluctuations and those intended to raise incomes.

The measures varied with such factors as the budgetary position of the government, the distribution of political forces, the attitudes to state intervention and so forth. But their form and scope were also affected by such factors as the relation between home-produced supplies and imports, the position of the particular product in the national economy (especially in the cash economy) and, for export products, the proportion which they bore to the actual or potential

producers are assisted by straight subsidies or import restrictions. Such measures may still reduce overall world output of primary products if the effects of re-distributing production between high-cost and low-cost primary producers exceeds the effects of the diversion of resources into primary production from other forms of activity.

158

supplies on the world market. Thus tariffs and quotas cannot be used to assist producers of export crops, and the former may be ineffective where the supply of imports is inelastic; straight subsidies financed out of general revenue are impracticable where the commodity is the most important cash product of the country; and unilateral restriction or stock-holding measures are likely to fail where the exporting country has no effective monopoly.

In general, these measures tended to maintain or to raise producer incomes by restricting supplies. This was particularly evident in the measures of assistance to producers of export crops where these products played such a large part in the national economy that producers could not be assisted effectively by subsidies financed out of general revenue, and had, therefore, to be helped by means of restriction schemes. In the 1930s and until the war these schemes covered such leading staples of international trade as rubber, tin, tea and sugar.

These were the most important governmental measures for maintaining the incomes of producers of commodities which were largely exported,[2] and they were to some extent the counterpart or obverse of the present-day stabilisation measures which curtail the incomes of producers. An examination of these two most important types of intervention serves to bring out their restrictive effects.

3

The restriction schemes were comprehensive cartels in which the participating countries were allocated shares, usually known as basic quotas, and the participants undertook to restrict production or exports to certain percentages of these quotas as prescribed by a central committee or council. Within the participating countries individual producers received shares in the basic quotas (usually known as assessments); the right to produce for sale or to export was statutorily confined to those in receipt of assessments; and producers were restricted to specified percentages of their assessments varying with the degree of restriction. Both the basic quotas and the assessments were generally fixed with reference largely to performance in a base period. Establishment of new capacity was prohibited or severely restricted and, again, confined largely to producers already established.

[2] Some of these schemes or their remnants are still formally in existence, and their revival is often canvassed. Whenever there is a substantial fall in the prices of primary products, their resuscitation can be expected.

As long as a scheme remained comprehensive these arrangements secured the objective of raising prices, which under some of the schemes were several times higher than they would have been in their absence. Indeed, they were so successful (within their formal terms of reference) that while at their inception some of the schemes were regarded as short-term emergency measures, by the late thirties they were seen as permanent organisations. Yet their operations were open to serious objections, some of which are familiar, while others are less well known.

These schemes raised costs as well as prices, and did so in several ways. They protected the high-cost producers and restricted the growth of lower-cost suppliers; they inflated costs of all producers by enforcing under-capacity working, which affected low-cost producers especially adversely, and in some instances the provisions of the schemes discriminated substantially against the lowest-cost producers. These results were especially marked when a particular section of producers had special influence in the establishment and administration of a restriction scheme. At times this had important political and social repercussions; it is an inevitable result of these schemes that, where they operate, political and administrative decisions directly influence not only the level of incomes but also the relative positions of different sections of producers.

The cost of these measures to consumers was clear. Less obvious was the burden borne by those would-be producers who were barred from entry by the operation of the schemes. Where the production of the commodity affected by restriction offered much the best available occupation (and it was often the only really profitable cash crop) the barrier bore harshly on large numbers of the local population; and where those excluded from the establishment of small plantations or smallholdings were forced back on subsistence production and/or more or less casual wage earning, this had serious adverse results on economic growth as well as on the political stability of the territories concerned. Under these schemes, and especially those for rubber and tin, there were rapid fluctuations in the value of exports, in the volume of production and in employment. This feature was inherent in their aims and methods of operation.

Most of the schemes were established as emergency measures to raise prices and, at least ostensibly, to enable readjustments in production to take place in the producing territories whose economies were threatened with collapse by the sharp fall in prices. But they became *quasi*-permanent organisations for the protection of high-cost producers, and in some cases for the suppression of low-cost rivals. And as their aims were only vaguely defined (e.g. to raise prices 'to levels reasonably remunerative to producers') both the target prices and the level of supplies fixed by the regulation committees were arbitrary and unpredictable.

Thus even as a method of raising incomes, regulation schemes have serious disadvantages; and these apply even more to the use of such schemes as a method for stabilising incomes.

4

With the rise in the price of primary products in recent years, measures have appeared designed to prevent or reduce the increase in prices and incomes received by producers.[3] In many countries governments have taken action, usually by differential exchange rates or export taxes, to withhold from primary producers part of the sales proceeds have received for their products. When, as is frequently the case, the proceeds of such taxes are used, directly or indirectly, to subsidise local secondary industries, the operation exercises a double effect on the terms of trade between manufactures and primary products; for, on the one hand, it reduces the output of food and raw materials, and on the other, it simultaneously stimulates the output of manufactures. Of such measures it can only be hoped that the continued worsening of the terms of trade for manufactured goods will ultimately counteract the *mystique* of industrialisation, and cause at least some of its believers to consider whether the greater real incomes to be obtained from developing the output of primary products may not justify a change in policy.

In addition to measures explicitly designed to reduce the incomes of primary producers, stabilisation schemes have been introduced in

[3] Some contrary tendencies still operate for certain products. Thus some pre-war restriction schemes remain technically in force; farm products are still subsidised in many importing countries, and the US parity scheme can be used to maintain farm prices, but not to reduce them. But this does not affect the present argument.

Since this was written, measures to maintain and raise agricultural income by restriction schemes, or in some instances by tariffs and subsidies, have been revived or extended. The statutory export monopolies of various under-developed countries, notably in West Africa, Uganda and Burma, have avowedly become instruments of taxation. For West Africa, this latter development is discussed in the Addendum.

recent years, with the ostensible objects of withholding temporarily part of their incomes in periods of high prices, and supplementing them in periods of low prices. The most drastic and ambitious schemes, both as regards the proportion of the prices retained and the size of the funds thus accumulated, operate in West Africa, where they cover practically all agricultural exports, notably cocoa, oil-palm produce, groundnuts and cotton. The history of these important organisations and schemes and of their methods serves exceptionally well to illustrate the difficulties latent in the idea of price stabilisation.

Statutory export boards with monopoly powers were set up in West Africa during the war for opposite reasons – for cocoa in 1939 because of a feared collapse in demand; for oilseeds in 1942 because of a diminution in supply after the loss of the Far East. The organisation responsible for cocoa was first the Cocoa Control of the Ministry of Food, then the West African Cocoa Control Board and from 1942 the West African Produce Control Board, which also assumed the control of oilseeds. For cocoa the boards secured approximately market prices, but almost from the beginning began to accumulate surpluses by withholding from producers part of the net proceeds. Oilseeds, on the other hand, the board sold to the Ministry of Food at prices far below those paid to other Empire producers for similar bulk supplies.

In 1947 the very low prices paid by the Ministry for oilseeds were raised somewhat, but a large part of the increase was withheld from the producers and the Board began to accumulate surpluses on oilseeds and palm oil as well as on cocoa.

Altogether, the West African Produce Control Board handed over £43 million to its successor boards in Nigeria and in the Gold Coast. For cocoa some three-eighths of the net distributable proceeds were withheld from 1939–40 to 1946–7 (when the Cocoa Boards began operations); for groundnuts about one-half, and for oil and palm produce about two-sevenths, were withheld from February 1947 to April 1949, when the successor boards took over. These proportions do not allow for export duty, or for sales effected below market prices.

In two White Papers, Cmd. 6554, published in 1944, and Cmd. 6950, published in 1946, the British Government announced the intention of continuing the export monopoly for cocoa after the war as

162

a device for price stabilisation.[4] The stated purpose of the policy is well set out in the following quotation from Cmd. 6950:

By fixing a steady buying price in advance of the sale of each season's crop the Boards will cut the link between the price of cocoa in West Africa and the day-to-day price on the world market. Accordingly, in some seasons when world prices are high, the price paid to the producer will be less than the average realisation on overseas sales. The Boards will, on such occasions, show a 'surplus'. There will, however, be other seasons in which the average world price is below the price paid to producers. On these occasions the Boards will make a 'loss', which will be financed from the 'surpluses' accrued in years of high world prices. The intention is that 'profits' will be utilised primarily to maintain the maximum possible stability in the price paid to the producer.

The period over which this levelling process would take place was left unspecified, but it was clearly expected to be short, and it was specifically and categorically stated that there could be no question of the boards making a profit at the expense of the producers. To quote Cmd. 6950 again (our italics):

It will be apparent from the above description of the boards' proposed method of operation that there will be no question of their making a profit at the expense of West African cocoa producers ... *thus on the average of a period of years ... the average price paid in West Africa will be substantially equal to the average net price realised on world markets, and the boards' buying and selling transactions will, therefore, approximately balance.*

Between 1947 and 1950 a number of other marketing boards were set up to take over the export of the other products handled by the West African Produce Control Board. Apart from their statutory monopoly powers of export, the boards also have extensive powers over the local operations of processors and dealers. They now cover practically all agricultural exports, including some quite insignificant products.

Rarely can official statements of policy have been more rapidly belied than those of the White Paper of 1946. From the time of its publication in November 1946 until March 1949, when the West African Produce Control Board concluded its operations, this organisation was accumulating large surpluses, which as we have seen

[4] *Report on Cocoa Control in West Africa 1939–1943 and Statement on Future Policy,* Cmd. 6554 of 1944; *Statement on Future Marketing of West African Cocoa,* Cmd. 6950 of 1946.

TABLE 1

Summary of the operations of the marketing boards[1]

	producer price per ton (£)	f.o.b. cost per ton[2] (£)	average f.o.b. price realised per ton (£)	surplus (including interest) per ton (£)	surplus per ton as % of producer price (i.e. (d) as % of (a))	total annual surplus (£m.)
	(a)	(b)	(c)	(d)	(e)	(f)
Gold Coast cocoa						
1947–8	75	83	201	117	183	24
1948–9	121	139	136	−0·5	−0·5	−0·1
1949–50	84	110	178	71	86	18
1950–1 (est.)	130	172	270	101	78	23
Nigerian cocoa						
1947–8	63	70	195	126	200	9
1948–9	120	135	138	8	7	0·8
1949–50	100	117	178	69	69	7
1950–1 (est.)	120	157	270	119	99	12
Nigerian palm oil						
1949	40	52	68	16	40	2·5
1950	40	52	65	13	32	2·1
1951 (est.)	53	70	88	18	34	2·7
Nigerian palm kernels						
1949	26	33	45	12	46	3·2
1950	26	34	41	8	31	2·9
1951 (est.)	33	42	60	18	55	5·4
Nigerian groundnuts						
1949–50	21	35	48	13	62	3
1950–1 (est.)	21	37	64	27	129	4·2
Nigerian cotton						
1949–50	37	43	82	39	105	1·2
1950–1 (est.)	37	47	107	60	162	1

1. Source for Tables 1–3: Annual Reports of the Marketing Boards.
2. Price paid to producers, plus transport and handling costs to port, plus export duty.

represented a substantial part of sales proceeds. And its policy was continued by its successors. Detailed review of the operations is not possible here, but the general effects of their activities are clearly shown in Table 1.

Thus only for one product (Gold Coast cocoa) and for one year (1948–9) has there been an infinitesimally small draft on the reserves. For all other products and other years the boards have had continual surpluses, usually very large. The great bulk of these surpluses are held in London, where they form part of the overseas-owned sterling balances. Column (*e*) shows the percentage[5] by which prices paid to producers could have been increased out of the receipts for the current year, without drawing on reserves. An unweighted average of the eighteen percentages is 78, and in eleven of the eighteen cases the percentage is over 50.

Table 2 shows the total surpluses[6] accumulated by the marketing boards up to the end of 1951. As the accounts for 1951 had not been published at the time of writing, the figures contain a small element of estimation:

TABLE 2
Surpluses of the marketing boards to the end of crop year 1950–1 (or calendar year 1951)

	(£ million)		
	taken over from the West African Produce Control Board	surplus on operations	total surpluses
Gold Coast Cocoa Board	14	67	81
Nigeria Cocoa Board	8	29	37
Nigeria Oil Palm Produce Board	11	20	31
Nigeria Groundnut Board	10	7	17
Nigeria Cotton Board	0·2	2	2
	45	125	168

[5] These percentages exclude export duties and also understate the burden on producers in various other ways; some of these are indicated below.

[6] The term 'surplus' is used instead of 'reserves', since in some instances a minor part of the accumulated surpluses has been allocated (though generally not yet spent) for specific purposes or to other organisations, and is, therefore, formally no longer part of the boards' general reserves. For this reason the figures

The aggregate of these surpluses is not far short of the total amounts paid to the producers since the inception of these boards in 1947 and 1949 respectively. The surpluses of these boards have been so large that they could maintain the average level of payments to producers paid since their inception for about three seasons (i.e. for about as long as they have been in existence) even if they gave the crops away.

When considering the burden of this system on producers certain factors are relevant which are not shown in the tables. Over the greater part of the period of statutory marketing the prices realised for oilseeds and cotton by the selling organisations were far below those received by other bulk suppliers. Secondly, the surpluses are computed after the payment of heavy export duties which are included in costs. These duties have been rising rapidly in recent years, and were raised sharply in 1950 and 1951. These increases were made politically possible by the operations of the boards, since in view of the large surpluses increases in the duties do not directly affect producers; thus the rates and levels of the duties are much affected by the accumulation of surpluses.

If we add to the amounts retained by the marketing boards the sums collected by the government in export taxes, we find that deductions from the incomes which producers would have received if the full proceeds of their output had been allowed to reach them are well over 50 per cent. If expressed as a percentage of net income, after payment of the expenses of production, the rate of tax would be still higher. This is a level of taxation incurred in this country only by those who earn incomes of well over £5,000 a year. In recent years the average annual cash income of Nigerian groundnut producers was perhaps of the order of £5.[7]

During these years, when the incomes of producers have been so severely restricted, prices of the imports on which they spend a large proportion of them have risen sharply. The terms of trade of the producers have therefore been depressed, not only relatively to what they would have been and to those enjoyed by producers of similar products in other countries, but often even absolutely.

In the long run this underpayment of producers cannot fail

do not agree in every case with the published reserves of the boards, though they do agree very closely with the figures of the annually accruing surpluses.

[7] It will be seen from Table 1 that the proportion of distributable proceeds withheld from groundnut producers since 1949 has been well over half.

166

adversely to affect the incentive to produce and to maintain and extend capacity. The implications of the damping of incentives inherent in these price policies are particularly serious because producers in other territories have for years been receiving far higher prices and have therefore been under a correspondingly greater inducement to plant, replant, extend and improve their holdings. Thus, the policy which in the short period depresses the standard of living of the producers, in the long run also tends to undermine their competitive position.

It might have been thought that by generally keeping prices to producers far below sales proceeds and below prices ruling in world markets the boards would have been able at least to increase their stability and reduce the violence of their fluctuations. Unfortunately, it is not possible to substantiate even this claim. As Table 3 shows, the annual amounts paid to producers by the Cocoa Boards have actually fluctuated considerably more from year to year than have the amounts received by the boards from the sale of the crops:

TABLE 3

Actual and potential combined money incomes[1] of cocoa producers in the Gold Coast and Nigeria

	actual		potential	
	£ million	as % of 1947–8	£ million	as % of 1947–8
1947–8	19·9	100	52·9	100
1948–9	46·6	234	46·3	88
1949–50	30·8	155	54·9	104
1950–1 (est.)	45·0	226	82·0	155

1. 'Actual Incomes' means the total proceeds paid out to producers. 'Potential Incomes' means the combined total receipts of the boards from the sale of the crops less the boards' expenses.

The de-stabilisation of the incomes of cocoa producers was largely the result of the steep reduction in the producer price in 1949, following a very slight draft of reserves in the Gold Coast for the previous season. This draft was less than 1 per cent of the accumulated surplus and also less than 1 per cent of the total proceeds for the season. This minute draft on reserves induced the board to cut

167

the producer price from 65s. to 45s. per 60 lb, or by about 30 per cent. This was the largest absolute and the second largest proportionate fall in annual cocoa prices in the Gold Coast since the compilation of official records.

It is not possible to prepare a similar table for the other major crops, for the other boards have not been in existence long enough for the construction of such a series. It is, however, possible to discern some tendency towards the de-stabilisation of incomes in the figures for groundnuts and cotton. The exportable crop of groundnuts was almost halved between 1948–9 and 1949–50 and declined further in 1950–1. Yet the producer price was increased only very slightly between the first two years and left unchanged between the next two years, with the result that incomes of producers were far less in 1949–50 and 1950–1 than they had been in 1948–9; their real incomes declined even further, as the price of consumer goods rose by about a quarter over this period. This policy was pursued in spite of the fact that in all three years the board had very large surpluses. The policy of the Cotton Board and the experience of the cotton producers have been similar.

The threat of inflation and the need for stabilisation are the principal lines of argument officially advanced in support of the price policies of the boards.[8]

The suggestion that, in order to prevent inflation, incomes have had to be severely restricted below the sales proceeds of exports implies, of course, that the British authorities have pursued a deliberately exploitative policy in accepting the essential products supplied by West Africa (or their foreign-exchange equivalent), while refusing to make available even an approximately equivalent volume of imports to the much poorer populations of West Africa. While there may have been elements of such a policy in the allocation of certain commodities, and while the price policies of the boards were no doubt welcome to the British authorities by reducing the claims on the British economy, it is clear that such a policy did not operate

[8] Compulsory saving for development has also been mentioned at times, but this would be the task of government and not of organisations established for quite different purposes. Actually only a small part of their funds has been set aside for this purpose, and very little has been spent; nor is it clear that worthwhile projects or suitable personnel will be available when the funds come to be spent, and what their real value will be at the time. An official statement in Parliament has re-affirmed that the funds of the Marketing Boards are not destined for development on a substantial scale, but are intended for stabilisation.

throughout this period over the whole range of imports;[9] and the suggestion that it did is an extremely grave accusation of British colonial policy.

Nor is it clear how far and in what sense the desire for stabilisation could have provided the basis of these policies. As will be suggested shortly, stabilisation is meaningless without a fairly precise definition and clarification of objectives and methods. But on no rational criterion can the price policies of the marketing boards be justified by stabilisation. As has already been shown, some of the boards, including the Gold Coast Cocoa Marketing Board, which is much the most important of the boards, have actually de-stabilised producer incomes. And as will be seen from Table 2, there have been wide and discontinuous price changes from year to year.[10]

Very probably a major factor influencing the price policies of these boards was a possibly unconscious inclination to place the interests of the organisations above that of their constituents. It is a familiar tendency of administrators of large-scale organisations to be more concerned with the strength, growth and progress of their organisations than with the interests of the members they supposedly represent. After a period, the administrators may even come to regard their constituents or members as being opposed to themselves or to the organisation, and they consider that funds paid out to their constituents are lost or dissipated. The policies of the boards and their statements alike suggest that their administrators are more concerned with the extension and strengthening of the organisations than with the interests of producers.[11]

[9] This can be seen from the response of the volume of imports to the level of producer prices over this period; from the share of West Africa in all British colonial imports, which was far less than its share of British colonial exports and shows that supplies were diverted elsewhere by the superior pull of unrestricted incomes; from the absence in other sterling-area territories of the measures and policies pursued in West Africa; and from the accumulation of stocks of merchandise (especially textiles) in West Africa in 1949–50, accompanied by reductions and cancellations of their commitments by merchants.

[10] The rise in the producer price of groundnuts in 1951 by 60 per cent was by far the largest absolute increase and almost certainly the largest proportionate increase from one season to the next recorded so far in the history of West African groundnut prices. It did not reflect a sudden change in market conditions, but only a long-delayed partial adjustment of producer prices to world levels.

[11] The surpluses are obviously merely a measure of the degree of the compulsory retention of part of the proceeds from producers, and this is possible even with an unsuccessful selling policy; yet in the reports of the boards large

169

The price policies of the boards may possibly reflect the idea (which is also at work in the sharp increase in the rates of export duties) that those who have recently had a rise in money incomes are better able to bear additional taxation (even if their incomes are still low) than others with higher incomes, even if the latter are much better off; this is presumably on the ground that what a man has never had he does not miss. Whether this 'excess profits' system of taxation is equitable is a question on which there may be a reasonable difference of opinion. Even those, however, who would regard recent increments of income as particularly suitable subjects of discriminatory taxation would hardly contend that it should be continued in perpetuity. There must surely come a time when past increments are regarded as ordinary income and taxed no more heavily than the rest.

5

From the foregoing discussion of their activities it seems clear that the West African Marketing Boards have largely lost sight of their primary function of stabilising producers' incomes over time without permanently reducing their average level. This is perhaps partly because, while stabilisation is widely regarded as desirable, there seems to be a general failure to appreciate the ambiguities of the concept, especially as a guide to policy.

Stabilisation may refer to prices, money incomes or real incomes. Stabilisation of any one of these may actually de-stabilise the others; and in certain likely circumstances, such as a rise in import prices or fluctuations in crops, it will necessarily do so.

The concept is meaningless without reference to a specific period over which the accumulated forced savings and their subsequent disbursement balance. As the future course of prices is uncertain, it can always be argued that the larger the surpluses, the greater is the ability of the organisation to weather possible storms. When there is no stated or even contemplated finite period over which stable prices are to be achieved, the continuous accumulation of increasing reserves can provide its own perpetual superficial justification.

Additionally, stabilisation is meaningless without some reference

surpluses are frequently referred to as evidence of profitable trading or of successful operations. Thus the recently published first *Annual Report of the Nigeria Groundnut Marketing Board* expressly congratulates the West African Produce Control Board on its successful marketing policy, which has resulted in the surpluses which it handed over to its successor.

to the relation between the price envisaged under stabilisation and the open-market level. The lower the absolute level received by the producer, the longer it can be maintained; a zero price would ensure the maximum safety and stability. This consideration is particularly relevant to the operation of statutory export monopolies in under-developed countries. Stabilisation may also refer to relative shares rather than to the absolute level of incomes, that is, to the maintenance of the position of a certain class of producers relatively to other groups in the national economy. Indeed, in recent years this has been laid down as the aim of agricultural policy in certain countries.

Again, stabilisation is often taken to refer simply to the maintenance of incomes at least at a certain level, i.e. to the establishment of a floor to incomes; and somewhat paradoxically it sometimes refers to the raising of incomes, especially of agricultural producers.

There also are fundamental difficulties of measurement and definition in the concept of stability; it is not clear whether a large number of frequent and small changes represent a greater or lesser measurement of stability than a smaller number of large and discontinuous jumps, such as are often found in the operation of the so-called stabilisation schemes.

Quite apart from these ambiguities, the desirability of stabilisation (whether of prices or incomes or real incomes) is not self-evident. First, the aim of policy cannot and should not be the permanent stabilisation of real incomes, which it is to be hoped will show a long-period upward trend in under-developed countries. The aim should be to remove or reduce random fluctuations round the long-period trend; and this is even more difficult than stabilisation at a particular level.

Secondly, an attempt to stabilise prices or incomes may result in a loss of contact with the long-term trend. This contingency, which has serious disadvantages, is particularly likely when there is a general change in the value of money or a change in the underlying factors of supply and demand of a particular commodity or group of commodities.

Thirdly, in the absence of a highly centralised and closely administered planned economy, prices and incomes serve to direct resources into and out of different lines of production; and stabilisation of prices may remove desirable inducements for expansion or contraction.

171

Finally, when the rate of exchange with the outside world is fixed, an improvement in the terms of trade postulates a rise in local prices and wages relatively to import prices; and if stabilisation is rigidly interpreted no improvement in the terms of trade due to a rise in export prices can be transmitted to the local population.[12]

There are thus substantial dangers implicit in stabilisation measures; and in certain fairly clearly defined circumstances these risks and difficulties are greatly increased, particularly when there is a change in the trend of prices or in the long-run equilibrium price, whether as a result of a general change in money values or of long-term shifts in supply and demand. And all these risks and disadvantages are much enhanced when the policies are pursued unilaterally and contact is severed with market prices in one territory or group of territories only, while it is retained elsewhere.[13]

These unresolved and often unrecognised ambiguities may have been responsible for the harmful and paradoxical result of the various stabilisation and regulation schemes which has already been mentioned in this paper: their tendency to reduce output. This effect is obvious in the operation of restriction schemes and other measures designed to raise prices. But it is also true of the stabilisation schemes, which have kept producer prices below market prices and have thereby discouraged output. The principal exceptions to this generalisation have occurred under certain measures for maintaining or raising prices, for in such conditions output has at times been stimulated, at least temporarily, either by the use of discriminating monopolies or by purchases for stock. In the former case any advantage the consumer may have obtained from the increase in output has been wholly or partially offset by restricted supplies and higher prices in the more preferred uses, while in the latter the fact that in some countries supplies, accumulated in order to maintain prices, have subsequently been available to relieve shortages has been attributable rather to fortune than to foresight. Despite these exceptions, there is every

[12] There is no reference in these paragraphs to the disadvantages or costs of restriction schemes, the primary concern of which is to raise rather than stabilise prices.

[13] These considerations suggest that indiscriminate quest for security and stability may often amount to the substitution of less obvious but equally real or even greater hazards for those it is intended to eliminate; and that after a point the covert risks increase cumulatively without compensating increase in safety. The relevance of this consideration extends well beyond policies of price and income stabilisation.

reason to believe that on balance the effects of government efforts to reduce fluctuations in producers' incomes by operating on prices have been to reduce both output and consumption, and thereby to reduce the world's standard of living.[14]

6

The ambiguities of the concept of stabilisation, the risks and disadvantages of the policies actually pursued and the patently unsatisfactory method of operation of these schemes in recent years may well give rise to the conclusion that on balance they have been definitely harmful, both to the countries concerned and to the world as a whole, and should be abandoned as soon as possible.

But while there is much to be said for this view when the producers concerned are companies or other substantial concerns, the position of the small peasant farmer, especially when he is largely dependent on the production and sale of a single crop, deserves further consideration. For such producers wide fluctuations in prices may involve changes in real incomes so drastic that they may imperil not only the health of the economy but also the social and political stability of the territories concerned. Small producers are unlikely to have the self-restraint and foresight to set aside in good times sufficient reserves to cushion the effects of worse ones, or, even if they have, may be debarred from doing so by social customs and obligations. Where the output of such producers is small in relation to the total national income, it may be possible for the rest of the community to provide in emergency the help necessary to enable them to adjust themselves to the changed conditions. But where their output forms a large proportion of the national product, and especially where it forms a high proportion of total exports, it may well be desirable to take steps to cause the producers themselves to set aside in good years the reserves which will give them time to adapt themselves to adverse change. This would be particularly desirable in the so-called under-developed countries, in many of which the strain of rapid transition from a subsistence to a money economy is

---

[14] The effect of straight subsidies financed from general taxation would be to stimulate the output of the subsidised product without curtailing consumption. Such subsidies have been unimportant as stabilisation measures, which have been concerned primarily with commodities which have been largely exported. We shall not be concerned here with the incidence or overall effects of straight subsidies.

greatly enhanced by violent fluctuation in money incomes, the reasons for which are quite outside the grasp of the population, and which may set up great political and social tension.

Although this is rarely stated explicitly, the aim of the advocates of stabilisation measures (when these are not intended as disguised forms of assistance or, conversely, as a permanent form of taxation) is clearly the removal of random fluctuations around the trend of incomes. It would be clearly beneficial if this could be achieved without the disadvantages which have been mentioned.

To fulfil these requirements without serious disadvantages and risks a stabilisation scheme would have to have the following characteristics:

The purposes of a stabilisation scheme need to be clearly and unambiguously specified as the smoothing of fluctuation in incomes around the trend. The relevant period over which stabilisation or smoothing is operative would also need to be specified; that is, the period over which proceeds are averaged and surpluses and deficits balanced. If possible it would be desirable to smooth fluctuation in incomes arising also from variations in the volume of the crop; a scheme covering prices only may often de-stabilise incomes. Removal of inflation, compulsory saving for development, the raising of incomes by monopolistic measures, the re-organisation or control of the industries covered, all of which may or may not be ends of policy, should be kept distinct from stabilisation and pursued by other measures. This is necessary to avoid confusion through the pursuit of contradictory policies.

It would be desirable to have stringent precautions and preferably automatic devices to safeguard against loss of contact with the trend of prices. And while it is of the essence of stabilisation or smoothing that price changes are not immediately transmitted to the producers in full, prolonged loss of contact has obvious dangers, such as a large accumulation of funds, failure to transmit incentive and the likelihood of the organisation becoming an end in itself. These increase cumulatively with time; and are especially harmful under a unilateral scheme.

As comprehensive international action is notoriously difficult in this sphere, there are important advantages in a scheme which could be applied locally, or in a few territories, without grave risk to the competitive position of these territories. As the scheme would be concerned with local producer prices and incomes, it would not affect world market prices directly. Accordingly, it would be desirable that it should not prejudice the acceptance of international schemes for smoothing fluctuations in market prices, such as the Graham–Hayek Commodity Reserve Scheme; and it would be desirable if it could be linked to such schemes if they came to be introduced.[15]

It would be desirable if the scheme could be operated without statutory export monopolies. These organisations retard the establishment of independent merchants with adverse effect on economic growth in various ways. There are also obvious political dangers in the dependence of the population on the decisions of statutory export monopolies. But if such organisations are found necessary for the administration of the scheme their price policies should be subject to rigid rules to make their decisions broadly predictable, and to eliminate possible clashes of loyalty.[16]

It would be highly advantageous if the flow of money incomes in the territories concerned could be forecast within fairly narrow limits for a year or two forward. If so it would be a singular and striking advantage if a scheme could be devised and administered which would combine the smoothing of fluctuations with a measure of predictability of the future flow of incomes.

In Section 7 there is outlined a scheme which seems to satisfy all these requirements.

7

Ultimately the difficulties of stabilisation all reduce to the problem of the maintenance of contact with the trend; the *desiderata* and dangers listed in previous sections flow from the likelihood of the loss of contact with the trend and from its consequences. Thus a stabilisation scheme or measure, while being of sufficient magnitude to be of real help to producers, must not seriously delay the process of adaptation of supply to change of demand, either during the period of the accumulation of reserves or during the process of their disbursement.

The danger of delaying or distorting the reaction of supply to changes in demand is clearly greatest where the elasticity of supply

[15] These schemes are concerned with market prices and not with producer income; they may de-stabilise local incomes if crops vary greatly.

[16] This point is a special instance of a wider problem. Some important objections to centralised governmental control of economic life flow from the wide, unpredictable and arbitrary nature of individual decisions; these objections would not apply where these are clearly circumscribed and predictable.

is large. Fortunately a high elasticity of supply makes assistance to producers unnecessary, for they can, by definition, adapt themselves rapidly to changes in demand and prices. Help is needed most in cases where it is least likely to be harmful. This applies to either of two different types of inelasticity of supply: lack of ability or readiness of producers to move into or out of a particular line of production or, as in the case of tree crops, a long period of production.[17]

But even where the short-term elasticity of supply is low, prolonged delay of the impact of a change in demand may have serious adverse distorting effects by preventing re-adjustment to changed conditions. The subsidy or levy under the scheme must therefore be temporary; and it must be known to be temporary, for the expectation of a future change in the income expected from a given activity may be almost as effective in securing the required adaptation to change in demand as an immediate change in income. Hitherto the duration of assistance or of levies under the various schemes has generally been unforeseeable, since this depended either on political decisions or on the discretion of administrators. Producers have therefore been induced to act as if the assistance or the levy was likely to be permanent; they were certainly not given any indication either of its duration or of its extent.

Changes in market conditions are often thought to be temporary when they first occur. Such a belief results in policies which are continued for a long period in the expectation of the temporary nature of the circumstances which brought about their adoption. As a result, the changed conditions are not transmitted to the producers for considerable periods, and their responses will be correspondingly delayed. While countries where the product concerned is only a small proportion of the national income may well continue assistance indefinitely, in countries where it constitutes a large proportion, the period over which assistance can be given is limited. On the other hand, there is nothing to prevent them from continuing indefinitely levies imposed in a period of rising prices, until what was started as a scheme for equalising producers' incomes over time becomes, almost insensibly, a system of taxation.

[17] This distinction is often neglected in discussions on the elasticity of supply. The short-period elasticity of supply of certain tree crops is much greater than that of others as the rate of capacity working can be subject to wider variation. Thus rubber production from a given area depends on the rate of tapping, while cocoa production is not subject to this kind of variation.

It is thus necessary to lay down in advance clear-cut mandates for those operating stabilisation schemes to ensure that accumulations should be limited and that this should be widely understood by producers.

An obvious form for such a mandate would be a prescription of a formal statistical method of smoothing fluctuations, such as a moving average covering a fixed number of years; that is, producer prices would be based on the moving average of net proceeds per ton as calculated by a clearly defined formula. The number of years to be averaged and the weight to be given to each year might well vary from scheme to scheme, according to the elasticity of supply of the product. In general, the higher the elasticity of supply, the higher should be the weight attached to the current year, and the lower the weights, or the smaller the number, of previous years.[18] The remainder of this section examines the outline and methods of operation of such a scheme.

In countries in which the administering authority is in direct contact with individual producers, and can keep accounts of individual deliveries and earnings, the smoothing process could be applied directly to the actual incomes earned from the production of a given product or group of products. The authority, perhaps a co-operative society, would retain part of the proceeds of the current year but simultaneously repay part of the proceeds retained in previous years.

In practice, it would probably not be convenient to wait until the final receipts from the sale of the crop were known before making payments to producers. This difficulty could be overcome by making a payment at the beginning of the selling season of the part carried forward from past years, and at the end of the season of the part earned in the current year. Alternatively, and probably more conveniently for producers, a whole year's payment could be made at the beginning of the selling season on the basis of an estimate of the

---

[18] The general formula for such a scheme is

$$I_t = \frac{Y_t}{x} + \frac{1}{n}\left[(Y_{t-1} + Y_{t-2} + \ldots Y_{t-n}) \times \frac{x-1}{x}\right]$$

where I_t = total amount distributed to producers in current year t;

Y_t = proceeds of crop for current year;

$\frac{1}{x}$ = fraction of proceeds for current year paid to producer;

n = number of previous years over which proceeds are averaged.

quantities and prices for the current year. Any errors in the estimate would be corrected in subsequent payments, the amount carried forward to the credit of the producer being the difference between the amount actually realised for his crop and the advance payment made to him.[19]

Such a system of averaging, applied to the income of each separate producer, would give him a measure of insurance, not only against falls in prices and other misfortunes shared with other producers, but also against those, such as a local crop failure, which affected him alone.

In many cases, however, including some where such a scheme is most needed, there is no possibility of that direct contact between the producer and the administering authority which would allow records to be kept of his individual deliveries. Instead, the authorities are obliged to operate entirely through the prices they pay. Even in such a case, however, it is possible to introduce the principle of averaging proceeds and thus smoothing fluctuations in incomes.

The way suggested of doing this is to prescribe a producer price each season calculated as the sum of two component elements. The first component would be a fraction of the estimated market price for the current year (or, more precisely, of the estimated net sales proceeds per ton). The second component, which would provide the smoothing element in the scheme, would be derived from the difference between the realised proceeds per ton in past years and the amounts paid out in those years on account of the first component. To obtain it, we should first subtract from aggregate actual proceeds of the crop over a given number of past years the amounts paid out on account of the first price component – that is to say, the aggregate of the first component of the price times the number of tons bought in each year. We then average this difference over the given number of past years, and so arrive at the aggregate amount to be distributed during the current year on account of the second component element in the price. This amount, divided by the estimated number of tons in the current crop, gives the second component element in the price per ton to be paid in the current year.

[19] The effect of the change from actual to estimates as the basis of the payment on account of the current year would modify the general formula as follows:

$$I_t = \frac{\overline{Y}_t}{x} + \frac{1}{n}\left[Y_{t-1} + Y_{t-2} + \dots Y_{t-n} - \frac{(\overline{Y}_{t-1} + \overline{Y}_{t-2} + \dots \overline{Y}_{t-n})}{x} \right],$$

where $\overline{Y}_t$ = estimated proceeds for the current year.

178

The general formula for this type of scheme is as follows:

$$S_t = \frac{\overline{P_t}}{X} + \frac{\left\{\frac{1}{n}P_{t-1}Q_{t-1}+P_{t-2}Q_{t-2}+...P_{t-n}Q_{t-n}-\frac{(\overline{P}_{t-1}Q_{t-1}+\overline{P}_{t-2}Q_{t-2}+...\overline{P}_{t-n}Q_{t-n})}{X}\right\}}{\overline{Q}_t},$$

where S_t = producer price;

P = market price (net proceeds per ton);

$\overline{P}$ = expected market price (net proceeds per ton);

Q = volume of crop;

$\overline{Q}$ = expected volume of crop;

$\dfrac{1}{X}$ = fraction of expected proceeds of current year paid out, i.e. included in calculation of producer price;

n = number of years over which proceeds are averaged for smoothing fluctuations.

This formula has the advantage of being self-adjusting for those errors of estimates which are likely to be of practical significance. It is self-adjusting in the sense that errors are self-liquidating over the number of years over which proceeds are smoothed. Thus an over-estimate of the price to be received for the current season automatically reduces the amounts carried forward, and thereby reduces the prices paid over the relevant number of ensuing years.[20]

[20] The only cases in which the operation of the formula is not completely self-adjusting is that of a large error in the estimate of the volume of the crop in the forthcoming year. This is because the producer price is calculated on the basis of expected prices and quantities but the payments are made for the actual crop realised. In certain special cases the results of errors in the estimates of the crop would not be fully liquidated over the smoothing period included in the formula. In practice, this is likely to be of very small importance, and could be provided for in either of two ways. It could be rectified by an *ad hoc* adjustment of the prices paid for subsequent crops. Alternatively, the formula could be made fully self-adjusting by the introduction of a correction factor in the subtraction in the second term. This would in fact be simple. But it would make the formula look rather cumbrous and, as it is required only in special circumstances, it is not included in the formula. If it were included the scheme would be completely and fully self-adjusting.

This scheme is obviously not quite so effective an insurance for the producer as one operating directly upon incomes, because, while it softens the impact of a fall in prices or of any general crop failure, it will not afford him protection against a crop failure which affects him either alone or together with only a proportion of producers. Indeed, if one section of producers experiences a crop failure while the rest have unusually good crops, the more fortunate producers will benefit from the misfortune of the rest, since (in addition to any effect on market

Under this scheme producer incomes in any one year depend to an appreciable extent on sums retained out of previous years' incomes. These sums are exactly known; and therefore producer incomes in the coming year and even in the year after that can be ascertained in advance far more closely than without such a scheme. This would considerably ease the task of those, whether merchants or government departments, whose responsibility it is to see that the supply of goods available for producers to buy is commensurate with their incomes. Where the merchants have to plan the import of consumer goods many months ahead (as they have to in many parts of the world) the economies to be obtained from a greater predictability of producers' incomes are very large indeed.

The method of operation of such a scheme with this formula would depend to some extent on the relative weights given to the two terms or component elements which determine the production price. If the first term is large (i.e. if in any one year a large part of expected proceeds is paid out) then the second term must necessarily be small, as the balances carried forward for distribution in subsequent years are necessarily small. Conversely, if the first term is small the second term is necessarily larger.

The relative importance to be attached to the two terms is a policy decision. The larger the first term, i.e. the greater the weight given to the current year in the calculation of the average, the less is the smoothing of producer incomes in the scheme. In the limiting case in which the denominator in the first term is one there is no smoothing. If it is thought desirable to effect a large measure of smoothing over a number of years the first term will have to be made small relative to the second. A large measure of smoothing has the advantage of smaller year-to-year variations in incomes at the cost of some delay in transmitting a change in the trend of prices to producers.

The operation of the general principles may be illustrated by a specific example. Let us assume that the producer price per ton is calculated by paying one-half of the expected proceeds per ton plus one third of the amounts retained over the previous three years; by

prices) the payments on account of previous years have to be distributed over a smaller output than if all had had good crops, and the price paid the fortunate producer is therefore higher. It is therefore desirable that, so far as administratively possible, areas subject to widely differing climatic conditions should be included in separate schemes.

CHART I

Hypothetical examples of use of formula
A. Changes in market price
(output constant)

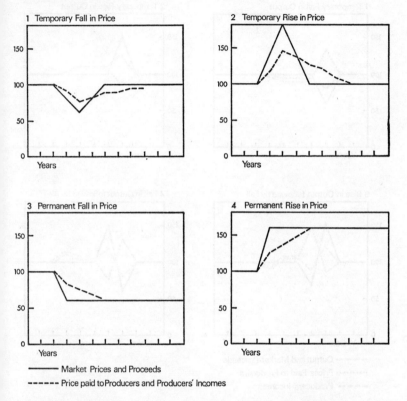

1 Temporary Fall in Price

2 Temporary Rise in Price

3 Permanent Fall in Price

4 Permanent Rise in Price

————— Market Prices and Proceeds

------- Price paid to Producers and Producers' Incomes

retained is meant the difference between the net proceeds per ton realised and the one-half of expected proceeds included in the actual producer price for the current year.[21]

This particular formulation is one which passes on to producers a substantial part of the impact of any change, and is therefore not likely seriously to affect its influence on supply; on the other hand, it appreciably mitigates its severity, reducing the degree of temporary

[21] This special application of the general formula is

$$S_t = \frac{\overline{P}_t}{2} + \frac{\frac{1}{3}\left[P_{t-1}Q_{t-1}+P_{t-2}Q_{t-2}+P_{t-3}Q_{t-3}-\dfrac{(\overline{P}_{-1}Q_{t-1}+\overline{P}_{t-2}Q_{t-2}+\overline{P}_{t-3}Q_{t-3})}{2}\right]}{\overline{Q}_t}.$$

181

CHART I

B. Changes in output
(market price constant)

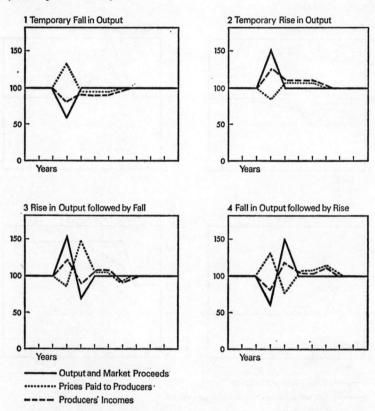

1 Temporary Fall in Output

2 Temporary Rise in Output

3 Rise in Output followed by Fall

4 Fall in Output followed by Rise

—————— Output and Market Proceeds
············ Prices Paid to Producers
– – – – Producers' Incomes

fluctuations in incomes and giving producers, more time to adapt themselves to permanent changes.

Chart I shows its application to eight different simple hypothetical cases, four of changes in prices and four of changes in output. The adjusted movements in producers' incomes seem to be rather similar to the changes in expenditure one would expect for a provident producer who had made provision for his own reserves. For purposes of simplicity the examples shown in the charts abstract from the effects of errors in estimating output and prices for the current year. These would, of course, automatically correct themselves in later years, since the scheme is self-adjusting.

TABLE 4

Gold Coast Cocoa

year	out-put (1,000 tons)	producers' prices per ton			producers' aggregate incomes			surplus retained by Board	
		earned (£)	paid (£)	payable on formula[1] (£)	earned (£m.)	paid (£m.)	payable on formula (£m.)	actual (£m.)	formula (£m.)
1942–3	207	17·6	11·6	16·8	3·6	2·4	3·5	1·2	0·1
1943–4	196	22·3	13·0	20·4	4·4	2·5	4·0	1·9	0·4
1944–5	229	28·2	22·4	22·2	6·4	5·1	5·1	1·3	1·3
1945–6	209	32·0	27·0	27·5	6·7	5·6	5·7	1·1	1·0
1946–7	192	100·8	51·3	65·6	19·4	9·8	12·6	9·6	6·8
1947–8	206	191·7	74·7	122·2	39·5	15·4	25·2	24·1	14·3
1948–9	275	120·8	121·3	100·1	33·1	33·3	27·5	−0·2	5·6
1949–50	253	155·0	84·0	138·1	39·2	21·2	34·9	18·0	4·3
1950–1 (est.)	247	231·0	130·0	190·9	57·0	32·0	47·1	25·0	9·9
Totals					209·3	127·3	165·6	82·0	43·7

1. In this Table it has been assumed that the estimates of price and output used in applying the formula turn out to be correct. With sufficiently erroneous estimates, it would, of course, be possible to arrive at prices which would increase the instability of incomes instead of reducing it. But even the most flagrant errors tend to cancel out over time. If we go so far as to assume that those making the estimates always expect the output and price realised in the previous year to be repeated in the current year, the aggregate amounts paid out to producers under the formula during the nine years from 1942–3 to 1950–1 would not be very different from those obtained by using correct estimates – £163 million, as against £166 million.

In addition, in Table 4 and Chart II are shown the prices which would have been paid for Gold Coast cocoa and the total receipts of producers if this scheme had been in operation since 1947, as compared both with the prices and amounts actually paid, and with those which would have ruled if the boards had distributed the whole of the available proceeds.

It will be seen that if this scheme had operated both producer prices and incomes would have been much higher and more stable than they actually were. In addition, they would have been more predictable, which, in the condition of the Gold Coast, would have been of much political, social and economic consequence.

One of the chief difficulties in starting such a scheme *de novo* would be the cost of building up the necessary reserves during the first few years, unless, indeed, it was inaugurated in a period of very steeply rising prices. If, however, it was given the initial help of a government guarantee, it would be possible to start it from the beginning as if it had already been running for an indefinite period, the prices paid being calculated on the basis of the size and prices of the crop in previous years. If the inauguration of the scheme were followed by a period of rising prices, it is unlikely that the government would ever

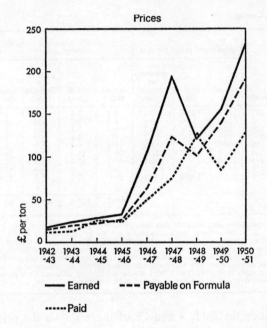

Prices

£ per ton

1942 -43　1943 -44　1944 -45　1945 -46　1946 -47　1947 -48　1948 -49　1949 -50　1950 -51

——— Earned　－－－ Payable on Formula

‥‥‥‥ Paid

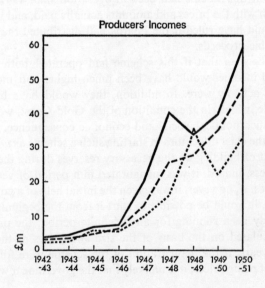

Producers' Incomes

£m

1942 -43　1943 -44　1944 -45　1945 -46　1946 -47　1947 -48　1948 -49　1949 -50　1950 -51

184

be called upon to implement its guarantee; but if it were followed by a period of falling prices, the government might well be at least temporarily out of pocket. The size of the reserve required depends on the precise variety of the scheme adopted. With the example used above the amount of the government's contingent liability would be limited to a maximum of about the value of one year's crop, which it would incur only if either the price or the output fell permanently to zero; in practice it would be unlikely to exceed half the value of a year's crop. The difficulty of providing an adequate reserve does not arise for those crops already being marketed through the West African and other marketing boards as these organisations already hold reserves far more than adequate for the purpose.

8

The scheme outlined above not only satisfies all the requirements for a stabilisation scheme set out in Section 5 above, but other important advantages can also be claimed for it.

1. There would be no loss of contact with the trend of prices. This scheme thus avoids the danger inherent in the usually canvassed stabilisation devices, since it is impossible to foretell whether a particular change is the beginning of a trend or whether it is a fluctuation likely to be reversed. Under the proposed scheme the only danger on this ground is a short lag in the transmission of the trend. Such a delay is of course inherent in any smoothing scheme. Any temporary divergence from the trend will be corrected by a smooth change over the next year or two, and not by means of large discontinuous changes as under other so-called stabilisation measures.

2. The scheme aims explicitly at smoothing fluctuations in incomes and not at stabilising prices. It provides a specific and clear meaning of the idea of stabilisation, and explicitly separates stabilisation or smoothing from measures designed to combat inflation or to enforce compulsory saving or disguided taxation. It also clearly distinguishes stabilisation and smoothing from monopolistic devices to raise producers' incomes. Such measures can be assessed on their merits and introduced irrespective of this scheme.

3. Under this scheme it would be possible to estimate the future level of money incomes far more closely and for far longer ahead than ever before. This follows from the operation of the second term of the formula. Importers will therefore be in a position to assess future demand far more closely and further ahead than in the past.

185

This would have the obvious very great advantages of substantial saving in capital and a reduction in the risks of trading. But it would also have important political advantages, since in backward countries both shortages and gluts of imported merchandise[22] are apt to have adverse political repercussions.

With a more accurate assessment of the future level of money incomes it will be possible to estimate more closely the future flow of tax receipts and of government revenue generally. This, in turn, will render possible greater stability and continuity of fiscal policy.

4. By smoothing fluctuations and by making possible much more accurate forecasts of the remaining movements in the flow of incomes, the operation of the scheme would go a long way to shield the economies of primary producing countries from the social, political and economic stresses and strains arising from discontinuous and unexpected fluctuations in money incomes.

5. Successful smoothing of fluctuations of incomes of primary producers may also serve to foster a sense of continuity in economic affairs, which for various reasons (among which the frequent and discontinuous fluctuations in incomes is one) is often very imperfectly developed in primary producing countries. As a sense of continuity is in different ways an important influence in promoting economic development, a measure which assists its growth may contribute to economic development in primary producing countries.

6. The scheme does not rely on the imposition of maximum or minimum prices, which among other disadvantages tend to enhance scarcities by stimulating demand and discouraging supply (maximum prices) or gluts by decreasing demand and stimulating supply (minimum prices).

7. Under this scheme there is no possibility of the indefinite accumulation of liquid balances. The very large balances of the West African boards raise serious economic and political issues, especially in view of the fiduciary relationship between the United Kingdom and the colonies. But they also involve political dangers locally, as they provide a strong temptation to local political parties, and will serve to give immense power to those parties which best appreciate their political possibilities. Again, such large funds accumulated

---

[22] Both shortages and gluts are apt to be ascribed to the malice of expatriate merchants. A shortage is said to be the result of monopolistic restriction of supplies in order to profiteer; a glut is said to be evidence of destructive dumping to eliminate the struggling local merchants.

without clear ideas on a long-term policy may come to be spent very wastefully. None of these dangers would arise under the proposed scheme. These implications or results of the accumulation of surpluses have been conspicuous in Nigeria and Ghana in the 1950s.

8. The scheme could be operated without statutory export monopolies by means of export taxes and subsidies at rates varying in accordance with the formula. The absence of statutory monopolies would have important social, political and economic advantages. But even if it were operated by statutory monopolies these organisations would function with definite, prescribed and known ends and methods. Among other advantages such rigid definition of functions would remove their actions from the political field. It would, of course, also remove any suspicion that the decisions had been influenced by pressure from the United Kingdom, and thus any suggestion of exploitation by means of compulsory accumulation of sterling balances.

9. The proposed scheme also has important advantages over the buffer-stock plans which are again widely canvassed. Buffer-stock schemes are concerned with prices and not with incomes (which they may actually de-stabilise); there is no real assurance that there will be no loss of contact with the trend of prices; the accumulation of buffer stocks tends to lead to a running down of private stocks; the price changes take the form of discontinuous movements; and there is no large measure of foreknowledge of the future flow of incomes as there would be under the proposed scheme. Moreover, a buffer-stock scheme would have to be operated internationally, while the scheme here envisaged could be operated either locally or internationally without any risk of damage to the long-term competitive position of the producers concerned.

9

The widespread adoption of schemes of this type, while primarily designed to reduce fluctuations in incomes of particular groups of producers, would also have appreciable effects on the economy of the world as a whole. These effects, unlike those of restriction or buffer-stock schemes, would not take the form of changes in the relative world prices of individual primary products, or of primary products as a whole in relation to those of other commodities. One of their main purposes, indeed, would be to reduce to the smallest possible limits their effects on the supply and price of particular products in the world market. They might, however, very well have a considerable influence on the magnitude of fluctuations in the general level of world prices and incomes.

The precise way in which such schemes might help to reduce fluctuations in the purchasing power of money on world markets would depend largely on the form in which the reserves were held. If a country instituting such schemes were a strong financial centre, with ample reserves of gold or foreign exchange, it would be reasonable for the reserves to be held within the country. They would thus help to reduce the inflationary pressures frequently associated with periods of rapidly rising prices of primary products. If, to take a simple instance, they were lent to the government, they would enable it to reduce its recourse to the banks, or to pay off existing government debt held by the banks, and so directly tend to keep down or reduce the quantity of money. In any subsequent depression the repayment of debt by the government and its distribution as income to producers would help to maintain both the quantity of money and the national money income. If the effect of this was to turn the balance of payments against the country concerned, its gold reserves would, by hypothesis, be adequate to meet the resulting losses, which would help to maintain incomes and prices in the rest of the world.

If the country introducing the schemes were not a strong financial centre, the repayment for use as income during a depression of reserves invested within the country might well cause so large an adverse balance of payments as to exhaust the gold or foreign-exchange reserves and to bring about a balance-of-payments crisis. It would therefore be necessary for the reserve funds to be invested either in gold or in liquid assets outside this country, preferably in a strong financial centre. These would then be available to cover any adverse balance created by their disbursement, which would incidentally help to maintain incomes and prices in whatever countries the foreign reserves were spent.

The effects of schemes of this nature on the general level of world prices would thus be very similar to those aimed at by a commodity reserve currency scheme, such as that suggested by Professors Graham and Hayek. Indeed, they provide a very convenient supplementary technique for achieving the same purpose, for the most convenient time for introducing them is during a period of rising prices and increasing scarcities of primary products, which is just the time when the setting up of a commodity reserve currency scheme would be most difficult. The two types of scheme might therefore very conveniently exist together, the producer-income stabilisation schemes doing their special work of reducing fluctuations in the incomes of particular groups of producers, and at the same time reinforcing the commodity reserve currency scheme in reducing fluctuations in the general level of world prices.

Addendum

In the 1950s Professor Paish and I published several joint articles on price and income stabilisation and on the operation of the West African marketing boards. Two of these articles were published in the *Economic Journal*. The first of these articles is reproduced here, with only minor stylistic changes. The second, almost as long as the first, was published in December 1954. This article was partly in reply to criticisms of the first paper which appeared in the *Economic Journal* in 1953–4, but it also developed further some of the arguments of the first paper. It is not reproduced here because much of it is in reply to criticisms of no general interest. In the *Journal of the Royal Statistical Society*, 1954, part I, I published a long article, 'Statistics of Statutory Marketing in West Africa, 1939–51', which examined the operation of the marketing boards up to 1951 in greater detail than is presented in the paper in this volume.

This Addendum deals first with some of the principal substantial issues which arose in the discussion initiated by the paper reproduced here. It also deals with some related relevant issues (including some of the arguments of the second *Economic Journal* paper by Professor Paish and myself) which were not the subject of critical comment. Thereafter some of the salient points of the article in the *Journal of the Royal Statistical Society* are summarised, and some major statistics on the operation of the marketing boards are brought up to date in summary form.

Two points of terminology may be noted. The repeated use in the paper of expressions such as 'should', 'desirable', and 'needed' imparts an unnecessarily normative flavour to certain parts of the discussion. In fact the normative connotation is more apparent than real.

These quasi-normative expressions occur mostly in contexts where they refer to the attainment of specific, explicitly stated or clearly implied objectives (usually accepted or advocated by supporters of stabilisation or of the marketing boards), such as the expansion of the production of the controlled crops or the assurance that no money would be withheld from the producers. At other times, the expressions refer to the attainment of objectives generally considered desirable in the context of public finance or of development economics, as for instance the avoidance of substantially regressive forms of taxation, or the minimisation of its disincentive effects. The quasi-normative expressions could have been replaced by other, often longer, formulations to indicate unambiguously their positive (distinct from normative) basis. Their positive basis is in fact clear throughout. The quasi-normative expressions thus refer to analysis or discussion which is positive, not normative; they are not simply expressions of preferences or of wider value judgments. But some readers may prefer a formulation from which all normative flavour, however faint, is removed.

We also refer in the paper to 'rising' and 'falling' prices. Here again the meaning is usually clear in the context, namely that the reference is to periods over which prices have risen or fallen, or over which they were or are expected to do so. Nevertheless, the use of the present participle is best avoided in economic discussion, especially in the context of price changes. Prices are in fact never rising and never falling. They may have risen, and for reasons to be specified the rise may be expected to continue. Similarly with a decline in prices. The use of the present participle implies a covert extrapolation from an unspecified base. Its use often reflects an implied invalid analogy with the concepts and methods of the physical sciences, perhaps a subconscious covert analogy with some of their concepts, such as the gravitational constant.

It is no longer disputed that since their inception the marketing boards have been instruments of taxation. This rather obvious point used to be much disputed, but has now come to be accepted both by academic writers and also by the West African authorities. When Professor Paish and I first suggested that the boards were instruments of taxation, this suggestion was received with indignation, and was countered by statements that they were instruments of stabilisation (in some indefinite sense). Such suggestions were clearly untenable in view of the large surpluses of the boards; the large increase in export duties specifically on exports controlled by the marketing boards; the diversion of large parts of their reserves to the governments; and the imposition in the Gold Coast in 1954 of a ceiling on the prices received, not only by the producer, but also by the Cocoa Marketing Board. Indeed, a supporter of the marketing boards, writing in *The Times* on 20 July 1951 explicitly claimed that their activities had prevented the emergence of a kulak class in West Africa. Thus this issue was never in legitimate doubt.

Various factors brought it about that the system ostensibly set up to promote the interests of producers by short-period price stabilisation promptly developed into an instrument for special taxation of those producers. Members of the marketing boards are not the first 'agents or trustees of the producers' (to quote the White Paper) to impose special burdens and levies on their charges, and to argue that this is for the benefit of the latter. The marketing board system was also welcome to those who from its inception appreciated its possibilities as an instrument for close state control over the economy. But as noted in the text, the vagueness of the concept of stabilisation, and its susceptibility to widely different and indeed conflicting interpretations, contributed to the smoothness with which the system became an instrument of taxation. Besides the ambiguities of the concept noted in the text, some further, related, problems were shown up by the operation of the system in the 1950s and 1960s, and these may be worth noting.

Even if no surpluses are accumulated under a comprehensive stabilisation or smoothing scheme, there must be a lack of correspondence between those producers from whom funds are collected and those to whom they are subsequently disbursed, unless the body of producers remains completely unchanged (which is impossible). For obvious reasons, the longer the period of accumulation of surpluses, the more pronounced this lack of correspondence, so that the scheme is then not one of smoothing of incomes of a group of producers, but taxation of one group and subsequent subsidisation of a different group. Moreover, a further complication of much substance arises if the period covered is one over which market prices have risen. The higher are prices, the larger are the absolute amounts required to maintain them at a given level over a stated period, and therefore a given sum is more likely to appear insufficient as a stabilisation reserve. Surpluses accumulated over a number of years of relatively low prices, and representing large percentages of producer prices at the time of their accumulation, may be held to

191

constitute an insufficient reserve at a subsequent date (by which time prices have risen greatly), even though the fear of a decline had been adduced as a reason for their initial accumulation. When prices have risen over a number of years, it is therefore quite likely (in the absence of a clear definition of stabilisation or of the period of accumulation) that the producers who received low prices in the early part of the period are called upon to surrender a large part of their incomes for the creation of reserves which may either be accumulated indefinitely, or used to subsidise much higher producer prices in face of a possible decline. This decline may represent a much smaller proportion of the higher prices than the proportion which the producers have had to surrender at a time of much lower prices. And, of course, the beneficiaries of this process are a group of persons different from those who have had to make the sacrifice.

If stabilisation of producer incomes is to have any meaning beyond serving as a political catch-phrase, it needs to be clearly defined as a smoothing of fluctuations around a trend over a clearly specified period. Unless the smoothing of fluctuations in incomes and prices is distinguished from other objectives and policy, and unless the period of smoothing is defined clearly, practically any course of action can be spuriously justified by a reference to one or other of different or even conflicting objectives of policy, or by reference to the need to provide for an unspecified contingency in the distant or undefined future. It is perhaps because it minimises the likelihood of a so-called stabilisation policy developing into a pursuit of wholly different objectives that the scheme we proposed was regarded as so objectionable by supporters of statutory export monopolies.

The scheme proposed by Professor Paish and myself unambiguously defines the concept as a smoothing of random fluctuations around a trend over a clearly specified period. The use of a formula is clearly essential to the scheme. The formula we proposed is rather simple though somewhat lengthy. Professor Harry G. Johnson has suggested to us that it could be expressed more briefly as follows:

$$S_t = \frac{\bar{P}_t}{X} + \frac{F}{n\bar{Q}_t}.$$

The notation is the same as in the other formulation except for F which refers to total reserves, i.e. the difference between total net proceeds and the amounts paid out over the previous n years.

Professor Johnson's formulation is simpler and briefer. The original formulation has the advantage of showing more clearly the underlying variables.

The only substantial criticism of our proposals came from Professor Milton Friedman in an article in the *Economic Journal*, December 1954. His main criticism was that our proposals were an unwarranted form of paternalism, since producers could themselves save part of their incomes in prosperity and draw on their reserves in adversity.[23] Professor Friedman argued that the appropriate action would be a removal of imperfections in the capital market to facilitate the accumulation of reserves by producers and their subsequent withdrawal.

Professor Friedman did not consider the practically important question whether, given large-scale government intervention in agricultural marketing in the name of stabilisation, a scheme of the type proposed by us might not be preferable (in the sense of promoting stabilisation) than previous arrangements. However, even if our contention that this is so is accepted, this acceptance still leaves open the more fundamental question of the justification of a compulsory, comprehensive smoothing scheme.

In the 1950s it seemed that the advantages of a rigorously defined compulsory smoothing scheme compared to complete non-intervention would outweigh the disadvantages. There would indeed be substantial advantages if the flow of incomes in many poor primary-producing countries could be made smoother and more predictable without offsetting disadvantages. These advantages would include the promotion of a sense of continuity, and also of a reduction in political tension often caused by wide and discontinuous price fluctuations.[24] Another advantage would be a reduction in the

[23] Professor Friedman also advanced certain secondary criticisms of our proposals, notably that they imply taxation of producers whose share in total sales is less when funds are disbursed than what they were in a period of accumulation. This disadvantage is inherent in comprehensive smoothing schemes without individual accounts, and need not be a serious disadvantage if the period is kept short and the withdrawals and subsequent disbursements relatively small. However, the point is undoubtedly valid.

[24] However, even wide fluctuations in domestic prices and incomes do not usually set up pronounced tensions when the elasticity of supply of imports reaching the domestic market is high, as is usually the case when there are no import, exchange or shipping controls.

volume of stocks import merchants have to carry, which is important when capital is expensive. Successful smoothing in the fluctuations of incomes may also promote saving by producers, because in under-developed countries they are often subject to strong social pressures to share a temporary increase in incomes with relatives (who are often distant) or even with mere acquaintances.

However, the experience of the last ten to fifteen years throughout the world has made it clear that, whatever specific assurances are given, a compulsory system is very likely to be used for large-scale taxation, or more generally as an instrument for close government control of the economy, partly because of the wide discrepancy in political effectiveness between the rulers and the ruled in under-developed countries. The potential benefits of compulsory smoothing are insufficient to offset the risks. This consideration does not affect the arguments in favour of the scheme of the kind proposed by us against arrangements which give unlimited discretionary powers to those in charge of statutory export monopolies.[25]

We note in Section 1 of this paper that governments are much readier to intervene to offset fluctuations in prices and incomes when these result from market changes than when they are caused by the weather or similar natural causes. This difference is probably an instance of a more general phenomenon. Even substantial adversity is more readily accepted and thus less conducive to political tension when it appears as the result of forces which are intelligible, and whose operation appears uncontrollable, than if it results from the operation of market forces which are often unintelligible, and any adverse effects of which appear to be avoidable.

As mentioned earlier in these notes, the operation of the marketing boards up to 1951 were reviewed in some detail in an article which appeared in the *Journal of the Royal Statistical Society* in 1954. That paper (to be referred to as the *JRSS* paper) is not reproduced in this volume, chiefly because the principal conclusions are embodied in the article by Professor Paish and myself. But some topics treated in that paper may deserve notice here, partly because they may facilitate the interpretation of the overall summary of the operations

[25] These arguments do not apply to general monetary and fiscal measures. Nor do they apply, of course, to voluntary smoothing schemes. See pp. 90 to 100, above, for a discussion of a voluntary scheme.

of the marketing boards presented in the concluding paragraphs of this addendum.

In the *JRSS* paper detailed evidence is provided on the levels of export duties on the controlled products up to 1951. These duties totalled £42 million from 1939 to 1951 on the controlled products. The close correspondence between the rates of export duty on the one hand and the level of surpluses on the other has become much clearer since the early 1950s when the paper reproduced here was written.

The rates of duties on the products controlled by the marketing boards in both Nigeria and Gold Coast-Ghana were repeatedly raised to levels much higher than those applying to the few products not controlled by the marketing boards. Moreover, a large part of the accumulated surpluses was transferred direct to the governments in both countries. In 1954 the Gold Coast government proceeded to prescribe not only producer prices but also the maximum prices receivable by the Cocoa Marketing Board, and diverted to itself direct the difference between commercial values and the prices prescribed for the marketing board. This was made politically possible because, when surpluses are accumulated, export duties diminish only the surplus and do not directly affect producer prices.[26]

The connection between the level of surpluses and the rates of export duty, and the treatment of both as levies on producers, have now come to be widely accepted. For instance, both export duties and marketing board surpluses are treated as levies on producers in two articles by Professor Helleiner and Mr Killick which will be referred to shortly.

In round figures the marketing board surpluses in Nigeria and the Gold Coast and the export duties together totalled some £200 million between 1939 and 1951 (the bulk arising between 1947 and 1951) against producers' gross proceeds of about £300 million. 'Gross proceeds' refers to the basic producer price multiplied by the

[26] Both in its effects on the economy as a whole, and from the standpoint of the individual producer, an increase in export duty to transfer part of the surplus from a marketing board to the government is purely a paper transaction which substitutes one type of compulsory levy for another. Surpluses are in principle available to subsidise producer prices in the future, or otherwise to help producers, while export duties become part of the general revenue. The practical significance of the distinction depends on the prospective price policies of the marketing boards.

tonnages marketed. The figure necessarily greatly exceeds producers' total receipts, since most of the output is sold by producers at stations where the prescribed prices are lower than the basic prices. Proceeds necessarily exceeded producer incomes from the crops because of the costs of production and often also of transport.

Until 1951 there was also a further substantial burden or cost falling on the producers. Up to that year the marketing boards sold the entire output of the controlled crops (other than cocoa) to the British Ministry of Food. Until 1947 they were sold at the cost price of the crops to the West African Produce Control Board (the predecessor of the marketing boards), which thus could not accumulate surpluses. Thereafter somewhat higher prices were obtained. But until 1951 the prices received by the West African marketing boards were much below those paid by the Ministry of Food for bulk supplies of these products from other sources and they were also much below market prices. The difference is termed under-realisation in the *JRSS* paper, and estimated at around £100 million on the sale of the controlled groups up to 1951. The basis of the calculation is set out in detail in that paper, where it is noted that these transactions were not simply forward sales, and that the comparisons do not refer to marginal quantities only. Under-realisation occurred only on crops controlled by marketing boards. The merchants selling the few products not subject to marketing boards (rubber, hides and skins and timber) secured market prices. When the under-realisation is added to the other levies, the three types of levy (shown separately throughout the *JRSS* paper) totalled around £300 million from 1939 to 1951. In round figures the surpluses were £160 million, the export duties about £40 million and under-realisation around £100 million. Producers' gross proceeds as noted and defined above were about £300 million.

Export duties and surpluses generally continued at high levels after 1951, but under-realisation terminated then, because thereafter open market prices were realised by the boards.

In the *JRSS* paper (p. 3) there is a table with the c.i.f. price of bulk supplies of groundnuts imported into the United Kingdom between 1939 and 1948 from Nigeria and India respectively. Throughout this period Indian groundnuts were shipped by merchants, while Nigerian supplies were shipped by merchants up to July 1942 and by the West African Produce Control Board thereafter. Before the take-over by the West African Produce Control Board, the market price of Nigerian and Indian groundnuts were practically identical; thereafter the prices of groundnuts from Nigeria were much lower at around 50 per cent to 75 per cent of the price of Indian groundnuts. This remarkable change came about as a result of the arrangement by which the Ministry of Food took over West African supplies at the cost price of the products to the West African Produce Control Board.

The *JRSS* paper also presents some detailed information on the effects of the marketing board system on the terms of trade for producers who have to pay the market price for the imported merchandise they buy while receiving much less than the market price for their produce. It is suggested there that, with the important exception of cocoa producers, the terms of trade of the producers were, as late as 1950, less favourable than they had been in the mid-1930s, and this conclusion may have applied even in 1951. The accumulation of surpluses and the high rates of export duties had necessarily depressed substantially the terms of trade of producers; and this effect has continued throughout the operation of the marketing board system. The *JRSS* paper also compares the prices received by the principal competitors of the West African producers with the prices received by these producers, and it is shown that the position of competitors was far more favourable than that of the West African suppliers. This situation has largely persisted until the present.

In the *JRSS* paper (p. 15) there is a brief reference to the effects of the taxation of producers on the volume of imports. More detailed information is presented in my book *West African Trade*, ch. 24, where it is shown that the volume of imports varied very largely with producer incomes, which in turn depended largely on the prescribed producer prices. It is also shown there that the share of West Africa in total colonial imports over this period was kept far below the corresponding share in colonial exports because the restriction of incomes in West Africa served to divert supplies to countries where incomes were not so curtailed. This information serves to refute the allegation mentioned in the article reproduced here (p. 168) that the policies of the boards were made necessary by a shortage of imports, i.e. by a refusal of the British authorities to make available supplies to these countries equivalent to the value of their exports. The argument is in any case irrelevant to the boards' price policies, since, if a deflation of incomes is thought necessary, this is appropriately carried out by the government by means of fiscal and monetary measures, not by marketing boards ostensibly established to serve the interests of their constituents by short-period price stabilisation.

Two students of the West African economies have recently presented information which makes possible the presentation of comparatively up-to-date, succinct summary of the taxation of producers under the marketing board system.

In an article 'The Fiscal Role of Marketing Boards in Nigerian Economic Development, 1947–61', *Economic Journal*, September 1964, Professor G.K. Helleiner has presented statistics of statutory marketing in Nigeria up to and including 1962. Professor Helleiner's statistics derive from official sources, mainly from the annual reports of the marketing boards which cover the major controlled groups in Nigeria, i.e. cocoa, groundnuts, palm kernels, palm oil and cotton.

Professor Helleiner found that the aggregate net proceeds (after all selling expenses) available for distribution to producers from 1947 to 1962 were £1,074 million. This sum is the total of payments of producers, export duties, marketing board surpluses and produce sales taxes.[27] This sum is termed by Professor Helleiner 'potential producer income'. Of the total of £1,074 million, £293 million (28 per cent) was withheld; surpluses totalled £126 million, export duties £149 million, and produce sales taxes £18 million. Between 1939 and 1947 the West African Produce Control Board secured £22 million from sales of Nigerian cocoa, of which it withheld £8 million. Thus, over the period 1939–62, out of available proceeds of £1,096 million, about £301 million (27 per cent) was withheld. These figures exclude the substantial under-realisation before 1951 mentioned earlier in this Addendum. They also exclude the export duties levied before 1947, when their level was not yet affected by the repercussions of statutory marketing, especially the accumulation of surpluses.

For Gold Coast-Ghana cocoa Mr A. T. Killick has similar information up to the end of 1961, the last year for which the Ghana Cocoa Marketing Board published annual reports.[28] His statistics are derived from the annual reports of the Cocoa Marketing Board throughout. Over the period 1947–61, net proceeds of cocoa, after

[27] These taxes are special taxes levied only on marketing board crops.

[28] The statistics are presented in a chapter by Mr Killick entitled 'The Economics of Cocoa', in W.B. Birmingham, I. Neustadt and E.N. Omaboe, *A Study of Contemporary Ghana: Vol. 1, The Economy of Ghana*, 1965.

all expenses other than taxes, totalled £768 million, of which £431 million was paid out to producers, and £337 million (44 per cent) was withheld. Export duties totalled £236 million, the marketing board surpluses £87 million, and a special tax on cocoa producers termed Farmers' Contribution to the Second Development Plan about £16 million. The West African Produce Control Board had left a surplus of about £14 million to the Gold Coast Cocoa Marketing Board out of available proceeds of £37 million. Thus from 1939 to 1961, out of total net cocoa proceeds of £805 million, producers' gross receipts totalled about £454 million and retentions £351 million (44 per cent).[29]

As the Ghana Cocoa Marketing Board ceased to issue annual reports in 1961, the amounts withheld from producers cannot be computed so clearly as they can up to that date. Moreover, it appears from fragmentary information that since about 1960 the board's expenses have risen sharply in acceleration of a tendency already in evidence before the reports ceased to be published. Various political influences seem to have been responsible for this increase in costs. In these conditions the levies cannot be computed readily because the expenses of the board do not reflect the economic cost of the marketing function. It is however clear that since 1961 further large sums have been withheld from producers, probably of the order of £50 million or more.

For various reasons the statistics presented by Professor Helleiner, Mr Killick and myself all overstate producer incomes, and correspondingly understate the percentage of potential pre-tax producer incomes represented by the various levies. Farmers' receipts or proceeds necessarily substantially overstate producer incomes, because of the presence of costs of production and distribution, including transport costs, which are often substantial. Professor Helleiner has suggested a further, and more sophisticated, reason why these figures under-estimate the burden of these levies on the producers. He points out (op. cit., p. 584) that potential producer incomes are higher than those shown in his statistics (as also in those presented in the *JRSS* paper) 'if, as is likely, there exists positive price elasticity of supply and greater than unit elasticity of world demand for Nigerian produce'.

Both Professor Helleiner and Mr Killick treat the surpluses and

[29] This calculation again excludes the under-realisation which, however, was relatively small for cocoa, about £8 million up to 1951.

the other levies as forms of taxation of producers. Indeed they regard the marketing boards primarily as instruments of taxation. Professor Helleiner writes: '. . . Within the last few years the Regional Governments of the Federation have stated quite explicitly that the marketing boards are an important source of revenues for their development budgets. . . . The discussion here will virtually ignore the questions as to how, what, or if, to stabilise – which were at the heart of the debates of a decade ago – in the belief that they are today, if not then, only of secondary interest. . . .' (p. 583).

10

CONCENTRATION IN TROPICAL TRADE: SOME ASPECTS AND IMPLICATIONS OF OLIGOPOLY*

1

In the course of an enquiry into the structure and organisation of the trade of British West Africa considerable quantitative information has become available on the degree of concentration in the import and export trade of Nigeria and the Gold Coast. Some of this information is presented and analysed in this paper. The information is both comprehensive and detailed, and offers what seems to be an exceptional opportunity for analysing the factors affecting the degree of concentration in trading activities, especially in the external trade of tropical territories.

Information on the shares of firms in a particular trade or industry is of interest chiefly where the degree of concentration is high. It provides some indication of the maximum number of suitable alternatives open to its suppliers and customers. The actual number may in some respects[1] be reduced by effective coalitions among some firms; and the degree of concentration is suggestive of the probability that coalitions may be formed and effectively maintained.

Indices of concentration may also be suggestive both of the degree of dependence and of the sense of dependence of those dealing with the monopolists and oligopolists; and of the power of the largest firms to influence prices ('make the market') which is a corollary of a high degree of concentration. Thus they are valuable pointers to important aspects of monopoly and oligopoly situations. But by themselves they cannot serve as reliable indices either of the reality

---

* *Economica*, November 1953, pp. 302–21.
[1] Where separate selling organisations are maintained alternatives of convenience and service remain. Even where the coalition between firms remains effective, some of their employees may be prepared to grant price concessions to some customers out of their own remuneration, and to that extent the effective range of alternatives is widened.

of dependence, or of the degree of monopoly power, or of the profitability of monopoly.[2] These depend on factors which usually cannot be expressed in a meaningful sense quantitatively or by means of a simple formula. They include such factors as the availability and suitability of substitutes (which are affected by the definition of the industry or the commodity); access of customers and of suppliers to alternative markets and occupations; conditions of entry; effectiveness of co-operation among the firms; and so forth. These factors require qualitative analysis.

2

There is a fairly high degree of concentration in the external trade of many even of the larger and more populous of the so-called underdeveloped countries. The principal reason for the predominance of a comparatively small number of large firms seems to be the advantages offered by the possession of large capital which appear to be pronounced in foreign trade with tropical or sub-tropical countries exporting primary products.

The risks of trading in these territories are greatly increased by the wide fluctuations in their purchasing power, combined with the long period between the placing of orders for supplies and their ultimate disposal. Firms short of liquid resources may be unable to weather temporary adversity, or to develop stable and continuous relationships with overseas suppliers. Unless reserves are ample, wide fluctuations in the prices of export produce may also result in losses on stocks and consequent financial embarrassment. Loans and loan capital are difficult to raise, particularly in times of strain; assets in foreign countries are not readily acceptable as security; certain types of lender, especially the British banker, prefer to lend to customers of whose activities they have fairly detailed information which tropical traders find it difficult to furnish; and lenders are aware of the general hazards of this type of enterprise. Firms with large capital of their

---

[2] The sense of dependence is often closely related to the degree of concentration and may be independent both of the reality of dependence and of the exercise of monopoly power.

With few exceptions the dependence is greater for sellers who are confronted by a monopolist buyer of their products or services than for buyers who are confronted by monopolistic sellers. This follows from the functioning of a specialised economy in which incomes are earned by individuals by selling specialised services or their products (or at most a few specialised services or their products), and in which they spend their incomes on a wide range of commodities.

own on the other hand, are likely to survive the frequent fluctuations in trade without severing established contacts. They are likely to be in a position to buy up the assets and/or the organisation of firms in financial difficulties; indeed at times they may almost be compelled to do so to prevent the demoralisation of the market by distress selling of stocks.

Other advantages also accrue to merchants in tropical trade from the possession of large capital. In many under-developed countries important ancillary services, especially warehousing and local transport, are poorly developed, and firms able to operate these are at an important advantage which favours firms with substantial capital. Possession of liquid resources also enables traders to take early advantage of new economic opportunities thrown up in a developing economy. Considerable opportunities are in this way frequently presented to the merchants in these territories, and developed and exploited by them both in the general interest and to their own advantage.

Entry into successful tropical trading is likely to require a considerable minimum capital. Once established, firms find it easier to raise money. Up to a point expansion tends to be cumulative, though beyond a certain size growth brings important disadvantages. In practice it is often difficult to distinguish between the advantages arising from the possession of capital and the mere size of the enterprise, and those accruing to firms already well established in the field.

In certain branches of tropical trade the advantages derived from the possession of large capital (especially the ability to survive vicissitudes) are reinforced by certain economies of large-scale operation. There are familiar economies from the bulk storage, handling and transport, especially of standardised products, such as flour, salt, cement, petroleum products. Similar economies to suppliers arising from large-scale transactions in these commodities enable them to grant quantity discounts to large-scale buyers which may represent genuine economies (especially in transportation) rather than extorted concessions.[3] Because most of these commodities are highly standardised a constant study of market requirements or contact with consumers is not quite so important as in other commodities, and it

[3] Somewhat analogous economies accrue to the substantial importer of textile prints, since printers often quote lower prices to buyers who place orders permitting long production runs on particular designs and specifications; they frequently refuse to consider orders below certain large minimum quantities.

is comparatively simple to administer and control even a very large trade.

But these advantages and economies are not unlimited. Beyond a point, which differs greatly among different activities, expansion of scale very largely involves duplication of available facilities, rather than the better use of facilities or the introduction of better methods. Even where improved methods are introduced the economies are eventually likely to be counterbalanced by higher costs of administration and control. The limit of the economies of size is likely to be reached soonest in trading in unstandardised commodities or services, and/or in markets in which supply and demand conditions change frequently and rapidly. These limitations are reinforced in the largest firms by the necessary reliance in senior posts on many executives whose financial interests are not bound up closely with the success of the enterprise, with the outcome of the decisions they themselves make, or with the fruits of their own efforts. The division of functions and of control between overseas head offices and the local establishments strengthen these considerations. Divided control and delayed decisions raise costs and impede rapid response to profitable opportunities.

In practice the disadvantages of large size and complexity in terms of economic efficiency are often counterbalanced by the strategic advantages enjoyed by firms partly by virtue of their early start but chiefly by virtue of their size. These often result in important advantages in the sphere of market strategy; and what is apt to be more important in contemporary conditions, more favourable treatment by officials. Important disabilities are often imposed on small and medium-sized and new firms by various types of administrative action and policy, in such spheres as the framing and administration of immigration regulations and of trade controls.

Developments in the last ten or twelve years have enhanced capital requirements in external trade in many parts of the world. Enforced reliance on more distant sources of supply as a result of interruptions of access to more convenient and customary sources slows down the rate of turnover of capital, thus placing an additional premium on the possession of large capital. Longer delays in deliveries produce a similar result. These factors are likely to be significant in long-distance trade, such as the external trade of many tropical countries.

Under conditions of full employment in the overseas supplying countries sellers show a particularly marked preference for dealing with firms able to place large orders, quite apart from their preference for confining available supplies to established customers. This incidental by-product of full employment, especially of hyper-employment, may substantially influence the trading situation and the prospects of different classes of trader. With higher costs of labour and equipment, suppliers are likely to demand increased charges for handling small orders, even when they are prepared to accept them.

In the external trade of West Africa local conditions tend particularly to favour firms in possession of large capital. Especially in Nigeria, the long distances and poor communications and the wide dispersal and small scale of individual production and consumption postulate a relatively large volume of stock in storage and transit to sustain a given volume of trade. The storage and movement of the stocks in turn call for larger fixed investments and more European supervisory and technical personnel.

The absence of a local capitalist class comparable to the Chinese or the Indians in the Eastern trade, has also increased the capital requirements of the merchant firms. They have not been able to dispose of imports in wholesale quantities to local intermediaries financing their own activities. They have found it necessary to finance many of their customers; and they have also been drawn into small-scale semi-wholesale or retail trade in widely dispersed establishments.[4] Thus directly or indirectly the firms have had to carry large stocks to secure a given volume of trade. The same forces have operated in the purchase of local produce for export which has had to be bought at up-country establishments frequently in small quantities, and financed by means of advances before purchase which increases both the capital required and the risk involved. For many years past the granting of advances has been an important prerequisite of successful entry into produce buying, especially in the purchase of cocoa and groundnuts.

The various influences increasing capital requirements in recent years which have already been listed have also operated in West African trade. Because of enforced dependence on more distant sources

[4] The vertical integration of the merchant firms has stemmed partly from motives of market strategy. Most of these motives have, however, been connected with the advantages of the possession of large capital and with the absence of a local capitalist class.

of supply and of shortages and bottlenecks of various kinds, much larger amounts of capital have had to be locked up by traders in the forms of stocks and storage facilities.

In common with the trade of other tropical regions the external trade of West Africa has been subject to wide fluctuations of fortune, and, as we have seen, capital requirements in West Africa are especially heavy. There are therefore certain underlying influences making for a high degree of concentration.[5]

For these reasons we should expect a comparatively high degree of concentration in the external trade of West Africa; and we should expect this to be particularly marked in the standardised staple lines of trade.

3

The degree of concentration in the import trade is very similar in Nigeria and in the Gold Coast. But the information is available for Nigeria in a more convenient and comprehensive form than the corresponding information for the Gold Coast. For this reason this section is confined to the presentation and discussion of the Nigerian data; the statistics available on the degree of concentration in the import trade in the Gold Coast are presented in a note appended to this paper.[6]

---

[5] In recent decades certain fortuitous circumstances have also played their part in promoting concentration in West African trade.

These included the conferment of powers of government on the Niger Company for a period of fourteen years from 1886 to 1900. The acquisition of the Niger Company by Lever Brothers in 1920 was also partly fortuitous as it was a by-product of the endeavours of the first Lord Leverhulme to establish plantations in West Africa.

The two most important amalgamations since 1920 were both precipitated by chance events. The amalgamation of the Niger Company and the African and Eastern Trade Corporation in 1929 to form the United Africa Company was brought about partly by heavy losses incurred by the African and Eastern Trade Corporation through unsuccessful cocoa speculations and the incomplete observance of a market sharing agreement by one important participant. The absorption of the substantial firm of G.B.Ollivant by Lever Brothers (the parent company of the United Africa Company) was an indirect result of the financial difficulties of the Royal Mail Shipping Company which resulted in financial embarrassment to G.B.Ollivant.

These various events and influences were in a sense chance occurrences; but they promoted concentration only because advantage was taken of them by organisations with large capital.

[6] The information underlying most of the material presented in this section

206

Some points of presentation need to be cleared up first. Practically all petroleum products and the larger part of the imports of cigarettes are imported by the oil companies and by the largest manufacturer, but are released through the merchant firms.[7] In assessing the shares of the merchant firms in the trade in imported merchandise their shares in the sale of these products need to be added to their shares in merchandise imports.

Associated firms and subsidiaries are treated as single firms.

The majority of the leading merchant firms in West Africa, denoted in this section by code letters A to F, have at various times participated in market sharing agreements, of which the Merchandise Agreement, concluded in 1937 and abandoned in 1946, was the most comprehensive. These firms have also been parties collectively to various agreements with suppliers. Though there still are periodic informal understandings of varying degrees of effectiveness to maintain pre-existing shares in the trade, there do not now seem to be any formal agreements between these firms. We shall refer to them as the Merchandise Agreement group. This, of course, is not intended as a term of abuse or even of criticism, but simply as a convenient collective noun for a distinct group of old-established European firms. Except where the contrary is specifically indicated, it does not imply concerted action by these firms.

In West Africa the first stage in the import trade, that is, direct importing, is largely in non-African hands. From information extracted by the Department of Statistics in Nigeria from Customs records it appears that in 1949 about 85 per cent of the import trade of that country was handled by European firms, about 10 per cent by Levantine and Indian firms and about 5 per cent by African firms.

The distribution of the import trade in Nigeria among the participating direct importers is shown in Table 1.

was assembled by the Department of Commerce and Industry and by the Department of Statistics in Nigeria, chiefly from customs records.

For most of the commodities the information was also provided from private sources. In every instance the figures provided independently by these sources agreed very closely with the information derived from official sources, which is reassuring about the reliability of those data derived from one of these sources only.

[7] Cigarettes manufactured in Nigeria by a subsidiary of the British American Tobacco Company are also released through the merchant firms. These supplies are treated as imports in the calculations in this article.

207

TABLE 1

Shares of principal importers in commercial merchandise imports into Nigeria, 1949

Firm	Percentage of values
A	34 ⎫
B	8 ⎪
C	7 ⎬ 58
D	4 ⎪
E	3 ⎪
F	2 ⎭
H	3
I	2
Z (aggregate of all other importers)	37

The firms A to F are the members of the Merchandise Agreement group.[8] The residual item Z includes all firms importing individually less than 1 per cent of all merchandise, and also the imports of petroleum and tobacco products by those importers who are not merchant firms. If these imports are divided among the merchant firms on the basis of commercial releases to them the shares of the largest firms in the sale of imported merchandise are raised quite considerably. The share of A becomes about 40 per cent and that of firms A–F is raised from 58 per cent to about 66 per cent.

Total imports include such items as mining equipment and supplies, marine and river vessels, ships' and aircraft stores and so forth imported by the mines and by the shipping and air lines; these supplies are not trade goods in the accepted sense of the term. If these items are excluded the share of A–F in the sales of imported trade goods in Nigeria in 1949 becomes about 70 per cent or slightly more.

The shares of firms in the aggregate imports of all commercial merchandise is information which is of limited meaning only. Quantitative information on the proportionate shares of the firms in individual commodities is in some ways of greater significance and interest than their shares in total imports. Table 2 presents this information for Nigeria for twenty-three commodities or commodity groups; in recent years these commodities have represented about three-fifths of the value of all merchandise imports.

As will be clear from Table 2 there are wide differences in the degree of concentration in different commodities which are of some general interest.

[8] The code letters are used consistently to denote the same firms.

TABLE 2
Shares of merchant firms in the import or distribution of certain commodities or commodity groups, Nigeria 1949

firms	all commercial imports (1)	cabin bread (2)	cement (3)	corrugated iron sheets (4)	dried fish (5)	matches (6)	salt (7)	sugar (8)	wheat flour (9)	all cotton piece goods (10)	white bleached cotton piece goods (11)	unbleached cotton piece goods (12)	dyed cotton piece goods (13)	coloured cotton piece goods (14)	printed cotton piece goods (15)	mixed rayon piece goods (16)	pure rayon piece goods (17)	sewing thread (18)	motor vehicles (19)	bicycles (20)	cigarettes (21)	petrol (22)	kerosene (23)
A	%34	%52	%48	%39	%52	%44	%58	%43	%46	%33	%41	%32	%33	%32	%30	%30	%16	%31	%28	%43	%74	%58	%59
B	8	16	11	18	4	11	6	10	16	8	11	9	11	5	7	5	2	14	12	7	1	12	14
C	7	17	16	12	9	12	20	11	9	7	11	10	4	4	5	5	—	13	—	11	13	12	14
D	4	3	3	2	3	7	4	2	5	5	4	4	7	3	6	2	2	8	20	4	3	5	6
E	3	9	2	2	5	7	3	3	5	5	6	7	4	3	5	—	—	13	—	2	—	6	3
F	2	—	3	3	—	—	—	1	3	1	—	2	1	—	1	2	—	3	12	—	1	1	2
	58	97	83	76	73	81	91	70	84	59	73	64	60	46	54	42	20	82	72	67	92	94	98
H	3	—	2	3	—	12	—	2	5	6	3	7	2	9	7	4	5	—	2	1	—	3	1
I	2	—	1	—	—	—	—	2	4	1	1	2	2	12	2	1	2	—	—	—	—	—	—
Z (all others)	37	3	14	21	27	7	9	26	7	31	23	27	36	33	37	53	73	18	26	32	8	3	1
	100	100	100	100	100	100	100	100	100	100	100	100	100	100	100	100	100	100	100	100	100	100	100

Notes:
1. The symbol — is used to indicate shares of less than 1 per cent.
2. Columns 1 to 20 refer to percentage shares of imports effected directly by the listed firms.
3. For cigarettes (column 21) the figures refer to the shares of the merchant firms in the sales of all cigarettes; the figures in this particular column include a very small element of estimate.
4. In columns 22 and 23 the figures refer to the shares of the distributors in the trade of petroleum products released by the oil companies from their bulk installations. About one-half to three-fifths of the total supply is handled by one oil company, approximately another one-third about equally by two companies, and the balance by the smallest supplier.

In the absence of licensing the degree of concentration tends to be specially high in standardised bulk staple lines, such as flour, cement, salt, cabin bread, and the other items in columns 2 to 9 in Table 2. This result is in accordance with expectations, since the economies of large-scale purchasing and bulk handling, transport and storage are marked in these commodities; moreover they offer few opportunities for the judicious gauging of the requirements of the consumer and the other advantages which flow from close contact with suppliers and with customers, and which tend to benefit smaller firms.

Flour and sugar imports in 1949 were subject to specific licensing and this also applied to corrugated iron sheets from certain sources. For reasons of policy, preferential treatment was granted to African importers in the allocation of import licences. It is certain that without this the share of the small firms (included in Z in the tables) would have been appreciably smaller. As direct importing requires considerable capital and skill, this particular form of assisting Africans has serious disadvantages, particularly when applied in a sphere of trading where small-scale operations tend to be inappropriate.

The tendency for the degree of concentration to be higher in standardised lower-grade merchandise emerges clearly in the trade in textiles. The share of the largest firm is greatest in the importation of bleached and unbleached textiles and becomes progressively smaller for those categories in which variety, design and colour are of greater importance, such as for printed cotton piece goods and rayon piece goods.

The table also provides quantitative information on another proposition which seems plausible on general grounds. A large measure of concentration among overseas suppliers conduces to concentration among importers. This is an instance of the general tendency of a high degree of concentration at one stage of production or distribution leading to similar conditions at subsequent stages. The influence towards concentration in distribution is especially strong where a product is standardised and the overseas supply is largely concentrated. In the West African merchandise trade petroleum products, cigarettes, salt and sewing thread provide obvious examples.[9]

[9] Most of the imports of sewing thread are derived from the United Kingdom where one producer holds a dominant position both in the home and the export trade.

4

The export of practically all agricultural products of both Nigeria and the Gold Coast is in the hands of marketing boards which are statutory export monopolies. In the actual export of these products the concentration is of course 100 per cent. The merchant firms act as buying agents for the boards, and for these commodities the statistics of concentration shown here refer to their operations as buying agents and not as actual exporters. For hides and skins and timber the information refers to the shares of firms in actual exports.[10]

With the exception of the buying of cocoa, confidential market sharing syndicates are operated by most of the licensed buying agents in the purchase of produce for export on behalf of the marketing boards.[11] In a review of statistics of the degree of concentration it is necessary for two reasons to take cognisance of such market sharing syndicates. First, the presence of a syndicate implies that in effect the syndicate members share their purchases. The shares of individual firms in total purchases do not give a full picture of the degree of concentration; in addition, the share of all the syndicate members taken together must be considered – because they act largely in concert and in their purchasing activities voluntarily limit their independence of action. Secondly, the share of an individual firm in total purchases in any year may give a misleading indication of its quantitative importance if it is a member of a syndicate. A firm may intentionally limit its purchases in accordance with the provisions of the syndicate arrangements. Such action tends to increase the tonnage bought by others, whether members of the syndicate or not. Conversely, a syndicate member which was buying less than its agreed share might make a special effort to recover its position; and this tends to reduce the tonnage bought by others.

These difficulties have been met by providing some supplementary information. Where appropriate, the combined share of syndicate

[10] There is much information available on the shares of individual firms in the export trade of West Africa. It is derived partly from returns furnished by the buying agents to the executives of the marketing boards and circulated by them, and partly from analysis of customs entries. Much information has also been made available by private sources. The reliability of these sources of information is confirmed by the close correspondence of the results with the degree of concentration shown by the wartime quotas in the export trade examined in Section 5 below.

[11] For palm kernels and palm oil see note 5 to Table 3.

TABLE 3
Shares of firms in purchases for export or in exports, Nigeria and the Gold Coast, 1949 or 1950

firms	Nigerian non-mineral exports a	Nigeria									Gold Coast
		cocoa 1949–50 (1)	palm kernels 1950 (2)	palm oil 1950 (3)	ground-nuts 1949–50 (4)	cotton 1949–50 (5)	timber in logs 1949 (6)	sawn timber 1949 (7)	skins 1949 (8)	hides 1949 (9)	cocoa 1949–50 (10)
	%	%	%	%	%	%	%	%	%	%	%
A	43·3	33·2	48·9	68·2	37·1	48·8	37	69	28	50	38·8
C	9·1	10·9	11·3	5·7	7·8	14·6			8	14	2·7
B	6·5	5·4	7·3	5·4	6·9	8·6			12	15	6·4
E	6·0	8·2	7·1	6·2	4·6	8·3			2	1	1·9
J	3·6	11·7	2·8								13·6
D	2·8	1·4	4·6	5·0	1·3	2·8			7		2·4
K	2·6				13·2						
L	2·3				6·0	15·4					
M	2·2	8·8							8	6	11·7
H	1·6	2·0	1·7		3·4						4·5
N	1·4			2·4							
O	1·3	1·1	3·0						24	11	5·0
P	1·3	3·1	2·3								
F	1·1	3·2	1·3								3·4
Q	0·9				4·5						
R	0·9				4·3						
S	0·8	1·5	1·0								
T	0·8			1·1							

212

	(1)						4		6		
	9·8	9·5	8·7	6·0	10·9	1·5	59	31	5	3	
U	0·7										3·7
V	0·6										3·3
W	0·4										2·6
X	0·0										
Y	0·0										
All others	9·8										
	100	100	100	100	100	100	100	100	100	100	100
Share of three largest firms	59	56	68	80	58	79	54	80	64	79	59
Share of five largest firms	69	78	82	93	76	96	71	83	87	97	75
Aggregate share of syndicate members			85	93	90	100					
Adjusted share of largest syndicate member			55	71	42	48					
Aggregate adjusted share of three largest syndicate members			71	83	58	72					

Notes:

1. The firms are listed here in order of their importance in total Nigerian non-mineral exports. Their order of importance in the import trade is not the same as in the export trade; for instance, there are one or two substantial firms engaged largely or wholly in one branch of the external trade only. As the code letters are used consistently throughout the article, this brings it about that the firms are not set out here in alphabetical order.

2. The figures in column (1) are averages of those in columns (2) to (9), weighted by the relative values of the individual commodities in aggregate exports in 1950.

3. The shares of the three and five largest firms exclude the shares of firm J, which refers to the African co-operatives.

4. Associated firms and subsidiaries have been grouped together as single firms. In groundnut buying one firm financially linked with another larger firm has, however, been treated separately, as their association is of a much looser character and does not include elements of ownership such as participation in profits. To this extent the degree of concentration is understated.

5. The figures referring to the buying syndicates in palm products are subject to a small margin of error. The shares of the individual firms in the syndicate refer to 1949 and the shares of the syndicates in total purchases refer to 1950. Moreover, the palm kernels syndicate, which in 1949 had still handled 95 per cent of all purchases, was apparently dissolved in the autumn of 1950 in the face of rapid progress by outside firms. The palm oil syndicate has also recently been dissolved.

members in total purchase is shown, as well as the *adjusted* shares of the largest firm and of the three largest firms together. The adjusted share for this purpose is the firm's participation share in the syndicate multiplied by the syndicate's share in total purchases.[12]

The available information is summarised in Table 3. Details of the shares in purchases for export[13] or in actual exports[14] are shown for each firm for the most important non-mineral exports. In addition the shares have been calculated of the firms in the total trade in these Nigerian non-mineral exports. No similar calculation for the Gold Coast is presented; in view of the preponderance of cocoa in non-mineral exports the shares of firms in cocoa buying are sufficient indication of their participation in produce buying generally. The products listed represent 92 per cent of all non-mineral exports from Nigeria; in the Gold Coast cocoa alone accounts for over 90 per cent of non-mineral exports.

A high degree of concentration is shown by the fact that in each case the three largest firms purchase more than one half of the quantity exported. The degree of concentration in the export trade is somewhat higher than in the import trade. The low value, bulkiness and standardised nature of the export products provide somewhat less scope for the activities of the smaller trader than does the more varied import trade, especially outside the bulky staple products. Institutional arrangements, notably the operation of the statutory export quotas during the war, more recently the establishment of marketing boards, have served to reinforce this influence. The very high degree of concentration in the purchase of oil palm produce, especially palm oil, seems to be the result of a combination of technical factors (the economies of bulk storage and transport), of historical factors (the Niger delta was the stronghold of the Niger Company) and of geographical factors (difficulties of communication in some of the most important producing areas).

As has already been suggested, the degree of concentration is an incomplete measure of monopoly power. This appears for instance from the prevalence of a fair degree of price competition in the

[12] For instance, if in a particular year the quota of firm X in the syndicate is 50 per cent and the syndicate in the aggregate has handled 90 per cent of all purchases, the adjusted share of firm X is taken as 45 per cent, even though its actual purchases may have been larger or smaller than this percentage.

[13] That is, their purchases as licensed buying agents on behalf of the marketing boards.

[14] That is, their exports as shippers on their own account.

purchase of several of the products covered by Table 3. This has been notable in groundnut buying and in the buying of palm kernels, activities which, statistically, appear to be dominated by a few large firms and where buying syndicates handle a large part of purchases. The statutory minimum prices of groundnuts and of palm kernels have frequently been appreciably exceeded.[15] Moreover, the progress of a comparatively small number of medium-sized and small firms has apparently brought about the dissolution of the palm kernel and palm oil buying syndicates.

5[16]

During the war and early post-war years practically all West African export produce was bought by the merchant firms on behalf of the authorities. Generally speaking the firms were reimbursed for their expenses in accordance with an agreed schedule of costs and remunerated for their services by a commission. Over this period the purchase for export (or the actual export) of these products was subject to official quotas; for oilseeds the system operated from 1939 to 1945 and for cocoa until 1947. The firms were allotted percentage quotas and were supposed to keep as near to these as possible. Those who purchased more than their quota were debited by the controlling authorities for the benefit of those who were under-bought. The penalty payments for over-purchases were equivalent to the sum of the commission and the overhead items in the schedule of expenses.[17]

The West African export quotas were among the most paradoxical of wartime controls. The quotas were imposed and maintained in the face of an unlimited market for export produce. The British government had undertaken to purchase all cocoa at the same price whether or not it could be shipped. Of oilseeds there was indeed an acute shortage. The fact that the market was unlimited was implicitly recognised in that no limit was placed on aggregate purchases or

[15] Cf. 'Competition and Prices: a study of groundnut buying in Nigeria', pp. 69 to 81, above.

[16] The first two paragraphs of this section summarise information presented in detail in, 'The Origins of Statutory Marketing in West Africa', pp. 138 to 155, above.

[17] This method of calculating penalties was exactly the same as that provided for in the cocoa buying agreement of 1937 and in the other agreements or syndicates of West African merchants in produce buying before the war. The quotas, the schedules of expenses and the method of computing were set out in circulars of various official bodies in charge of wartime export control.

TABLE 4

Changes in participation in produce buying since the abolition of the quota system

	purchases of firms which started buying since 1947 as percentages of total purchases in 1949–50 or 1950 (a)	combined share of three largest wartime quota holders		
		share in wartime quotas (b)	share in actual purchases 1949–50 or 1950 (c)	effective share in purchases, 1949–50, or 1950, allowing for syndicate arrangements (d)
	%	%	%	%
Cocoa, Gold Coast	1	63	49	no syndicate
Cocoa, Nigeria	9	65	56	no syndicate
Palm kernels, Nigeria	14	82	67	71
Palm oil, Nigeria	5	86	79	83
Groundnuts, Nigeria	11	70	57	58

Notes:

1. In the purchase of oilseeds the quotas were abolished in July 1945, but the prohibition of the entry of new firms continued until 1947. In cocoa buying the quota system and bar on entry were removed together in 1947.

2. Both in the Gold Coast and in Nigeria certain classes of small cocoa buyer (so-called B shippers and agents) were in receipt of fixed specific tonnage quotas as distinct from percentage quotas. In the Gold Coast after several revisions these tonnage quotas came to total about 10 per cent of the crop exported. In Nigeria eventually only the co-operatives remained with tonnage quotas and all other buyers received percentage quotas. The tonnage quotas of the co-operative societies were about 10 per cent of the total crop exported.

In the table allowance has been made for the tonnage quotas by reducing the percentage quotas of the three largest quota holders by the appropriate amount, i.e. by deflating the percentage quotas by one-tenth. Thus the percentages are comparable throughout the table.

3. The figures in the column headed 'Effective share in purchases' are in the nature of a refinement and are the result of certain adjustments which are useful to illustrate the position of firms where market sharing syndicates are in operation (as they were for the purchase of products in the table, with the exception of cocoa). The nature and purpose of the adjustments have already been indicated.

216

shipments; the quotas simply referred to shares in an unspecified and unlimited total. The quota system was in fact simply an official recognition with statutory sanctions of the private produce buying syndicates which operated before the war.

The quota system has had various far-reaching effects on West African economies which, however, will not be considered here. But in conjunction with the shares of the firms in purchases of export products shown in Table 3 the quotas offer an exceptional opportunity for presenting quantitative information on the effects of such a system in freezing the pattern of trade and in preventing the growth of new firms. By comparing the quotas of the firms with their shares in purchases shown in Table 3 it is possible to measure the effects of the entry of new firms and the expansion of some established firms which have taken place since the quota system was abolished. In the circumstances of West African trade in the late 1930s it is reasonable to assume that these or similar developments, probably on a larger scale, would have taken place sooner if the quota system had not been imposed.[18]

The salient facts are summarised in Table 4 which should be read together with the accompanying notes.

The table suggests that the share of newcomers who entered the various branches of produce buying since 1947 is about equal to the reduction in the shares of the largest quota holders since the abolition of official quotas. There has been a general decline in the relative participation of the principal wartime quota holders, which is pronounced in the purchase of Nigerian cocoa, palm kernels, and groundnuts. This loss of ground is noteworthy in view of the comparatively short period since the lifting of the ban on new entry, and in view of the various obstacles (of which the immigration restrictions are much the most important) to the establishment and growth of the smaller non-African firms.[19]

[18] This is a reasonable assumption in view of the rapid progress in 1938–9 of certain non-syndicate members in the purchase of cocoa and groundnuts, and in view of the proposed establishment in 1939 of a cocoa buying organisation by a large American user. In that year a large American firm was on the point of entering the cocoa trade in Nigeria and was prevented from doing so by the introduction of export controls which confined the trade to quota holders with past performance in the trade. There were several other prospective newcomers, but this was the most important.

[19] With the exception of Gold Coast cocoa, the loss of ground cannot be ascribed to official assistance given to African produce buyers, especially to the

217

6

The data of the earlier sections of this article, especially the statistics in Table 2, show the strong connection between the standardised nature of the product and the degree of concentration in its handling.[20] The high degree of concentration in the export trade points in the same direction. These data tend if anything to understate the connection between the degree of standardisation and the degree of effective monopoly power, since the more highly standardised the commodity the easier is the conclusion and operation of market sharing agreements. With a given degree of concentration market sharing agreements are more likely to be concluded and operated effectively the more standardised the commodity; while the degree of concentration is likely to be higher the more standardised the commodity.

These considerations apply fully to both branches of the external trade of West Africa. In the import trade market sharing agreements were first applied to the more standardised commodities; even when extended to other commodities they were rarely effective outside their range.[21]

Interesting examples of the operation of this tendency can be seen in the export trade. Produce buying syndicates or pools have always been confined to the more standardised exports such as cocoa, groundnuts, cotton, oil palm products, and they never operated in hides and skins, or timber. Similarly, the wartime export quotas applied largely to the former class of commodity and only intermittently and imperfectly to the latter. The tendency has continued to the present, since the former commodities are subject to statutory export monopolies while the latter are not.[22]

co-operative societies; in Nigeria the most important instances of relative gains have been registered by independent firms, chiefly expatriate enterprises not assisted by the government.

[20] These influences also operate among the overseas suppliers of these commodities. The production of these is often in the hands of large numbers of small-scale units producing under conditions of near perfect competition. But the advantages in the bulk transport, storage and processing of these commodities often result in a high degree of concentration in their export from the supplying countries to West Africa. Sugar is an obvious example.

[21] The barriers to entry of competitors are also likely to be more effective in the more standardised branches of trade.

[22] These considerations are only one of several reasons for suggesting that the identification of standardisation with the perfection of competition is not only meaningless and misleading, but may actually imply the reverse of the truth.

Before considering certain implications for the structure of West African trade of the statistics shown in this article it may be useful to emphasise again the limitations of quantitative analysis; in particular to stress that the degree of concentration may exaggerate the powers of the larger firms.

The tables show that one firm is dominant in the economic and statistical sense of handling a significantly large share of the total and it therefore necessarily substantially influences the market. But although the dominant firm stands out clearly, its position in the market is not so overwhelming as is widely believed in West Africa.[23]

In addition to the dominant position of one firm, a comparatively small group of firms (including the dominant firm) imports and distributes some two-thirds of merchandise imports and an even larger proportion of the principal staples of West African trade. This is a high degree of concentration in trading activities in such large and diverse markets.

This degree of concentration would be high even if the firms were of approximately equal size and always acted independently. In an important sense it is even higher in West African trade. First there is one dominant firm; and secondly, most of the large firms have often acted in concert. Thirdly, with few exceptions the same large firms participate in the import trade and in the purchase of export produce more or less in the same proportions. The degree of concentration is therefore greater than would be suggested by the shares of the largest firms in the import or export trades separately. Altogether the picture presented by these statistics suggests a degree of concentration in trade which is rather exceptional and noteworthy.

The structure of the trade suggests an oligopolistic situation. And indeed for some years past some of the more characteristic features and methods of West African trade have been the expected accompaniments of oligopoly. Firms have been intensely preoccupied with the activities and conduct of individual competitors; they have acted in the knowledge that a price change initiated by one of their number was likely to bring about retaliation on the part of others; there have been recurrent phases of intense competition followed by market

[23] This general warning must suffice here. Detailed qualitative discussion of the structure of West African trade is not possible here.

sharing arrangements; and there have been occasional spectacular attempts to keep out or destroy particular competitors.

The wide range of diverse types of merchandise handled by the large firms, and the forward integration of the importing firms into the semi-wholesale and retail trade, which are prominent in West Africa, seem also to be connected with the oligopolistic structure of the market. Although they may originally have been adopted for different reasons (notably the necessity for diversifying operations in areas where the scope for specialisation is limited), they are in part devices to pre-empt the market, which is a well-known feature of oligopolistic market strategy.

The oligopolistic (and occasionally monopolistic) nature of West African trade has exerted considerable influence on political life and events in West Africa; the Gold Coast cocoa hold-up of 1937–8, which was promoted partly or largely by the publication of a market sharing agreement, is only one familiar example.[24] The relatively high degree of concentration has also influenced the attitude of the administrators and of the local population in many different directions.

Distrust of middlemen and traders is widespread in most societies; foreigners are also generally the objects of misgiving; expatriate traders attract hostility for both these reasons. A large measure of concentration suggests a substantial measure of economic dependence, which is likely to be felt and resented particularly keenly where the predominant firms act both as buyers and sellers and are powerful expatriate merchant houses; and this feeling is largely unaffected by the very real limitations imposed on the firms by potential competition, whether from new entry or from the expansion of smaller rivals. Where prices, whether of imported merchandise or of export produce, are liable to frequent and market fluctuations, feelings of dependence and resentment lead the local population to ascribe any adverse price changes to the malice of foreign firms pursuing their selfish ends. Increased prices for imported merchandise, for instance, are seen as evidence of monopolistic exaction, while price reductions are ascribed to attempts to destroy the struggling local merchants. Superficial plausibility is lent to these charges by the undeniable and indeed

[24] The commercial rivalry between the leading firms also influenced considerably the events which led to the Accra riots of 1948 and to subsequent political developments in the Gold Coast. Discussion of these events would be too lengthy in an article.

inevitable power of the firms to influence prices. The high degree of concentration, especially the large share of the total trade handled by one firm, also brings it about that a strike against one firm may paralyse the economic life of extensive areas.

A high degree of concentration once established may have cumulative or at least self-perpetuating elements, since in various ways it may serve to raise barriers to entry. Although such influences have been at work in West African trade, especially in the late 1930s, they have not been very effective in stifling competition or in barring new entry.

In recent years, however, the predominant influence has been the operation of certain official controls, especially trade controls and immigration regulations, which have served to preserve a high degree of concentration. The very rigid restrictions on the immigration of expatriate personnel (especially for small businesses) and on the establishment of new trading firms, particularly small or medium-sized businesses by immigrants or by employees of established enterprises, have served to shield the larger firms from the growth of competitors.[25]

Since about 1949 the operation of specific licensing in the import trade in certain staples has increased materially the shares of the African traders in this activity. The system has served to reduce the degree of concentration but in a manner which has secured guaranteed and riskless profits to all recipients of licences large and small.[26]

APPENDIX

THE STRUCTURE OF THE IMPORT TRADE IN THE GOLD COAST

The information on the structure of the import trade in the Gold Coast is not available in quite such a comprehensive and convenient form as it is for Nigeria. The material is presented in Tables 5 and 6.

Table 5 refers to 1949 and is based partly on the records of the Director of Supplies and partly on information derived from private

[25] Shielding from competition is not the same as raising their profits. It is quite possible that the total profits of the large trading firms would have been greater if they had had a smaller share in a larger trade which would have resulted from the growth of the economy brought about by the activities of the immigrants.

[26] This is only one instance in which the sectional interests of African importers benefit at the expense of the African population at large. The operation of the immigration regulations is another example. It is often overlooked that the African interest vis-à-vis the activities of the expatriate firms is not homogeneous.

221

TABLE 5

Shares of firms in the import or distribution of certain commodities or groups of commodities, Gold Coast 1949 (percentage of values)

firms	sugar %	flour %	cotton manufactures %	cigarettes %
A	31	40	40	57
B				
C				
D	36	20	18	32
E				
F				
G¹				
H	12	8	10	8
Z (all others)	21	32	32	8

1. G refers to a member of the Merchandise Agreement group not established in Nigeria.

TABLE 6

Shares of merchant firms in the imports of certain commodities into the Gold Coast, May–August 1950 and January–May 1951 (nine months)
(percentages of values)

firms	cement %	corrugated iron sheets %	sugar %	wheat flour %	cotton manu- factures %	cycle and tricycles %	unmanu- factured tobacco %
A	49	28	12	30	45	43	39
B	7	7	3	5	9	4	12
C	5	2	2	3	3	12	—
D	4	16	3	5	6	—	14
E	1	6	1	1	3	1	7
F	2	11	2	4	5	—	8
G	—	8	2	2	1	11	7
	68	78	25	50	72	71	87
H	4	8	4	5	6	1	3
Z (all others)	28	14	71	45	22	28	10
	100	100	100	100	100	100	100

sources. The information is not quite comprehensive because in some cases the records of the Director of Supplies covered only those imports which were subject to specific licensing which applies to imports from certain sources but not from others.

Table 6 is based largely on the records of the Customs Department. It shows the shares of firms in the imports of certain commodities into the Gold Coast for the nine months May–August 1950 and January–May 1951, i.e. nine months out of the thirteen months May 1950–May 1951.

The figures are to a small extent affected by the fact that the first table is not quite comprehensive, while the second does not cover a consecutive period of twelve months. The figures in Table 5 probably slightly understate the combined share of B to F in the imports of cotton manufactures, while Table 6 certainly overstates both the share of A and the combined shares of A to G in the imports of this commodity. Again, the fact that Table 6 does not refer to twelve consecutive months also affects to some extent the shares of the different groups in the imports of sugar and flour. It is almost certain that for various technical reasons connected with the issue and expiry of licences and with the trading methods of African importers Table 6 somewhat overstates the share of the residual group Z (firms individually handling less than 1 per cent of total imports) in the imports of sugar and flour. If statistics were available for twelve consecutive months it is probable that the share of Z in the imports of sugar in 1951 would be about 60–65 per cent and of flour about 40 per cent, instead of 71 per cent and 45 per cent as shown in the table.

But in spite of these imperfections in the data, they show that the broad pattern of participation of the firms in the import trade in the Gold Coast is similar to that shown for Nigeria in Tables 1 and 2.

The large share of Z in the imports of sugar and flour reflects the strong discrimination in favour of Africans in the operation of specific licensing which applied to these commodities; this has become much more marked in 1950 and 1951, as is obvious from a comparison of their shares in the import of these commodities as shown in Tables 2 and 5, the former of which refers to 1949 and the latter to 1950–1. In the absence of this discrimination the African share in the direct importation of these commodities would be small; this is evident from a consideration of the small share of all other importers in those staple imports in Nigeria which are not subject to specific licensing.

Addendum

The statistics in this paper refer to 1949–50 or to earlier years. The factual information is not only out of date but is doubtfully relevant to present-day conditions in West Africa. I do not know of any subsequent work on concentration in West African trade. Certain radical changes in conditions, especially in policy, have affected both the degree of concentration and the profitability of trading operations, sometimes in the same direction, sometimes in opposite directions. Official measures to promote the interests of African traders, for instance by specific licensing, have at times reduced the degree of concentration in certain branches of the import trade, while simultaneously increasing its profitability to all participants. At other times the reduction in the share of the trade in non-African hands, or higher taxation of company profits, have more than offset higher profits under controlled conditions.

The degree of concentration in certain branches of the import trade has also been reduced as a result of the expansion of the market, and perhaps also as a result of various methods of export promotion in supplying countries; these are influences which operate independently of any reduction in concentration brought about by preferential treatment of Africans under import licensing. The expansion in the market has been the result partly or largely of the long-term progress of the economy, especially in Nigeria, principally through the spread of the exchange economy. The running down of accumulated sterling balances and the generally favourable export prices were among other factors which played a part in extending the size of the market.

In the export trade all agricultural exports are handled by statutory export monopolies. Several of the larger firms have withdrawn from buying these crops as agents of the marketing boards, partly as a result of official pressure and partly because they found the activity unprofitable.

Thus the present market structure differs substantially from that of the late 1940s. I hope that some of the information presented here, though out of date in the sense that it does not describe present conditions, is still of some interest and relevance. This may apply to the discussion of the factors behind the high degree of concentration here described; the examination of the differences in the degree of concentration in the different branches of trading activity, notabyl in different types of merchandise and export produce (such as the appreciably higher degree of concentration and the greater effectiveness of market sharing agreements in the trade in standardised bulky commodities, and the reverse conditions in the more varied and differentiated commodities); the relation between the wartime controls and the degree of concentration; and the quantitative effects of the abolition of export quotas on the degree of concentration.

11

REGULATED WAGES IN UNDER-DEVELOPED COUNTRIES*

In an unregulated market, the available supplies or numbers determine the wage, but, under regulated conditions, wages determine the numbers.
Report of the South African Industrial Legislation Commission, 1935.

I shall discuss some major implications and results of wage regulation[1] in under-developed countries. Besides examining the factors behind its introduction, I shall consider such economic effects of wage regulation as its influence on economic development, on the structure and location of industry, and on the occupational distribution of the population. I shall examine these economic issues both on the basis of general economic analysis and by reference to specific examples from various parts of the under-developed world. Beyond the more narrowly economic implications, the establishment of regulated wages often has far-reaching and pervasive social and political results which I shall also discuss, albeit briefly.[2]

1

In most under-developed countries wages are regulated in important sectors of the economy. The principal instruments of regulation are:

* *The Public Stake in Union Power*, ed. Philip D. Bradley. University of Virginia Press, Charlottesville, 1961, pp. 324–49.

[1] The term regulated wages is used in this paper to refer to wages determined by government, statutory authorities, and trade unions, in contrast to those emerging from the play of market forces. Even without such organised prescription of wages, the institutions of society affect wages, as they do all other prices. But such general influences act by affecting the conditions of supply and demand, and not by setting rates with given conditions of supply and demand, or by monopolistic measures restricting the supply reaching the market.

Monopsonists, that is employers or employers' associations with some power of monopoly in the hiring of labour, can depress wages below the rates which measure what labour is worth to them (the marginal value product). They can do this by diminishing the amount of employment they offer, which in these conditions reduces the wage rate. The special problems raised by monopsony are examined in Section 5, below.

[2] The analysis of this paper represents largely an application of a branch of price theory to conditions in under-developed countries. The basis of the analysis

225

minimum wage legislation; promotion of binding wage arbitration; official insistence on, or promotion of, payment of wages above the supply price of labour, as for instance by fair wages clauses in government contracts and in protected industries; and also trade union action, often sponsored or facilitated by government, notably by the granting of special legal rights and immunities. Regulated wages, when they are effective, are instruments of restriction, irrespective of the agency which has established them; their introduction implies the withholding from employment in the regulated activity of part of the labour supply available at the regulated wage or at lower rates. By thus curtailing supplies which can be offered compared to the total available supply, regulated wages create, and indeed are often designed to create, a situation which may be conveniently called a contrived scarcity (again in the regulated activity).[3]

Wage regulation in under-developed countries dates from the inter-war period, and has become very widespread since the Second World War. It is neither possible nor necessary to estimate its extent quantitatively. There are several reasons why specific quantification is not possible. These include the presence of much subsistence activity in most under-developed countries, frequent shifts between activities, and imperfect occupational specialisation. Moreover, it is often difficult to discover whether a particular wage is above the supply price of labour (i.e. whether it is a regulated wage), and also the extent and effectiveness of its enforcement. However, these difficulties do not vitiate the general discussion or the confident general conclusion that

and the major relevant aspects of local conditions are set out in the text. Thus, although the argument bears on issues of economic policy, its validity can be assessed on the basis of positive (as distinct from normative) reasoning. Where normative expressions are used (such as uneconomic or wasteful use of resources), the meaning will be clear from the context; the reference is generally to the enforced employment of resources in uses where their contribution to the value of output is less than it would be if those who control them were free to deploy the resources in directions where their contribution would be greater.

[3] Unavoidable scarcity, sometimes termed natural scarcity, reflects the limitation of the total available supply, while a contrived scarcity results from the withholding from the market of part of the total supply. A contrived scarcity is usually superimposed on a natural scarcity because economic resources are normally in limited supply. But the two concepts are logically distinct and have very different implications for policy. The distinction corresponds to the traditional distinction between rents on the one hand and monopoly earnings or prices on the other. The convenient terms of natural and contrived scarcity have been proposed by Professor W. H. Hutt of the University of Cape Town.

regulated wages affect economic activity over a wide area of the under-developed world.[4]

Industry-wide collective bargaining by trade unions is officially encouraged throughout the under-developed world, notably in Latin America, Asia, and the British Commonwealth.[5] In important and controllable sectors where collective bargaining is not yet effective, the government generally regulates wages either by statute or by the other measures already mentioned. Thus there is wage regulation either by official action or by industry-wide collective bargaining. This is the pattern officially and explicitly promoted by the International Labour Office (ILO), the British Colonial Office, and the Indian government. In most under-developed countries, official action is as yet more important than the activities of trade unions. There are statutory minimum wages in important sectors of practically every Latin American and Caribbean country, coupled generally with maximum hours and frequently with fines for discharging workers.[6] In Asia statutory minimum wages are in force in several countries, including India, where they are supplemented by maximum hours, binding arbitration and at times by compulsory bonuses varying with company profits. In many African territories there are statutory minimum wages as well as compulsory arbitration, and their establishment elsewhere is proposed or foreshadowed. There are fair wages clauses in government contracts in practically all British dependencies; their adoption is a condition for the receipt of Colonial Development and Welfare funds.

[4] For instance, according to a recent report by the International Labour Office on *Minimum Wages in Latin America*, Geneva, 1954, p. 22, 'Brazil, Chile, Costa Rica, Cuba, Haiti, Mexico, Paraguay and Uruguay have had considerable experience in the fixing and enforcement of minimum wage rates. In each of these countries it may be said that, taken together, the rates fixed have had a substantial influence on wages as a whole.'

[5] Throughout this chapter the discussion refers to industry-wide bargaining and wage determination. It does not bear on collective negotiation by workers of a single enterprise, which raises issues quite different from those here considered. The relevance of this distinction has been noted by writers as different as Henry C. Simons and Sumner H. Slichter.

[6] The ILO report on *Labour Policies in the West Indies*, Geneva, 1952, says (p. 173), 'The regulation of hours of work, whether by collective agreement, by administrative order or by general legislation, has developed during the period 1939–49 as part of the general process of the introduction and strengthening of modern labour legislation in the area, and of the development of collective bargaining.'

The comprehensive labour legislation in India which, as just noted, provides, among other matters, for minimum wages, maximum hours, and compulsory and binding arbitration, and compulsory profit sharing, affects the interests and prospects of vast numbers. Some of this legislation dates from the inter-war period or very exceptionally from before 1919, but the bulk, including the most important items, has been introduced since 1948.[7] The industries covered include, among others, agriculture, cotton manufacturing, motor transport, tanning, vegetable oil milling, rice milling, and tobacco manufacture. The legislation applies to the whole of India, and the rates are prescribed for entire states with populations up to sixty million. The areas covered include a large part of the poorest regions of this very poor country. In many of the areas there is ample evidence of much lower incomes earned in unregulated activities compared to the statutory minimum wages.

Regulated wages are not always effectively applied and observed; there are in this respect significant differences both between countries and also between different sectors within a single country. They apply widely to the larger enterprises and are usually observed by them. The same is true of enterprises owned by foreigners or by members of distinct ethnic, linguistic, or religious minorities, an important category in most under-developed countries. The smaller local enterprises are often legally exempt. In other instances the legislation is enforced only on foreigners or minorities. In yet other circumstances it applies nominally to all employers, even to those operating in tribal conditions, but is unenforced or even unenforceable over large sectors. Such a situation presents opportunities for corruption and extortion, as many people are always technically in breach of the law.

2

Many of the reasons behind the spread of restrictionism in the labour market of under-developed countries are familiar from experience elsewhere. They include the influence of the organised employee beneficiaries of such policies; the influence of established employers,

[7] India ratified in 1921 the Convention for a 48-hour week which was adopted in principle by the Washington Labour Conference of 1919. It was not, however, generally introduced in India until 1948.

That Convention was ratified in the 1920s by a number of under-developed countries which were then, or are even now, at very early stages of economic development. Yet in British industry the 48-hour week was not adopted generally until after the First World War.

especially the largest employers, who benefit from such measures when they impede actual or potential competitors much more than themselves, as is often the case; the influence of those who favour a more closely controlled economy; the influence of vested interests in the organisation and administration of wage regulation; and humanitarian sentiment, which habitually ignores the serious adverse effects of these measures on the poorest people. Moreover, these influences are rarely counteracted effectively, partly because those who are most adversely affected are usually not aware of the causal sequence, and they are in any case unorganised and politically impotent.

But there is a further major factor operative in this particular sphere of restrictionism. This factor is an international emulation effect which suggests to politicians, administrators and others that their country is backward unless it has labour legislation and organisation modelled on those of the most advanced industrial countries; that is, that the introduction and extension of wage regulation and other labour controls (for instance, of hours and conditions of work) are evidence of development.

This influence operates pervasively in the under-developed world. It can be conveniently illustrated by quoting some statements of prominent Indian spokesmen. Thus, according to N. M. Joshi, a prominent Indian labour leader, 'India's desire to prevent being classed at the International Labour Conference as a backward country in matters of social policy has led to the initiation of labour measures which might not otherwise have come up for consideration at all.'[8] And according to Sir Atul Chatterjee, 'The eyes of the world, of the democracies of every country in the world, are at the moment on us. I am confident that the Council has a full sense of its responsibility for the good name and dignity of India in international councils. We do not want to be considered a backward nation always and for ever.'[9]

This emulation effect is both recognised and magnified by the ILO. According to one of its publications, 'Every State . . . now knows that

[8] Mr Joshi was addressing the Preparatory Asiatic Regional Conference of the International Labour Organisation, New Delhi, 1947.

[9] Quoted by P. P. Pillai, 'India and the ILO', in A. N. Agarwala, *Indian Labour Problems*, 1947, p. 111.

The text of these and a number of similar passages are reproduced in Robert L. Aronson and John P. Windmuller (eds.), *Labor, Management, and Economic Growth*, Institute of International Industrial and Labour Relations, Cornell University, Ithaca, NY, 1954, p. 175 et seq.

the measures by which it applies the Convention's provisions will be closely scrutinised by authorised bodies at Geneva, and that any serious discrepancy will in all probability be discussed in public debate.'[10]

And a commentator has concluded justifiably, 'It may not then be far-fetched to attribute to the ILO a decisive role in accelerating Indian labour legislation if one realises that, in the days immediately after the First World War, the ILO possessed the incomparable prestige of the international organisations in Geneva.'[11]

Thus there are powerful political, social, intellectual, economic and administrative forces behind the imposition and extension of wage regulation. A recent, and in some ways illuminating, example of this influence is mentioned in another ILO publication:

As a sequel to technical assistance provided to Burma by the International Labour Office, the first wage council, for the cigar and cheroot manufacturing industry, was established by the Government in 1953. This council has prepared proposals for fixing minimum rates of wages . . . the Government of Burma plans to extend the system progressively to other industries and other parts of the country.[12]

3

The relative abundance of manual labour compared to capital, developed natural resources, and administrative and technical skills, is a general characteristic of under-developed countries. Indeed, the possession of – or access to – comparatively cheap labour is among their few economic advantages compared to more developed and richer countries. Wage regulation raises the price of labour and endows it with some element of contrived scarcity, and it thus reduces this advantage and injures these countries' prospects of economic progress. This conclusion applies whenever labour costs affect the establishment of economic activities and their scale of operation, an effect which is practically universal. The presence of costs and their relevance to the establishment, location, and scale of economic activities, ultimately flow from the limitation of resources and of incomes, and are thus general; only the extent and readiness of the

[10] *The International Labour Organisation, the First Decade*, Geneva, 1931, p. 314.

[11] Subbiah Kannappan, 'The Impact of the ILO on Labor Legislation and Policy in India', in *Labor, Management, and Economic Growth*, p. 188.

[12] ILO, *Problems of Wage Policy in Asian Countries*, Geneva, 1956, p. 64.

responses vary with different conditions and activities.[13] A few illustrations will demonstrate the relevance of this obvious consideration to the under-developed world.

The history of the rubber growing industry and of its impact on South-east Asia is an outstanding example of the attractive power of cheap labour and of the profound economic and social transformation brought about with its aid.

The rapid and massive development of rubber production in South-east Asia is comparatively recent. There were no exports of rubber from South-east Asia in 1900; they are now (1958) about 1·8 million tons annually, worth over one billion dollars. Rubber is the most important North American import from the eastern hemisphere. Its rise has transformed the economic life of South-east Asia. For instance, around 1900 Malaya was a sparsely populated country, largely of Malays living in hamlets and engaged in subsistence cultivation, where tribal warfare and endemic and epidemic disease were widespread. It is now a thriving country with populous cities linked by excellent communications. Since the 1890s the population has increased by natural growth and by immigration from about two million people to over seven million people, living longer and at a far higher standard of living. National income is about $300 per head annually, by far the highest in South-east Asia. Rubber is the basis of the cash economy, of government revenues, and of further progress throughout the area.

Cheap labour was the principal attractive force which brought the industry to South-east Asia; this has been widely and explicitly recognised throughout its history.[14] The rubber tree (*Hevea brasiliensis*)

---

[13] The relevance of the level of labour costs is often denied implicitly and at times explicitly. For instance, Gunnar Myrdal in a recent book *Economic Theory and Under-developed Regions*, 1957, p. 31, expresses a widely held view, 'All history shows that the cheap and often docile labour of under-developed regions does not usually attract industry.'

If this suggests simply that industrial production requires more than one factor of production, it is truistic but not interesting. If it suggests that labour costs are irrelevant, it is untrue.

[14] The first issue, in 1906, of *Rubber Producing Companies*, an annual reference book of the rubber industry, designed in part to attract capital into the industry contained the following passage: 'It may therefore be well for intending investors to consider what advantages the cultivated rubber of the East may have over the wild and uncultivated rubber of the West.

'The first consideration is that of labour. This is in favour of the Malay Peninsula and Ceylon, both countries being conveniently situated for the supplies of cheap coolie labour to be drawn from Southern India.'

was not indigenous in South-east Asia. Until the beginning of the century the small quantity of exports came from South America. The hardy rubber tree thrives practically anywhere in the tropical rain forest. Cheap labour is important in this industry, the main phases of which are labour intensive (labour costs are about two-thirds of production costs), and even on American-owned estates have not yet been mechanised. Most of the labour supply which attracted the industry to South-east Asia was not in the principal producing territories but in other countries, which themselves were not so suitable for rubber cultivation, but from which labour could be obtained. Cheap labour in turn attracted to South-east Asia large amounts of capital and specialised administrative and technical skills. Rapid economic development and pervasive social changes resulted from the interplay of these forces. Had cheap labour not been available this development would have been obstructed or prevented altogether. The relevance of cost is indisputable.

The very high profits of the few rubber companies in the early years of the century, especially from 1908 to 1912, greatly stimulated expansion. The total planted area, which was about 8,000 acres in 1900 (almost all of which was still immature), increased to about 250,000 acres in 1906 and to about $2\frac{1}{4}$ million acres in 1914. The high profits were secured by a small volume of capital on a small output, about 2 per cent of present production. If wages had been raised greatly, whether directly or by compulsory profit sharing systems, such as are now operated in many Indian industries, the incentive for rapid expansion would have been greatly reduced. This experience bears on the proposals and measures in under-developed countries designed to raise regulated wages and incomes in specific activities, whether by direct wage increases or by bonuses, when these activities are specially profitable. Such measures obstruct the flow of capital into industries the expansion of which would be economic, and which would raise labour incomes generally.

There are many other specific examples in under-developed countries of the relevance and importance of labour costs. A large and elastic supply of cheap and efficient labour has been a major factor, probably the major factor, in the emergence and growth of Hong Kong as a producer and exporter of manufactures. This tiny country has practically no raw materials, fuel, hydro-electric power, and only a very restricted domestic market. In spite of these limitations, often said to be crippling to development of manufacturing in under-developed countries, unsubsidised manufacturing industry has advanced rapidly in Hong Kong. The annual output of manufactures is now about 300 million US dollars, about half of which is exported. Hong Kong is now a major textile exporter to the United Kingdom, and, indeed, these textile imports have become a major issue in British home politics. Cheap labour has also been important in the growth of the cotton textile industries of India and Pakistan.

Low labour costs have also played a major part in Japanese industrialisation. For instance, the textile industry relied extensively on young girls from rural areas who accepted industrial employment at very low wages for a few years before marriage. Such activities are now obstructed or even prevented by wage regulation.

Conversely, there are many examples of the inhibiting effects of high labour costs on the establishment and expansion of enterprises. For instance, the British Colonial Development Corporation has recently (in 1957 and 1958) contemplated the establishment of various industrial projects in Fiji. But these proved uneconomic in view of the high rates of wages (about $1.50 a day) prescribed by powerful trade unions of Indian labourers.

Indeed, the relevance of labour costs to the establishment and operation of overseas enterprises is a commonplace of British and American business literature.[15]

The recognition is not new of the relevance of the level of costs to the establishment and prospects of manufacturing industry in under-developed countries; indeed it goes back to the nineteenth century. Indian experience provides an instructive example. Although the introduction of comprehensive labour legislation in India is relatively recent (chiefly the 1940s and 1950s), the merits and implications of the imposition of maximum hours and minimum wages have been discussed for about a century. Factory production of textiles in India began in the 1850s, and it developed rapidly. From the 1870s the establishment of minimum wages and particularly of maximum hours for Indian industry (especially textiles and jute) was frequently proposed by manufacturing interests in Britain. These proposals were resisted in India, where it was often pointed out that they were designed to reduce the effectiveness of Indian competition by inflating industrial costs. Indian manufacturers and effective public opinion at the time were well aware of the relevance of costs for attracting

[15] For instance, E. R. Barlow, *Management of Foreign Manufacturing Subsidiaries*, Cambridge, Mass., 1953, especially chapter 2.

capital, securing markets and providing employment.[16] It is ironic that under the influence of the international emulation effect the measures which were resisted fifty years ago, and the implications of which were then so clearly realised, are now vigorously espoused. These effects and implications remain the same. The deliberate inflation of industrial costs is paradoxical in view of the insistence in Indian economic planning on accelerated industrialisation.[17] And there is probably no country where contrived barriers to industrialisation are more seriously damaging than in India, because of the severe population pressure, the poor quality of the soil, the abject rural poverty, the social obstacles to economic mobility and to the raising of agricultural productivity, and the barriers to emigration.[18]

[16] The *Report of the Indian Factory Labour Commission of 1908*, 1908, refers explicitly to the adverse effects on industrialisation of restrictive measures. The Commission was especially concerned with working hours, but its remarks apply equally to other restrictive measures: '. . . We are strongly opposed to the imposition of any unnecessary restriction on the employment of labour in factories, especially at a time when the further industrial development of the country is of such vital importance . . . the strongest practical objections exist to the general enforcement in India of any law rigidly restricting the working hours of adult males . . . the imposition of a direct restriction on the hours of adult labour would be repugnant to the great majority of capitalists, both in India and abroad, who have invested, or are considering the question of investing money in India . . . the opinion is widely and strongly held that, if interference with adult labour be permitted, pressure will be brought to bear in order to utilise that power of interference in a manner calculated to promote the interests of Lancashire and Dundee, rather than of India . . . [and this] would undoubtedly adversely affect India's industrial development . . . we are strongly opposed to any direct limitation of adult working hours, because we consider there is no necessity for the adoption of this drastic course, because we are convinced that it would cause the gravest inconvenience to existing industries.' Pp. 32–3.

[17] The importance of labour costs in Indian manufacturing is shown by the share of wages in the net product (value added), which for manufacturing industry as a whole in India was 44 per cent in 1950. In cotton textiles, a major industry affected by minimum wages, it was 64 per cent; in tanning it was 64 per cent; in jute manufacture 51 per cent; and in rice milling 45 per cent. These are all regulated activities. These are official figures quoted by S.A.Palekar, 'Real Wages and Profits in India, 1939–50', *Indian Economic Review*, August 1957.

[18] These simple considerations are no new discoveries: 'Whatever, besides, tends to diminish in any country the number of artificers and manufacturers, tends to diminish the home market, the most important of all markets for the rude produce of the land, and thereby still further to discourage agriculture.' Adam Smith, *Wealth of Nations*, book IV, chapter viii.

4

The required economic analysis of the results of regulated wages is straightforward, and it can be found in easily accessible publications.

Regulated wages and other restrictions on the supply of labour reaching the market raise the wage above the supply price of labour which measures its highest contribution to output in alternative uses, which in turn reflects its economic scarcity.[19]

Unless it is either redundant or unobserved, wage regulation raises wage rates in the industries in which it is introduced. This effect reduces the volume of employment in the regulated industry compared to what it would be otherwise. This decrease[20] of employment will vary directly with three factors: the readiness of the consumers of the product to turn to alternatives (elasticity of demand); the readiness of the other productive resources employed in the regulated activity to withdraw from that activity if their rewards are reduced (elasticity of supply); and the ease of substitution of other productive resources for labour when its cost is raised (elasticity of substitution). The influence of these factors is often accentuated when labour costs are a large proportion of total costs. The cost of wage regulation, that is the excess of the wage over the supply price of labour to the regulated activity, falls on those consumers and owners of factors of production who cannot turn easily to alternative commodities or activities. In under-developed economies the effect on employment is usually considerable, and, further, a large share of the cost is borne by very poor people.

The elasticity of demand for the products of the regulated industries is often very high, as in export industries, such as mines, plantations, and simple manufactures. In under-developed countries these export industries, especially mining and plantation industries, are the most prominent and easily controllable activities, and are likely to attract wage regulation. The elasticity of demand for the product is

[19] The supply price itself may exceed this productivity. Thus members of agricultural families often share in the family or group income even though their contribution to output is very small. Their supply price to industry may be governed by the average productivity of the group, which may much exceed their marginal productivity.

[20] It seems necessary to say explicitly that this refers to the curtailment in the volume of employment compared to what it would be otherwise, that is, it refers to a functional relationship and not to an observed change in employment during the relevant period.

often likely to be high also in the domestic market for local industries, though not so high as in the export markets. These products have to compete for the low cash incomes of consumers with products of unregulated activities, often including cottage industry, handicrafts, and even imports.[21] When the elasticity of demand for the product is high, the effect on the volume of employment will be substantial. In practice this effect usually takes the form of a retardation of the growth of employment in that industry (or possibly a decline in a subsequent recession) rather than an immediate reduction in the number of those already employed, which is one reason why the effect is so often overlooked. On the other hand, when the elasticity of demand is low, the main burden falls on consumers in the form of higher prices. In under-developed countries most of the consumers of local industrial products are themselves very poor.

The supply of capital, enterprise, and skills, whether domestic or foreign, but more particularly when foreign, is likely to be elastic to the regulated industry. This response may not operate immediately. For example, capital invested in specific assets cannot be withdrawn promptly when returns are reduced, even to levels below those which would induce initial investment. But after a while investment commitments and employment contracts will not be renewed, and fresh resources will not be directed to the regulated industry, at least not in the volume in which they would have been in the absence of the regulation. Moreover, even if much of production remains profitable, part of the output is normally marginal, and it is thus affected adversely by higher costs. For instance, the large variations in the amount of payable ore with variations in cost is a well documented theme of the literature of gold mining. This reasoning applies even when the employers have a substantial measure of selling monopoly,

[21] Even the products of subsistence agriculture can be at times substitutes for the output of the regulated industries. This effect is obvious when agriculture is among the regulated activities, as in India. Moreover, where production for the market is only slightly more profitable than subsistence production, as often happens in small-scale agriculture, higher prices of consumer goods in the exchange sector reduce the attractiveness of agricultural production for sale compared to subsistence production, which may discourage agriculturalists from producing for sale. This influence may at times affect the elasticity of demand and thus the incidence of higher labour costs. This effect of regulated wages is analogous to that of a tax on production which is likely to retard the development of the exchange economy. A fuller treatment of this type of problem will be found in P.T.Bauer and B.S.Yamey, *The Economics of Under-developed Countries*, chapter 7.

as part of the output will still be marginal in terms of the maximisation of monopoly profits.[22]

The extent of factor substitution is less easy to assess. It depends on technical and economic factors as well as on legal and social influences. It is often likely to be important, as is shown by differences in methods of production in different firms or in similar industries in different countries.[23] Of course, such substitution may be prevented by further restrictive measures limiting the replacement of the regulated labour by unregulated categories of labour or by machinery. Examples of such measures, which are familiar also in highly industrialised countries, range from the prescription of ratios between European and non-European labour in some branches of South African mining and manufacturing industry to the regulation of the ratio of machinery to labour in the Mexican textile industry.

Even if the extent of factor substitution is small, the other responses (the elasticities of consumer demand and of the supply of other factors) ensure a high elasticity of demand to labour. Thus wage regulation generally affects employment appreciably. As already noted, in practice this effect expresses itself in a retardation of growth rather than in an actual contraction. The effect on employment is increased further by the fact that those responsible for wage regulation, especially when wages are regulated by government rather than by trade unions, do not take into account the relevant factors influencing the growth of employment opportunities, so that the adverse effects on employment are not minimised by selecting for regulation those industries in which the elasticity of demand for labour is relatively small. Indeed, in the under-developed countries regulated wages are especially likely to be introduced in activities in which the elasticity of demand for labour is likely to be high. I have already instanced the liability of export industries to wage regulation. For different reasons, to be noted in the next section, competitive industries in which wage rates are relatively low. and labour costs a comparatively large part of total cost. are also likely to attract wage regulation, and the elasticity of demand for labour in such industries is usually comparatively high.

[22] This argument does not apply when there is monopoly in the hiring of labour. This problem is considered below.

[23] Differences in factor availability are often reflected in differences in methods of production even when at first sight there seems to be little scope for such variations. Differences in planting density in rubber production on estates and smallholdings are an example discussed in some detail in Bauer and Yamey, op. cit., chapter 4.

The decrease in employment opportunities in the regulated activity implies that much or most of the cost of its introduction falls on those who have to accept less preferred employment, either in another grade of the same industry or, more likely, in some other activity.

5[24]

At this point it is necessary to take cognisance of a category of situations in which wage regulation need not, in principle, contract employment, and in which the cost will fall entirely on employers. This is the case of monopsony, that is monopoly in the purchase of labour, whether exercised by a single dominant firm or by a group of firms acting in concert. Where a monopsonist is confronted by a rising supply curve of labour, the wage rate can be reduced by decreasing the amount of labour employed, and up to a point the advantage of the reduction in costs exceeds the disadvantage of the smaller gross proceeds resulting from the reduction of output.[25] The imposition of minimum wages may then raise wages without increasing the marginal cost of labour (because the employment of additional labour no longer raises wage rates) and thereby secure more employment and higher wages.

Such conditions are not unknown. The arrangements in the recruitment, wage determination, and allocation of labour in the South African mining industry are an example. However, regulated wages are unlikely to be the most effective remedy for monopsony. For instance, there is the difficulty of setting and adjusting the dose, that is of determining the wage which transfers monopsony profits without affecting employment adversely. Moreover, it does not affect the source of monopsony, which is the absence of accessible employment alternatives for the workers. Development of a wider range of such alternatives is likely to be the more appropriate policy. Lastly, even if monopsony did call for wage regulation, it would do so generally on a plant or local level and not on an industry-wide or national level, since monopsony, even where it exists, is essentially a local phenomenon.

[24] The argument of this section, which is in part somewhat technical, is intended only to forestall a possible objection to the main argument of this paper. The subsequent argument does not depend on this section which can be omitted by the non-technical reader.

[25] If the monopsonist is a group of employers acting in concert, the labour has to be rationed among them formally or informally.

Monopsony, though not unknown, is exceptional in under-developed countries, as elsewhere. The high degree of concentration in an industry or trade often encountered in under-developed countries does not imply even effective monopoly power, since such power is also affected by ease of entry and access of customers to alternatives, and these are not measured by the degree of concentration. And even monopoly in the product market does not indicate monopsony in the labour market, since industries producing widely different commodities compete for the same factor of production, so that a monopolistic industry may have no monopsony power whatever. Again, even wide disparities in wealth, knowledge, literacy or commercial sophistication between employers and workers are not evidence of monopsony, or of differences in bargaining power which would result in exploitation. Liability to exploitation results from lack of independent competing alternatives, and not from differences in wealth or commercial sophistication. Even illiterate poor workers will be paid what they are worth to their employers if these employers can obtain their services only by competing for them, that is attracting them from other employers.

Monopsony is clearly absent in most of the sectors in under-developed countries in which wages are regulated. Throughout the under-developed world wages have been regulated in many highly competitive industries into which entry is easy and in which producers act independently, both in the purchase of labour, which is relatively undifferentiated and occupationally mobile, and in the sale of the products. They have also been introduced in areas in which there are many alternative forms of employment. Minimum wages have been established in India in agriculture, cotton manufacture, leather manufacture, simple food processing; and in Burma in the manufacture of cigars and cheroots; and in Latin America in many small-scale industries, including handicrafts. In these activities there is no monopoly, still less monopsony. Thus, wage regulation in under-developed countries is neither required to counteract the effects of monopsony, nor is it designed for this purpose. And, as already noted, industry or nation-wide wage regulation (as distinct from regulation on a plant or local basis) is in any event especially irrelevant to action designed to counter monopsony or its effects.

The irrelevance of monopsony to wage regulation as practised in under-developed countries is evident from the absence in the literature of the ILO, the British Colonial Office, and the Indian government, of references to this phenomenon as a condition or requirement or argument for the establishment of regulated wages. On the contrary, this literature often deplores the absence of employers' organisations, on the ground that the multiplicity of independent employers obstructs the introduction of industry-wide collective bargaining, and even the establishment of statutory wage determination. Indeed such measures often issue in the formation of employers' associations, the influence of which may extend beyond the labour market.[26]

Indeed, wage regulation is especially likely to be introduced in competitive industries. For instance, in Great Britain statutory minimum wages were first introduced in the so-called sweated trades, which were highly competitive. This connection is not accidental. Industries in which labour costs are relatively large are likely to be highly competitive because of the comparative unimportance of fixed capital. Moreover, wage rates in these industries are likely to be low compared to less competitive industries. The firms in competitive activities cannot afford to pay more than the market rate. The lower wages in the competitive activities lend plausibility to the demands for official intervention. On the other hand, firms with some measure of monopoly are often anxious to placate public opinion by paying wages higher than are necessary, and they are often well placed to do so by virtue of monopoly profits and scarcity rents.

Thus, although in principle a case might be made out for wage regulation to counter the presence and effects of monopsony, it is essentially irrelevant to the actual establishment and operation of wage regulation in under-developed countries.

6

The regulated wage creates a contrived scarcity which overstates its unavoidable or natural scarcity, and which induces economy in the use of labour in the regulated activity, both through curtailment of production and by the substitution of other factors. The economy in

[26] According to a multigraphed memorandum by the Information Department of the British Colonial Office, *Notes on the Development of Trade Unionism and Labour Relations in the Colonies*, 1953, p. 5: 'The degree of employer organisation varies considerably between territories, but in general it can be said that the greatest degree of organisation is to be found where either the formation of workers' associations has demonstrated the need for combination on the part of the employers, or the common problems of an industry . . . have brought about co-operation.'

the use of labour in this activity increases its availability elsewhere, where its contribution to output is less because the supply price which measures its highest contribution elsewhere is less than the prescribed wage. The contrived scarcity results in uneconomic allocation of resources and thus diminishes aggregate output. Besides this effect on current production, regulated wages and similar measures retard the growth of output by reducing the national income and thus the volume of investible resources, and also by reducing the flexibility and adaptability of the economy.

In under-developed countries special factors reinforce these results of regulated wages. The diversity of supply and demand conditions of labour is one of these. Such diversity does not reflect generally, or even primarily, institutional barriers to movement, but rather differences in aptitudes, resources and customs, and also the undeveloped state of transport facilities. Even within apparently undifferentiated unskilled labour there are wide differences in attitudes, adaptability, skill and productivity, which are reflected in wide differences in earnings of workers on piece rates in particular enterprises as, for instance, the earnings of rubber tappers on Malayan estates. These earnings differ widely even within the same ethnic group, and much more so between workers of different ethnic groups, such as Chinese, Indian, and Malay tappers. Again, the efficiency of newcomers to town and industry from rural and tribal areas is usually far lower than that of more experienced workers.

The supply price of different types of unskilled labour also differs widely. For instance, the supply price of migrant labour from rural to urban areas varies with distance, family circumstances, the length of stay envisaged, agricultural prosperity, employment opportunities of dependants, and other factors.

In these conditions the compulsory standardisation implied in regulated wages is very wasteful in terms both of the allocation and the growth of resources. For instance, it prevents the migration of prospective newcomers to industry and the acquisition of skill by them, because in view of their inexperience they are not worth the prescribed wage. Thus the incomes of the would-be migrants are depressed, and they are also disqualified from improving their condition. Not only is there an uneconomic allocation of resources, but their growth is manifestly inhibited.

Thus in under-developed countries the adverse economic results of regulated wages are likely to be specially pronounced. Moreover,

241

this affects the factor of which the relatively ample supply is among the few economic assets of these countries. And they can least afford wasteful policies.

7

It is sometimes urged that the adverse effects of regulated wages on development are offset by benefits resulting from the adoption of more capital-intensive methods induced by raising the money cost of labour, notably by the impetus this provides to technical change. Among other relevant factors, this reasoning ignores the retardation of technical change in the activities where wages are depressed as a result of overcrowding brought about by the curtailment of employment opportunities in the regulated activities, the effect on investment resulting from the reduction in the current national income, and the reduced flexibility and mobility resulting from institutional wage determination. Although criteria based on the allocation of resources may conceivably be inadequate guides for policy designed to promote their growth (especially in the field of public finance), it does not follow that indiscriminate inflation of the money cost of labour somehow conduces to growth to offset the wasteful allocation of resources to which it gives rise.[27]

There are some arguments in support of wage regulation which may be noted in passing because of their popularity. One is that such measures maintain or increase purchasing power. But they only transfer purchasing power from some individuals and groups to others

[27] W. Galenson and H. Leibenstein have ingeniously suggested in an important article, 'Investment Criteria, Productivity, and Economic Development', *Quarterly Journal of Economics*, August 1955, that higher capital intensity in certain activities brought about by higher wage costs may promote development even when there is surplus labour. The suggestion is that although the current national income may be reduced, the difference between production and consumption, that is the volume of investible resources, may be increased. The formal validity of this argument depends in part on an assumed equivalence of future and present output, and on specific assumptions on factor productivities and consumption habits in different sectors, and on the irrelevance of consumer preferences. Acceptance of these assumptions and premises raises large questions of political judgment as well as matters of empirical fact. However, even if these assumptions and premises are accepted, the policy appropriate to the promotion of development would be a tax proportionate to the wage bill, rather than the indiscriminate imposition of minimum wages and conditions, since such taxation would conduce to the most efficient deployment of different types of labour, and possibly of other resources, within individual enterprises.

without increasing it. In fact they necessarily diminish aggregate demand because they affect adversely the total national income, the ultimate source of real purchasing power. The unemployment of unskilled labour in these countries, which reflects the lack of co-operant factors of production, is also aggravated by the wasteful results of these measures. The further suggestion that prescribed higher wages increase the productivity of under-nourished workers ignores the effect of wage regulation on the incomes of those excluded from the regulated activity. These are people poorer than those protected by the regulated wages, and their low incomes are depressed still further by them. As such measures both tend to diminish the total national income, and especially the incomes of the poorest people (that is, those excluded from the regulated activities), they are unlikely to improve nutritional standards.[28] The suggestion also implies that the incidental results of the activities of outside bodies are required to correct the misjudgment of those personally and constantly engaged in conducting industry or in managing their own private lives.

It is sometimes urged that restrictions such as the imposition of regulated wages are required to protect the welfare of poor, illiterate workers in under-developed countries, as they cannot perceive their own interests, much less protect them. As already mentioned, this line of argument is irrelevant to exploitation which reflects monopsony power of employers, since the possibility of this depends on the absence of alternative employment opportunities and not on the ignorance or poverty of workers; and, again, wage regulation is not generally the appropriate instrument to counteract monopsony, nor is it generally introduced for that purpose. Further, wage regulation is generally calculated to harm rather than benefit the poorest sections of the community whose employment opportunities it restricts. Nor is the assumption of the woekers' ignorance of suitable alternatives and of their lack of response to opportunities generally valid. Throughout the under-developed world there is much detailed evidence of the awareness of poor and illiterate people of differences in economic conditions and in net advantages of different occupations

---

[28] The argument criticised in the text could be valid if there was a rise in the workers' efficiency simultaneous with the announcement of the higher wage rates, and proportional to the rise in wage rates. This consideration is unlikely to be of practical significance, especially as it is not a factor taken into account in the imposition of wage regulation.

and of their readiness to respond to these differences within the opportunities open to them. For instance, in the early decades of this century hundreds of thousands of South Indian labourers migrated from the rural areas of Madras to Malaya and Ceylon. The volume and direction of this migration responded promptly and markedly to changes in economic conditions in these countries; the illiterate rural population was remarkably well informed of working conditions and employment opportunities in these countries.

8

The creation of the contrived scarcity diminishes the volume of employment in the regulated activity compared to what it would be otherwise. As a result some people whose preferred occupation would have been the regulated activity have to seek alternative employment. This effect on monopolistic action is widely ignored in discussions on the incidence of the cost of monopoly. In practice, this cost is often heaviest on people who are barred from supplying the monopolised commodity and service; it often bears more harshly on such people than it does on the buyers of the commodity or service. This aspect or result of contrived scarcity is both significant and manifest in wage regulation in under-developed countries.

The gap between prescribed wages and the incomes and earnings of those excluded from the regulated trades is generally wide in under-developed countries, proportionately much wider than in developed countries. The gap cannot be attributed to differences in skills and aptitudes: if this were the reason, the wage regulation would be redundant. The workers who cannot secure employment in the regulated industries are forced to accept other employment on less attractive terms.[29] The most important of these overflow activities are agriculture, petty trading, domestic service and casual labour, and participation in them takes the form of self-employment, full-time or

[29] Without seniority rules or other barriers to entry, the inflow of labour attracted by the prescribed wage rate tends to reduce earnings by the sharing of employment, since by definition the rate is above the level at which supply and demand balance. It could even reduce earnings over a period to the level prevailing in the absence of prescribed rates if entry is easy and labour is hired entirely indiscriminately. In practice, however, differences in efficiency between established and outside labour, together with preference for those already employed, maintain at least part of the privileged or monopoly incomes. Inflow of labour does not affect the adverse effects of minimum wages on the volume of employment, but only the distribution of the privileged earnings among employees.

part-time employment, under-employment or virtual unemployment. Unless they are either redundant or flouted, regulated wages and other restrictive devices curtail employment in these activities and thus enhance the over-crowding in the over-flow occupations. Further depression of the very low incomes in these occupations is the general result of the overcrowding of the lowest level of the labour market.[30]

The very low incomes in the overflow activities have often been reported in widely different conditions, and they have been noted in various publications of the ILO. For instance, the ILO study on *Problems of Wage Policy in Asian Countries* quotes several official Indian and Indonesian reports which show regulated unskilled wages exceeding, by a factor of over three, wages and earnings of similar labour in unregulated activities in the same area. The extremely low incomes in unregulated activities are usually attributed in this literature to the absence of regulation, and its extension is urged accordingly. The legislation of several Latin American countries, including the Argentine and Uruguay, specifically provides for the extension of minimum wages to cottage industry at rates comparable to those in the corresponding factory trades. Such measures, if they could be carried to their logical conclusion, would deny all sources of earned income to those who fail to secure employment at the regulated wages; they would be reduced to the cold comfort of public relief or private charity, or would have to face starvation.

The burden of wage regulation on the poorest people is a noteworthy but not accidental outcome of measures promoted by social reformers motivated by an allegedly sensitive and rational social conscience. In part it reflects the popular failure to perceive effects which are inevitable but do not occur immediately; nor are these effects or their cause immediately obvious when they do occur. It probably also reflects differences in political effectiveness between the beneficiaries of these measures and those harmed by them. The former include, besides the protected workers, influential employers (whom such measures protect from competition by firms relying on cheap labour, and who also gain prestige from paying comparatively high wages), and also those politicians, administrators and other public figures

[30] There may be exceptions to this proposition which are unimportant, especially in under-developed countries. There may be a number of distinct types of unregulated labour. An increase in the supply of one type brought about by the establishment of regulated wages for another type may increase the demand for a third type which is complementary to the first.

who benefit politically and personally from the administration of such measures. Those who are harmed are the consumers of the products of the regulated activity, and, more substantially, those who are forced into the overflow activities or compelled to remain there. The difference in effectiveness is obvious.

9

The restrictive effects of minimum wage regulation are thrown into exceptionally clear relief by the arrangements in the labour market in South Africa. They help to identify the operation and effects of forces at work elsewhere, more especially to show that the cost falls primarily on those excluded from the regulated activities.

The rapid expansion of South African gold and diamond mining in the closing decades of the nineteenth century created a great scarcity of skilled white labour with correspondingly high wages. The scarcity value was subsequently threatened by various factors, notably by immigration from Europe, by exodus of South African Europeans from rural areas, and by the acquisition of some industrial experience and settled habits by Africans. To replace the lost natural scarcity by contrived scarcity, and scarcity rents by monopoly earnings, the skilled European workers, especially miners, promoted and enforced severe restrictions, among them minimum wages, and an industrial colour bar enforced by custom and trade unions. These measures aggravated the overcrowding of the unskilled labour market and depressed unskilled wages, at that time earned chiefly by Africans. But many Europeans were unable to secure skilled employment because they lacked the qualifications. Moreover, the increase in wages restricted the demand for labour. The excess supply in the labour market depressed the unskilled wages of Europeans to levels which alarmed public opinion. This led to the establishment of minimum wages in a number of trades in the hope of securing employment to Europeans at so-called civilised rates. But each stage of this process restricted further the opportunities and depressed the wages of those who could not find employment at the prescribed rates. Employment was then specifically created for poor whites in government enterprises, especially the railway, and in private industry by official pressure on employers by various means, including threats of the removal of protection from industries not employing a sufficient proportion of Europeans. Moreover, non-Europeans came to be excluded from an ever-widening range of activities by various devices, including prescription of minimum wages above unskilled rates, which in effect excluded non-Europeans. This, however, again also barred many Europeans who were not worth the prescribed minimum wages for various reasons, such as their inadqueate education or rural background.

The imposition of statutory minimum wages was among the restrictive measures adopted. Not only has this restrictive device been employed widely, but its effects have been publicly discussed and understood. For instance, a section in an important report, that of the Economic and Wage Commission of 1925, is headed 'The minimum wage as an instrument of the colour bar'.

In several instances statutory minimum wages were at first confined to Europeans. But this sometimes led to the substitution of non-Europeans at unregulated wages for white labour at regulated wages, and the wage fixing machinery was deliberately extended to cover non-European labour. This measure effectively barred non-Europeans because it removed the incentive to employ them. The effect is well documented on both the volume of employment and on the racial composition of the labour force of the prescription of minimum wages at equal rates for European and non-European labour. For instance, a survey of poor relief in Cape Town found that in the district surveyed the majority of those unemployed and on relief were people insufficiently qualified to earn the prescribed minimum wage, though they were worth employing at a lower wage. A survey of the confectionery trade in Pietermaritzburg found that the prescription of minimum wages in 1931 both decreased total employment and reduced the proportion of non-Europeans. The establishment of minimum wages for non-Europeans in truck driving led to their dismissal and replacement by Europeans over a wide area in the 1930s.[31]

Gold mining has been the most important single industry affected by these measures. As the price of gold is fixed, no part of the cost falls on the user. Part of the cost of the inflated wages of European miners falls on capital. But there is always a grade of ore which is only just payable. Many detailed surveys have shown the wide variations in the amounts of payable ore with variations in costs. It is much easier for capital to find alternative employment at comparable returns than it is for labour excluded from the mines, so that the greater

[31] These examples are from Sheila T. Van Der Horst, *Native Labour in South Africa*, 1942, chapter 13. The argument of this section owes much to Dr Van Der Horst's excellent study.

part of the burden is clearly borne by those Europeans and Africans who fail to secure employment in mining. The same principle applies throughout the scale. The overcrowding of the labour market has, however, also depressed the wages in employments specially created for Europeans. The large proportion of the cost of such measures borne by those excluded from the regulated activities stands out exceptionally clearly in South Africa.

The repercussions of this process, outlined here only very briefly, have extended far beyond the economic life of the country and also well beyond its frontiers. The process has been a major factor in the political development of the country. A leading historian of the British Commonwealth has written on this subject:

The colour bar in industry originated among British workers under the Union Jack. 'It was at the diamond fields that the gate to all but low-paid and unskilled labour was slammed against the native in industry.' (C.W. de Kiewiet, *The Imperial Factor in South Africa*). From the Kimberley diggings the colour bar was carried by English-speaking workers into the mining areas of the South African Republic. . . .

South Africa's national historian, if ever he should arise to tell with pride the story of how his country rejected a liberal doctrine which was foreign to her blood and soil, will not, if he is just, give all the glory to the descendants of the Voortrekkers. The triumph, if ever it be completely won, will belong in part to those sturdy British workmen who made themselves at home on South African soil. The historian will not forget their vindication of the colour bar. Nor will he omit to record that it was their labour party which first appealed to the white voters of South Africa with a full-blooded programme of racial segregation.[32]

This is only one pertinent and striking instance of the far-reaching political repercussions of restrictionism in the labour market of under-developed countries, including wage regulation. These implications and results of restrictionism cannot be discussed here. But it is important to remember that the effects of such policies pervade social life well beyond what is usually regarded as the sphere of economics.

10

The basic analysis of the implications of regulated wages is not complicated. Yet it is largely ignored in the influential literature on under-developed countries. This is perhaps strange in view of the concern

[32] W.K.Hancock, *Survey of British Commonwealth Affairs*, 1941, vol. II, part 2, pp. 40 and 42.

in this literature with enterprise monopoly and with imperfections in product markets. The neglect is certainly unwarranted in view of the wide scope and pervasive influence of restrictions in the labour markets in under-developed countries. Both the intellectual interest and the practical importance of the subject would justify and reward sustained and disinterested enquiry in this sphere.

The investigator who will turn his attention to the field of restrictionism in the labour markets of under-developed countries will have to reckon with the ingrained neglect of the basic analysis. Moreover, he must be prepared to face intense hostility directed from entrenched intellectual, political and economic interests and influences. He will do well to remember certain pertinent remarks by Adam Smith:

This monopoly has so much increased the number of some particular tribes of them, that, like an overgrown standing army, they have become formidable to the government, and upon many occasions intimidate the legislature. .... If he opposes them ... and still more if he has authority enough to be able to thwart them, neither the most acknowledged probity, nor the highest rank, nor the greatest public services, can protect him from the most infamous abuse and detraction, from personal insults, nor sometimes from real danger, arising from the insolent outrage of furious and disappointed monopolists.[33]

Academic economists are exceptionally well placed to appreciate the truth of these observations – and also to ignore the warning they imply.

Addendum

A few supplementary remarks by way of clarification may be in order on the relation between the level of wages on the one hand, and the introduction and effects of wage regulation on the other.

Public discussion on the merits of wage regulation, notably on the need for its introduction or maintenance, generally focuses on the level of wages, notably on the level of wage incomes. The important distinction is usually ignored whether the workers receive their marginal value productivity (which may be low) or whether they receive less than their marginal value productivity. The second type of situation reflects monopsony, the presence of which cannot, however, be inferred from the level of wages: specialised employees with

---

[33] *Wealth of Nations*, book IV, chapter ii.

high incomes may nevertheless be subject to monopsony. Conversely, workers may be paid what their services are worth (the marginal value product) and yet receive very low wages if their services are worth little because their supply is abundant relatively to the demand. Indeed, as is suggested in the text, wages are apt to be relatively low in highly competitive industries. For reasons also indicated in the text, in the absence of monopsony wage regulation depresses wage rates in activities in which they are lower than in the regulated activities, thus defeating the ostensible or avowed objective of the regulation, namely to increase the wages of the lowest paid workers. Failure to distinguish between situations in which monopsony is present or absent, and the habit of focussing attention simply on the level of wages, thus issue in policies the results of which defeat their ostensible purpose.

12

PRICE CONTROL IN UNDER-DEVELOPED COUNTRIES*[1]

In Western Europe, North America and Australasia the wartime and post-war price controls were largely dismantled in the 1950s. But in many parts of Asia, Africa and Latin America they have been retained or reimposed. This article discusses certain implications and results of these controls.[2] It is chiefly concerned with price controls in conditions where they are more effective at one stage of distribution than at others.

The problems and situations discussed have been suggested largely by the experience of West Africa and India, and to a lesser extent Pakistan and Cyprus in the 1940s and 1950s. But the analysis is more generally relevant.

1

Certain features of the economic scene of many poor countries bear on this discussion.

* *Journal of Development Studies*, October 1965, pp. 19–37.
[1] In accordance with current practice the term 'under-developed' is used here to refer to most of Africa, Asia and Latin America; it is in fact a synonym for 'poor'. The line of distinction between developed and under-developed (i.e. rich and poor) countries is arbitrary and imprecise. This imprecision does not, however, affect the discussion. The characteristics of under-developed countries relevant to the argument are set out in Section 1, and they will be found to apply widely in the conditions of these countries.

[2] The discussion is mostly in terms of price control over imports, as this throws into clearest relief certain issues of practical interest. Most of the discussion would, however, apply also to price control over locally produced commodities, including manufactured goods.

This article is not concerned with, and therefore disregards, the possibility that effective price control over a monopolist producer or distributor can serve to increase his output. The usual type of price control over commodities in under-developed countries is not introduced for this reason, but to deal with situations, often called colloquially short-supply situations, in which the relevant supply (usually total supply, but at times supply from certain sources) is fixed; cf. Section 3 in the text.

Although sustained or substantial monopoly or monopoly profits are unusual in trading in these countries because of the comparative ease of entry and the ineffectiveness of market sharing agreements, there is often a high degree of concentration in the import and export trades, and to a lesser extent in the local wholesale trade.[3] This reflects chiefly the advantages of substantial capital in the conduct of long-distance trade. Much of this trading activity is in the hands of people different in nationality, language or race from the majority of the population. They are sufficiently distinct from most of the local population for the distinction to be habitually recognised in public life and social intercourse. Such differences, at times unnoticed by external observers (for instance, membership of different African tribes), are often clearly and habitually recognised locally. The prominence of foreigners, strangers or other ethnic groups distinct from the local population reflects advantages derived from the possession of skills, attitudes (including commercial aptitudes), capital and from wider commercial contacts.

In this article importers are referred to as *merchants*; they are the first stage in the internal distribution system. In this context they include wholesalers who obtain supplies at controlled prices from producers, from the government or from other domestic sources. Firms and individuals operating in the distributive chain between the merchants and the ultimate consumers will be termed *intermediaries*. Reference to *traders* may be either to merchants or to intermediaries, according to the context.

Effective rationing at the final consumer stage is rarely possible in these countries. This is partly because the majority of consumers are illiterate, and also because the ideas behind rationing often conflict with the mores, values and customs of the community. As a result, the ultimate consumer, especially in the rural areas, almost invariably pays the open market price, that is the price at which the quantity on offer and the quantity demanded balance. This price will be referred to as the open market price, and it may be quite unrelated to the controlled price. Indeed, most of the transactions *after* the stage of sale by the merchants to their customers (usually the larger intermediaries) are at this open market price, that is either at the price

---

[3] The concentration in the import and export trade of West Africa in the early 1950s, and the reason for its high degree there as in many under-developed countries, are discussed in my book, *West African Trade*, Cambridge, 1954, especially chapters 5, 7, 8 and 17, and also in an article, reprinted above, pp. 201 to 224.

paid by the final consumer, or at a price differing from this only by the costs of transport and distribution to the point of final sale. This is at times implicitly recognised in the arrangements for price control, in that prices are often not fixed beyond the wholesale or semi-wholesale stage. But whether or not formal price control extends beyond the wholesale stage rarely affects the prices actually paid by the majority of the, usually numerous, small-scale intermediaries or the bulk of final consumers.[4]

Chiefly because of the dispersal of consumers and the poverty of the individual consumer, ultimate retail transactions are on a very small scale. For these and certain other reasons, there are a large number of successive stages in the distributive process, and a large number of traders at each stage. Most of the sales of merchants are to intermediaries, especially large intermediaries, who are a small proportion of the *total* number of intermediaries operating in the country.[5] This is partly because consumers and the smaller

[4] The following passages from a thesis submitted by Mr B. G. Kavalsky for the M.Sc. degree at London University illustrate the ineffectiveness of price control in Northern Rhodesia in the 1940s, besides other aspects of economic life there.

'The case of Mufulira in 1944 provides an interesting example of the operation of price control. The control price was set for grain and meal and immediately evaded through a change in the measure given to customers. The management then introduced special cups and dishes, which when filled with grain or meal gave the correct weight, and enforced their use. The marketeers next step was to cut round pieces of cardboard of the same colour as the meal and fit them as a shelf some inches up from the bottom of the mug. When the authorities cottoned on to this, the marketeers switched to beating up the bottoms of the mugs, and when this was stopped, they cut down the tops gradually over a long period, so as not to be immediately noticeable. The effect of all this was that in 1945 none of the measuring cups bore any relation to the original size, and the price had been restored to its earlier level.

'Other managements tried similarly to control the price by the introduction of scales. The figures on the scale were quickly scratched out and the old prices charged till eventually the matter was settled by the breaking of the scales. When the controlled price of fish was made 8d. a lb as against the actual selling price of 2s. a lb and the riverside price of 6d. a lb, the fish sellers simply left the market and refused to operate at that price. The customers were most unhappy about the situation and asked the management to stop the controls as they would rather have higher prices than no fish at all.'

The passages are Mr Kavalsky's summary of a longer discussion of this subject in W. V. Brelsford, *Copper Belt Markets*, Lusaka, 1947, pp. 22–3.

[5] Meaningful specific quantitative estimates of this point are difficult to secure because the occupational statistics of most poor countries are very wide of the mark, chiefly owing to the incomplete occupational specialisation in these

intermediaries often buy in smaller individual quantities than the minimum quantities which it is economic for merchants to sell; and also because many of the consumers are far from the merchants' establishments. Some of the merchants' sales, however, are to final consumers, especially to certain categories whose position is considered in Section 6 below.

In many of these countries specialisation, especially occupational specialisation, is as yet imperfectly developed. In trade there is usually no clear cut specialisation by stages, at any rate after the merchant stage; traders are likely to operate at each of several successives stages. Further, large numbers of people are apt to shift at short notice from other occupations into trading, both full-time and part-time, and they equally readily shift their activities from one commodity to another.

Lastly, intermediaries and the larger-scale traders generally are among the most vocal and politically influential elements of the local population. They tend to be literate, or at any rate more literate than the population at large; they are often closely connected with the local newspapers, and their views are prominent in the local press and in political assemblies.

2

Before 1939 supply and demand conditions of imports into poor countries changed rarely so rapidly and discontinuously as to bring about sudden sharp increases in either retail prices or the profit margins of merchants. There were no substantial short-period fluctuations in the condition of supply of imports. There were wide fluctuations in demand according to variations in the flow of money incomes. But the elasticity of supply of imports into any one country was high, and increased supplies of imports were readily forthcoming. And when import prices did rise, this was part of a general rise in the prices of these commodities, and did not result in a significant increase in profit margins of merchants. Again, increases in the prices

countries where a significant proportion of the people not classified as traders nevertheless do trade, at least part-time or intermittently. This subject is examined in 'Economic Progress and Occupational Distribution', above, pp. 3 to 17, and also in *West African Trade*, ch. 2. However, it was found in 1950 that the number of traders operating in three markets of Eastern Nigeria was about 14,000, which was more than the total number of the regular customers of the eight merchant firms which at the time handled about five-eighths of all commercial imports into Nigeria.

of imports in a boom tended to be less marked than those in the prices of exports, or in the incomes of the great bulk of the local population. Lastly, such increases in the prices of imports were on the whole gradual, chiefly because of the high elasticity of supply of imports. In these circumstances such increases in prices of imports as did occur were usually gradual and were not accompanied by such high profit margins as to yield obviously abnormally high returns, nor did they impose serious strain on any substantial section of the local population. Accordingly such price increases in imports as occurred did not usually result in demands for price control.

Since 1939, however, there have been frequent, rapid and substantial changes in the supply of and demand for imports in many poor countries. Many of these changes bring about discontinuous sharp increases in the local open market price of imported commodities. Such situations have resulted either from a sharp contraction in supply and/or an expansion of demand. The principal reasons for these changes are familiar. During the Second World War and the first post-war decade they were chiefly the temporary eclipse of certain sources of supply; enforced reliance on higher cost sources of supply because of licensing of foreign exchange or scarcity of shipping; longer delivery dates for imports, especially from sources not subject to licensing; expansion of money demand; and discontinuous variations in producer prices subject to official determination.[6] Since about 1955 domestic inflation and changes in import licensing and exchange control policies have been the principal factors bringing about discontinuous changes in the supply–demand relationships of imported commodities in under-developed countries. The resulting sharp increases in the local prices of imported commodities have often affected adversely the interests, notably the standard of living, of influential, though not necessarily large, groups of consumers.

3

A rise in the local open market price of imported commodities may or may not be accompanied by abnormally high profit margins of merchants. It may reflect simply a general rise in the cost of imports,

---

[6] The distinction between an increase in demand and a contraction in supply, though often important both for analysis and for policy, is not directly relevant to this article. For simplicity of exposition, the discussion is confined to a contraction of supply with an unchanged demand.

i.e. a shift of the supply curve to the left, without abnormal profits. This situation does not raise issues of analytical interest, nor does it usually issue in the imposition of price control.

But a change in supply may take certain forms under which the new equilibrium price will secure abnormal profits to merchants, which may be more than accidental or short-term, since there are no, or practically no, elements of self-correction in the situation. Such instances have been frequent since 1939; and although they all belong substantially to one genus, for the purpose of this discussion they may be considered under two headings.

First, there are arrangements (case A) under which a certain amount of the goods is made available at a given import price, and additional supplies are unobtainable. This occurs when the volume of the commodity to be imported is fixed by direct control, or indirectly by control of the issue of foreign exchange, or the allocation of shipping space.

Case B is a variant of such arrangements. Under this certain strictly limited supplies may be available from some sources, while additional supplies are obtainable at higher cost from other sources.

During and since the Second World War both these types of arrangement have been frequent in the import trade of many underdeveloped countries, notably in many British colonies. Locally, their counterpart is a system of licensing or allocation of supplies among merchants, usually on some basis of past trading performance. Frequently, however, a proportion of licences or of supplies is reserved for members of the local population, who had not previously been merchants; the favoured individuals usually are from the ranks of past or present intermediaries.

Both cases A and B imply that (in the absence of effective price control) merchants who obtain supplies at a cost (including their own selling expenses) below the new local open market price will secure abnormal profits, which may be very large. In both these cases the abnormal profits have their roots in the system of allocation or licensing of supplies; or in other words, in the inability or unwillingness of the original sellers and/or the authorities to raise the cost of these supplies to the merchants, or to impose or raise taxes to equate supply and demand at the merchant stage. These profits arising from the difference between the supply price and the open market price will be referred to as *windfall profits*. This term seems more appropriate than monopoly profits, or profits of scarcity, or abnormal profits.[7]

4

Recipients of licences (a term used here to include allocations of supplies) are generally subject to price control of varying degrees of effectiveness. The declared aim of price control is generally to skim off the windfall profits inherent in any system of licensing, and to reduce margins to a level yielding no more than normal profits. It is, however, rarely, if ever, possible to achieve this; for various reasons the licensees are almost certain to be left with more than normal profits. First, the permitted profit margins are likely to err on the side of leniency, since otherwise there is a danger that the service might not be forthcoming. Further, it is very difficult to allow for the various indirect advantages accruing from the receipt of licences or supplies in times of general stringency and in conditions of riskless trading. Thus even if price control were effectively enforced, it would be unlikely to eliminate windfall profits completely.

But price control is unlikely to be completely effective even over the sales of the larger merchants; and it is much less likely to be effective over the operations of those local intermediaries who have been promoted to the status of merchants through the receipt of licences. Thus even if the recipients are subjected to price control, there is likely to be an insistent demand for licences for amounts far in excess of those the applicants would want to handle in the absence of windfall profits.[8]

These aspects and results of import licensing are familiar. There are other results which are particularly characteristic of the economic, political and administrative scene in many under-developed countries. Certain important and characteristic repercussions arise from the differing degree of effectiveness of price control over the various classes of trader, notably its much greater effectiveness over merchants, especially foreign merchants (or those who are at any rate

[7] It should be clear from the context whether the reference is to profit margins or to rates of return on capital.

[8] This type of situation is vividly described in certain official reports, especially locally published reports. Examples include the *Report of the Commission on Enquiry into the Distribution and Prices of Essential Imported Goods*, Accra, 1943; the *Report of the Commission of Enquiry into Conditional Sales*, Lagos, 1948; and also the *Report of the Commission of Enquiry into Disturbances in the Gold Coast*, 1948.

ethnically distinct from the majority of the population), than over intermediaries.

Price control is likely to be at least partially effective when applied to the transactions of merchants, both to their sales in bulk and to their sales in smaller quantities. There are various political and administrative reasons for the comparative effectiveness of price control over merchants. These are generally substantial firms who keep regular accounts, and who employ large staffs. Thus control of their activities is comparatively easy, while evasion is more likely to be detected or denounced. Moreover, the political risks of evasion tend to be great.[9]

But price control is often ineffective even over the transactions of the larger merchants. This is partly because of the difficulty of effective control over the actions of the employees of merchants, either by the employers or by the authorities. However, there is another and more important reason. It will be recalled that the bulk of the sales of merchants (including sales through stores as well as ex warehouse) are to intermediaries, that is to customers who are themselves re-sellers and not final consumers. These re-seller customers of the merchants dispose of the commodities at open market prices, since for reasons stated in Section 1 price control is usually inoperative beyond the stage at which the merchants operate.[10] As their customers re-sell in markets in which price control is inoperative, merchants and their employees are strongly tempted to evade price control. Indeed, pressure by their customers for the allocation of supplies at controlled prices may be so insistent that some evasion of price control may be well-nigh unavoidable; and even when avoidable, evasion might involve merchants in less trouble and unpopularity than observance.

Not much can be said in general terms about the form and extent which the evasion of price control is likely to assume, except perhaps

[9] These considerations apply much less to the transactions of local traders specially promoted to the status of merchants by the operation of import licensing, i.e. traders who would not normally import directly, and who are attracted into this activity by the operation of licensing and enabled to participate in it by the allocation of licences.

[10] Scattered information on the level of controlled and open market prices in India will be found in R.G.Agrawal, *Price Controls in India*, New Delhi, 1956, and in B.R.Shenoy, *Indian Planning and Economic Development*, Bombay, 1963.

Some information on controlled and actual prices of consumer goods in West Africa in the late 1940s is presented in *West African Trade*, p. 437. There is also some sporadic information on this subject in the reports mentioned in footnote 8.

that the device of conditional sales is often used. This amounts to a restriction of sales of the price controlled commodity to buyers who undertake to purchase another commodity or range of commodities, which otherwise they would not buy, or at least not at the price which they are required to pay. This type of evasion is generally difficult to prove formally; and further, as merchants usually sell a range of imported commodities in their normal course of business, it is easier to subject their customers to conditional sales than if trading were more specialised.[11]

Of the total windfall profits inherent in a situation in which the supply price of imported goods is kept below the open market price, the merchants generally can secure a part only, and often the smaller part. The balance accrues to the intermediaries to whom the merchants sell at prices below the open market price, which is the price at which the intermediaries can generally dispose of the commodities. While the distribution of the windfall between the merchants, their employees, and the intermediaries is often not easy to assess, it seems generally true that both the first and the last secure a significant share; and further, where the merchants are foreigners (or, at least, ethnically distinct from the majority of the population), and relatively vulnerable to political pressure, the share of the intermediaries is generally considerable. These are safe approximations; and they are sufficient for our analysis.

In such circumstances the demands for price control, which might in any case arise if vocal sections of the population (as consumers) find that the prices of important items in their expenditure have risen substantially, are likely to be reinforced by two factors.

First, it is likely to be widely realised that, in the absence of price control, the merchants (many of whom, it will be recalled, are often clearly distinct from the rest of the population) secure windfall profits which are likely to persist while licensing continues. Secondly, the intermediaries will appreciate that price control, if imposed, would be ineffective at the later stages of distribution so that its (more effective) operation over the transactions of merchants will secure for them (the intermediaries) an appreciable part of the windfall profits

[11] The beneficiaries of conditional sales, as indeed of other types of evasion, are often the employees of the merchants rather than the merchants themselves. Where the beneficiaries are employees belonging to the local population, their position under price control and their interest in its maintenance are analogous to those of the local intermediaries.

inherent in the situation. They will thus press vigorously for its imposition. Plausibility is lent to these demands by the rise in the prices of imports and the emergence of windfall profits for merchants.

5

Thus, in the circumstances of many poor countries, the windfall profits inherent in cases A and B are likely to result in three types of demand or pressure: demands for licences; demands for the imposition of price control over the merchants; and demands for the allocation of supplies by merchants at controlled prices. As many intermediaries operate on such a small scale that they cannot hope to secure import licences (even under preferential treatment of the local population), their demands tend to be largely for price control and for allocation; and these demands may be more vocal and prominent than demands for import licences.

Price control, unless it is either ineffective or redundant, implies a situation in which the quantity demanded is in excess of the quantity offered. As in these countries there can generally be no effective system of rationing, and often there is not even formal rationing, the merchants have to ration informally the price-controlled commodities. This in turn brings about an inflation in apparent demand, a speculative shift in the demand curve, i.e. over-statement by customers of their requirements at particular prices in order to secure larger quantities than they would otherwise obtain. For several distinct reasons this familiar phenomenon tends to emerge much more readily, and to be quantitatively more important, in under-developed countries than in more advanced countries.

First, as already stated, a large proportion of the beneficiaries from the difference between the controlled price and the open market price are likely to be re-sellers who secure a cash gain from any allocation of supplies at less than the open market price.[12] Thus the demands of individual re-sellers, unlike those of individual consumers, have practically no saturation point at the controlled prices (up to the point where the open market price is reduced to the controlled price by additional supplies). Further, the gains accruing from securing commodities at controlled prices and re-selling them at open market prices are manifest and easily calculable. Indeed, the allocation of the commodity at the controlled price (or more generally at any price

[12] There are certain favoured groups of consumers who benefit from price control; they are considered in Section 6.

below the open market price) is tantamount to a cash gift. In conditions of imperfect specialisation the possibility of this obvious gain brings about the appearance of large numbers of *ad hoc* traders[13] applying for supplies of the price-controlled commodity. In these conditions the apparent excess of demand over supply at the controlled price is much greater than the actual excess of effective final consumer demand.

Such a situation conduces to political tension. The merchants are likely to be accused of evasion of price control, conditional selling, and of favouritism towards particular individuals and groups, especially towards intermediaries and of their own nationality or race. In the circumstances there are many disgruntled traders and would-be traders.

6

The effects of price control on the ultimate consumer are very different from what is usually implied by those demanding its imposition. In case A the great majority of consumers do not benefit. They buy at the open market price which is not reduced by price control, however effective or ineffective at earlier stages.[14] Indeed, it may even be increased slightly. The transfer of windfall profits from merchants to intermediaries may increase total money expenditure. The merchants' profits are less likely to be spent locally than are those of the intermediaries; and further, they are usually subjected to heavier taxation (often *de jure* and very generally *de facto*). If the transfer of the windfalls from merchants to intermediaries results in an appreciable increase in money demand, the general level of prices is likely to be higher than it would be otherwise, and consumers paying open market prices would be worse off as a result of price control.[15]

[13] These *ad hoc* traders may either be individuals who are not usually engaged in trade at all, or traders who do not normally deal in this particular commodity. In West Africa in the 1940s and 50s schoolboys often acted as *ad hoc* intermediaries either individually or in small groups. The same phenomenon seems also to have occurred in some other under-developed countries, including Pakistan.

[14] We are considering here case A, that is, instances in which the supply is perfectly inelastic beyond the quantity already imported. When additional supplies are obtainable at higher prices (case B) the open market price will certainly be *raised*. This is considered later in this section.

[15] This neglects any satisfaction they may get from the knowledge that some windfalls have been transferred from foreigners to compatriots.

There are, however, certain classes of consumer who are likely to secure supplies at controlled prices. These include civil servants, members of the police force, politicians and public men generally, and employees of the merchants. These favoured consumers, together with the intermediaries buying from the merchants, are generally a small proportion of the total population.

They are, however, politically, socially, and administratively influential groups. As they benefit appreciably from price control, they are likely to favour it, even though open market prices are unchanged or may even have been raised; and their advocacy of price control is not likely to be affected by its political and social results. Moreover, they rarely understand the factors behind the situation. Alongside other sections of local opinion, they are likely to ascribe these results to the selfishness and malice of the merchants.

Under case B the reasons and motives of demands for price control are likely to be very similar to those under case A: a sharp rise in the local prices of imported goods and the emergence of large profits for some merchants. And most of the results of the imposition of price control are similar to those observed in case A: excess of demand over supply, inflation of demand, informal rationing by merchants, and obvious discrepancy between the open market price and the controlled price.

But there is one significant difference. The open market price will now certainly be higher than it would have been without price control. The supply of imports is now not completely inelastic; additional supplies can be obtained from higher cost sources. Unless price control is completely ineffective over the operations of merchants, some merchants will not be able to realise such high average prices as they would otherwise, and it will not pay some merchants to tap certain high cost sources which they would have tapped without price control.

7

Even wide fluctuations in aggregate money incomes in the importing countries, or wide fluctuations in the supply of imports, need not require, or even render desirable, intervention in the markets for particular commodities. Thus if the cost of imports rises greatly, but the supply is elastic, the only way to assist consumers is by direct subsidy. Even if situations designated as case A or B threaten to emerge, it may still be possible to deal with them or forestall them without intervention in particular markets. It may be possible by suitable fiscal or monetary action to deflate aggregate money incomes sufficiently to equate demand and supply for imports. Or again in certain circumstances it may be thought desirable to leave the traders with windfall profits. Thus somes licences may be granted to members of the local population, and the high profits may be thought desirable to strengthen the resources of these traders in their years of apprenticeship in foreign trade, even though they represent windfall profits secured at the expense of the rest of the population.

But in many instances these courses would not be practicable, desirable or sufficient. The fiscal machinery or the monetary mechanism may not be sufficiently developed or responsive for a general control of the flow of incomes. Auctioning of licences might serve to increase further an already high degree of concentration. Complete non-intervention may secure very high and persistent windfall profits to the recipients of licences.

Thus other measures may have to be adopted, affecting particular commodities or those dealing with them. In practice it will be necessary to consider the effects and relative merits of price control (Sections 8 and 9), of the imposition of particular indirect taxes and of the taxation of merchants' profits (Section 10), and of government purchase and sale of the imports affected (Section 11).

8

There is a certain superficial political and administrative attractiveness in a system of licensing combined with price control. It is usually demanded by influential sections of the local population. The merchants are also likely to favour it. In spite of price control they will make larger (and relatively riskless) profits than they would in more usual conditions. Moreover, licensing shields them from competition from new entrants. These demands are reinforced by superficial rough justice, since one class of beneficiaries (the favoured groups of consumers who succeed in buying at the controlled prices) include individuals who are generally adversely affected when prices have risen, especially if their money incomes have not risen correspondingly. Governments may also often welcome a system of licensing to promote the entry of local traders into direct importing. For political reasons participation of some members of the local population in external trade may be deemed desirable and in the absence of licensing the entrants may be unsuccessful.[16] Again, the salaries and wages of government employees are often linked to cost of living indices based on controlled prices, so that governments have a financial interest in formal price control, even when it is ineffective. And lastly, a system of licensing and allocation may appeal to influential groups for political and administrative reasons, generally because it promises closer official control over various branches of economic life ; and also because it creates posts and positions of influence and power.

9

In spite of these attractions there are severe disadvantages in such a system, some of which are familiar under any system of licensing with or without price control. Others are peculiar to under-developed countries, and stem chiefly from the fact that price control is so largely ineffective at the final consumer stage.

A system of licensing tends to freeze the pattern of trade. This may be modified to some extent if licences are not confined to established firms. In this case, however, they are likely to be given to politically influential members or groups of the local population who would not be able to survive in trade without licensing.

The system tends to ensure riskless windfall profits to the licensees. Price control may remove some of these. But the more effective is the price control over the activities of merchants, the greater are the riskless profits accruing to the intermediaries at the next stage. This poses problems peculiar to the operation of price control in many under-developed countries.

For reasons discussed in Section 2, the differential effectiveness of price control over merchants and intermediaries respectively largely inflates the demand of the customers of merchants, with the result that frequently only a small fraction of the expressed demand can be satisfied.

The more rigorously the merchants observe price control, the greater and more obvious is the profit accruing to intermediaries, and the larger becomes the excess demand, and the smaller the fraction of the demand which can be met. The merchants will be accused of favouritism, illegitimate preference, and possibly also

---

[16] This might to some extent counteract the advantages to established merchants from the operation of licensing. However, the merchants rarely oppose restrictive licensing on this account.

corruption. If, on the other hand, they evade price control by conditional sales or similar devices, they will be accused of profiteering by those who are disappointed of part of their expected profits. A further concomitant of such a situation is an increase in the volume and stridency of the demands by the local population, especially intermediaries, for a larger share in supplies.

The operation of these forces is intensified by a genuine failure of public opinion to appreciate essential features of the situation, in particular the reasons for the absence of effective rationing at consumer level and the consequent ineffectiveness of price control at that stage. The prominence among merchants and their employees of foreigners, strangers and of members of other ethnic groups distinct from the local population, tends further to exacerbate the situation.[17] These circumstances can bring about severe political tension.[18]

Such a situation is also likely to engender misleading ideas about the nature of trading activity and the sources of trading profits. It is likely to be believed that trade is a fixed quantity in which an increased share for some necessarily implies a smaller quantity available to others. Trading profits take on the appearance of riskless and almost effortless windfalls or monopoly profits. This serves both to attract large numbers into trading activity, while at the same time it discredits the work of the merchants.

Lastly, there is the familiar result of self-perpetuation under any system of licensing. In the circumstances described, there are special factors reinforcing the familiar tendency. The local traders and intermediaries who receive licences or supplies below the open market price from the merchants may not be able to survive in business without these favourable conditions. They will emphatically oppose their removal.

[17] Many books and reports could be quoted showing the failure to understand the essentials of this type of situation, especially the reasons for the discrepancy between the open market and the controlled prices and the resulting pressure on merchants for additional supplies which makes conditional sales or other types of evasion practically unavoidable. Locally published official reports are particularly revealing on these points; the reports listed in footnote 8 above are examples.

[18] The disturbances in the Gold Coast in 1948 which culminated in the Accra riots in which more than twenty people lost their lives were closely connected with such a situation.

10

Taxation may serve to avert some of the difficulties just described.[19] Where no further supplies are available or admitted (case A), the imposition of taxes to raise the supply price to the open market price will not raise the latter, and may even lower it; and as the bulk of consumers pay this price they cannot be affected adversely.

The imposition or raising of taxes to reduce or eliminate the gap between the supply price and the open market price is certain to be strongly resisted by those affected. Even in more sophisticated communities such measures are often resisted on the argument that they would raise retail prices. In under-developed countries the opposition is likely to be much stronger, from merchants, from intermediaries, and from favoured consumers. Between them these groups are often much the most important section of vocal public opinion.

The opposition to this use of indirect taxation is likely to be even stronger if it is imposed before the emergence of the windfall profits and of the short supply situation. The rise in the open market price will be ascribed to the higher taxation. This view is less likely to gain currency if the gap between open market price and the supply price has persisted for some time.

But even if the imposition of sufficient additional indirect taxation is politically practicable, it will not be the most effective instrument in dealing with the short supply situation of case A.

Indirect taxes cannot easily be altered frequently, and rarely more than once a year. If they are levied at rates designed to skim off the entire difference between the supply price and the open market price at the time of their imposition, supplies may disappear if subsequently there is a fall in the open market price. Thus even if political conditions permit the imposition of indirect taxes to equate the quantities supplied and demanded, this may be inadvisable. It may be thought preferable to leave the merchants with slightly more than the normal profit margin, and leave it to profits taxation to deal with any surplus profits which it is desired to remove.

In case B the tension and difficulties brought about by price control

[19] In principle, similar effects can be secured by the auctioning by the authorities of the limited supplies or the licences to import. However, in the conditions of many under-developed countries this may have results undesired by the authorities, for example an increase in the degree of concentration in the import trade.

are very similar to those under case A, with the added factor that the open market price itself will have been raised by the operation of price control. The resistance to the removal of licensing and price control, and to its replacement by additional taxation, are also likely to be very similar. In this case, however, the open market price will also be affected by the imposition of additional indirect taxation. It will clearly be higher than it would have been in the absence of price control and the absence of indirect taxation. In this type of situation it may be preferable to rely principally on income and company taxation to skim off the abnormal profits of those who have secured intra-marginal supplies to which access is barred to others. If this form of taxation is not highly developed, it can be supplemented or even replaced by the imposition of additional indirect taxes, which will, however, raise the open market price.

11

Government purchase of supplies for resale may be used as an alternative method for bridging the gap between open market prices and supply prices.[20] In substance this is, of course, closely similar to additional indirect taxes. It differs from it in certain aspects which may be important in the conditions prevailing in many under-developed countries.

First, while indirect taxes can usually be changed only once a year, the selling prices of commodities handled by the government can be altered frequently. In rapidly changing conditions of supply and demand this consideration is often important, especially in countries where, for reasons already stated, a relatively small discrepancy between supply price and open market price may result in a tense situation.

Secondly, in case B this method could deal with the situation without raising the open market price. For reasons suggested in Sections 9 and 10, both the imposition of price control and of additional taxation is bound to raise the open market price when it discourages supplies from higher cost sources; and where consumer demand is inelastic, the rise in the open market price may be substantial. Government trading may make it possible to avoid raising the open market price, and it may even be possible to lower it, since there need

---

[20] State trading is, of course, no novelty. The discussion is intended only to examine its merits and defects compared to the other principle methods of dealing with certain specified problems.

be no contraction of supplies from marginal sources. Moreover, the profits on the sale of supplies from lower cost sources (which, it will be remembered, cannot be expanded) may be used to subsidise purchases from higher cost sources, thus reducing the open market price.[21]

Third, the political opposition to this method may be less pronounced than to the imposition of indirect taxes. This attitude may be irrational, but it may nevertheless be present; witness the very different attitude of the British public to the trading profits of the British Ministry of Food, and to the suggestions for using the purchase tax to deflate the excess demand for motor cars in the early post-war years. Conversely, of course, the opposition of traders may be stronger if they see in this measure not only a device for skimming off windfall profits, but the beginning of permanent state trading.

The disadvantages and difficulties of the adoption of this method stem essentially from obvious political and administrative considerations. The machinery may not be equal to the task of organising and operating the scheme. Or the integrity of the local civil service, especially at the middle or lower levels, may be unequal to the evident temptations.

This method may also clearly set up strong influences of self-perpetuation or extension. Its adoption creates influential and remunerative positions yielding to their holders incomes or power far greater than they would enjoy otherwise. This influence is likely to retard the adoption of other measures for dealing with the situation whether by the deflation of aggregate money demand and/or by the development of new sources of supplies. Indeed, once established the scheme may be so attractive to those in administrative and political control that they may seek to extend it to other activities.

If these political and administrative dangers and defects could be avoided, this method may prove the least disadvantageous solution in some under-developed countries for dealing with a situation of excess demand for a range of commodities.

12

The factors behind the short supply situation, that is the situation of excess demand, and the principal implications both of the situation and of the methods for dealing with it are generally reasonably clear.

[21] Such purchases could, of course, also be subsidised out of general revenue if this were thought desirable.

But the choice of different measures requires delicate assessment of political conditions and of economic effects. Measures affecting specific activities or commodities are likely to be more effective and cause less friction if the discrepancy between aggregate money demand and the total volume of supplies is small, so that the burden of adjustment borne by particular indirect taxes or the taxation of merchants' profits is not too great. Thus other things being equal, these measures are likely to be most effective when used in conjunction with more general measures for deflating aggregate money demand.

Addendum

Section 11 discusses the introduction of state trading amongst other methods for dealing with some of the adverse consequences of partially effective price control in under-developed countries. Various dangers and defects of that method are noted. I now feel, partly as a result of further study of conditions in both East and West Africa, as well as in India and Ceylon, that the political, administrative and financial dangers, disadvantages and costs of state trading in under-developed countries almost certainly outweigh the advantages, and that the alternative methods discussed in that section, and even non-intervention, are to be preferred. I probably under-rated the political disadvantages of state monopoly in major sections of the economy, which, especially in under-developed countries, implies close control over large sections of the population. Moreover, the inherent tendency towards self-perpetuation and extension of state trading seems in practice irresistible. Further, the diversion of capital and personnel from more essential government functions is likely to prove costly.

Part 3

B.S. YAMEY

13

THE ORIGINS OF RESALE PRICE MAINTENANCE: A STUDY OF THREE BRANCHES OF RETAIL TRADE*

1

The movement in many branches of retailing to foster the practice of resale price maintenance dates from the last two decades of the nineteenth century. Though the development was not the same in every respect, it is possible to discern uniformities in the mainsprings of the movement and in the resistances it encountered in several trades. This paper examines the motives and pressures which gave rise to demands for resale price maintenance in the grocery, drug and patent medicine, and tobacco trades,[1] and the considerations which prompted manufacturers to satisfy or to reject these demands. It is not suggested that the account would necessarily be the same for all other branches of industry and distribution; on the other hand, there is much evidence that the factors and influences, which are discussed here, were not peculiar to the selected trades.[2]

The discussion is based upon information which has been obtained from retail trade journals,[3] covering the formative years of resale price maintenance up to about 1906. During the period the journals contain fairly full details of the activities of trade organisations and

* *Economic Journal*, September 1952, pp. 522–45.

[1] No detailed or chronological account is presented of the course of developments in the selected trades.

[2] Two articles, 'Manufacturers and Retail Prices', in *The Times: Financial and Commercial Supplement*, 1 October 1906 and 8 October 1906, contain an excellent general survey of the forces behind the price maintenance movement. The present study fully bears out the analysis presented there. The two articles aroused considerable discussion in the retail trade press. It was suggested that *The Times* was not impartial, because at that time the Times Book Club was engaged in its historic war against price maintenance in the book trade.

[3] The following are the principal journals used (the abbreviations used in this paper are indicated in parentheses):

The Grocer (*G.*)
The Chemist and Druggist (*C. & D.*)

the results of negotiations between manufacturers and trade organisations, as well as numerous comments on developments by trade organisers, retailers and manufacturers. In particular, the opinions and observations of the most influential figure in the history of resale price maintenance, the late Sir William Glyn-Jones, are valuable for revealing the atmosphere in which the price maintenance movement was launched and the difficulties it had to overcome. Glyn-Jones was the founder in 1895 of the Proprietary Articles Trade Association (PATA) for promoting and administering resale price maintenance in the chemists' trade; he influenced developments in the grocery trade, and was consulted by associations in other trades which were anxious to safeguard retail profit margins. He also played an important part in the organisation of a chemists' PATA in Canada in 1926; this association dissolved itself after an official investigation had concluded that its activities were against the public interest.[4]

2

The last quarter (and more) of the nineteenth century was a period of growing price competition in many branches of retailing. New types of retailing establishments were rapidly gaining ground. The 'middle class' co-operative stores (e.g. the Civil Service Supply Association and Army and Navy Stores), the universal providers (department stores such as Whiteleys and Harrods) and the multiples (e.g. Home and Colonial Stores, Boots and Salmon and Gluckstein) were making use of their trading advantages to secure patronage by offering inducements to the public largely in the form of extensive and significant price reductions,[5] and large sections of the public

Anti-Cutting Record *(ACR)*
The Tobacco Trade Review *(TTR)*

The *Anti-Cutting Record* was the official organ of the Proprietary Articles Trade Association in the chemists' trade.

[4] Some biographical details concerning Glyn-Jones may be of interest. Born 1869; after serving as chemist's assistant in the Mile End Road, carried on business as chemist in Poplar; active in organisation of PATA from 1895 onwards; called to the Bar, 1904; Liberal Member of Parliament for Stepney, 1911–18; Parliamentary Secretary to Minister of Munitions, 1916, and to Minister of Reconstruction, 1917; knighted 1919; secretary, Pharmaceutical Society, 1918–26; died in Vancouver, 1927.

[5] The lower prices were widely publicised in advertisements and price lists. Some multiples appear to have used the appeal of low prices with a vigour which is startling to modern eyes. When Lewis and Burrows Ltd opened branches in the Pimlico area, circulars were distributed announcing that the firm, 'the popular

responded to the attraction of lower prices.[6] The 'working-men's' co-operative societies were steadily expanding and extending their operations geographically. The competition provided by new methods of retailing was superimposed upon the probably more leisurely competition that existed among the typical small-scale retailers of an earlier period. The so-called 'legitimate' retailers (operating on a small or medium scale along traditional lines) felt the severe effects of the enhanced competition: the smaller share of the trade that remained for them had to be transacted at lower prices and margins of profit. Moreover, they had as before to contend with competition within their own ranks. The intensity of this kind of competition increased, for some were quick to follow some of the methods of their large-scale rivals. Prices and margins tended to be reduced even where the more substantial competitors had not yet made their presence felt.[7]

The branding or trade-marking of merchandise on a growing scale[8] increased the severity of retail competition. The advertising of

store chemists, have declared war against the extortionate prices charged by chemists in the district'. *C. & D.*, 28 May 1898, p. 895. Boots Ltd used an advertisement in Guernsey, headed, 'Great Robbery in the Drug Trade at Guernsey – Thousands of Pounds'. *C. & D.*, 4 June 1898, p. 933.

[6] It would be otiose to document the nature of the public response to the offer of lower prices. An unusual example may be of interest. Glyn-Jones noted that some patients would tear off the bottom part of a doctor's prescription form, on which some proprietary article had been prescribed. Only the remainder of the prescription, requiring something to be dispensed, would be presented to the chemist, because the proprietary article itself could be obtained more cheaply at stores which could not dispense. *C. & D.*, 2 May 1896, p. 630.

[7] A grocer in a reminiscing letter on the origin of price cutting noted that 'severe and senseless cutting was rife years before "companies' branch shops" [multiples] were in every street'. *G.*, 7 March 1914, p. 694. An article on 'Company Chemists' pointed out that 'the cutter was with us before the company chemist appeared on the scene, but except in his own immediate locality he was loftily ignored'. *C. & D.*, 30 January 1897, p. 163.

Some of the new types of retailing establishment affected prices over a large area. The London stores, for example, had to be taken into account by provincial grocers and chemists. Changes in their price lists were regularly reported in *The Chemist and Druggist* in the 1890s.

At the first annual conference of the Federation of Grocers' Associations in 1891 there was some discussion on the appropriate level of grocers' profit margins. A grocer of Leamington pointed out that 'it was of no use to talk of 8 per cent, or any other percentage, for they had to follow in the lines which were set by the Army and Navy and other stores'. *G.*, 21 November 1891, p. 963. The Army and Navy Stores were (and are) in London.

[8] In the period under review branded goods were not equally important in the

branded goods by manufacturers and their acceptance by consumers made it relatively easy for the retail trade to handle the merchandise. The large-scale retailing firms could make use of relatively unskilled labour for the simplified tasks of selling; and the entry of new firms into retailing became even easier than it had been before. Further, branding made it possible, for example, for grocers and publicans to sell tobacco products and for grocers to sell proprietary medicines, since no special knowledge of the merchandise was necessary to sell the branded goods of other trades. The universal providers had weakened the traditional division of types of merchandise among different retail trades; the success of proprietary articles tended to hasten the process, and to sharpen competition still further. Not only was competition keener within each trade, but those in different trades also competed with one another.

The evils of 'cutting' were a dominant and recurrent theme in contemporary retail trade journals which reflected the views of the ordinary or 'legitimate' small-scale retailers. Retail associations spent many hours in denunciations of cutting and the cutters. The evils were attributed to the activities of the several types of retailing innovators and to new-comers generally,[9] and to the less co-operative members of the 'legitimate' trade. Further, the chemists blamed the grocers for the unsatisfactory prices of patent medicines, and each trade was apprehensive of the 'illegitimate' competition of out-siders.[10]

It was frequently alleged that the cutters were practising what today is called loss-leader selling (which term appears to be of more recent origin). The practice of selling some items of merchandise at very low prices in order to attract custom was said to show that the new types of firm were using unfair or deceptive methods of trading.

three trades. It would seem that branded goods were of greatest importance (as a percentage of total trade) in the chemists' trade, and of the least in the grocery trade.

[9] On the latter point, for example, Glyn-Jones remarked that 'he had come across a trader occasionally who had really advocated cutting, but that was generally a young man who entertained the idea that he could only get a footing by cutting below the present prices'. *G.*, 19 February 1898, p. 468.

[10] The importance of the different types of 'cutting' firms – stores, multiples, aggressive small-scale retailers and 'dabblers' – was not the same in each trade, or in the various branches of each trade (branded and unbranded goods), or in different areas. The common feature in the three trades was the strength and effectiveness of price-cutting generally.

276

From the evidence there can be little doubt that, as it was often expressed, sprats were thrown to catch mackerel. The practice was used by all kinds of retailers, large and small; and branded as well as unbranded goods were used for the purpose. But the effects of general price-cutting and of selective price-cutting were substantially the same: price competition and price reductions were effective over a considerable range of goods. It was this that caused alarm among the retailers. Glyn-Jones noted that cutting made it necessary for retailers to conduct 'a large portion of their trade on lines which left no profit whatever'.[11] A prominent provincial grocer reported that his firm 'found that we had successively reduced one article after another ... until nearly every article was sold at barely over cost. This arose from the usual cause: a grocer in one district would cut three or four of them; a grocer in another district would, in retaliation, cut five or six of another lot; and so at last it came about that we were all selling alike.'[12] Some years later a grocer who 'flattered himself that he could purchase on the very best terms' confessed his inability to match the prices of 'some of the big shops'. 'Instead of throwing a sprat to catch a mackerel, they would really have to throw a mackerel to catch a sprat, for it was difficult to find an article that was not cut by these shops.'[13]

Many of the numerous contemporary references to loss-leader practices may be discounted. The complaining retailers would naturally have been unwilling to concede that their competitors could undersell them generally, since such an admission would have implied that their rivals were more efficient or more successful in meeting the requirements of large numbers of consumers.[14] Many of the allegations about selling below cost were equally unfounded. Retailers did not always know at what prices their principal competitors were able to buy proprietary articles or other goods from

[11] *G.*, 17 July 1897, Supplement, p. 21.

[12] John Williams, in *G.*, 27 December 1901, p. 1597. He referred to twenty-nine proprietaries made by one firm; and indicated that more than 1,500 brands were in a similar unprofitable condition.

[13] *G.*, 16 December 1911, p. 1647.

[14] The universal providers were sometimes said to use entire departments as loss-leaders, and this might have been so in some cases. But where the same firm was said by different groups of retailers to be using several different departments in the same way, one may suspect exaggeration.

In the grocery trade some of the larger multiples handled only a small number of staple lines. The scope for loss-leader tactics would have been limited.

suppliers. Manufacturers were generally prepared to grant large discounts to large buyers. 'Many a time a grocer is led to think that at a company shop some article is being cut at a ruinous price, whereas the real truth is that the multiple-shop firm is enjoying more advantageous terms of purchase.'[15] The practice of granting substantial quantity discounts encouraged price competition at retail, and manufacturers were often censured for supporting the cutters and making cutting possible. 'It was the owners of "proprietaries" who made the cutting movement possible to the stores' because discounts were granted so generously that '. . . it came about that those places [the stores] could get such terms from the suppliers . . . as permitted them to cut the goods down to, and sometimes below, the prices which the retailer had to pay the selfsame supplier'.[16]

3

The hard-pressed retailers attempted to improve their own competitive position or to neutralise the competitive advantages of their rivals in a variety of ways. For example, schemes were canvassed, particularly in the grocery trade, for groups of small traders to combine their purchases to secure the better terms which their bulk-buying rivals enjoyed. Attempts were sometimes made to persuade manufacturers not to grant favourable discounts to large-scale buyers. Local agreements on retail prices appeared to be a promising method of preserving profit margins, and local associations of grocers, chemists or tobacconists attempted to introduce minimum price lists and to secure adherence to them. But not all retailers belonged to the sponsoring associations, and the larger firms generally refused to be parties to price agreements. Members themselves found it difficult to honour their undertakings when non-members were cutting below the agreed prices, whose one-sided maintenance made new entry and price-cutting profitable. The numerous reports of the failure of price-fixing agreements constantly refer to the 'troublesome minority' and to the fact that 'one cutter makes many'.[17] There were no effective measures of enforcement against members or non-members.

[15] Editorial, *G.*, 9 January 1904, p. 86.

[16] Letter in *C. & D.*, 2 May 1896, p. 643. For a similar view, see *TTR*, June 1895, p. 212.

It would be incorrect to ascribe the success of the new types of establishment wholly to their buying power.

[17] Quoted from *TTR*, January 1895, p. 2.

The success of proprietary articles gave new hope to retailers after other attempts at meeting or neutralising the competition of larger or more efficient or enterprising firms had met with limited success. The attitude of the 'legitimate' trade towards proprietary articles tended to become ambivalent. On the one hand the retailer saw in them a threat to the value of skill and experience in retailing and a direct means to intensified competition. On the other hand, branded goods offered prospects of securely enforced minimum retail prices because each manufacturer was in a position to control the supply of his brands to retailers and so to discipline price-cutters by withholding supplies.[18] According to Glyn-Jones the 'first axiom is that the key to the situation lies in the manufacturer's hands; he it is who can control supplies, and without this control . . . it would be impossible to arrange matters by mutual consent of the traders'.[19] Retailers who were anxious to proscribe retail price competition perceived that the manufacturer of a proprietary, by virtue of being its sole source of supply, had the means of withholding supplies from particular retailers; and that this power was not enjoyed by any one manufacturer of an unbranded staple line.[20]

Two specific examples of the numerous reported failures may be mentioned. A member of Southampton Grocers' Association: 'We have in the past endeavoured to do all in our power to regulate somewhat the retail prices of goods, especially what we term leading articles or well-known brands of goods. This, we regret to say, has not been so successful as we should have hoped it would be; and since fresh difficulties have cropped up in the shape of new competition, it has made our scheme still more unworkable.' *G.*, 16 August 1890, p. 269.

'It has often been said that it is impossible to maintain prices for any length of time by purely voluntary agreement amongst local chemists, and the position in Glasgow proves the case.' Here all chemists had agreed to charge certain minimum prices for some brands, and the arrangements worked well for two years. Then Boots Ltd opened a branch and could not see their way clear to join the arrangement, which came to grief. *PATA Yearbook*, 1904, p. 94.

[18] Thus the decision of Tate's, in 1898, to brand and packet their sugar in 2-lb and 4-lb packages had a mixed reception from grocers. Some complained of an 'attempt to capture a most important source of profit by making it a proprietary article'. *G.*, 18 June 1898, p. 1666. Others appear to have favoured the decision, because the refiners undertook to guarantee a minimum retail gross margin on an article that was notoriously subject to price-cutting. See 'Notes on Novelties', *G.*, 11 June 1898, Supplement, p. 12.

[19] *G.*, 10 October 1896, Supplement, p. 40.

[20] See, for example, the remarks of John Williams, a leader of the price maintenance movement in the grocery trade, in *ACR*, February 1898, p. 65; and of Glyn-Jones in *G.*, 19 February 1898, p. 468.

Resale price maintenance or protected prices (to use the earlier term) for branded goods came to be regarded by large numbers of retailers as the most promising device by which gross profits could be maintained or raised, and by which competitors could be deprived of their most important method of attracting customers and of enlarging their trade. Glyn-Jones was aware that 'the public did not expect chemists to work for nothing, but they would certainly go where they could get things cheapest. That was the only reason of their forsaking the chemist for the stores. But if the prices were all fixed, there would be no inducement to go to the stores or such places.'[21] To him resale price maintenance '. . . was not only a question of ensuring a better profit on proprietary articles, but, what was more important to them, to rob the cutter and stores of the advantage which followed their sale of these goods to the public'.[22]

4

Retailers who were in favour of resale price maintenance had to persuade manufacturers that a system of protected prices for proprietary articles was in their own interests as well as in the interests of the retail trade. The arguments used to support what proved to be a difficult task of persuasion were a mixture of offers of friendship and support, of cajolery and of threats.

The manufacturers were told that they had to choose between the 'legitimate trader or retailer of proprietary articles and the stores, and that they could not obtain the friendship and goodwill of both'.[23] 'The case of the retail druggist must be considered by manufacturers and wholesale dealers, spite of the fact that Mr Boot and similar pushing men are valuable customers . . .'[24] It was argued that in the long run the support of the numerous 'legitimate' retailers was more valuable to manufacturers than that of the large stores, the multiples and other price-cutters. It was contended that the large stores and cutters generally used proprietary articles to build up a reputation

[21] *C. & D.*, 22 May 1897, p. 803.
[22] *C. & D.*, 23 May 1896, p. 748.
In 1896 Boots Ltd advertised their protests against the 'price ring' of the PATA. The fact that 'Boots and company were evidently aware of its importance' made cautious retailers see 'more in this Association than they had thought'. *C. & D.*, 29 August 1896, p. 337. This caused many chemists to join the Association.
[23] Glyn-Jones in *C. & D.*, 2 May 1896, p. 630.
[24] Editorial in *C. & D.*, 3 October 1896, p. 521.

for low prices; but that, having built up a large business, they would progressively dispense with the proprietary articles, when they had served their purpose, and substitute their own productions for them.

Somewhat paradoxically the practice of substitution, which the retailers demonstrated was detrimental to the interests of manufacturers when practised by their successful retail competitors, also served to support their other main line of argument. It was argued that 'the interests of the manufacturers and the retailers are identical ... and if the former can insure a fair profit for the latter, they will at the same time directly benefit themselves'. But if the manufacturers were not prepared to help the retailers to secure a 'living' profit, 'it is possible for the grocers to influence the public in their demands, and to direct them into channels which are profitable – for the grocers'.[25]

5

It was realised that the arguments would not impress manufacturers favourably unless they were presented and reiterated by organised bodies representing large numbers of retailers. The demand for protection would have been ineffective without strong organised backing; neither the offers of friendship nor the threats of trade opposition would have appeared substantial. What was insignificant when practised loosely by individual small-scale retailers would become more serious when retailers were organised and could speak and act with some measure of solidarity. 'The retailers held a powerful weapon, for it was evident that manufacturers must join [the PATA] if retailers combined to boycott their goods.'[26] It would be apparent to manufacturers 'if chemists joined the association in sufficient numbers that they could not withstand the organised opposition of a combined trade'.[27]

By the early 1890s there were numerous local associations of retail traders in various branches of retailing. Many of these interested themselves in the prices of branded goods. National federations of the local grocers' and tobacconists' associations were founded in 1891; both attempted to further the cause of price maintenance and were responsible in the 1890s and subsequently for negotiations with

[25] Editorial in *G.*, 17 September 1887, p. 464.
[26] Glyn-Jones at PATA dinner, reported in *C. & D.*, 25 June 1898, p. 1016. Generally the word 'boycott' was not used by leaders of the movement.
[27] Glyn-Jones in *C. & D.*, 20 February 1897, p. 317.

manufacturers. In the chemists' trade the Proprietary Articles Trade Association (PATA) was founded in 1895 by Glyn-Jones and came into operation in 1896. At first its functions were narrowly confined to resale price maintenance and related issues. It was composed of manufacturers, wholesalers and retailers pledged to the promotion of the practice of price protection; but there is no reason to doubt its founder's denial 'that the movement was a manufacturers' movement in its origin. It started with the retail trade.'[28]

The various trade associations gathered strength slowly, and some of them suffered occasional setbacks. At the end of the period under consideration many 'legitimate' retailers (almost certainly the majority) were not subscribing members of their respective local and national trade organisations. Nevertheless, from the beginning these organisations were formulating the demands and pressing for them on behalf of larger numbers of retailers than their membership lists would have indicated.[29] Apart from the PATA, they were not solely concerned with price protection, but also presented the views of the 'legitimate' trade on other matters, such as the enactment and administration of legislation affecting the trade.

It was Glyn-Jones's wish to form one large organisation for propagating and administering resale price maintenance in as many branches of trade as possible. 'The advantages of joining forces under one organisation instead of the various trades each running its own separate organisation goes without saying. Our agitation is only one feature of what sooner or later must be a keen fight between individual traders as a class and the huge trading companies which are daily being formed to utilise cheap money. The struggle between the one-shop trader and the would-be trading monopoliser [i.e. the multiples] is common to all businesses, and, in so far as chemists are traders, they have interests in common with the single-shop dealer, whether grocer or ironmonger. Each trade has its grievances against another. These must be sunk in order to effect a union of forces in the common interests of all traders. The wider and more diffused the influence of the PATA the better will be its chance of

[28] Glyn-Jones in *G.*, 5 June 1897, p. 1411.

This assurance of the origins of the association was given on many occasions; some retailers were apprehensive of any association which they believed to be a product of the initiative of manufacturers.

[29] On the other hand not all members of the National Federation of Grocers' Associations were in favour of its declared policy of promoting price protection.

complete success. At present the law allows us to combine, but an attempt may be made to alter that law. In such a case it would be of immense advantage to be able to influence our legislators through a united organisation of shop-keepers.'[30] The grandiose objective was not achieved; but the gradual success of the PATA greatly influenced developments in other trades.

6

The manufacturer, when considering whether or not to yield to retailer demands to protect his prices, faced a difficult problem of assessment. Some but not all retailers were in favour of the proscription of price competition; the manufacturer had to judge the relative strengths of the two broad groups of supporters and opponents, as well as the relative severity of the damage each group was likely to inflict upon him if dissatisfied with his decision.

Several of the important retailers who opposed resale price maintenance made known their views to the manufacturers; in the chemists' trade the battle of words between the supporters and opponents of protected prices was waged in the trade press with much skill and vigour. The opponents included the large stores and multiples as well as price-cutting firms generally. In addition, the co-operative societies and private firms paying patronage dividends to customers were against resale price maintenance, particularly (or only)[31] if the payment of dividends on purchases to customers was interpreted (as the 'legitimate' trade demanded) as an infringement of minimum resale price stipulations.

[30] Interview reported in *C. & D.*, 19 June 1897, p. 947.
The statement quoted above was made as a partial answer to the question which worried many chemists, why Glyn-Jones was so active at the time in efforts to organise an anti-cutting movement among grocers, who were regarded by many chemists as their most serious adversaries after the stores and multiples. The rest of the answer was that those manufacturers who sold their products through both chemists and grocers would not protect their prices unless grocers, too, pressed their demands for protection.
The 'grievances' referred to in the statement would seem to point to the chemists' traditional complaint about the sale of patent medicines by grocers.
[31] See circular letter issued by the Co-operative Wholesale Societies after the PATA had decided that customer dividends infringed the principle of minimum retail prices. The circular stated that 'we have never refused to conform to the conditions imposed by manufacturers so long as they did not affect any co-operative interest or infringe any co-operative principle'. The circular is reproduced in *G.*, 7 April 1906, Supplement, p. 8.

Manufacturers were almost certainly aware that the opponents of resale price maintenance, if thwarted by its introduction, would be in a strong position to extend the sales of substitute brands. Frequently they were large firms, well able to advertise widely and to finance production. Fears of their ability and determination to commence or to extend their own production or to promote substitute brands, if particular proprietaries were protected, would in retrospect have been justified. After six leading tobacco manufacturers in 1896 had entered into an 'anti-cutting compact' with the organised retailers to protect the resale prices of packet tobaccos,[32] the leading multiple firm (Salmon and Gluckstein Ltd) extended the range of its own manufactures. A circular was issued to customers announcing 'a series of new tobaccos' brought out 'as a means of meeting the inevitable demand consequent upon the attempted artificial inflation in prices of proprietary tobaccos'.[33] Harrods, the department store, appear to have withdrawn protected articles from their widely circulated price lists.[34] In 1906, after the PATA had decided that the payment of dividends to consumers was a breach of minimum price stipulations, the Co-operative Wholesale Societies notified the retail societies that they would cease to sell PATA articles: 'Wherever practicable, we propose to manufacture or pack articles to replace those withdrawn, which, together with preparations manufactured by firms unconnected with the PATA, will enable you to supply your members with little, if any, inconvenience.'[35]

On the other hand, 'legitimate' retailers could express their displeasure with non-protected brands by attempting to substitute other brands, by refusing to co-operate in manufacturers' sales-promotion efforts and, generally, by keeping 'unprofitable' lines in the back of the shop or under the counter. In the drug trade dispensing chemists had the facilities and skill to devise and prepare substitutes for many proprietary lines;[36] and many tobacconists and grocers had selections

[32] For an account of the 'compact', see footnote 62.

[33] *TTR*, January 1897, p. 4.

[34] See letter reproduced in *The Stationery Trades Journal*, September 1905, p. 444.

[35] Circular reproduced in *G.*, 7 April 1906, Supplement, p. 8. In a later circular the Co-operative Wholesale Society indicated its own preparations and the brands for which they were replacements. The list included substitutes for some brands which were not on the PATA list, *ACR*, September 1906, p. 185.

[36] The proprietors of Beecham's Pills withdrew their membership of the PATA (to which they belonged though their product was not protected) after

of 'own brand' merchandise.[37] Moreover, combinations of retailers could sponsor the production of brands to be distributed solely by members. For example, the London and District Tobacconists' Association introduced a range of its own branded packet tobaccos in 1892,[38] and the Birmingham Association marketed its own brands in 1895.[39] Price maintenance was a much-publicised feature of the last two ventures. Though these attempts were not markedly successful, they served to show that organised retailers could take direct action against the interests of the manufacturers of branded goods. The sponsors of the Birmingham tobacco scheme believed that 'we can only hope to receive practical consideration from others whose proprietary goods are cut, and bear little or no profit, when we learn to work for the good of all tobacconists in enabling them to own their own brands'.[40] According to a leading London tobacconist the manufacturers 'did not seem inclined to do anything until the retailers could show them something to make them alter their views'.[41]

Manufacturers had to take into account the likely effects of the increased retail prices which would follow the adoption of price protection. Sales were likely to be affected adversely. Moreover, it was not unlikely that an increase in retail price would make it easier for retailers to substitute other brands; the public would be less

the *Anti-Cutting Record*, the organ of the PATA, had published a letter from a chemist giving his formula for a pill which he substituted for Beecham's. See *ACR*, November 1898, p. 3.

[37] In some cases the initiative was taken by manufacturers who were prepared to pack articles carrying the retail buyer's name. A cocoa manufacturer advertised such services under the heading, 'War to Proprietary Cocoas'. *G.*, 2 March 1901, pp.40–1.

[38] It was resolved to follow this course after a motion to approach the manufacturers once more to secure price protection had been defeated. *TTR*, June 1892, p. 160.

[39] Other tobacconists' associations were encouraged to handle the brands.

[40] Statement by sponsors of Birmingham scheme, *TTR*, November 1896, p. 502.

[41] *TTR*, June 1897, p. 292.

In negotiations with retail organisations, tobacco manufacturers were apt to express their resentment of the practice of retailers having their 'own brands'. In a conference in 1896 a group of manufacturers complained that the retailers were 'taking up arms against the manufacturers'. *TTR*, September 1896, p. 383. In 1901 another group made acceptance of proposals for price protection of their goods conditional upon an undertaking that 'every retailer . . . would forfeit the right of using brands of tobaccos, cigars, and cigarettes in his own name'. *TTR*. September 1901, p. 406.

unwilling to accept substitutes if their otherwise preferred brands had become more expensive.[42]

Finally, manufacturers could not be certain that those retailers who were agitating for price maintenance would refrain from substitution once resale prices were protected. In the chemists' trade, for example, in the earlier years of the PATA, there is evidence that substitution by the 'legitimate' trade continued even after brands had been added to the protected list. Retail members of the PATA were not required to bind themselves not to substitute for protected articles.[43]

7

The relevance of the considerations enumerated in the preceding section is evident from the explanations of manufacturers who were not willing to introduce resale price maintenance. For example, a chocolate and cocoa manufacturer explained that 'we have never adopted the system of compulsory selling prices, as we find that a large number of our friends prefer to be free'.[44] Another manufacturer complained in a retail trade journal that 'it is not a pleasant experience to have to refuse business from buyers who are in a position to place large orders, simply because they are cutting grocers, and the task of following up retailers who are not adhering to regular rates, and endeavouring to induce them to fall into line, is a very thankless and sometimes a very hopeless one'.[45] A manufacturer of a popular proprietary medicine, in turning down an invitation to join the PATA, noted that the association had 'considerably under 2,000 retail members, and that 2,000 could not be placed in the balance for sales of proprietaries against the various

[42] This consequence of higher prices was stressed by Jesse Boot, the founder of Boots Ltd, and by the Managing Director of Day's Southern Drug Company Ltd, of Southampton, in *C. & D.*, 31 October 1896, p. 666, and 24 October 1896, p. 612.

[43] The chairman at a PATA meeting announced that 'there was an impression abroad that the members of the association must agree not to substitute. Nothing of the kind would be asked, and it would be left to the discretion of the members.' *C. & D.*, 18 April 1896, p. 560. When the PATA contemplated a change in its policy by ruling that patronage dividends were a form of price-cutting, a firmer attitude towards substitution by retailers was promised as a *quid pro quo* for the sacrifice required of manufacturers.

[44] Letter of Fry and Sons, in *G.*, 2 February 1901, p. 299. The firm added that 'whenever the trade in any town desire to regulate prices we have done our best to assist them'.

[45] Letter of BP Co. Ltd, in *G.*, 12 December 1903, p. 1582.

big firms'.[46] Leading tobacco manufacturers in 1896 were reported as having said that 'on account of the very large purchases of packet tobaccos made by these cutting firms all over the country, they did not think they could afford to say that unless these firms would raise their prices they must close their accounts'.[47]

There is much evidence pointing to the importance attached to the damaging effects of retail price increases. The proprietors of Pears soap in a letter to the PATA pointed out that the adoption of price maintenance 'would necessitate one of two courses: increasing the price to the public or diminishing it to the trade – both of which are impossible, as should be obvious to you'.[48] Jas. Hennessy and Company of Cognac explained to a grocer who appealed for price protection that 'there are two sides to the question. Yours, from the trade point of view [in favour of protection], is undoubtedly sound, and [protected prices] would make the retailer more anxious to sell our brandy. But from our point of view, the point is, would the public buy less if the price was raised?'[49]

The importance of the effect of resale price maintenance on the level of the retail price is further borne out by the fact that many manufacturers were unwilling to risk their brands under resale price maintenance unless their competitors did likewise. They seem to have been anxious not to give their rivals any competitive advantage in the retail market. This reluctance to act alone was particularly strong in the tobacco trade. A retail trade journal noted 'that little assistance is to be expected from them [the manufacturers]. In these competitive times they have to fight for their own hand, and when they profess to be eager to block the channels of supply, so far as the cutters are concerned, we may applaud their sentiments (which are splendid), but we may doubt whether they will have any practical effect.'[50] Leading tobacconists expressed the view that nothing useful would come of the retail trade agitation for protected prices until the manufacturers were combined for the purpose;[51] and the retail

[46] *ACR*, April 1904, p. 94.　　[47] *TTR*, September 1896, p. 382.
[48] *ACR*, September 1906, p. 185.

The editorial comment was that 'any one of the 220 something members of the PATA Manufacturers' Section might with as much truth (or as little) say that his goods were entirely exceptional and should be used as cheap sprats for catching dearer mackerel'.

[49] Correspondence published in *G.*, 16 December 1905, p. 1631.
[50] Editorial, *TTR*, November 1891, p. 339.
[51] *TTR*, February 1893, p. 47.

organisations were active in attempting to promote such combinations among the reluctant manufacturers. The first step to introduce resale price maintenance was taken by six manufacturers in concert (in 1896) only after several meetings had been arranged by the principal retail trade organisation.

The fear of being placed at a competitive disadvantage in the consumer market because of price maintenance was also present in other trades. A manufacturer of chemists' goods and a member of the PATA stated that 'they were not without competitors, but if the proprietors of kindred articles agreed to add their articles to the list [of protected articles] his firm would be most happy to do so'.[52] A manufacturer of grocery products stated that 'we have frequently tried to protect prices of our own brands, but found it was impossible, as the grocers themselves were only too ready to buy elsewhere for a cutting line. . . . The only conclusion we can come to is that it is impossible for the manufacturer to protect prices of his own specialities unless both the wholesaler and retailer are willing to meet him half-way by binding themselves not to buy goods of a similar nature from other firms and this we have not up to now found them willing to do.'[53]

The introduction of resale price maintenance could be successful only if the active support of the 'legitimate' retail trade outweighed all the disadvantages. The testimony of firms who discovered that the policy of protection was rewarding is therefore of interest. The proprietors of Hall's coca wine, one of the first items on the PATA protected list, announced that 'we are more than satisfied that it pays us to support the ordinary shopkeeper in a fair minimum profit. In maintaining this position we have lost the goodwill of some of the large co-operative societies, but our loss in this direction has been more than made up by the increased sales of the retail trade.'[54] The proprietors of Scott's pills were 'glad to say that the increased sales of their pills proved that they were right in their belief' that the public would not resent a higher retail price. They added that 'formerly they had the greatest difficulty in getting [retailers] . . . to exhibit showcards or distribute handbills, or in any way assist the sale of their pills. Now, however, they were having applications for

[52] Representative of Oppenheimer, Sons & Co. Ltd, at PATA meeting, *C. & D.*, 26 September 1896, p. 487.
[53] *Advertising*, March 1903, pp. 449, 450.
[54] Circular quoted in *C. & D.*, 20 November 1897, p. 808.

handbills, etc., from hundreds of retailers in all parts of the country.'[55]

8

The difficulty of assigning weights to the various conflicting considerations and the uncertainty of the outcome of the adoption of price maintenance were reflected in the hesitant approaches of manufacturers. The opinion of the trade was frequently canvassed. For example, Lever Brothers in a letter to the trade press asked, 'what support would be given by the trade generally to the manufacturer who risked his trade in order to put a stop to the cutting evil?'[56] Sanitas Co. Ltd conducted a poll of the trade to discover whether it should place its products on the PATA list.[57]

Many manufacturers were careful not to offend the 'legitimate' trade, even if the demands for price protection were to be left unsatisfied. Rejections tended to be conciliatory. Firms expressed their regrets, stressed the difficulties, asked for information, postponed decisions or sheltered behind the obvious division of opinion in the retail trade on the subject of price protection.[58]

Some manufacturers adopted compromise solutions, apparently in an endeavour to retain as much as possible of the goodwill of *all* retailers with the minimum of sacrifices. The following are some of the compromises which were adopted by manufacturers: some became subscribing members of the PATA but did not place their brands on the protected list;[59] some introduced price maintenance with very low margins of retail profits,[60] sometimes after having

[55] Statement at PATA meeting, *C. & D.*, 26 September 1896, p. 487.
[56] Letter of Lever Brothers, *G.*, 10 September 1887, p. 414.
[57] Advertisement, *C. & D.*, 16 October 1897, p. xviii.
Partly as a result of the replies the firm decided not to introduce resale price maintenance; instead, some concessions were made to the trade. See *C. & D.*, 1 January 1898, p. 16, and Advertisement, p. 7; and footnote 63, below. The firm joined the PATA in May 1898 and protected the prices of its products.
[58] For example, see letter of Bovril Ltd to Hull Retail Grocers' Association, *G.*, 16 September 1899, p. 698.
[59] See discussion, *C. & D.*, 26 September 1896, p. 487.
[60] For example, Allen and Hanbury introduced resale price maintenance in 1895 after they had 'been pressed in many quarters to adopt some measures to prevent the cutting prices . . .'. *G.*, 13 April 1895, p. 882. The stipulated minima were cutting prices, according to an editorial in *C. & D.*, 23 March 1895, p. 419, commenting upon a statement to that effect by a leading wholesaler, *C. & D.*, 9 March 1895, p. 352.

obtained the agreement of leading price-cutting firms; in some cases price maintenance was applied to particular regions only, often after consultations with local retail associations;[61] manufacturers sometimes protected some but not all of their brands;[62] some adjusted discount terms to be more favourable for smaller retailers, without any price protection;[63] some firms granted special discount terms to retailers who would undertake to advertise and display the brand, without resale price maintenance being introduced;[64] and many manufacturers introduced price protection schemes without effective enforcement and with numerous protestations of the difficulties.[65] But the main type of compromise was for manufacturers to disregard the payment of patronage dividends as a form of price-cutting, despite the protests of the trade that it was an injurious exception

[61] For example, the proprietors of Beecham's pills, on the initiative of Southampton chemists, introduced price maintenance in that area; the protected margin was low, and the terms had been agreed with an important 'cutting' multiple firm, Day's Southern Drug Co. Ltd. *C. & D.*, 2 October 1897, p. 565. The arrangement was subsequently extended to London after consultations with some of the leading cutters. *C. & D.*, 27 August 1898, p. 383.

[62] The anti-cutting compact of 1896 in the tobacco trade illustrates this and the preceding two types of compromise arrangements. The rates of retail gross margin allowed for in the price schedule were regarded as wholly inadequate by the 'legitimate' trade; the terms had been settled only after the manufacturers had adjourned the negotiations with the retail delegates in order to obtain the views of one of the leading 'cutting' firms, Salmon and Gluckstein Ltd; at first the minimum prices did not apply to the London area; and the compact covered packet tobaccos only, and not cigarettes.

Some patent-medicine manufacturers were members of price maintenance associations or protected the prices of their brands in some other countries but refused to join the PATA or to protect prices in England. See *ACR*, September 1900, p. 209, and October 1900, p. 225.

[63] This was done by Sanitas Ltd, after its poll of trade opinion had been taken (see footnote 57).

[64] See discussion, *ACR*, January 1900, p. 45. The PATA claimed credit for indirectly bringing about the granting of this and other types of compromise concessions in the chemists' trade.

Special discounts for co-operating retailers were granted by some manufacturers after price maintenance had been adopted. Thus one firm (Gosnell's), which was an original member of the PATA though it added its brands to the protected list only in 1898, had special discounts for 'special retail agents' who had to undertake 'not only to stock, but also to push the sale of ... [the] ... specialities in every reasonable way' and 'not to substitute or attempt to supply other than ... [the] ... specialities when asked for them ...', *ACR*, October 1898, p. 241.

[65] This was widespread in the grocery trade, but not confined to it.

to the desired uniformity of retail prices. This compromise was generally adopted until the PATA, in its momentous decision in 1906, reversed its earlier tolerant attitude.

9

Apart from the advantages flowing from the fact that some (possibly influential) sections of the retail trade favoured price protection, there is no evidence that manufacturers believed that uniform retail prices for any one brand carried any other advantages for them. They do not appear to have considered other alleged advantages which today are sometimes adduced in favour of price maintenance. For example, they do not appear to have thought that uniformity of retail prices was necessary for the most effective advertising on a national scale; or that uniform prices eased the consumer's shopping tasks and so disposed him favourably towards the product; or that consumers, judging quality by price, tended to look down upon the cut-price brand. Such arguments were not advanced by those promoting the extension of resale price maintenance;[66] and the behaviour and attitude of manufacturers indicate that they, at best, originally regarded price maintenance as an unfortunate restriction sometimes necessary in order to placate influential sections of the retail trade.

The widespread practice of having 'advertised prices' for branded goods was in use long before the coming of resale price maintenance; and when resale price maintenance came to be introduced the proprietors frequently stipulated minimum resale prices below the advertised prices, which were still marked on containers and referred to in advertisements.[67] It would seem that the advertised price was

[66] Only one reference has been found to this kind of argument in the period under consideration. A correspondent in *The Grocer* observed that he knew of many manufacturers 'who do not like their goods priced lower than those of other makers in the same trade, as this causes it to appear that the higher-priced article is the best'. *G.*, 30 June 1888, p. 1207.

[67] In the grocery trade the use of advertised prices in the advertisements of manufacturers appears to have started in the 1860s. In 1868 a correspondent in *The Grocer* complained of the 'growing practice among manufacturers of advertising retail prices'. It was called an 'unfair and unbusinesslike system', because, so it appears, the practice made it difficult for the grocer to charge his customers *more* than the advertised price. The prevention of 'over-charging' may have been the original purpose of advertised prices. An editorial, commenting on the letter, conceded the force of the complaint in many cases, but considered that 'in the case of specialities uniformity in price is of as much importance as the name of a celebrated maker'. *G.*, 4 January 1868, p. 9. Nevertheless, celebrated

put out as an index of the 'value' of the product,[68] or an indication of the size of the package, and not as an indication of the price at which it was available to the public at retail. In the PATA there appears to have been resistance by some manufacturers against equating their minimum and advertised prices. Elliman's Ltd, perhaps the first manufacturers of branded medicines to have had effective resale price maintenance even before the establishment of the PATA, nevertheless refused to place their brands on the PATA list. The head of the firm objected, *inter alia*, to joining hands with manufacturers, some of whom insisted that the 'advertised price should be the minimum price. He was of opinion that it was absolutely necessary to allow a discount to cash customers, and he thought that it would be found impossible to insist upon full prices being obtained.'[69]

When price maintenance was adopted, manufacturers did not require or insist that their minimum prices should also be maximum prices;[70] though competition tended to bring about this result. Some manufacturer pioneers of price maintenance appear to have envisaged that retail price-cutting of their brands would continue. Their object were merely to prevent what they considered to be excessive cutting, and not to proscribe price competition altogether.[71]

10

Three general tendencies may be discerned in a survey of developments during the period 1885 to 1906. First, the initiative to introduce manufacturers permitted the retail prices of their goods to be cut far below their advertised prices until the beginnings of the price maintenance movement. Until then there does not appear to have been any effort to adopt more realistic advertised prices or to prevent retail price-cutting.

[68] A wholesale chemist expressed his disapproval of the practice: 'They [the public] are deceived into the belief that they are getting 2s. 9d. worth for 2s. 6d., thus making the chemist and other retailer the vehicle for a fraudulent delusion'. *C. & D.*, 8 February 1896, p. 236.

[69] *ACR*, July 1896, p. 13.

He indicated, further, that he was unwilling to join the PATA list because he would not co-operate with manufacturers 'who did not protect the article for which they had the most sale'.

[70] Thus W.D. and H.O.Wills, tobacco manufacturers, when publishing their minimum price schedule in 1899 (a continuation, largely, of the low minimum prices agreed by them and five other firms in 1896) stated: 'In cases where better prices have been obtained we have no desire that they shall be disturbed, our sole object being to fix prices *below* which no retailer must sell'. *TTR*, March 1899, p. 92.

[71] For example, see letter of Lever Brothers, *G.*, 27 September 1890, p. 513.

resale price maintenance did not come from manufacturers, the great majority of whom were reluctant to move in the matter. Secondly, the pace at which the reluctance of manufacturers was overcome depended largely upon the strength of retail organisation. Thirdly, the most effective resistance to the introduction of protected prices came from owners of well-established brands.[72]

Before 1892 few manufacturers were prepared to stop retail cutting of the prices of their brands.[73] There are references in trade journals to the 'masterly inaction' of manufacturers.[74] Proprietors of successful brands had had many years of a highly competitive retail market with considerable and sustained price-cutting, in which the severity of price-cutting was a fair index of the popularity of the brand. New brands had been launched in these conditions, and the successful ones had prospered greatly. There is little wonder that some manufacturers 'have been inclined rather to encourage cutting than otherwise, in the belief that low prices directly lead to increased consumption'.[75]

The manufacturers would not lightly interfere with retail competition or with the supply of their goods to the most successful

[72] The general tendencies were present in the three trades up to 1901; but from 1901 there were changes in the structure of the tobacco-manufacturing industry which broke the continuity of developments in manufacturer–distributor relationships in the tobacco trade. In 1901–2 the American Tobacco Company entered the British market, and its principal British competitors united to form the Imperial Tobacco Company. In the struggle between the two large firms to secure or to enlarge their share of the market the value of the sympathy of the 'legitimate' trade went up considerably. The trade was wooed in many ways, of which the protection of prices by resale price maintenance was an important one. Moreover, the Imperial Tobacco Company, as one move in the struggle, acquired control of the multiple tobacconists, Salmon and Gluckstein, who had been among the most formidable of price-cutters.

The amalgamation of the American and Imperial interests in 1902 put an end to the duopoly struggle and produced a high degree of concentration with one dominant firm in the industry. The firm continued maintaining resale prices. The scope of this article does not make it possible to attempt to trace the development of the dominant firm's marketing policy and the role of resale price maintenance after 1902.

[73] There were few exceptions. The important pioneers appear to have been Elliman's Ltd (medical preparations), Blondeau et Cie (toilet preparations) and Lever Brothers (Sunlight soap).

[74] e.g. editorials in *G.*, 16 August 1890, p. 280, and in *TTR*, August 1895, p. 273.

[75] Editorial, *TTR*, June 1889, p. 155.

retail competitors. The risks of any drastic change in marketing policy, and the uncertainty of the response of different groups of retailers and of the consuming public, were sufficiently great for manufacturers to avoid action until the inducements held out to them by retail organisations or the pressure exerted by them could no longer be ignored. Those supporters of resale price maintenance 'who expected an immediate capitulation of the great proprietors expected a very foolish thing'.[76] Glyn-Jones reported in 1899 that 'the negotiations are exceedingly tedious, but we find there is no help for it. The issues for the large firms are very grave, and they are naturally cautious.'[77]

Glyn-Jones correctly 'emphasised the fact that the size, length and importance of the [PATA] protected list would be almost in direct proportion to the support given to the movement by retailers'.[78] He himself in 1896–7 conducted what was aptly called an anti-cutting crusade in the chemists' trade as well as in the grocery trade; and a similar country-wide tour to solicit support for the tobacconists' organisation was made by its sponsors in 1900–1. The more conspicuous gatherings of retail traders and their demonstrations in favour of price maintenance were apt to convert wavering manufacturers. The Grocery Exhibition of 1896 is said to have persuaded several manufacturers to introduce price maintenance.[79] In 1902 the PATA convened a conference which was attended by delegates from forty-four local chemists' associations. A strong resolution in favour of the PATA method of securing retail profits was carried. 'The result has been that since the conference about fifty proprietors have joined the association, some of them representing articles of largest sale.'[80]

The proprietors of well-established brands were least susceptible to the inducements and pressures of organised retailers. New brands tended to be price maintained from the outset once retail demands for protection were well organised; but the owners of popular lines were more cautious and even defiant. The PATA in 1901 regretted that 'more articles of prime importance have not been included in

[76] Editorial on first protected list of PATA, *C. & D.*, 25 July 1896, p.124. See also editorials, *G.*, 24 June 1893, p. 1386, and 7 September 1893, p. 518.

[77] *G.*, 21 January 1899, p. 143.

[78] *C. & D.*, 23 January 1897, p. 118.

[79] Statement by John Williams, *G.*, 10 February 1900, p. 366.

[80] *PATA Yearbook*, 1904, pp. 22–3.

the list [of protected articles], but it is a matter of satisfaction to note that new proprietaries, as they come out, are placed on the list'.[81]

The reasons for the particularly strong disinclination of owners to place well-known brands under price maintenance are clear. An importer who believed in the wisdom of price maintenance had to concede that this did not apply to the 'mammoth advertisers who claim to create such a demand for their brands that retailers must keep them, and who consequently think it unnecessary to consider the retailing interest'.[82] It was not easy for retailers to substitute other brands for brands whose names were household words; any retailer who attempted to boycott such brands would merely have driven customers away from his establishment. Advertisements which warned against substitution were not uncommon.[83] Moreover, manufacturers were loath to disturb low prices and channels of distribution which had been established for long periods.[84] On the other hand, the owner of a new brand could select his methods of distribution and his retail price without having to interfere with existing arrangements; and he was more dependent upon the goodwill of substantial sections of the retail trade.

The policy of Bovril Ltd provides a useful illustration of the operation of the forces described in this section. This firm produced various products, some of which were sold mainly by chemists and others mainly by grocers. None of its products appears to have been protected before the establishment of the PATA. The PATA was

---

[81] Report of PATA in *G.*, 20 July 1901, p. 143. For the grocery trade, see John Williams' remarks, *G.*, 10 February 1900, p. 366, and Glyn-Jones's remarks, *G.*, 19 October 1901, p. 928.

[82] Managing director of Australian Wine Importers Ltd, *G.*, 18 October 1890, p. 662.

An editorial in *Advertising* (May 1903, p. 599) noted that 'not one of the largest advertising concerns is among the manufacturing members of the PATA'.

[83] The proprietors of Beecham's pills issued an advertisement warning the public 'if an effort is made by any retailer to induce them to take any other remedy when Beecham's Pills have been asked for – that the article offered as a substitute invariably carries more profit, and will not give the same satisfaction to the purchaser'. *ACR*, December 1898, p. 23.

[84] The strength of the position of well-established brands was recognised by the PATA at an early date. From 1898 well-known brands were admitted on the protected list even though they carried lower margins of retail gross profit than that originally laid down as a minimum. Sometimes further concessions were made.

originally intended to cover both branches of the retail trade; but in fact its support came almost wholly from chemists. Bovril Ltd placed its chemists' trade line, Invalid Bovril, on the PATA's first protected list; but it did not introduce price maintenance for its predominantly grocery line, Bovril, at the same time. The reason for this differential treatment was 'that they would not put the other in the [protected] list until the grocers took the matter up themselves'.[85] Requests for protection from grocers or local associations met with the reply that price-cutting was 'solely due to the short-sighted policy of the retailers themselves' and that no scheme of price protection was 'free from dangers or difficulties'.[86] Later the firm explained that it could not protect its prices because the grocery trade as a whole had not made up its mind.[87] Finally, in 1901, price protection was introduced for the grocery line, after representations had been made by several active local grocers' associations.[88] In the meantime the firm had added a 'new nutritive', Virol, to the PATA list in 1899 at the time of its appearance on the market.[89]

11

This study of the formative years of resale price maintenance in selected branches of the retail trade points to conclusions, some of which are at variance with views which are sometimes advanced in present-day discussions. It may be useful, therefore, to couch these conclusions, where relevant, in terms of the language of controversies of today.

Before the introduction of resale price maintenance retail price competition was intense. The price-cutters were not ephemeral intruders temporarily upsetting the retail market; they included substantial firms, many of which have survived to this day. The movement for price maintenance grew out of the dangers which price-cutting firms and their successful price policies presented to the profits and existence of large numbers of retailers employing traditional methods of doing business. It was in origin a retailers' movement designed to preserve (or even to enlarge) the share of the retail

[85] According to Glyn-Jones, *G.*, 9 January 1897, p. 76.

[86] Letter of Bovril Ltd, *G.*, 20 March 1897, p. 738.

[87] Letter from Bovril Ltd to a grocers' association, quoted in *G.*, 16 September 1899, p. 698.

[88] See, for example, report of Birmingham Grocers' Association, *G.*, 27 July 1901, p. 234.

[89] *ACR*, May 1899, p. 131.

market served by the threatened group of retailers and to improve the profitability of that share. Its object was to prevent competitors from using the offer of low prices in the competitive struggle for business, and its method was to induce manufacturers by persuasion, organised threats and by offers of support to introduce and to enforce minimum retail prices for branded goods.

The retail price competition, which organised retailers sought to remove, was not considered by the owners of branded goods to have been prejudicial to their interests. Manufacturers were reluctant to obstruct price-cutting. The adoption of resale price maintenance was not the inevitable or indispensable adjunct of the policy of branding and advertising. The persuasion of manufacturers to the point of view that it was in their interests to protect retail prices was a slow and difficult process, in which the strength of retail sentiment and organisation in favour of the practice appears to have been among the decisive considerations. Manufacturers protected prices not because of the 'damage' their brands suffered at the hands of price-cutting retailers; they appear to have done so because of the reactions of the numerous retailers who disliked the results of price competition.

Some present-day advocates of resale price maintenance contend that retail price competition produces 'chaos' and 'instability' in retail markets, which are harmful to consumers. However, there is no evidence that, before the introduction and spread of resale price maintenance, consumer interests were injured and not promoted by the prevailing competition. It was because consumers showed their appreciation of low prices by supporting the price-cutting retailers that the competitors of the latter wished to have resale prices protected. For the same reason manufacturers were not eager to raise the prices of their brands or interfere with the business policies of successful retailers.

Addendum

As is stated in the intoductory paragraph of the article, the forces at work in the three selected branches of retailing were also present in other branches. Small-scale retailers using traditional methods of trading were under strong and increasing competitive pressures. Their stock response was to organise, to urge manufacturers to protect them against competition and to impress upon them that it was in their own interests to do so.

'The tones of a few individuals, however dulcet and sweet, will not charm the soul of the manufacturer who seeks his own ends and has no care for his customers. ... But let the gentle tones of the feeble be transformed in the ponderous clamour of the strong, and respectful attention will be shown.'[90] In words such as these (quoted from a journal in the hardware trade) retailers in various trades who were threatened or injured by competition were urged to join forces. A few years later the same trade journal quoted the following words of the general secretary of the Ironmongers Federated Association: 'This matter [price maintenance] ... I view as one of the main planks of our programme, and it is to a great extent the salvation, at any rate, of the small retail shopkeeper. Unless it is vigorously prosecuted, and kept to the fore, and where manufacturers who have adopted it are given all the support we possibly can, the small shopkeeper will, year by year, have a greater struggle to exist.'[91] Shortly afterwards the journal reported that the association and 'the other retail trade organisations have very seriously hampered the London stores in the carrying out of the policy which controls their business by the progress which has been made in price maintenance'.[92]

It is clear that the movement for price maintenance was directed in large measure against the large-scale retailing firms. The manufacturers whose co-operation was sought had to choose between the organised supporters of price maintenance and those, largely unorganised, who were opposed to the practice. After Reeves and Sons had introduced price maintenance for their colour boxes, the firm reported that it lost business with such large firms as Boots, Harrods and the Army and Navy Stores which had withdrawn the brand from their catalogues. But the over-all results were 'entirely satisfactory, for ... the great increase in trade from other sources *far out-balances* our loss of business with those houses'.[93] The firm's principal competitors in manufacturing had not then price-maintained their rival brands. Price-maintaining manufacturers were sometimes less fortunate in that they tended on balance to lose business to their competitors who had not introduced price maintenance. An interesting example relates to pens. The makers of certain pens had introduced price maintenance, but had to set their

[90] *Hardware Trade Journal*, April 1900, p. 36.
[91] Ibid., 11 May 1906, p. 142.   [92] Ibid., 29 June 1906, p. 342.
[93] *Stationers' Gazette*, November 1906, p. 385.

resale prices at about 25 per cent lower in 'certain large centres' than in the rest of the country. The explanation was that competing manufacturers refused to price-maintain their brands which were resold at relatively low prices in the more competitive large centres.[94] Another example relates to sporting cartridges. Kynochs, having introduced price maintenance for one of their brands, lost business because the 'cutters' were selling non-maintained brands more cheaply. The firm introduced a new brand, also price-maintained it, but priced it to resell more cheaply than its established brand.[95]

It was therefore important for organised retailers to support co-operative manufacturers. '. . . They must be consistent. If manufacturers gave them a guaranteed profit they must support them. When one manufacturer gave them fair play and another was pandering to their opponents they must encourage the one who was doing the fair things. . . .'[96] This is how the matter was viewed by one ink manufacturer: 'At the present moment there were many ink firms quite willing to fall into line with the [price maintenance] association, but there were other firms who did not yet see their way clear. It was for the retailers to force the hands of the manufacturers.'[97]

The development of resale price maintenance in the book trade in the 1890s was broadly similar to that in other trades. Some differences may be noted. First, retail price competition on a large scale developed rather earlier in the book trade. Once books were being published in standardised form – with all copies of an edition being identical in format and binding – the basis was established for effective price competition among retailers. By the middle of the nineteenth century price competition was common, and the attempts at resale price maintenance, abandoned after public protest in 1852, were largely ineffective. Second, the retail price competition in books in the second half of the nineteenth century was primarily within the ranks of small and medium-scale retailers. Large-scale retailing firms were relatively unimportant, although some of the large department stores helped to extend the area of competitive prices through their catalogues. The largest retailing firm in the book trade, W. H. Smith

---

[94] *Stationers' Gazette*, June 1906, p. 195.

[95] *Hardware Trade Journal*, 28 September 1906, p. 319.

[96] *The Ironmonger*, 7 May 1904, quoted in W. H. B. Court, *British Economic History 1870–1914: Commentary and Documents*, Cambridge, 1965, p. 249.

[97] *Stationers' Gazette*, November 1906, p. 371.

and Son, in fact remained largely aloof from price competition in the 1890s, presumably because its numerous railway bookstalls were insulated by location from the pressures of price competition. Third, in the book trade, unlike in some other retail trades, there was little if any scope for retailers to influence sales away from or in favour of particular publishers. Bookseller pressure for resale price maintenance had to be directed at publishers as a body, since there was little opportunity for one publisher to be played off against another.

The Net Book Agreement, concluded in 1899, introduced organised resale price maintenance with collectively administered sanctions. The agreement was a triumph for the organised booksellers. The scheme for the maintenance of resale prices was 'drawn up in the interests of the booksellers, as urged by the majority of them and their representatives'. The pressure exercised by the national organisation of booksellers, supported by numerous district associations, was the key to the submission of the publishers, whose spokesman 'made it very clear to the booksellers that we did not enter on this step through any wish of our own. We should be content to let matters go on as they are.' The achievement of their goal, albeit at first on a modest scale, by the organised booksellers was a tribute to their increasing strength. For, only a few years earlier the first president of the publishers' trade organisation, the Publishers' Association, had declared that similar proposals for organised resale price maintenance were neither 'practical' nor 'desirable', and had expressed the hope that the association would 'never fall to the level of a ring' to 'raise prices, and to maintain them by the coercion of those who did not obey its regulations'. The arrangements agreed to in 1899 provided for just such a ring.[98]

The introduction of resale price maintenance in the various trades involved the raising of resale prices. It is not easy to measure the extent of the increase in prices, although there is evidence that in some cases retail prices went up by as much as a third. The general order of magnitude of price increase in the book trade can be indicated more readily. The scheme accepted in 1899 recommended that existing titles, if placed under resale price maintenance, should have their published prices (off which retailers were giving dis-

[98] For a detailed discussion, with documentation, of the origins of resale price maintenance in books, see my 'Price Maintenance of Books in Britain: The Historical Background', in *Essays in Honour of Marco Fanno*, Padua, 1966, pp. 754–76.

counts of 25 per cent, and occasionally more) reduced by one-sixth and treated as the 'net' maintained resale price. This implied an effective increase of one-ninth in the retail price paid by the public. New titles issued *ab initio* as net books generally carried higher retail gross margins than books converted into net books after 1899.

It is surprising that the widespread adoption of resale price maintenance in various trades in the period 1890–1910 did not provoke more public protest – for little interest appears to have been displayed in the press or elsewhere. (This is in marked contrast to the agitation against the attempts to enforce price maintenance in the book trade in 1851–2.) Perhaps what Alfred Marshall said in 1898 about resale price maintenance in the book trade applied more generally: 'I find people to whom I talk generally approve the net system, in so far as it aims at raising the status of the bookseller in a moderate way. But they do not know what the net system is: and when I tell them they are incredulous.'[99] But it is difficult to believe that consumers were unaware of the increases in price occasioned by the introduction of price maintenance. These could be observed directly, and attention was drawn to them by some of the large retailer opponents of the practice. (The supporters of price maintenance certainly made no attempt to argue that the practice did not raise prices.)[100] Perhaps the spread of price maintenance was not rapid enough to excite protest. Or perhaps there was widespread sympathy with small-scale retailers and recognition of their right to organise in their own interests at a time when other economic groups, manufacturers as well as workers, were freely engaged in collective action in the promotion of their sectional interests.

[99] Letter from A. Marshall to F. Macmillan, in C. W. Guillebaud, 'The Marshall–Macmillan Correspondence over the Net Book System', *Economic Journal*, September 1965, p. 532.

[100] Thus supporters of price maintenance often argued to the effect that the cutting of retail prices was not in response to any expressed desire on the part of the consuming public. For example: 'It seems ridiculous that all those [dealers] handling cartridges should have to handle them at cut profits when there is no demand on the part of the shooting public for a decreased price of sport.' *Hardware Trade Journal*, 11 May 1906, p. 156.

14

THE RAW COTTON COMMISSION, 1948–52*

On 1 January 1948 the Raw Cotton Commission became the sole importer and seller of raw cotton in Great Britain. The Act setting up the commission[1] provided for the appointment of a chairman, either one or two full-time members (the 'independent members'), and not more than ten part-time members. All but two of the part-time members were required to have special knowledge of the cotton textile industry, and the independent members could, but need not, be similarly qualified.[2] The commission had a monopoly of the importation and sale of raw cotton until September 1952, when, on the recommendation of the Cotton Import Committee[3] set up to review the position, private importation was again permitted as an alternative to purchase from the commission. After a further committee[4] had reviewed the working of this arrangement, the Conservative government introduced a Bill in November 1953 providing for the winding up of the commission, and it is now in process of liquidation. The time is appropriate, therefore, to consider the extent to which the expectations both of those who advocated the creation of the commission and of those who opposed it have been borne out by the commission's activities and experience during its life as a monopolist trading in raw cotton.[5]

* (With J. Wiseman): *Oxford Economic Papers*, February 1956, pp. 1–34.

[1] The Cotton (Centralised Buying) Act, 1947, 10 and 11 Geo. 6, ch. 26.

[2] The Board of Trade was responsible for appointments to the commission, and (together with the Treasury) for general regulation of its financial activities. It also had powers to direct the commission 'on matters appearing to the Board to affect the public interest', but there is no evidence that it did so.

[3] *Report of the Cotton Import Committee*, Cmd. 8510, April 1952.

[4] *Report of the Cotton Import (Review) Committee*, Cmd. 8861, June 1953.

[5] We do not consider, save incidentally, the activities of the commission after the withdrawal of its monopoly power. We also do not attempt to appraise the wisdom of the decision to restore private trading in cotton in September 1952 rather than earlier or later. Further, we do not consider whether a body like the commission might not be used for purposes other than those contemplated by

1. THE ORIGINS OF THE COMMISSION

Private trading in raw cotton and in cotton futures was suspended during the Second World War, and was replaced by a government agency, the Cotton Control. The problem facing the control was, simply, to ensure adequate supplies of reasonable cottons to enable the cotton textile industry to fulfil its wartime functions. Price, though of some relevance, became a secondary consideration. The control accordingly began to negotiate bulk contracts from 1942, and succeeded by this policy in building up stocks from the danger-ously low 1941 level of 178,000 tons to a peak of 411,000 tons in 1945. Cotton textile production was concentrated on utility goods and on material for the armed forces, with emphasis on quantity rather than quality in production. Cotton was sold to spinners in bulk by description only; prior sampling and selection were pre-cluded by the need for speedy removal of goods from dangerous port areas.[6] The system worked fairly smoothly in wartime. Market conditions were quite different from those of peacetime. Prices were decided by use of a formula such that spinners, operating to guaran-teed margins, had no special incentive to make careful selection of the type of cotton to be used in manufacture.

This procurement system was similar to that adopted for other raw materials. After the war, however, when other raw material markets were reopened, or indications given that reopening waited solely upon suitable trading conditions, the cotton market was singled out for special treatment as a relatively small and unobtrusive element in the Labour Party's nationalisation programme. Cotton purchasing and trading were nationalised by the Cotton (Centralised

its creators; in particular, we do not discuss whether a body like the Raw Cotton Commission could be used as an instrument for subsidising the cotton textile industry.

[6] Cotton is not a homogeneous commodity; growths from different regions vary in the length of the cotton fibre (staple) and in the intrinsic qualities of the cotton (grade): some fibres, for example, spin a 'softer' yarn than others and are thereby better suited to particular spinning and weaving purposes. Also, cotton can be more or less well packed, unstained, free from dirt, and so on (see n. 14). In these circumstances, the accurate description of cottons, and (for those with very special requirements) such facilities as sampling of the cotton before delivery, are an integral part of the peacetime cotton market (see Section 4). Even in the quite different wartime conditions being described, the Cotton Control did arrange to have the cotton it purchased classed and passed in the country of origin.

Buying) Act, 1947. The Act was passed at a time when nationalisation was popular *per se*; it was nevertheless unusual in that raw cotton trading exhibited none of the features the presence of which was used to justify the nationalisation of other branches of economic activity. Raw cotton trading was not significant as a potential source of concentration of economic power; there was in any case no evidence of monopoly in raw cotton buying or selling. It was not a key industry the operations of which might have important effects on many other industries, and no capital investments, of a kind likely to have important secondary effects on general levels of income and employment, were involved. There was no unrest among the trade unions directly concerned,[7] and the operations of the pre-war organised markets had met with only isolated criticism from spinners.[8]

The government's reasons for nationalisation were not entirely unambiguous or unequivocal, but it was clear that the major argument related to the direct economic advantages (in buying, selling, and cover facilities) expected to follow from the creation of a statutory monopoly.[9] In both buying and selling, it was argued, it would be possible to make use of 'centralised knowledge'. In cotton *buying*, the experience of the Cotton Control and the examples of multiple stores and the co-operative movement were adduced as evidence that economies of bulk buying were possible.[10] Long-term bulk-buying agreements with empire producers would not only benefit Britain by providing increased and assured supplies, but would also be of advantage to the producers themselves, by providing an assured market for their produce. Improvement in the actual cotton bought was expected: cotton stocks would be more varied, 'bad

[7] The only unions to express strong views on the matter were concerned with textile *manufacturing*, and had little direct contact with the raw material markets. See, for example, the *Report on Ways and Means of Improving the Economic Stability of the Cotton Textile Industry*, prepared for the President of the Board of Trade in 1943 by the United Textile Factory Workers Association.

[8] See quotation in *House of Commons Debates*, 28 March 1946, col. 630, for an example.

[9] The summary of views (and the comment on their ambiguity) which follows is elicited from *House of Commons Debates*, 28 March 1946 and 2 December 1946, and from the reports of a speech on the subject by Mr Marquand (Secretary for Overseas Trade) to the United Textile Factory Workers Association in May 1946.

[10] See *House of Commons Debates*, 2 December 1946, col. 42 (speech by Mr Marquand).

spinning' prevented,[11] and the buying programme would be decided 'with knowledge of the requirements of the whole industry'. Despite these claims, no more was expected from the buying economies than that they would enable purchase 'at least as economically as by private importation'. When *selling* cotton to spinners, the commission would be able both to 'assure long-term stability for spinners in the price of their materials', and to operate a cover scheme affording 'a very high degree of protection against price changes', including cover of a kind 'which was not afforded . . . before the war' by the Liverpool Cotton Exchange.[12] While there was no direct condemnation of speculation *per se*, the frequent references in parliamentary and other political debate to gambling and to the effect of speculation on cotton prices revealed the dislike on the government side of *private* speculation.

The claims made for a centralised buying agency were received with considerable scepticism by the Opposition party in Parliament and by most spinners.[13] It was pointed out that the Cotton Control provided no reliable evidence about peacetime trading, since it had never operated in a commercial environment. The government buyer, said the critics, would be 'seen a mile off', and attempts by a bulk buyer to exert pressure in world markets would both create political problems and stimulate monopolistic combination among producers. Far from having precise foreknowledge of the industry's requirements, the agency would have to rely on global statistics and would

[11] This practice is explained on pp. 325–6.

[12] See, in particular, *House of Commons Debates*, 2 December 1946, cols. 42–52 (Mr Marquand).

[13] The government made some attempt to claim support among the spinners, and cited a Report of the Federation of Master Cotton Spinners, circulated as long ago as 1928, to the effect that a benefit of grouping or amalgamation of mills was the 'bulk buying of cotton in whichever market offers the best possibilities'. In fact, the Federation joined with the Liverpool and Manchester Cotton Associations in a deputation of protest against the creation of the commission to the Lord President of the Council, and also submitted a memorandum of protest to the Board of Trade. A questionnaire elicited that owners of around 90 per cent of the industry's spindles preferred the pre-war system. The statement of the Cotton Board Committee on Post-War Problems, 1944, on the subject of bulk buying by amalgamations of mills is of interest:

'. . . experience in Lancashire tends to establish that the individual unit, if in efficient hands, has never been at any disadvantage vis-à-vis the combines in these respects. In point of fact the larger concerns have either not resorted to these policies or have not done so on a large scale.'

be unable to deal with small-scale or 'special' requirements.[14] Furthermore, it was argued that raw cotton prices at home could be stabilised only by requiring the government to bear the risks caused by fluctuations in world prices. Speculation would not be prevented by the Act, but would be transferred from informed private specialist dealers to the central agency, which would also be a permanent 'unhedged bull', as it must necessarily bear sole responsibility for ensuring the availability of cotton stocks.

Any appraisal of the commission's activities must take account of the environmental factors set out in the next section. These make it difficult to arrive at completely firm conclusions. Nevertheless, the commission's history does provide useful evidence by which to test the validity of these diverse views and expectations of its original creators and opponents.

2. THE MARKET ENVIRONMENT

World markets were characterised throughout the duration of the commission's monopoly by dollar shortage and by the intervention of governments in the marketing process. About 80 per cent of world cotton production is of American-type cottons. This is composed of US-produced cotton (normally about half the cotton entering world trade is exported from the US) and of broadly substitutable types from other sources. Egypt is the principal producer of another large group of longer-stapled cottons, known as Egyptian-type. The consequence of the world dollar shortage was a shift in the pattern of demand and consumption away from dollar and towards non-dollar sources of cotton. The shift was brought about largely by means of currency controls imposed by cotton-consuming countries, and not by the rationing of dollar cotton supplies by their relative prices. For much of the post-war period non-dollar cottons have been high in price relative to dollar cotton; up to 1951 (i.e.

---

[14] See *House of Commons Debates*, 2 December 1946, col. 138 (Mr Fletcher), for an illustration of this.

The Liverpool Cotton Association illustrated the difficulty of trading in bulk or simply by description in this way:

'. . . one can buy cotton in the United States standardised as Middling in grade, 1-inch in staple. This type of cotton . . . will vary as to colour, bloom, character and strength of staple. One mill may require a bright style of cotton of soft staple, while another may require a rough style with hard staple. Both . . . might be quite correctly shipped as Middling 1-inch. . . .' *Liverpool Cotton Association Pamphlet*, May 1946.

even after devaluation) dollar cotton was still regarded as 'the cheapest cotton in the world'.[15] This situation gave a cost advantage to countries having both supplies of dollars and a cotton textile industry able to use American-type cottons.[16] It also led other cotton-growing countries, which were themselves short of dollars, to favour 'hard-currency' buyers either by creating dual price levels or by prohibiting non-dollar sales. These conditions, together with the various quota schemes described in the next paragraph, so restricted British use of US cotton that only about 21 per cent of British imports of cotton came from the US in the period 1946–8, as against 42 per cent in 1935–8.[17] There is a general belief in the industry that the pre-war proportion would have been approached after the war in the absence of the currency shortages and quota schemes, with favourable effects on the industry's efficiency and competitive position.

Government intervention in the world cotton market during the life of the commission was most important (in terms of results) in the case of America. The US government offered loans to growers on the security of their cotton, conditional upon acreage quota agreements between government and growers. In this way a floor was provided for the price of American cotton, in the absence of which 'it seems certain that the general world level would be substantially lower'.[18] The drawbacks of this scheme from the point of view of the international textile industry were very clearly demonstrated in 1951, when acreage quota restrictions together with low yields per acre reduced the volume of American cotton available so drastically that quantitative export restrictions were imposed and cotton allocated to importing countries by the US government by

[15] See report of speech by H.O.R.Hindley (chairman of the commission) to the Liverpool Economic and Statistical Society. *Manchester Guardian*, 29 October 1949.

[16] Japan and Belgium were in this position.

[17] There was a great increase in the proportion of retained imports coming from the Commonwealth. Empire sources provided 6·3 per cent of the total in 1930–4, and 30·1 per cent in 1952. The proportion fell to 25·2 per cent in the following year, when private importation was permitted as an alternative to purchase through the commission.

[18] See reports of speech by H.O.R.Hindley, loc. cit. While Mr Hindley is perhaps too certain, the view is not unreasonable. To the extent that his argument is valid, there was the piquant situation of the world price of cotton being bolstered by quota restrictions imposed by a country whose own cotton was relatively undervalued in world markets.

means of yet another quota scheme. This had important effects upon the policy of the Raw Cotton Commission and on the British textile industry in general; more dollars were available for the purchase of cotton in 1951 than the commission was able to spend. In Egypt, the government also intervened in the cotton market by the operation of a guaranteed minimum price scheme for growers, and further affected the market at different times by the imposition of export taxes and by direct trading in cotton.[19]

Disturbed market conditions existed when the commission was created. Indeed, the government pointed out that currency shortages would prevent completely free trading in cotton whether the commission existed or not. But general machinery intended to be of a temporary character already existed for dealing with problems of currency shortage, and it was not suggested by the government that the setting up of a permanent commission to trade in this one commodity could be justified by the contemporary scarcity of dollars. It was foreseen that the commission itself might be prevented by the currency situation from providing a complete service to spinners; critics went further and suggested that the dollar shortage would be aggravated by the commission's inability to mobilise and utilise individual buying skills as efficiently as private traders could have done.[20]

In the event, reference to difficulties in world markets came to be the commission's most frequent and general answer to adverse criticism of its activities,[21] and it came to be believed widely that

[19] Soon after the setting up of the Raw Cotton Commission, Egypt reimposed the export tax on cotton, which had been in abeyance for two years, and increased it from the former level of $\frac{1}{2}$d. per lb to $2\frac{1}{2}$d. per lb. Direct intervention was resorted to in 1951–2, when Egyptian prices were falling rapidly. The government entered the market as a heavy buyer in July and September 1951, and again in 1952. These purchases failed to stem the decline, and the Alexandria futures market threatened to break down, some large dealers being unable to meet differences. The government then took up July futures at $125, and removed the export tax for several months.

[20] See, for example, *Memorandum of the Federation of Master Cotton Spinners' Associations, Ltd, to the Board of Trade*, 7 November 1945, para. 15.

[21] '... the commission has been widely and unjustly blamed for shortcomings wholly outside its control. The sensitive fluctuations of demand in relation to price cannot easily be adjusted to the availability of foreign currencies.... In other cotton-growing countries, small crops have created a shortage for domestic use and have led to severe export restrictions. Similarly, the world shortage of dollars has caused increasing competition for non-dollar growths, which may be expected to become even more intense in the future.' *Annual Report of the Raw Cotton Commission*, July 1948, para. 20.

dollar shortages and intervention in the market by foreign governments were the major reasons for the commission's creation and
existence, though this view is not in accord with the facts.[22] Nevertheless, a balanced judgment of the efficiency of the commission's
operations requires that these market conditions be kept in mind,
so that problems created by them can be distinguished from problems
inherent in the nature of public monopoly in cotton trading.

3. THE COMMISSION'S PURCHASING METHODS

After the end of the war the Cotton Control began to replace its
wartime practice of purchasing in bulk quantities by the purchase
of cotton in relatively small individual lots from the agents in
Liverpool of foreign cotton shippers. By the end of 1947 cotton
from America, India, and the Belgian Congo, amounting in that
year to about 33 per cent of total purchases, was being bought by
this means. In Egypt and Brazil the control (and afterwards the
commission) maintained buying offices which classed cotton in the
country of origin and made purchases in that country in direct
competition with other buyers. These offices accounted for 47 per
cent of total purchases in 1947. An essentially similar arrangement
existed in Peru, except that a private British firm acted as buying
agent. Bulk purchasing was being used only in respect of Sudan
cotton (11 per cent of total purchases) and of cotton from other
empire sources (7 per cent of the total).

During its first year the commission abandoned its buying office
in Sao Paulo and the services of its Lima agent, and the method of
purchase through shippers' agents in the UK was extended to
Brazilian and Peruvian cottons. These changes left a buying office
only in Egypt. This office purchased around 40 per cent of the total
Egyptian crop annually; the commission believed it to cause less
disturbance of the market than would the use of shippers' agents. In
any case political considerations, and in particular the censorship
of cables and letters, were thought to make immediate changes
impracticable.[23] The first modifications were made in 1951, when it
was arranged that Egyptian cotton should continue to be purchased
in Alexandria, but against shippers' types approved at the beginning

---

[22] Cf. e.g. *House of Commons Debates*, 18 January 1948 and 7 July 1949.

[23] *Annual Reports*, July 1948, paras. 18 and 19, 1948–9, para. 11, and 1949–50,
para. 11. There is some indication in the 1950 Report that political conditions had
become the main reason for there being no change in methods.

of the cotton season in Liverpool. The quality of shipments was to be passed in Liverpool, and arbitration was to be transferred to that city from Alexandria.[24] In the same season the commission took the further step of inviting offers of cotton in Liverpool as well as in Alexandria, and by the 1952–3 season all requirements were being met by Liverpool offers.[25]

By 1952, then, the commission had largely abandoned the practice of centralised bulk buying which had been so prominent in the minds of its creators;[26] purchase of cotton through shippers' agents at home accounted for all but 18 per cent of the total amount bought,[27] the remainder being obtained mostly through bulk-purchase agreements from the Colonial Empire. These agreements with colonial territories were a continuation of those entered into earlier by the Cotton Control. In view of the claims advanced for bulk purchase when the commission was created, it is worth while to study the subsequent development of the agreements more closely, even though only about one-fifth of total purchases was affected by them. We examine in turn the arrangements made for purchasing cotton from Nigeria, Uganda, and the Sudan.[28] These areas were the important sources of cotton purchased in bulk; they were also areas in which the sale of exported cotton was in the hands of official or semi-official marketing authorities.

From 1940, Nigeria's exportable cotton crop was bought in bulk by the (British) Cotton Control at prices agreed with the colonial marketing authority in advance of each season. The commission took over the outstanding obligations of the Cotton Control, and

[24] *Annual Report*, 1950–1, para. 10.

[25] *Annual Report*, 1951–2, para. 3.

[26] In its *Annual Report*, 1950–1 the commission writes of buying Brazilian on a 'hand to mouth' basis.

[27] The changes in buying methods seem to have brought satisfactory results: the 1948–9 Report says of Brazilian purchases that 'as far as price is concerned it is clear that the change has not been disadvantageous' (para. 29). Some improvement also occurred during the period as a consequence of the growing experience and acumen of the commission itself. This showed itself, for example, in the introduction of a policy of selection of American shippers on the basis of their past record in an effort to improve the quality of shipments, which proved to be 'an unqualified success'. The commission also introduced new Egyptian cotton standards when dissatisfied with the cotton being tendered against Alexandria standards.

[28] On what follows, see the sections of the commission's *Annual Reports* dealing with buying in the regions concerned.

310

at first continued the existing practice of bulk purchase by fixed-price agreements. In 1949 the Nigeria Cotton Marketing Board was established as a statutory marketing monopoly to replace the earlier authority, and in that year the commission and the board entered into an agreement covering the Nigerian exportable surplus of cotton for a period of three years, beginning with the 1949–50 crop. Prices for the year's exportable[29] crop were fixed each October, and it was agreed that the price fixed in any year was not to diverge by more than 15 per cent from the previous year's price. The commission also undertook to pay a development premium for each bale purchased over 40,000.[30] The board were pleased with the fact that this contract provided a guaranteed minimum price.[31] In the event, however, more favourable prices could have been obtained on world markets than those negotiated with the commission during the whole of the period covered by the arrangement. This was recognised when the agreement was extended in October 1950 to cover the 1952–3 and 1953–4 seasons, with a rolling clause providing for further extension at each October negotiation. In consequence of these negotiations the permitted annual price variation was increased to about 25 per cent, with an agreed lower price limit for any season covered by the agreement.[32] The development premium was also altered, becoming a fixed sum of £4 per bale for each bale purchased over 60,000.[33] The price-fixing arrangements were made even more flexible in October 1951; for the 1951–2 season the commission undertook to buy 40,000 bales at an agreed price, the rest of the export crop[34] to be bought at 'seller's call'. With this arrangement the seller had the option to fix the price of lots of 10,000 bales or more from time to time on the basis of price quotations in the US cotton market, subject only to observance of the agreed maximum

[29] A small proportion of the total crop was sold for local manufacturing use.

[30] A Nigerian bale is approximately 410 lb. The premium was on a rising scale: £1 per bale from 40,000 to 60,000 bales, then £1½ per bale up to 80,000 bales, over 80,000 bales to be fixed by negotiation if necessary.

[31] 'It will be noted that the main advantage to the board from this agreement was that the prices for cotton lint for the 1950–1 and 1951–2 seasons could not fall below the levels of the percentage limit.' *Annual Report of the Nigerian Cotton Marketing Board, 1949–50.*

[32] The price of NA1 grade cotton was not to fall below 19d. per lb c.i.f. UK for any season covered by the agreement.

[33] £4 per bale is approximately 2·3d. per lb.

[34] In the event this excess amounted to 60,000 bales.

and minimum levels.[35] This scheme enabled the board to take 'advantage of rising cotton prices during the latter part of the season'.[36] The seller's call arrangement was continued in later seasons; it was considered by the marketing authority to 'ensure that the best possible prices are obtained for Nigerian cotton'.[37]

In short, the Raw Cotton Commission's buying practices in Nigeria evolved from fairly specific advance price fixing to arrangements in which the price paid was closely linked to that prevailing in world markets, and in which the revenue obtained by the colonial marketing authority was determined largely by its skill in deciding when to sell. There can be little doubt that the Nigerian authority gained from the change. This is suggested not simply by the board's own satisfaction with the evolution, but also by the statistical evidence of the average value of British imports of cotton of similar staple from Nigeria, Peru, and the US between 1936 and 1954 (Table 1). In comparison with pre-war price relationships, the average prices paid for Nigerian cotton during the period 1948–51 were low;[38] the price relationship moved in Nigeria's favour from 1952 onwards, when advance price fixing was abandoned progressively. While statistics of this kind can give only a rough indication of the position, the changes are large enough for the inference to carry conviction.

Superficially, it might appear that the bulk-buying scheme was successful in another direction: the Nigerian cotton crop rose from 30–35,000 bales before the war to 140,000 bales in 1953–4. It is clear, however, that this increase could not have been due either to the level of prices negotiated between the Nigeria Cotton Marketing Board and the commission or to the development premium payments scheme later introduced. In fact the prices paid to the producers by the board were far below those realized by it on the sale

[35] The price was to be fixed on the basis of the US March futures quotations up to 20 February 1952, and on the basis of US May quotations from 20 February to 20 April 1952.

[36] *Annual Report* of the Board, 1951–2: 'In the face of the unpredictable trends of the market, this arrangement provided a reasonable safeguard. At the worst, the position was satisfactory and secure while at the best it could be very advantageous.'

[37] *Annual Report* of the Board, 1952–3.

[38] It may be added that in this period, and particularly in 1951, the world price of US cotton was at times restrained by various controls. The statistics therefore understate the relative lowness of Nigerian cotton prices.

of cotton to the Raw Cotton Commission, and were also below the prices producers could have obtained had they been free to sell in world markets. During the years 1949–53 only about two-thirds of the net proceeds of the marketing board's sales to the commission was passed on to the growers, most of the rest[39] of the board's revenues being retained in a reserve fund.[40] There is indeed evidence that the Nigerian cotton marketing authority was concerned to co-ordinate its policies with those of other authorities dealing with other agricultural products in order to preserve what was called the 'balance' of agricultural production, and that this sometimes involved the quite deliberate inhibition of any possible incentive effects of high world prices on cotton production.[41] Growers were clearly not

TABLE 1

Volume and value of imports of raw cotton, under $1\frac{1}{4}$ in. staple and over $\frac{7}{8}$ in. staple, imported into Great Britain from Nigeria, Peru, and US

	Nigeria		Peru		US	
	volume (000 centals)[1]	average (c.i.f.) value (£ per cental)	volume (000 centals)	average (c.i.f.) value (£ per cental)	volume (000 centals)	average (c.i.f.) value (£ per cental)
1936	110·7	2·8	713·4	3·3	6,010·6	2·7
1937	148·4	3·0	835·6	3·3	7,466·5	2·6
1938	94·8	2·1	789·8	2·8	4,329·7	2·1
1948	109·4	4·3	330·2	13·1	1,834·5	9·6
1949	220·8	5·8	441·2	14·2	4,121·2	9·9
1950	274·0	11·0	621·3	17·0	2,810·3	13·7
1951	307·2	14·9	662·0	29·5	2,106·4	15·5
1952	431·6	16·5	249·9	20·2	2,162·4	15·2
1953	392·9	14·7	350·6	14·6	1,919·2	13·2
1954	568·9	13·7	478·8	15·9	2,574·4	13·7

Source: Board of Trade and HM Customs and Excise.
1. 1 cental = 100 lb.

[39] Some small part of the surplus was spent on investment projects (including research into cotton growing) autonomously decided upon by the board.

[40] Moreover, it may be noted that the price guarantees in the agreements between board and commission were not at all necessary for any policy of *producer* price stabilisation which may have been envisaged by the Nigeria Board; the board's power as sole buyer for export enabled it to divorce the prices paid to producers from the fluctuating prices of the world market, whether such guarantees existed or not.

[41] 'In deciding the provisional minimum prices to be paid for the 1952–3 crop, an important consideration taken into account was the need to fix prices at a level which would not adversely affect food production and result in shortages

313

unaware of the advantages of circumventing the board's buying monopoly; some cotton appears to have passed directly and illegally into neighbouring territories. This general situation was not altered by the introduction of development premia into the bulk contracts between board and commission, since no similar incentive scheme appeared in the board's own arrangements for payments to growers.[42]

The evolution of buying agreements in Uganda was essentially the same as in Nigeria. The marketing authority was the Uganda Lint Marketing Board, which began to function at the end of 1949. The 1949–50 crop was sold in bulk on terms agreed earlier by the British government and the colonial authorities. In the following season, four-fifths of the exportable crop was sold in bulk to the Raw Cotton Commission and the government of India, the remainder being disposed of in the free market. The bulk agreement provided for sale at fixed prices. These conditions of sale were altered for the 1951–2 crop: the new pricing formula stipulated an agreed price, but permitted a variation from this determined by the average movement of cotton futures prices on the New York market. Also, the new agreement provided for the sale of 200,000 bales of cotton to the commission and India jointly. This was based upon an estimated crop of 300,000 bales; if there was an excess over this latter amount (as there eventually was), 50 per cent of it was to be sold under the bulk agreement, and the rest on the free market as before.

Like the Nigeria Board, the Uganda Lint Marketing Board passed on to growers only a portion of its net receipts (about two-thirds in the three years 1949–50 to 1951–2), and the commission's agreements gave no direct incentive to growers. Moreover, at first the Uganda Board, in continuance of previous practice, bought cotton from growers without offering any additional return for superior grades or condition. In consequence, the crop deteriorated,[43] and

which would in turn lead to increases in the cost of corn and other staple food-stuffs.' Also, the Nigeria Groundnut Marketing Board had not changed its producer prices, and '. . . some measure of relative uniformity should exist between the two price structures if the economic balance of the Northern Region was to be maintained'. *Annual Report* of the Board, 1952–3.

[42] It is not suggested that the commission could be held responsible for the cotton buying policy of the colonial marketing authorities.

[43] '. . . many [ginneries] just do not care what happens to the cotton because they are paid by weight. Everywhere I went, I heard nothing but wholesale condemnation of the system of bulk buying, except from ginners. . . . What does it matter as long as they are paid by weight?'

the effects were serious enough to cause a change in policy. The agreement between the board and the commission for 1950–1 provided for sale 'on the basis of physical standards . . . instead of the former basis of description',[44] and the board itself introduced grading schemes, with premium and discount payments by quality.

The contracts with the Sudan were the commission's largest single agreements. Until June 1950 most Sudan cotton was purchased by bulk contract from the Sudan Plantations Syndicate and the Kassala Cotton Company, which were private concerns with concession rights from the Sudan government. Other cotton (such as White Nile and Nuba Mountain) was bought directly from the Sudan government. When the concessions expired in 1950, the companies were replaced by the Gezira Board, a Sudanese body with substantial independence in contractual matters. None of the Sudan authorities accumulated reserves by following policies similar to those described for Nigeria and Uganda.

Each year the Cotton Control, and later the commission, obtained and took up an option on 60–70 per cent of the total crop. Until 1948 a contract price was fixed in advance, but in that year the Egyptian price of comparable cottons rose after the contract price had been settled, and the commission had to agree to pay a higher price. Thereafter, the contract was used simply to ensure supplies; prices were not negotiated in advance, but were settled by agreement by reference to the concurrent prices ruling in the free Alexandria spot cotton market. The Sudan government also made a point of holding back some part of its crop for sale by auction each year 'with the object of conserving their other overseas markets'.[45]

'There is no incentive to the grower to grow good cotton – he just gets paid the same price whether it is pure BP 52 or mixed.'

'Up in the North they are fetching cotton from across the Nile and mixing it with the Buganda cotton against all regulations. . . .' J. Littlewood, chairman, at the annual meeting of the Empire Cotton Growing Corporation, July 1949. The statements refer to the system of payments existing before the Uganda Lint Marketing Board was established; the board adopted this system in its first year.

[44] *Annual Report* of the Board, 1949–50.

[45] *Annual Report* of the Commission, 1949–50, para. 14.

The marketing of the British West Indies crop during the period is of some interest. Like those discussed in the text, this crop is grown mainly by small producers; it is, however, much smaller in volume and is mostly long-staple high quality cotton. The commission purchased the whole of the BWI export surplus, but was never able to negotiate firm prices in advance. A price was in fact negotiated with the British West Indies Cotton Association in the United

The failure of the bulk contract system (and particularly of fixed-price arrangements) to fulfil the expectations of its advocates, and the resultant movement towards less 'planned' alternatives, cannot be regarded as particularly surprising; the notion that such contracts must benefit both buyer and seller in circumstances such as those described is unconvincing. Buyers are interested in a low price for cotton, sellers in a high one; their mutual interest could be served only if the bulk contract altered the trading environment for the better in other respects while leaving unaffected this prime conflict of interest. This might (but need not) be the case if (for example) fixed-price bulk contracts could be used (as there is no evidence that they can) to secure long-run price stability without any long-run loss of revenue to either party. There seems to have been little belief in the existence or value of such mutual benefits in other countries; no bulk contracts, fixed price or otherwise, were negotiated by the commission outside the colonial territories. Indeed, the commission negotiated no such contracts at all except in regions where some kind of bulk-purchasing arrangement was already in being when the commission was created. Where long-term agreements with fixed prices were made, their subsequent history was uniformly one of modification to permit greater flexibility in price fixing, until the contract price was quite closely linked with free market prices. The bulk contracts then became largely pre-emptive agreements with little value to the sellers, who could still have disposed of their crop at the market price if the agreement had not been made. This is exemplified by experience in the sale of Uganda cotton. No bulk agreement was made in 1952–3 following upon the British government's decision to allow private importation of raw cotton as an alternative to purchase through the commission. There was some anxiety in Uganda, encouraged by the sudden need to re-create marketing facilities. But the fears were groundless: the crop was

Kingdom and sanctioned by the Colonial Office, and from 1949 this was done at the time of ploughing in order to stimulate cotton growing. This price could only be recommended to growers, however, and was not binding upon them, although in the event the whole of the crop was usually sold to the commission, whatever the price ruling in world markets. The reasons for this are not altogether clear. Attempts were made to create more formal contract arrangements. In 1948 the commission suggested to the colonial governors that they should encourage the creation of a Cotton Marketing Board, and when this failed, a limited company to negotiate contracts was proposed, but no progress seems to have been made. See successive *Annual Reports* of the Commission.

316

disposed of without difficulty 'at prices ... comparable to those obtaining for comparable growths in world markets'.[46]

It might be argued that the fixed-price agreements existed for too short a period for their benefits to have been felt, since, as we have seen, the original inflexible arrangements were soon modified. Thus, it could be contended that the prices paid by the commission might have been as high as those obtainable in the free market if averaged over a long enough period of years, and that the quantity and quality of the crops might have been raised as a result of the consequent stability. Such an argument would be unconvincing on two grounds. First, there is no evidence that the commission was pursuing a policy with this aim; the indications (e.g. the market-sharing agreement with India)[47] do not suggest a policy designed to bolster the price of colonial cotton when world prices were falling. Such a policy would certainly have aggravated the commission's already intractable problems of selling price policy. Second, the success of a long-term scheme of this kind would have required the continuous co-operation of the colonial selling authorities for the whole of the requisite period, entailing a willingness to accept less than world prices, possibly for years at a stretch. The successive modifications that were in fact made to the original fixed-price agreements indicate that an attempt to obtain such co-operation could not but have produced considerable strain both in the relations between the commission and the boards and between the boards and the better-informed of the colonial growers.[48]

[46] 'There was some little local apprehension that Uganda exporters might not be able to find overseas markets for the whole crop at reasonable prices following such a long period of trading with only a very small proportion of the crop. The absence of a reliable market on which to hedge accentuated fears in this direction. In the event these fears proved groundless. ...' *Annual Report of the Uganda Lint Marketing Board, 1952–3.*

[47] Possibly inadvertently, Mr Harold Wilson, in the Standing Committee on the Cotton Bill, made quite clear the ability of the commission to keep prices below world levels by its actions: '... if we are to have not bulk buying but private buying of the raw cotton, with every mill competing against every other mill ... the result will be not only to put up the price but to endanger supplies in this country.' Parliamentary Debates, Cotton Bill, Standing Committee A (First Sitting), col. 30.

[48] Indeed, the payment of fixed prices below world market prices produced charges that the transactions were in fact compulsory sales, the colony having 'no option but to acquiesce in wishes forcibly expressed from Downing Street'. See Protest to the Colonial Secretary by the Liverpool Chamber of Commerce, November 1949.

4. SERVICE TO SPINNERS

Cotton spinners require of their raw material supply that there should be a range of suitable raw cottons from which to choose, while at the same time types particularly suited to special purposes are available. They also require a variety of contractual arrangements sufficient to enable continuous adaptation of purchasing policy to changes in the position of the firm and to ensure that contractual undertakings are satisfactorily fulfilled. Cottons grown in different geographical locations differ in length of fibre (staple) and in quality (grade); they also possess other individual characteristics making them more or less suitable for the purposes of particular spinners. The great geographical extension of cotton growing during the last 150 years has both increased the possibilities of substitution of one growth for another and produced cottons more peculiarly adapted to the special requirements of individual spinners. The possibilities of substitution depend upon the use to which the yarn is to be put. Thus, spinners of yarn for cotton sheeting have a good deal of latitude; it might be to their advantage to switch from one growth to another in consequence of a change in relative prices at the cost of suitable adjustment of their processing machinery. On the other hand, satisfactory production of yarn for the manufacture of fine velvets, super poplins and laces depends upon adequate supplies of a quite narrow range of suitable cottons. To ensure that the cotton he purchased would be suitable for his requirements, the cotton spinner before the war could, if he chose, make use of the market's sampling facilities, which enabled prior inspection of agreed proportions of the cotton delivered against sample or specification. He could also utilise the services of merchants with special knowledge of his needs, since merchants were numerous and tended to specialise and to experiment with new types. To safeguard his supplies, the spinner could also enter into contracts to buy cotton for deferred delivery, either at an agreed price or 'on call'. The on call contract enabled the buyer to 'fix' the price to be paid for his cotton at any time during the stipulated delivery period, by reference to the price ruling in the futures market at the time of fixing. It served the same purpose as an actual purchase of cotton and the off-setting sale of a futures contract, to hedge against the risk that the price of the cotton might change before the yarn made from it was sold. The on call contract was a convenient device enabling the spinner to make a yarn price for a customer with safety at any moment simply by reference to the ruling futures prices.

The commission's creators had expected that it would improve upon the pre-war service, since it would 'adjust the forward buying programme with knowledge of the requirements of the whole industry'. As the commission discovered, 'size works no such magic in foreknowledge'. The information had to be discovered, and large-scale buying could magnify the consequences of erroneous forecasting. Initially, the commission based its estimates of future requirements on the weekly returns provided by spinners for cover purposes,[49] which gave details of the mill stock and consumption of each spinner by growth and type.[50] But such returns, even if accurate, were unsatisfactory in that they gave historical information only, so that a purchasing policy based upon trends in the figures could take no account of current changes in the expectations and requirements of spinners. There was found to be a need to reintroduce the sampling, delivery and other facilities of the pre-war market, not only in the interest of efficient production by spinners, but also to provide information and guidance for the commission's own buying activities.[51]

[49] Cf. Section 6.

[50] The procedure was broadly as follows:
From its information about weekly consumption rates by growth and quality, mill stocks, its own stocks in this country, abroad and afloat, the commission assessed the minimum stock holding (including mill stocks) required in this country (thirteen to seventeen weeks) and the buying programme was framed to provide a monthly build-up of stock over future months to ensure that this minimum stock holding was always maintained. The weekly consumption by growth and quality was carefully watched and if there was any appreciable change in an upward or downward direction, the quantities defined in the buying programme for shipment in later months were adjusted accordingly.

This system applied in the main to the larger growths such as American, Indian, Pakistan, Egyptian, and Brazilian and mainly to qualities of which purchases could normally be made throughout the season. In the case of speciality cotton such as high-grade Karnak, which normally had to be bought in quantity at the beginning of the season or not at all, arrangements were made, *after consultation*, to enter the market for quantities of cotton in excess of the thirteen to seventeen weeks minimum stock holding.

[51] In the commission's own words: 'The commission has always recognised the importance of introducing deferred delivery and forward contracts. Only the largest spinners could afford to lock up substantial sums so as to ensure continuity of quality in their supplies of raw material, and the majority of unit mills were obliged to declare themselves "short" in their weekly price cover

Sampling facilities were provided early in the commission's life. The antecedent Cotton Control had introduced a choice of three alternative contracts for users of Egyptian cotton. Cotton bought on description only against the control's standard types was offered at a discount on the published selling price for the cotton concerned. By paying the full published price a buyer could take samples of 10 per cent of the cotton he wished to purchase, and by paying a premium in addition he could purchase the right to sample all bales before delivery and to exchange all bales falling below standard, or, alternatively, demand a fresh tender of cotton. Extension of these facilities to other growths by the commission was delayed only by the need to create centralised sampling and storage facilities (to replace the decentralised arrangements of the pre-war market), and by the unwillingness of the spinners to accept a cancellation clause enabling the commission to avoid contracts it was unable to fulfil because of circumstances outside its control. It was felt that as the contract was for the actual delivery of cotton it should bind the commission to deliver the exact cotton specified. Finally, a condition was accepted permitting cancellation after three trial tenders, and contracts similar to the Egyptian ones came into use on 1 October 1948. Apart from the escape clause, these facilities were comparable to those afforded to spinners by the pre-war market.

Forward buying through 'deferred delivery' or 'on call' contracts took a good deal longer to arrange. The commission proposed the use of such contracts in 1948, and expected facilities to be made available within the first quarter of 1949, as part of the proposed new cover arrangements.[52] In fact, the negotiations on the cover scheme were protracted, and in May 1949 a 'partial' deferred delivery scheme was introduced as an interim measure. This contract enabled returns, without specifying their exact requirements. The commission was thus deprived of advance information on spinners' requirements which would have been invaluable in framing its purchasing programme, because the movement of prices might lead a spinner to buy a different growth from that specified in his cover return. . . .' *Annual Report*, 1948–9, para. 49.

[52] The commission's reasons for not providing such facilities earlier are interesting, particularly for the light they throw upon the effects of the 'parity of treatment' principle (pp. 321–2, below): '. . . it would clearly be disastrous to lull spinners into a sense of false security by entering into such contracts without first being reasonably certain that they could be fulfilled. The commission had not been able to accumulate *a visible supply in every growth* which would be sufficient to justify the introduction of these facilities' (authors' italics). *Annual Report*, 1948, para. 46.

spinners to make purchases for forward delivery at the price ruling at the date of contract.[53] As a result of uncertainties about supplies of American cotton, the contract was little used in the early stages except for Egyptian cotton, so that it did not become a useful source of information for the commission's cotton buyers, and many spinners continued to find difficulty in planning forward[54] without incurring the costs of carrying large stocks – when these were obtainable. However, the scheme was gradually extended to other growths. In November 1949 the commission broadened the contract to permit purchase for deferred or forward delivery either at fixed prices or on call, provided that adequate supplies were available of the growth and quality of cotton required. On paper these services approached those of the pre-war market. The new scheme was very welcome to spinners and of great potential value to the commission as a guide to buying policy. Unfortunately, the scheme was launched in unpropitious circumstances; the requisite 'adequate supplies' were unobtainable in the ensuing crop period for an important range of growths. In particular, the commission was handicapped by a short Brazilian crop and by the continuing ban on Indian raw cotton exports. These troubles were followed in 1950–1 by the quite general supply difficulties caused by the disastrously small American crop and the small quota of that crop allocated to Great Britain.

The commission also offered facilities for the selection ('ear-marking') of the actual cotton bought for forward delivery at the time of first purchase. This facility was most important in relation to purchases, for deferred delivery, of cotton from the commission's own stocks. But the value of the service was much reduced as a result of the commission's policy of 'parity of treatment'; earmarking facilities could be made available to individual spinners only if the commission's stocks of the particular cotton required were large enough to permit the offer of like facilities to the industry as a

[53] A further scheme permitting spinners of Egyptian cotton to 'liquidate forward yarn sales at a price corresponding to the Alexandria discount' was withdrawn because spinners feared that it would encourage their customers to cancel yarn orders placed at 'old crop' prices. *Annual Report*, 1948–9, para. 52. (The problems of new crop discounts are examined in the discussion of cover schemes, Section 6.)

[54] The yarn quota system, introduced during the war, was still in operation at this time. This effectively restricted the stocks spinners could carry and the period for which they could plan forward, and so reduced the importance of the commission's policies in this respect.

whole.[55] Such a principle of equal treatment was probably un-avoidable for a public authority[56] enjoined to serve an undefined public interest; it was apparently considered to be in the best interests of the industry[57] to restrict earmarking in such a way as to prevent the large combines from 'creaming the stock' of scarce types to the disadvantage of the 'less wealthy' unit mills.[58] But the policy could not but deprive the commission of buying information, and place British spinners at a disadvantage in relation to such foreign competitors as could 'buy' these facilities if they thought it worthwhile.

Despite the arrangements described, then, the commission's service to spinners appears to have been deficient in at least three respects. First, spinners' cotton requirements (by way of staple, suitability and continuity of quality, and ability to make purchases when their own stock position and assessment of world market conditions made it desirable) were never met as precisely as they had been by the free market; there were continuing complaints on this score, particularly but by no means exclusively from spinners in the fine trade with a highly specialised demand.[59] Second, deferred delivery and on call

[55] Otherwise, deferred delivery purchase had to be by reference to sample, in accordance with one or other of the three buying contracts already described.

[56] A statement to the House of Commons in May 1948 gave this principle governmental approval, at least as regards the Cotton Control.

[57] This concern to take care of the 'interests of the industry' appears frequently in the commission's statements. But there is clearly no such interest except, at most, on a few very special issues. What is in the interests of one firm will often be contrary to the interests of another. For example, some firms liked the parity of treatment principle because they came out of it better than they would have come out of competition for supplies; others felt that the principle deprived them of services they would willingly have paid for.

[58] This argument is in interesting contrast with those advanced by the creators of the commission, which could itself be described as a large buying combine.

[59] Firms stated regularly that difficulties of this kind were raising their costs, either by stimulating attempts to ensure continuity of supply by the carrying of larger stocks, or by encouraging the use of higher-priced cottons if their supply seemed better assured, or simply by enforced acceptance of the inconveniences and losses consequent upon the non-availability of desirable types. Irregularities in supply hindered redeployment by destroying the confidence of labour in new work systems, and made spinners unwilling to undertake to give continuity of quality. Two quotations may emphasise the nature and importance of these problems:

'Our only worry, and it has been a big worry, is to obtain the right quality of cotton from the Raw Cotton Commission. Never since the government took over the buying of raw cotton have we been able to purchase adequate qualities of the right type for spinning velvet yarns. The government's excuse is shortage of

facilities were never as useful as had been expected, either to spinners or to the commission, as they could never be made available automatically, or to the extent that they would probably have been provided by the free market, throughout the commission's monopoly. Third, the principle of parity of treatment severely restricted the provision of such facilities as earmarking.

Difficult world trading conditions complicated the commission's task, and unquestionably bear some of the responsibility for the shortcomings of its service. But it is fairly clear that the commission's position as a statutory monopolist and sole cotton importer was also not without importance in this respect. Thus the principle of parity

dollars ... it is regrettable that we are not able to obtain the right type of American cotton when so much of the finished cloth is sold to America and Canada. ... The government and the Raw Cotton Commission have been approached on this subject over and over again.' Annual Report of Messrs Balstone, Cooke-Rayonese Ltd, April 1952.

The frustration created by the inability to act upon judgments about world markets is well brought out in the following extract from the Annual Report of Messrs J. and P.Coats, May 1948:

'Last autumn, when it would have been possible to purchase high-grade Karnak of suitable quality for our requirements at about 29d. per lb, we made repeated requests to the control authorities to purchase for us approximately two years' requirements. We do not know why they did not do so. ... Over the period referred to replacement deliveries of this type of cotton to the mills were less than one-third of what we were consuming.

'I can offer no explanation as to why we were kept in such short supply ... had we been free agents we would have made sure of an adequate supply of cotton at a time when market prices were much more favourable than they are now. We have now ... received sufficient cotton ... but at prices up to 60d.'

Questions about this stimulated the government's statement of the principle of equality of treatment (see n. 56).

There are many other illustrations: e.g. Reports of Combined Egyptian Mills Ltd, November 1950; Calico Printers Association Ltd, November 1949; Lancashire Cotton Corporation, January 1949; J. and P.Coats Ltd, June 1949; and Belgrave Mills Co. (1926) Ltd, November 1951.

Apart from referring to difficult trading conditions in world markets, the commission's most general answer to complaints of this kind, and particularly to complaints about quality, was that 100 per cent sampling facilities were available for those who chose to use them, and that since their use was in fact negligible the quality problem could not be serious. While the spinners on their part may have overstated their case, this evidence is not unambiguous proof of the skill of the commission's cotton classers; it can equally well be interpreted as evidence of the lack of value of a 100 per cent sampling contract that had to be purchased at a cost, but did not offer a firm quality guarantee since the commission had no binding obligation to supply a suitable cotton.

of treatment, probably incumbent upon a statutory monopolist, was relaxed when that monopoly was ended, and cover arrangements[60] were also modified to increase the flexibility of producers' hedging arrangements. It is also not without significance that the commission experienced great difficulties of internal organisation and administration. These warrant more detailed examination as they can reasonably be held to provide supporting evidence for the view that not all the commission's deficiencies were attributable to world conditions, since many of the difficulties sprang directly from the existence of a centralised buying and selling agency.

The commission took over from the Cotton Control an organisation similar to that generally adopted by cotton merchanting houses, with growth managers responsible for both the buying and the selling arrangements for particular growths. But the commission's growth managers had to maintain contact with growers and buyers on a far greater scale than in any merchanting house, and there was an inevitable loss of detailed knowledge and efficiency.[61] Dissatisfied with the system, the commission took the advice of a firm of industrial consultants[62] and reorganised its work into three main departments, buying, sales, and finance and administration, each under the

[60] See Section 6.

[61] See *Annual Report*, 1948, para. 15. Merchanting houses were '. . . mostly comparatively small units, in which the principals maintained a close and intimate contact both with their suppliers and with their customers'.

The nature of the commission's problem appears to be illustrated by the policy for the buying of Egyptian cotton in 1948 which was much criticised. After letting it be known that they would not be buying, the commission had to enter the market late and buy at much higher prices in order to maintain stocks. This appears to have been the consequence of a failure of the internal administrative arrangements.

A difficulty of another type arose in respect of cotton for velvet manufacture. The commission invited representatives of the velvet trade to approve types of suitable cotton (SM $1\frac{1}{8}$ in., $1\frac{1}{16}$ in. Memphis). After the commission had bought about 7,000 bales of cotton to match these types, the velvet trade turned to other cottons that it found better, and the commission had to carry the stock for some years. No private trader would have placed himself in so vulnerable a position.

The size of the commission's own stocks alone was enough to create problems of administrative control. For example, there is no evidence that even a physical check of the stock taken over from the Cotton Control was accomplished inside the commission's first year of existence.

[62] It may be noted that this advice was taken in preference to that offered by the trade, which would have involved the employment of merchant firms to act on behalf of the commission. *Annual Report*, 1948–9, para. 10.

control of a senior executive, with the independent members of the commission left free to decide major policy questions. This scheme was fully implemented in November 1949, when the general buying manager was appointed. Buyers and sellers were expected to become specialised in their functions, with benefit to efficiency; but in fact the difficulties of co-ordination between departments seem to have been no less than the difficulties of large-scale co-ordination by individual growth managers.[63] By the end of 1951 the commission had reverted to the type of organisation earlier found to be unsatisfactory, with four managers responsible for both the buying and selling of four distinct groups of cottons. The administrative problems do not appear to have been solved by organisational change; they would appear to be a manifestation of the general diseconomies of very large size in this kind of business. It is certainly clear that the difficulties relate rather to centralised buying and selling *per se* than to the world trading conditions faced by the commission.

In contrast to these deficiencies, it has been suggested that the commission's service did succeed in improving upon the pre-war service from the point of view of the spinning *operative*. It is claimed to have eliminated the 'bad spinning' that had occurred from time to time before its creation. However, this claim is dubious. Bad spinning is the spinning of particular yarns from cottons that are inferior from the point of view of the operative, in that they reduce his earnings, increase his work-load, or do both. It would appear that the possibility of bad spinning must indicate a defect in the system of wage-payment rather than in the method of cotton supply; no one has suggested that either the commission or the free market refused to supply the types of cotton asked for by spinners if that cotton could be made available. Further, while the defect might be difficult to remedy, no employer would have an incentive to take advantage of it unless he was not worried about losing his operatives by doing so. This suggests that full employment and a textile labour shortage, rather than the methods of cotton supply, were responsible for the disappearance of bad spinning. This view is strengthened by

[63] For the departmental scheme to function it was essential for the sales department to have enough authority to ensure that its knowledge was acted upon by buyers. It has been suggested, not implausibly, that the fact that the head of the buying department was a member of the commission while the head of the sales department was not, may have been a contributory (though not a fundamental) cause of the failure of the experiment.

the fact that complaints about the practice did begin to reappear during the one short but severe textile recession that occurred during the commission's period of monopoly.[64]

5. PRICE POLICY

The government, in setting up the commission, had expected it to pursue a price policy such that spinners would be 'assured of a long-term stability in the price of their materials'. The Act itself required that cotton be sold at prices 'best calculated to further the public interest in all respects', and also that the commission should balance revenues and expenditures 'on an average of good years and bad'. The commission, it seems, did not expect that these requirements would necessarily be compatible.[65] It placed emphasis upon its obligation to further the public interest, and interpreted that obligation in the broadest sense.[66] This was particularly important in the formulation of price policy. In the words of the commission's first chairman:[67]

In fixing selling prices, the three full-time members[68] of the commission had to take into account not only replacement cost and relative spinning values but also the cost at which the cotton was bought, which, in the end, limited the extent of its price manipulation. They had, moreover, to give supreme regard to the public interest, which covered a wide range of subjects, including the availability of foreign currency, the necessity to stimulate exports, the maintenance of employment in the industry, the avoidance of labour troubles ... and the necessity to preserve good relations with suppliers.

The commission took over a functioning policy of long-term price stabilisation from the Cotton Control, and continued for some time

[64] The impression in the trade is that spinners 'went higher in grade' (i.e. used better quality cottons) in the period of good trade after the war. Revival of complaints about bad spinning coincided with a reversal of this movement when the recession encouraged a search for usable but lower grade and cheaper cottons.

In any case, the trade unions agreed that only a minority of firms had ever been affected.

On the bad spinning question as a whole, see correspondence in the *Manchester Guardian*, 5–16 June 1953.

[65] 'These two provisions may, of course, prove to be mutually inconsistent in certain circumstances.' *Annual Report*, 1948, para. 48.

[66] The Act itself contains no definition or explanation of the public interest.

[67] Speech by the chairman, H. O. R. Hindley (see n. 15).

[68] The fixing of selling prices was reserved to the full-time members by directive of the Board of Trade under para. 6 (3) of the Act.

to change prices relatively infrequently; the price of individual cottons was not normally being changed more than once weekly at the end of 1949. But the trading situation had changed a good deal since the introduction of price stabilisation by the Cotton Control. The control had held large stocks, accumulated for strategic reasons, and had sold to customers with a negligible (though developing) interest in the export trade. Further, the trend of world prices during its life had been generally upward. In those circumstances, the control was able 'to balance profits on one growth against losses on another, thus maintaining a balanced relation between selling prices and spinning values'.[69] Prices could remain unchanged for long periods; only seven changes were made between 31 March 1941 and 31 December 1947, and two of these were decreases made specifically to offset wage increases in the cotton textile industry. By the time the commission inherited the control's policy, trading circumstances had become very different. Exports and foreign competition were once more of importance, and losses on one growth could be offset by profits on others only by raising the home price of the profit-making growth above that paid by foreign spinners buying in world markets, so that 'exporters in that section of the trade would be at a crippling disadvantage with their foreign competitors'.[70] Accordingly, considerable dissatisfaction was caused by the conspicuous lack of correspondence between the commission's price and the world market price of Egyptian cotton in the early months of the commission's activities. The divergences in prices for American-type cottons were in general less marked, but could be significant; in March 1948 spinners found themselves faced with increases in the prices of American types at a time when their world market prices were falling.[71]

The commission was early aware of the dangers and disadvantages of *long-term* price stabilisation; the policy was abandoned, in principle, as early as the end of March 1948, when the commission decided that 'the only practicable policy was to fix prices approximately in line with the replacement price ruling from time to time in the world's markets'.[72] The full implementation of a policy of

[69] *Annual Report*, 1948, para. 50.   [70] Ibid., para. 51.

[71] The extent of the price divergences in both Egyptian and American is well brought out by the price charts given in the commission's annual reports.

[72] *Annual Report*, 1948, para. 52. It is noteworthy that the commission did not consider this to be a complete abandonment of the stabilisation principle, but

more flexible prices waited upon the acquisition by the commission of the requisite skill and experience; it was also inhibited by the administrative difficulties created by the commission's cover scheme,[73] and by the existence of controls in other parts of the cotton textile industry. In particular, price changes were made more difficult for the commission by the government's price-control arrangements, and especially by those concerned with utility cloths. These controlled prices were based upon the Cotton Control's wartime policy of administered price stability for raw cotton, and it seems to have taken a considerable time to get them adjusted to the new situation. As these obstacles were overcome, price changes became more frequent, and the commission moved gradually towards an imitation of one of the significant characteristics of the pre-war market, in that the commission's selling prices came to be changed more and more rapidly in response to changes in world market conditions. When stability was first abandoned, prices were changed weekly at most and on Mondays only. By the end of 1949 changes were being made on any day, and in September 1951 five new price lists were issued in one week. Thenceforward a policy of changing prices daily if necessary (as compared with minute-to-minute changes in the pre-war market) obtained. As a corollary, individual price changes became smaller.

Although long-term price stabilisation was abandoned, and despite the growing efficiency of the commission in implementing a broad policy of selling prices based on replacement costs, the relationship between the commission's prices and those prevailing in world markets never became exact of predictable.

There were four kinds of reasons for this.[74] Two arose directly from the fact that pricing at replacement cost was never the commission's sole or over-riding aim. First, the commission always felt itself free to depart from replacement-cost pricing if some other

rather as a replacement of long-period by short-period stabilisation. This seems to have meant in practice that the commission's prices for spot cotton were always in force as a matter of policy for at least a single business day, in contrast with the minute-to-minute fluctuations in the free market. But stabilisation of this minimal kind is almost inevitable for a monopolistic seller; no one else can quote a price and more frequent changes by the single seller would be administratively difficult.

[73] See Section 6.

[74] An additional but less fundamental reason was the fact that some cotton-growing countries did not have continuously operating spot markets.

objective (such as its desire to use 'skilful or fortunate' purchases below world levels[75] for the purpose of stabilising prices) was thought more important in the light of its assumed responsibilities in regard to the public interest. Second, the commission was unwilling to ignore the relative spinning values of different cottons when deciding prices. If world replacement prices at any time failed to reflect relative spinning values in the British industry, a strict replacement-cost policy was likely both to cause unwelcome shifts in demand towards the favoured growths and make for difficult relations with the spinning industry. Consequently, the replacement-cost principle was always subject to modification to take account of spinning values.

The third reason for divergence from replacement-cost pricing concerns the fact that the commission, while wishing to price at replacement cost, was driven to depart from that principle in order to protect itself, in its position as a central stock-holder, from losses consequent upon the unpredictability of changes in demand and price. This question is important enough to merit more detailed consideration. It has been predicted when the commission was created that it would be an unhedged bull, carrying large stocks and susceptible to large gains or losses as world cotton prices changed. Those who were unimpressed by this proposition argued that, by carrying such gains and losses internally, a body as large as the commission should be able to balance its long-term position, particularly if it abandoned price-stabilisation policies. Thus, if world price movements were followed closely, and if price fluctuations were regular, then (if the price *trend* was not rising or falling),[76] the commission would not gain or lose in the long run if the stock from which it met spinners' requirements remained constant. Unfortunately, the postulates of this 'internal compensation' argument have little relation to the conditions in which the commission had to trade. The argument only holds if the price trend is horizontal and if fluctuations are regular – conditions not be to expected in the world cotton market. In any other circumstances, even if a constant stock is held, large gains or losses must be a possible, even likely, contingency, and it would at best have required a very long period for gains and losses to balance one another, if such a balance were achieved at all.

[75] *Annual Report*, 1948, para. 52.
[76] With a constant stock and regular fluctuations, a rising or falling trend would result in a long-term gain or loss.

Furthermore, the commission did not in fact keep a constant stock of cotton. It tried to maintain a reserve of approximately four months' consumption of all the main growths, but modified this to take advantage of any opportunities to purchase particular cottons whose supply might be affected by currency difficulties or disturbed trading conditions.[77] This policy naturally resulted from time to time in the commission having an unusually large 'long' speculative interest in some cottons. For example, very large stocks of Egyptian cotton were built up in this way, and the commission suffered heavy losses when the price of the cotton in this 'strategic reserve' fell. In any case the commission's *ability* (as distinct from its *desire*) to control its stock position was inevitably affected by unpredictable variations in demand from spinners. It may also be noted that whenever the commission's prices were below world prices, as a consequence of any departure from a strict replacement-cost policy, the commission's stocks were liable to be depleted by spinners demanding cotton freely in the expectation that the commission's prices would rise. If quick orders could be obtained for the yarn, the spinners could avoid the need to make difference payments under the cover scheme[78] when the price in fact rose, and so could gain a competitive advantage.

Lastly, the commission's pricing policy had to take account of the peculiar position of US cotton in world markets. Purchases of US cotton were an important item of British dollar expenditure, and the volume of imports of US cottons (which varied around half the total volume of imports of American type) was fixed by the government by reference to the country's foreign exchange position, and not by the Raw Cotton Commission's estimate of the demand for US cotton at the sterling equivalent of the ruling US market prices. The commission therefore had less US cotton than spinners would have taken at such prices. It also kept stocks of other American-type cottons of similar spinning values bought, up to 1952, at significantly higher sterling prices.[79] It met this situation by selling not at approximate replacement prices for such cottons but at an 'averaged' replacement price, arrived at by combining the prices of all comparable growths.[80] Spinners thus had to buy their cotton at

---

[77] See n. 50.   [78] See Section 6.   [79] See Section 2.

[80] The commission also practised another form of averaging which it thought reasonable for 'a monopoly owner of a stock'. This consisted of the spreading of the charges incurred in holding the whole of its cotton stock over the cotton actually sold. Criticisms based on comparisons of commission and world prices

administered prices determined largely by the relative proportions of dollar cotton and more expensive outside growths that resulted from the government's import programme. In consequence, dollar cottons were more expensive in Britain than in countries with no controls on dollar expenditure, and non-dollar cottons (e.g. Brazilian) were generally less expensive. Exporters were at a disadvantage in relation to those of other countries such as Belgium and Japan which could use dollar cottons more freely.

There can be little doubt about the wisdom – indeed inevitability – of the commission's abandonment of long-term price stabilisation. Nevertheless, the policy actually pursued, which took account both of buying prices and replacement costs and also permitted adjustments on account of the other factors just explained, was never an unqualified success either from the point of view of the spinners who purchased the cotton or from that of the commission itself. The difficulties and uncertainties created by the commission's price policies were the source of continuing complaints from individual spinners – complaints that did not fail to point out that only a monopolist would be able either to treat buying prices as relevant to the fixing of selling prices or to indulge in averaging. Not all the complaints were reasonable; some spinners seem to have expected a policy of price stabilisation when prices were rising and one of quick price adjustment when prices were falling. But apart from complaints from users of American cotton who felt themselves at a disadvantage in world markets, and general comment on the handling of the price increases that followed the short American crop of 1950, criticism of the commission's pricing policy did not become widespread during its first $3\frac{1}{2}$ years, largely because a world seller's market made the effects of that policy less noticeable. However, the criticism became frequent and insistent in the summer of 1951 when American prices were affected by the expectation of a large cotton crop to follow upon the current small one. This situation coincided with the beginning of a decline in world demand for cotton textiles. The combination of circumstances directed the attention of British spinners to the excess of the commission's American price quotations over US new crop prices, and to the commission's price policy in

which ignored or took imperfect account of this averaging were thus thought by the commission to be misleading and unjust (see *Annual Report*, 1952–3, para. 101). But it is not without significance that the possibility of such criticisms depended entirely upon the commission's position as a monopolist.

general, and produced a widespread and not altogether justified outburst of criticism.[81]

At the same time the commission was not able to protect itself from the consequences of its vulnerability as a central stockholder. The annual accounts showed large profits from its operations in some years and large losses in others, the differences being accounted for by changes in the market value of the commission's stocks, and, to a smaller extent, by the gains and losses from the operation of its cover scheme. An important part of these gains and losses must be regarded primarily as the consequence of the existence of the commission, since it is unlikely that private traders, with their greater freedom of action, would have held cotton stocks of anything like the size of those held by the commission, and there is no reason to suppose that this would have been economically disadvantageous. The commission was under no *legal* obligation to maintain stocks; but its position as a statutory monopolist and its interpretation of its own responsibilities in regard to the furthering of the public interest made the carrying of such stocks unavoidable.[82] It may be suggested, further, that the exceptional size of the stocks on which major losses were incurred,[83] and to some extent the price policy pursued by the commission in certain periods, may also have been influenced by the strength and views of the spinning interest on the commission itself.[84]

In spite of the commission's experiences, a belief has persisted that there was no reason why a policy of long-term price stabilisation should not have been successfully pursued. It will therefore be useful, in completing the examination of price policy, to consider what other types of stabilisation (different from the policy inherited from the Cotton Control) might have been pursued, and what would have

[81] The events of 1951 are revealing not only for the light they throw on the commission's price policy but also in regard to its cover schemes. Accordingly, they will be explained more fully after the cover schemes have been outlined in the next section.

[82] 'A body charged, like the commission, with a responsibility to enable the industry to keep in production cannot be wholly guided by purely commercial motives when considering the desirability of purchasing cotton ... ordinary commercial prudence would preclude the building up of a long position of any magnitude.' *Annual Report*, 1952–3, para. 101.

[83] They are believed to have reached over two million bales.

[84] In contrast with other nationalised enterprises, the interests of customers were well protected. The constitution of the commission was such that the independent members were greatly outnumbered by the trade representation.

been their probable consequences. There were two main possibilities: the commission might have tried to stabilise world prices by using its influence as a large buyer in world markets, or it might have tried to insulate the British spinner from world fluctuations by an internal price-stabilisation policy for each type of cotton. The first alternative would have put the commission in the position of a speculator going against price movements in world markets, and making heavy losses if its expectations were incorrect.[85] The second alternative, of 'internal' stabilisation, would have meant buying at world market prices and selling to spinners at an averaged cost price for each designation of cotton. The averaged price would have been fixed to cover total buying costs over a period. But here also the commission would have had to distinguish between price movements of a short-run nature and changes in long-run equilibrium conditions when computing the averaged price; failure to guess correctly would have resulted in a speculative gain (or loss) at the expense (or in favour) of the spinners. Also, this second type of policy would have caused difficulties similar to those already explained, by causing divergences between the commission's prices and world prices. Spinners and others would have needed to set aside the additional gains made in times of rising prices to offset the British industry's buying disadvantage when world prices were falling, and this financial problem would have been exacerbated to the extent that falling prices coincided with difficult world trading conditions.

6. COVER

In the preceding section we discussed the position of the commission as a speculator, vulnerable to risks of gain or loss because of changes in the price and volume of its raw cotton stocks. Risks of this type are of course inseparable from economic activity requiring the purchase of materials for sale (in whatever form) at some subsequent point in time, so that the price of the material can change between the time of purchase and the later sale. Such risks are taken, for example, by any spinner who purchases cotton to spin for stock. Futures markets, by providing facilities for individuals (speculators) to specialise in the taking of price risks, enable those who wish to

---

[85] Its position would have been similar to that of an international commodity price-stabilisation authority with control of only a portion of total trade and relying on one country alone to meet any losses.

have only a 'trading' interest in the goods concerned (the hedgers) to offset such risks. Markets of this kind have developed the world over; they illustrate the possibilities and advantages of division of labour.

The Liverpool Cotton Exchange provided the pre-war facilities for futures trading in raw cotton. Futures contracts were available and in general use in respect of American, long-staple Egyptian, and short-staple Egyptian cotton; there were also less popular contracts for Empire and Miscellaneous and for Indian cottons. A spinner working for stock could, in the absence of an on call arrangement of the kind described earlier, hedge the price-risk consequent upon his cotton purchase by the simultaneous sale of a futures contract for an appropriate quantity of cotton. When the yarn was sold, the transaction was completed by buying back the futures contract. Others with an interest in cotton such as growers, merchants, converters and manufacturers could use the facilities in a similar way, buying futures to offset selling risks, or selling them to offset buying risks in respect of the raw cotton content of their new materials or products. With minor limitations, all concerned were in a position to choose that combination of price-risk bearing and price-risk avoidance that they thought best.

To the extent that a loss (gain) from a change in price of actual cotton was exactly offset by a gain (loss) from a change in the price of the futures contract, the hedger would be in the same position as if the purchase price of his 'actuals' cotton had continued unchanged. There was no certainty that this would be the case; the protection from risk provided by any particular futures transaction was incomplete. The hedger continued to carry residual risks of two kinds. First, the relationship between the actuals market for raw cotton and the futures market was such as to ensure that prices in them moved roughly together, but there was no reason for the movements to correspond exactly in any given time-period. Second, the futures contract fixed the price of a 'basis grade' cotton, and the payments due or owing on the contract at maturity were determined by the behaviour of the price of that cotton in the actuals market. But the hedger's actuals interest[86] would often be in some other cotton, so that he continued to bear the risk that the changes in the prices of the two cottons over the contract period might be dissimilar. Residual risks of this second type do not seem to have been of

[86] e.g. the raw cotton he held for use in his manufacturing operations.

major importance for raw cotton users.[87] In fact, such empirical evidence as is available suggests that, despite both types of residual risk, the pre-war futures market provided a high degree of cover for a *consistent* hedger[88] whether his spot interest was in the basis grade or in a cotton or commodity not even deliverable against the futures contract concerned.

During the war the futures market was closed, and cover facilities were provided for most of the period by the Cotton Control. The control had to take cotton as and when it could be obtained, and wanted it decentralised in the hands of spinners as quickly as possible. Spinners thus came to be in possession of larger stocks of cotton than they would have taken voluntarily, and of qualities that they would not necessarily have selected themselves. The control's cover arrangements relieved spinners of the price risks created by this situation. All varieties of cotton were altered in price simultaneously and by the same amount. Spinners made weekly returns of their stock and sales commitments to the control and paid or received price differences, according to their net 'short' or 'long' position, on the occasion of price changes. The control maintained a staff of inspectors, but although unintentional errors were discovered from time to time, no complete check on returns was made, as price changes were infrequent and the control was able to restrict the volume of transactions in the period immediately before they occurred. Conditions after the war caused this scheme to be modified. In May 1946 a 'cover symbol' was allotted to each of the main growths, and prices began to be quoted and cover provided separately for each symbol. Spinners were able to remain covered under the old scheme, and some few opted to do so; some also decided to remain without cover altogether rather than undertake to cover the whole of their transactions with the control, as was required of participants. This system, which was the one taken over by the commission, had a number of drawbacks. No cover at all was provided for people other than spinners with an interest in cotton, and the spinners' scheme was itself defective. The rendering of weekly returns and the administrative complexity of the cover

[87] Their significance was minimised by the possibilities of substitution between cottons in manufacture, which tended to prevent undue divergences between the prices of different cottons in the spot market.

[88] i.e. one undertaking a series of hedging transactions rather than a single one, so that residual losses and gains would tend to cancel out over time.

scheme made it impossible to change prices more than once weekly, so that the cover arrangements provided an important reason for the slow implementation of the new price policy described in the last section.[89] At the same time the large size of the price changes which sometimes were made caused great difficulties for spinners caught long or short of the cotton concerned.[90]. With price changes made once weekly on Mondays, it therefore became worth while for spinners to make a guess during the preceding week as to likely price changes and to endeavour to adjust their trading activities (and with them their net long or short position) so as to anticipate and take advantage of the change.[91] It was also possible, with this system, for long spinners to use the cover scheme to obtain cover against a new crop discount;[92] such a discount could not have been hedged in a futures market by those choosing to carry cotton over the relevant period.

The commission introduced a new cover scheme at the end of 1949 to remove these faults.[93] This gave spinners complete cover against price changes in the particular growth in which their actuals interest lay, the spinner being required in return to maintain a balanced position (within prescribed limits, and on call purchases apart) between raw cotton purchases and yarn sales. The scheme provided for the deferred delivery and on call arrangements already discussed,[94] and also provided cover for spinners buying cotton to spin for stock by allowing them to fix the price of the cotton at a later date. This scheme persisted almost unchanged throughout the rest of the period of the commission's monopoly.[95]

[89] See Section 5.

[90] The importance of this can be assessed from the fact that the great increases in Egyptian prices during 1948 caused such distress to some fine spinners called upon to produce large sums to meet differences that the commission had to provide special financial accommodation.

[91] Spinners could also adjust the timing of their returns to show the best possible position, though it is not suggested that this happened on any very general scale.

[92] A discount of this kind actually occurred in 1948, and was hedged against by spinners carrying stocks.

[93] The necessary six months' notice to terminate the earlier scheme had been given as long before as May 1948, but the discussion of the new arrangements with the trade was protracted. In the interim, the commission tried to 'check abuses' by seeking agreement to amendments in the method of submitting returns, but without success.　　　[94] See Section 4.

[95] The most important amendment was made in 1952 to take care of the fact

The commission also began to create separate cover schemes to take care of other interests. The first of these was the Cover Contract Scheme for converters. The converters wanted a scheme that would afford them protection when running dangerously long positions.[96] They made it clear that they had no wish to cover the whole of such holdings, but only particular types and for particular markets. The scheme enabled a converter who bought cloth to sell nominal futures to the commission, provided he did not rebuy in less than three months or more than twelve months. While the scheme provided some flexibility, restrictions were imposed by the commission 'to limit the possibilities of speculation at its expense'.[97] The scheme was useful during the post-war boom period, but less so after 1951 when converters could buy cloth for immediate delivery and have it processed at once. Another scheme, similar in principle, but designed to take care of different kinds of interest and separately administered, was developed for weavers and doublers, and three distinct schemes were introduced to cope with the cover problems of vertically integrated organisations. In addition, from the end of 1949 the commission operated an overnight export offer cover scheme, to provide overnight cover for spinners with interests in the export market. All the schemes offered complete protection against changes in raw cotton prices in respect of the cotton content of the goods traded, thus eliminating some of the residual price risks carried by the hedger in the pre-war market.

The commission's price and cover policies were the subject of great controversy in 1951. In the summer of that year a large American crop was expected, and the New York futures market showed a heavy forward discount. After July, when 'old crop' prices ceased to be quoted in New York, there was a very marked difference between the New York prices quoted for the new crop cotton and the commission's spot prices for American cottons. This provoked criticism

that spinners, affected by the recession and spinning for stock in preference to closing down, began to extend the period of call of their 'on call' cotton further and further. A new 'long position' cover arrangement was then introduced, which enabled such cotton to be finally invoiced, while affording protection for yarn stocks by making provision for the settlement of differences.

[96] It should be pointed out that risks of other kinds were sometimes more important to converters – e.g. the risk that foreign buyers might cancel orders placed at very high prices. No market or body could be expected to provide cover against this kind of risk on reasonable terms.

[97] *Report of the Cotton Import Committee*, para. 15.

of the commission's practice of averaging and also of the operation of cover schemes which did not afford protection against the forward discount. It was argued that the commission should begin to quote and sell its existing stocks at new crop prices before the new crop cotton became available on world markets. If it did not do so, it was suggested, it would be using its monopoly powers to force those spinners who had to buy at the higher prices to carry losses that should rightly be borne by the commission. The commission refused to adopt such a policy. It supported its replacement-cost principle on the grounds that new crop prices were irrelevant until the cotton began to reach the market, and that there was no old crop American cotton to be bought in world markets at New York prices quoted after July. In this the commission was probably right; the free market did not afford protection to spinners carrying cotton 'into the discount', and the natural result of a short crop followed by the expectation of a long one is progressively to reduce spot stocks as the new crop months approach. Thus the commission's best policy would appear to have been one designed to reduce its stocks to their minimum operational level, by successive price reductions, by the time new crop cotton became available. The losses of those constrained to carry cotton would then have been borne as in a free market. However, the commission advanced other arguments in defence of its policy; it argued that it was acting in the long-run interests of the trade as a whole, since, if it yielded, expectation of a large crop in future years would cause trade to stagnate even longer, as buyers would wait for the commission's reductions. Spinners suggested that such an attitude was only possible for a monopolist, that the policy was influenced by a Treasury desire to avoid loss, that foreign buyers of textiles were being discouraged by the commission's price lists (which, they said, made evident the price handicap under which the British producer laboured and indicated that exporters elsewhere were likely to be cheaper) and that the decline in trade (which was in fact the beginning of a world-wide textile recession) was attributable directly to the commission's activities.

The commission felt and stated that many of the criticisms of the price and cover policy pursued in 1951 were unjust and ill-informed,[98] and this view was not without justification. But the criticism was encouraged by the 'moral' flavour of the commission's attitude to a commercial matter, by its attempts to safeguard *the* interests of an

[98] *Annual Report*, 1950–1, ch. v.

industry with many divergent interests and (as was pointed out earlier) by the fact that a statutory monopoly of this kind provides a natural focus for complaint and attracts blame for circumstances often outside its control.

In some respects the commission's cover facilities were superior to those of the pre-war market. Spinners were given complete protection against the residual price risks that they had had to carry in the free market, and participants in other schemes were able to avoid some residual risks that had formerly been unavoidable. Many traders found these cover facilities very valuable; some of the textile combines, which had been continuously critical of the commission, expressed anxiety when its abolition was projected lest they be left without comparable cover facilities. There were offsetting disadvantages. The commission's cover arrangements required a separate set of rules and administrative arrangements for each type of risk covered, as against the unified organisation of the futures market. The schemes also required, broadly, that the trader should cover all his transactions or none, whereas the Liverpool futures market could be used to obtain that degree of protection that individual traders thought most appropriate at any time. This meant a great loss of flexibility in the hedging arrangements. There is evidence that some firms considered this loss to be not without importance, and, when its monopoly was terminated and private importation permitted, the commission showed its own appreciation of the value of less rigid arrangements by introducing modified arrangements that allowed producers to have an uncovered long interest if they so desired.

Price risks were not abolished by the commission's cover schemes. Rather, speculative activity was denied to traders by the requirement that they keep a balanced position, and the commission, through its cover scheme, took the price risks instead. Thus, in addition to being a speculator on the grand scale as the central stockholder, the commission had to speculate to a significant though relatively less important extent in providing cover facilities. Nevertheless, it has been claimed that, quite apart from the excellence of the cover they provided, the commission's schemes served a useful purpose in preventing 'harmful' speculation by private individuals. But the nature and existence of such harmful speculation is difficult to establish. The pre-war private speculator performed an economic function; condemnation of his activity as 'gambling' ignores the fact that the risks he specialised in taking were not created by him but had to be

borne whether or not such specialisation existed. The only proposition of interest is that the activity of private speculators may
have had harmful (i.e. destabilising) effects on spot prices through
'speculation about speculation' as made familiar by Keynes. While
evidence about this is not easy to collect, since speculative behaviour
per se is difficult to isolate, it appears probable that such destabilising
speculation is of less importance in commodity markets, in which spot
market trading provides a continuous check on expectations, than
in the security markets that Keynes himself had in mind.

Lastly, it is apparent that, with these cover arrangements, any price
change made by the commission affected not only the world competitive position of British spinners and the value of the commission's
own sales, but also the size of its gains and losses under its cover
schemes. The wisdom of allowing these three separate and possibly
conflicting interests to be reconciled by a unified authority such as
the commission is open to question.

7. GENERAL CONCLUSIONS

There is one respect only in which the commission appears to have
provided facilities superior to those of the free market. This is in the
provision of cover facilities. Since the reopening of the Liverpool
Cotton Exchange, circumstances in world markets beyond the control of the Lancashire industry have created difficulties for those
requiring cover facilities from the free futures market,[99] and there
must be many spinners who look back wistfully to this aspect of the
commission's activities. From the community's point of view, however, a clear issue of principle arises: the excellence of the commission's cover arrangements depended in the last analysis upon their
reliance upon the public purse.

In many other respects the Raw Cotton Commission fell short of
the ideals of its creators, justified the forebodings of its early opponents, and provided spinners with services that they considered
inferior to those they would have expected of the free market. The
strength and sincerity of the spinners' views in the matter were
demonstrated when the efficiency of the statutory monopoly was put
to the test. After the publication in April 1952 of the Report of the
Cotton Import Committee set up to examine the operations of the
commission, all growths of cotton were divided into four broad
groups, and spinners were permitted to opt whether to buy their

[99] See below, pp. 371–83.

cotton requirements entirely from the commission or entirely privately in respect of each group. Cover continued to be provided by the commission. Twenty-nine per cent of the industry (in terms of previous year's consumption) contracted-out of purchase from the commission in the first year that this was permitted, and the figure rose to around 60 per cent in the second year.[100] The statistics underestimate the importance of contracting-out, particularly in the first year, since they include single mills being used as 'pilot' buyers for combines, and since some cottons continued to be bought in bulk on the commission's long-term contracts and so were not easily obtainable by private purchase. It is clear, however, that spinners were prepared to take the opportunity to buy privately despite the short-run difficulties such buying entailed, and that (on the evidence of the increase in contracting out in the second year) they were not dissatisfied with the results.[101] The government appears to have taken such a view: it did not adopt the recommendation of the Cotton Import (Review) Committee in June 1953 that the contracting out system by continued. Instead, legislation was introduced to wind up the commission.

The commission's deficiencies cannot be attributed to its personnel, whose technical competence and good intentions were generally accepted; nor can they be attributed entirely to the world trading conditions that obtained during the commission's life, difficult though these sometimes were. Rather, the evidence suggests that many of the commission's shortcomings related directly to its position as a statutory monopolist and sole seller, committed by the government to serve an undefined public interest and required by the cotton textile industry to fulfil technical requirements of some complexity with at least the same precision and flexibility as the free market had done. Its position as a monopoly also made it peculiarly vulnerable to influence, complaints and criticism. Further, its position as a *statutory* body permitted the intrusion of non-commercial considerations into what were essentially commercial operations.

[100] *Annual Report*, 1952–3, paras. 24 and 40.
[101] The reaction of spinners in the first year of the option may have been influenced to some extent by exaggerated claims on behalf of private buying and by exaggerated criticisms of the commission. But these influences could have had no effect in the second year.

15

AN INVESTIGATION OF HEDGING ON AN ORGANISED PRODUCE EXCHANGE*

1

The practice of 'hedging', by buying and selling futures contracts on organised produce exchanges, enables manufacturers and merchants to cover themselves against adverse movements of prices of raw materials in which they deal. The hedging facilities have always been recognised as one of the principal justifications for the existence of organised produce exchanges, even by those who look upon these institutions with disfavour. It is also generally recognised that the cover against unfavourable price movements that is provided by hedging may not always be perfect or sufficient. The hedger may be left with a balance of profit or loss on his hedged transaction – the cover may be too much or too little. It is the object of this note to attempt to give some indication of the extent of the inaccuracies in hedging on the pre-war cotton market in Liverpool.

In organised produce exchanges there are two related markets – the 'spot' ('cash' or 'actuals') market in which the actual commodity is bought and sold;[1] and the 'futures' market in which highly standardised contracts for future delivery are negotiated. Hedging consists of balancing an open position in the spot market by an open but opposite position in the futures market. Thus if a processor or dealer buys a quantity of the commodity he takes up a 'long' position in the spot market, and he is exposed to the risk of loss should the price fall before he sells. He hedges by selling a futures contract of the same quantity, thereby taking up a 'short' position in the futures market. When he sells the commodity in the spot

* *Manchester School of Economics and Social Studies*, September 1951, pp. 305–19.
[1] Transactions in the actuals market can be for either immediate or forward delivery. A forward actuals contract is not to be confused with a 'futures' contract.

market he concludes his transactions by buying back the futures contract he had previously sold as a hedge. (The 'short-seller' in the spot market – e.g. a manufacturer who undertakes to deliver at a future date without having the necessary supplies when he gives the undertaking – is in the opposite position: he buys a futures contract as hedge against the risk of a rise in price before he obtains the necessary supplies.)

If the costs of holding stocks of the commodity and the costs of dealing in the two markets are omitted, the hedger finishes with neither profit nor loss only when the prices in the two markets have moved in the same direction and by the same amount. Only then is his loss (or profit) on his spot dealings exactly compensated for by an equivalent profit (or loss) on his futures dealings. In fact the two prices rarely move precisely in step with each other, and the hedger is usually left with a balance of profit or loss. Expressed differently, the outcome to the hedger depends upon the relationship (i.e. difference) between the spot price and the futures price at the opening and closing dates of the set of transactions. If the difference between the two prices is the same at the two dates, the hedge is perfect and the hedger neither loses nor gains on balance. Any change in the difference between spot and futures prices (called the 'basis' in the trade) produces a loss or gain for the hedger.

The basis may change for a variety of reasons. Some changes in basis are connected with the technicalities of the futures contract. Others, and probably the more important ones, are due to the fact that the two markets, spot and futures, are not indentical though they are related; and that arbitrage transactions (through time) between the two markets cannot assure a rigid and unchanging relationship between prices in them. Thus for example if there is a tightness of immediate supplies in the spot market and promise or expectations of easier supplies in the near future, spot prices are likely to be high relatively to futures prices. On the other hand futures prices are likely to be high relatively to spot if, towards the end of a crop-year, the new crop looks unpromising. Supply and demand conditions do not affect the two markets equally, and changes in these conditions may bring about changes in the basis. Arbitrage operations affecting the two markets (effected by accumulating and carrying stocks and selling futures; or by liquidating stocks, deferring consumption and buying futures) may mitigate but cannot entirely prevent divergent or unequal movements in the two markets.

The practice of hedging is founded upon the assumption that the prices in the two markets are likely to move in fairly close correspondence with each other, so that changes in basis are relatively small. The investigation of price movements in selected sample periods has been made in order to test the validity of the assumption.

2

Before turning to an account of the investigation and the findings it may be useful to tabulate possible hedging situations, and the results to the hedger in each case (Table 1).

TABLE 1

Classification of hedging situations

	price movements		results			
			to one who is 'long' in the spot market		to one who is 'short' in the spot market	
type	spot price	futures price	unhedged	hedged	unhedged	hedged
1A	falls	falls by same amount as spot	loss	neither profit nor loss	profit	neither profit nor loss
1B	falls	falls by greater amount than spot	loss	profit	profit	loss
1C	falls	falls by smaller amount than spot	loss	loss, but smaller than unhedged loss	profit	profit, but smaller than unhedged profit
1D	falls	rises	loss	loss, but greater than unhedged loss	profit	profit, but greater than unhedged profit
2A	rises	rises by same amount as spot	profit	neither profit nor loss	loss	neither profit nor loss
2B	rises	rises by greater amount than spot	profit	loss	loss	profit
2C	rises	rises by smaller amount than spot	profit	profit, but smaller than unhedged profit	loss	loss, but smaller than unhedged loss
2D	rises	falls	profit	profit, but greater than unhedged profit	loss	loss, but greater than unhedged loss

It will be seen that there are four pairs of symmetrical situations: Types 1A and 2A, 1B and 2B, 1C and 2C, and 1D and 2D. These pairs may be called, respectively, perfect hedges, over-compensating hedges, under-compensating hedges, and aggravating hedges. With perfect hedges neither long nor short interest in the spot market suffers any loss. The cover is complete. The hedger is compensated for any loss but forfeits any profit arising from price movements in the spot market. With over-compensating hedges the loser in the spot market becomes, with hedging, a net gainer, and vice versa. With under-compensating hedges the loser (or gainer) in the spot market remains a loser (or gainer) but a smaller loser (or gainer) in the hedged position. The aggravating hedge is a special kind of under-compensating hedge. The loser (or gainer) in the spot market remains a loser (or gainer) in the hedged position, but his loss (or gain) is greater with hedging than without it.

It would be futile and unreasonable to hedge as a means of risk reduction if all hedges were of the aggravating type and were known to be so. On the other hand, if all hedges were either perfect or under-compensating, and known to be so, hedging would be a useful and reliable method of risk reduction. With over-compensating hedges the position is not clear-cut. Where price movements are over-compensating, firms who would have gained without hedging become net losers with hedging. And the amount of the loss of the loser with hedging may be smaller or greater than the amount of the loss of the (different) loser without hedging, depending upon the extent of the over-compensating movements. If the losses were *smaller* with hedging than without it, over-compensating hedges transform larger losses and gains into smaller gains and losses; and if all hedges were of this type and known to be so, the practice of hedging would still offer opportunities of risk reduction to dealers who are uncertain about price fluctuations and anxious to minimise or avoid the consequences of particularly unfavourable price changes in the spot market. On the other hand if over-compensating price movements produced greater gains and losses than those without hedging, the practice would not commend itself to the type of dealer described.

3

The statistical analysis of the results of hedging in cotton futures on the Liverpool Cotton Exchange has been limited to two periods, each of two years: August 1930 to July 1932 and March 1938 to February 1940. For each period dealings in two futures contracts have been selected: in the American Middling contract for both periods, in the Egyptian Sakellaridis contract for 1930–2, and in the Egyptian Uppers contract for 1938–40. There are thus four samples. The two periods have been selected because in each there were major fluctuations in cotton prices. The periods include such sharply disturbing events as the departure of several countries from the gold standard

345

and the outbreak of the Second World War. The first period was one of falling prices on balance, and the second period one of rising prices; but in both periods there were both rises and falls.

The data, analysed below, purport to show the results of hypothetical sets of dealings in the cotton markets. For each sample the following situations have been assumed and their results calculated: On each Friday[2] within the period a spinner bought (or sold) cotton, of the description and grade forming the basis of the futures contract, at the closing price in the spot market.[3] He hedged by selling (or buying) an equivalent futures contract at the closing price on the same day. Eight weeks later he reversed his earlier transactions in the two markets, again at the closing prices. Since at any time there are several futures contracts for the same basic description of cotton, differing from one another only in that they fall due in different stated future months, the hypothetical spinner is assumed to have selected the particular futures 'month' (contract) by following a simple rule.[4] The rule ensures that the selected contract continued to have an active market for several weeks after the hedging transaction had been completed.

All results are expressed in hundredths of a penny per pound of raw cotton. In fact futures contracts were sold in units of substantial size. The American cotton contract, for example, was sold in multiples of 48,000 lb (0·01d. per lb equals £2 per contract in this case).

4

The limitations of the findings are listed before the statistics are presented. First, the hedger is assumed to have dealt in raw cotton of the description and grade forming the basis of the particular futures contract (e.g. American middling cotton 'equal in colour to the standard and of not less than fair staple' for the American futures contract). If dealings in other descriptions, growths, or qualities of cotton had been assumed, additional profits or losses might have resulted. Secondly, the statistics are based upon the assumption that the hedger did not attempt to gauge which of the available futures 'months' (contracts) would undergo the most favourable change in

---

[2] Or Thursday if the Exchange was closed on Friday.

[3] All price quotations have been taken from *Tattersall's Cotton Trade Review*.

[4] For eight-week periods beginning on or before the tenth day of any month, the futures contract postulating delivery two months hence was selected; after the tenth day, the futures contract falling due three months hence was taken.

basis. Thirdly, the hedger is assumed to have refrained from switching his hedge from one 'month' to another during the eight-week transaction period. Additional gains or losses might have resulted from speculations about the most appropriate 'month' to use as hedge, or from switching. Tests have indicated that simple switches from one 'month' to another would not have produced significantly different results, and that dealings in any other near-month futures contracts, rather than the particular ones selected, would not have changed the picture much. But on occasions the skilful hedger, if his anticipations were correct, could have secured much better results than those of the routine hedging incorporated in the present findings.

The costs of using the futures market are ignored in the calculations. Brokerage payments would have been from 0·02 to 0·04 pence per lb for each transaction in the case of American contracts, according to the status of the spinner on the Exchange. The costs of storing cotton for eight weeks, which would have been incurred by our 'long' spinner, are also omitted. Carrying costs would have varied a good deal; if they are calculated at 10 per cent per annum on value, they would have been from 0·02 to 0·06 pence per lb for each venture.

5

In Table 2 the results of hedging are classified into types on the basis of associated spot and futures price movements (as tabulated in Table 1). Data are presented for each of the four samples, each of which is sub-divided according to the amount of the price change in the spot market.

Aggregating the results of the four samples the findings may be summarised as follows:

Percentage distribution of hedged results

	with spot price changes of less than 1d. per lb	with spot price changes of more than 1d. per lb	all cases
Perfect hedges	5	2	4
Over-compensating hedges	41	42	41
Under-compensating hedges	45	56	48
Aggravating hedges	9	—	7
	100	100	100

TABLE 2

Analysis of related movements of spot and future prices
(over eight-week periods)

change in spot price (in hundredths of a penny per lb)	number of times				
	futures price moved in same direction as spot price			futures price and spot price moved in opposite directions	
	by the same amount as spot price	by a greater amount than spot price	by a smaller amount than spot price		
	col. (1)	col. (2)	col. (3)	col. (4)	totals
American (middling) 1930–2					
1–29	0	9	10	8	27
30–59	2	13	13	0	28
60–99	6	14	10	0	30
100–149	1	3	10	0	14
150–199	0	5	1	0	6
Totals	9	44	44	8	105
American (middling) 1938–40					
1–29	3	18	18	8	47
30–59	1	10	17	0	28
60–99	0	3	9	0	12
100–149	0	4	3	0	7
150–199	0	5	0	0	5
200 and over	1	3	0	0	4
Totals	5	43	47	8	103 (b)
Egyptian (sakel) 1930–2					
1–29	0	6	4	5	15
30–59	0	8	7	0	15
60–99	0	9	12	0	21
100–149	0	7	12	0	19
150–199	0	4	16	0	20
200 and over	0	5	9	0	14
Totals	0	39	60	5	104 (b)
Egyptian (upper) 1938–40					
1–29	2	20	16	5	43
30–59	1	11	23	1	36
60–99	0	6	3	0	9
100–159	0	1	4	0	5
150–199	0	1	3	0	4
200 and over	0	6	1	0	7
Totals	3	45	50	6	104

Notes:
 (a) Columns (1) to (4) indicate, respectively, 'perfect', 'over-compensating', 'under-compensating', and 'aggravating' hedges.
 (b) Two results, where there were no spot price changes, are omitted. The futures price movements were 0·03 and 0·18d. respectively.

The results were much the same for small and large spot price changes (particularly when it is remembered that aggravating hedges are in a sense under-compensating hedges – in both types the loser in the spot market remains the loser in the hedged position). Under-compensating hedges occurred somewhat more frequently than over-compensating hedges, particularly in the Egyptian samples. An analysis of the data reveals, further, that under-compensating hedges occurred relatively more frequently in association with increases than with decreases in spot prices, and again this was more marked in the Egyptian samples.[5]

It may be noted that aggravating hedges – 7 per cent of the total – were confined to spot price changes of less than 1d. per lb. In fact all except one of these cases occurred with price changes of less than 0·30d. per lb. For the larger price changes the futures prices always moved in the appropriate direction, though the movement was generally too large or too small for perfect hedges.

The amount by which a change in futures prices exceeds or falls short of the related change in spot prices measures the imperfection or inaccuracy of the hedge. Table 3 sets out the average imperfection for the four samples sub-divided according to the amount of the change in spot prices. In each case the average imperfection is expressed in absolute terms as well as relatively to the average change in spot prices.

TABLE 3
The extent of imperfection in hedging

change in spot price (in hundredths of a penny per lb)	average amount of imperfection (in hundredths of a penny per lb)				average amount of imperfection as percentage of average change in spot price			
	American middling 1930–2	American middling 1938–40	Egyptian sakel 1930–2	Egyptian upper 1938–40	American middling 1930–2	American middling 1938–40	Egyptian sakel 1930–2	Egyptian upper 1938–40
					%	%	%	%
0 to 29	10	9	15	9	62	62	99	59
30 to 59	9	15	16	9	19	37	37	20
60 to 99	9	18	16	16	12	25	20	21
100 to 149	20	15	16	36	15	12	13	27
150 and over	23	19	26	27	13	9	14	12
All	11	13	19	13	17	25	17	21

[5] Forty-five per cent of the hedged results associated with spot price decreases were under-compensating or aggravating, against 64 per cent of the hedged results with spot price increases. For the American samples alone the percentages were 47 and 54 respectively; and for the Egyptian samples, 41 and 75, respectively.

On the average hedging provided a high degree of cover, except for the smallest spot price changes. The effectiveness of hedging varied almost directly with the amount of spot price change; the practice was least effective in times of small movements in spot prices.[6] This finding speaks well for hedging, since the hedger is naturally particularly anxious that large spot losses should be effectively covered.

6

In Table 4 the results of the 416 individual hedged transactions are analysed in greater detail. The amount of the gain or loss, with hedging, is shown for each eight-week period, from the point of view of the spinner who, unhedged, would have been on the losing side of the spot market (i.e. the holder of stocks in periods of falling prices and the short-seller in periods of rising prices). Net gains are recorded for over-compensating hedges, and net losses for under-compensating and aggravating hedges. The net gains or losses indicate the amount of imperfection in the hedging.

The contents of the table may be summarised as follows: of cases where the spot price changed by less than 1d. per lb, 55 per cent showed imperfections of less than 0·10d. per lb and 85 per cent of less than 0·20d. per lb;[7] of cases where the spot price changed by more than 1d. per lb, 18 per cent showed imperfections of less than 0·10d. per lb, 50 per cent of less than 0·20d. per lb, and 75 per cent of less than 0·30d. per lb.

There were of course occasions when the results were unsatisfactory to the hedger. In the twenty-seven aggravating hedges (indicated in Table 2) the hedged loss was naturally greater than the unhedged loss. In addition there were fourteen over-compensating hedges (out of 171) where the loss with hedging (of the gainer in

---

[6] Further calculations indicate the following:

(a) The relative imperfection was greater for under-compensating than for over-compensating hedges. Under-compensating hedges were not only more frequent than over-compensating hedges, but also less accurate.

(b) The degree of imperfection was not on the average influenced by the direction of price movements.

[7] For spot price changes under 0·30d. per lb, imperfections were less than 0·05d. per lb in 30 per cent of cases, and less than 0·10d. per lb in 60 per cent of cases. For spot price changes between 0·30 and 0·99d. per lb, imperfections were less than 0·05d. per lb in 25 per cent of cases, less than 0·10d. per lb in 50 per cent of cases, and less than 0·20d. per lb in 70 per cent of cases.

TABLE 4

Analysis of results of hedged transactions

(Results expressed from point of view of hedger who suffered loss in the spot market)

All amounts of gain or loss expressed in hundredths of a penny per lb

loss in the spot market	number of times hedging resulted in											totals
	loss of					loss or profit less than 10	profit of					
	60–69	40–59	30–39	20–29	10–19		10–19	20–29	30–39	40–59	60–69	
American (middling) 1930–2												
1–29	–	–	1	3	5	16	1	1	–	–	–	27
30–59	–	–	1	1	–	21	3	2	–	–	–	28
60–99	–	1	–	1	2	18	8	–	–	–	–	30
100–149	–	1	2	4	2	3	2	–	–	–	–	14
150 and over	1	–	–	–	–	1	2	2	–	–	–	6
Totals	1	2	4	9	9	59	16	5	–	–	–	105
American (middling) 1938–40												
1–29	–	1	1	–	10	29	5	1	–	–	–	47
30–59	–	–	2	5	8	9	3	–	–	1	–	28
60–99	–	1	–	1	4	4	1	–	–	–	1	12
100–149	–	–	–	1	2	3	–	1	–	–	–	7
150–199	–	–	–	–	–	1	2	–	2	–	–	5
200 and over	–	–	–	–	–	1	1	2	–	–	–	4
Totals	–	2	3	7	24	47	12	4	2	1	1	103
Egyptian (sakel) 1930–2												
1–29	–	–	–	3	3	6	1	1	1	–	–	15
30–59	–	–	–	–	4	3	6	1	–	1	–	15
60–99	–	1	–	4	4	7	4	–	1	–	–	21
100–149	–	–	–	5	5	5	3	1	–	–	–	19
150–199	–	2	2	3	7	2	2	2	–	–	–	20
200 and over	–	3	3	2	1	1	–	2	–	2	–	14
Totals	–	6	5	17	24	24	16	7	2	3	–	104
Egyptian (upper) 1938–40												
1–29	1	–	–	–	3	30	8	1	–	–	–	43
30–59	–	1	–	2	9	22	2	–	–	–	–	36
60–99	1	–	–	–	–	6	1	–	–	1	–	9
100–149	–	–	3	1	–	–	–	–	–	1	–	5
150–199	–	2	–	–	1	–	–	–	–	1	–	4
200 and over	–	–	1	–	–	2	3	–	1	–	–	7
Totals	2	3	4	3	13	60	14	1	1	3	–	104

the spot market) was greater than the loss without hedging (of the loser in the spot market). In all except three of these cases the results were associated with spot price changes of less than 0·30d. per lb.

There were twenty-four results (6 per cent of the total) where the imperfections in hedging were of the order of 0·40d. per lb or more. Of these ten were in respect of eight-week periods commencing within the first eight weeks of the war. Eight were in respect of eight-week periods covering the end of one crop-year and the beginning of the next, when uncertainty about supplies is greatest. Apart from the results affected by the outbreak of the war, most of the imperfections in excess of 0·40d. per lb (ten out of fourteen cases) occurred with spot price movements of over 1½d. per lb.

7

A somewhat misleading impression will be gained if results of hedging are examined for isolated hedges alone (as in Table 3). A spinner or merchant is likely to have several hedging transactions at different times within any period, so that the imperfections of individual hedges, some being to his advantage and others not, may tend to even out. Calculations have therefore been made for the four samples to measure the extent to which individual gains and losses, with hedging, cancelled one another.

The calculations are based on the assumption that the hypothetical spinner had the same quantity of cotton at risk in each of the eight-week transaction periods in which the samples are sub-divided. The spinner is assumed to have been 'long' in the spot market, i.e. a holder of raw or processed cotton. The results of his operations are shown in the aggregate, comparing the results without hedging and the results with hedging. Three sets of calculations are presented in Table 5 in respect of each of the samples. The first shows the aggregated results of the transactions in eight-week periods in which spot prices fell (i.e. in which closing price was smaller than opening price). The second shows the results for eight-week periods in which spot prices rose. The third shows the aggregate results for all the eight-week transactions in each sample, and consists of summations of the first two sets of results.[8] (The results would have been reversed in the case of a spinner who was 'short' in the spot market.)

Though there were variations from sample to sample (and for

[8] The results here are calculated on the basis that the hedger hedged every successive spot purchase.

TABLE 5

Aggregated results, with and without hedging, of hypothetical transactions (see text, above)

(in hundredths of a penny per lb; $+$ = profit, $-$ = loss)

sample	results (aggregated) of transactions					
	in eight-week periods in which spot prices fell		in eight-week periods in which spot prices rose		in all eight-week periods	
	without hedging	with hedging	without hedging	with hedging	without hedging	with hedging
	col. (i)	col. (ii)	col. (iii)	col. (iv)	col. (v)	col. (vi)
American middling 1930–2	−3782	−115	+3136	+218	−646	+103
American middling 1938–40	−1547	−313	+3868	−71	+2321	−384
Egyptian sakel 1930–2	−6775	+51	+4625	+660	−2150	+711
Egyptian upper 1938–40	−1365	−86	+4847	+234	+3482	+148

sub-divisions of the two-year periods of each sample) the general conclusion is that, for spot price increases and decreases considered separately, the hedging imperfections tended to balance out to a considerable extent,[9] leaving a relatively small remainder of under-compensated hedging (see cols. (i) to (iv) in Table 5), meaning that on balance the loser in the spot market remained a loser, but a very much smaller loser, with hedging.

A particular spinner is not likely to suffer adverse price changes in the spot market all the time. Even without hedging, gains on favourable price movements will offset losses on unfavourable price movements. The results of such off-setting are shown in column (v) of Table 5, revealing that substantial profits or losses, without hedging, remained for our hypothetical spinner. Column (vi) of Table 4 shows the results with hedging. Though, in the terminology

[9] The following calculations relating to the American samples indicate the extent of the improvement brought about by the balancing of the imperfections on individual hedges. Without such balancing (i.e. without taking into account whether the imperfection was to the hedger's advantage or disadvantage) the average imperfection for spot price decreases, expressed as a percentage of the average spot price change, was 14 per cent in 1930–2 and 39 per cent in 1938–40; taking balancing into account the corresponding figures were 3 per cent and 20 per cent, respectively. For spot price increases the figures were 22 per cent, without balancing, against 7 per cent, with balancing, in 1930–2; and 19 per cent against 2 per cent in 1938–40.

adopted in this paper, hedging was on balance under-compensating (see preceding paragraph), the inaccuracies of hedging together with the (net) direction of spot price movements caused the net loser without hedging to become a net gainer with hedging (and vice versa) in three samples out of four. However, this result is less significant than that the magnitudes of the gains and losses with hedging were much smaller than the gains and losses without hedging, and were, indeed, small in absolute terms. This last conclusion, if it were true generally as well as for the selected samples, would provide strong justification for the practice of hedging as a means of reducing the risks of loss from price fluctuations.

Addendum[10]

1. THE CLASSIFICATION AND ASSESSMENT OF HEDGING OUTCOMES

A four-fold classification of hedging outcomes has been used in the preceding article. The classification can be made more elaborate. Thus the classification 'over-compensating hedges' can be subdivided according as to whether the movement of the futures price is less than twice, twice, or more than twice the movement of the spot price; the loss (gain) with hedging is, respectively, smaller, equal to, or greater than the gain (loss) without hedging, and it may be said that there is correspondingly an improvement, an unaltered situation, or a deterioration in the results from the hedger's point of view (see above, p. 345). For convenience let us refer to these sub-categories as type 1, 2 and 3 respectively. Again, the four-fold classification omits two possible types of situation, one where the spot price remains unchanged while the futures price changes (leading to a deterioration in outcome), and the other where the spot price changes while the futures price does not change (causing no change in outcome). In all, the four-fold classification can be expanded into an eight-fold classification.

A distribution of hedging outcomes, classified into the preceding eight categories, can be re-arranged to yield a different three-fold

[10] I am indebted to Dr R. H. Snape of Monash University who has given me the benefit of helpful suggestions and criticism in numerous discussions concerning the matters raised in these Notes.

classification, based not on the extent and direction of associated price changes but on the nature of the outcome, namely whether hedging improved or worsened the position or left it unchanged. Improvement may be said to come from perfect, under-compensating and type 1 over-compensating hedges; and deterioration from aggravating and type 3 over-compensating hedges, and cases where the futures price alone moves. The remaining two cases may be said to leave the situation unchanged by hedging, that is type 2 over-compensating hedges and cases where the futures price alone does not move. On this basis, the following are the outcomes for the two US samples:

	1930–2	1938–40
Improvement	96	89
Deterioration	7	14
No change	2	1
	105[11]	104

Except on one occasion, cases of deterioration occurred where the change in the spot price was relatively small, that is, less than 0·20 pence per pound. Nine-tenths of the over-compensating hedges were of type 1, that is, they were 'improving' hedges in the sense that the loss (gain) with hedging was smaller than the gain (loss) without hedging.

The final section of the paper (pp. 352 to 354, above) discusses the *aggregate* of the outcomes of the four samples of hypothetical trading, the earlier sections having been concerned with the *distribution* of individual transaction outcomes. It concludes with some comments on the comparison between the aggregated outcome of the series of unhedged transactions in a sample and the aggregated outcome of the corresponding series of hedged transactions for a holder of a stock of cotton. In my view this sort of comparison can be misleading. It may give rise to interpretations of the kind that, where the former net gain was larger than the latter (or the former loss was smaller than the latter), hedging was unprofitable or of

[11] One case where the spot price changed while the futures price did not was for convenience recorded in the article as an aggravating hedge. This explains why the number of instances of deterioration is less than the number of aggravating hedges, whereas the former should be equal to or exceed the latter.

negative value to the hedger, and that he would have been better off without hedging. Such an interpretation would be invalid. It would ignore the fact that the hedgers under consideration are presumed to wish to reduce their exposure to risk and to avoid the adverse consequences of unforeseen unfavourable price movements. To infer from a comparison of aggregated unhedged and hedged outcomes that the short hedger would have been better off without hedging in two of the four samples (see Table 5, p. 353, above) would be the same as to say, after the event, that it was unprofitable to have had the expense of fire insurance cover during a period in which the insured did not suffer a fire. The comparison in question tells us nothing about the efficiency with which the cover was provided. The analysis in the remainder of the paper is relevant for an answer to this question.

In Table 5, above, the aggregated results of the hedging outcomes are presented. The average values of the outcomes can be derived, and standard statistical tests applied to determine the probability that the observed averages do not differ significantly from zero, that is that the observed differences from zero are due to the chances of sampling. Since a (statistically significant) average value of zero implies that on the average the hedges were perfect, and that the observed imperfections were of the kind likely to occur at random, this test is of some interest. From it one may conclude with a high level of confidence that the average outcome in the US 1930–2 sample did not differ significantly from zero. For the US 1938–40 sample, on the other hand, the observed average is so large relatively to the dispersion of individual outcomes that it would be unsound to conclude that the observed imperfections were due to chance factors alone and that they did not reflect a systematic bias in spot–futures price relationships in the period. The probable explanation of the 'poorer' performance of the market in this second period is that it included the outbreak of the Second World War, the expectation and impact of which disturbed price relationships.[12]

[12] The salient data for the two US samples are:

	1930–2	1938–40
Number of outcomes	105	104
Mean outcome (hundredths of a penny)	+0·98	−3·67
Standard deviation (hundredths of a penny)	15·88	16·57
Value of t	0·63	2·25

2. DIFFERENT CONCEPTS OF HEDGING

The paper reprinted above is concerned with hedging as a device for avoiding or reducing the impact of market (price) risks, and the terminology is developed in terms of such hedging objectives. Hedging is 'perfect' when the spot and futures prices move in parallel. Expressed in terms of 'basis' changes, hedging is perfect when the opening basis (i.e. the difference between spot and futures prices when the hedge is placed) is the same as the closing basis (i.e. the difference between the spot and futures prices when the hedge is lifted). The hedge is perfect because both a 'short' hedger (i.e. one carrying a stock of the commodity) and a 'long' hedger (i.e. one with an uncovered forward sales commitment) would obtain complete cover against adverse changes in the spot price. For convenience we will refer to this type of risk-avoiding hedging as 'insurance hedging'. This term is useful in that it identifies the motive or intention of the hedging transaction. It is this type of hedging which is most commonly referred to in discussions of the uses of futures markets.

The approach used in my paper and in similar studies made before and after its publication has been criticised by Professor Holbrook Working and also by Professor Roger Gray.[13] 'The basic idea that complete effectiveness of hedging depends on parallelism of movement of spot and futures prices is false, and an improper standard by which to test the effectiveness of hedging.'[14] The criticism is, however, altogether misconceived in so far as the stability-of-basis measurement or test of hedging is used in relation to insurance hedging, as was done in my paper.

Working has, however, performed a valuable service in drawing attention to another type of, or motive for, hedging in futures markets; and had his articles on the subject appeared before mine was written, I would have been more careful to stipulate the type

When the 1938–40 sample is truncated by omitting all outcomes after the end of August 1939, the mean is $+2\cdot06$, the standard deviation $12\cdot08$, and the value of t, $1\cdot50$.

[13] See Holbrook Working, 'Futures Trading and Hedging', *American Economic Review*, June 1953, and 'Hedging Reconsidered', *Journal of Farm Economics*, November 1953; and Roger W. Gray, 'The Importance of Hedging in Futures Trading, and the Effectiveness of Futures Trading for Hedging', in *Futures Trading Seminar*, vol. 1, Madison, Wis., 1960.

[14] Working, 'Hedging Reconsidered', p. 547.

of hedging I had in mind, and would have made it clear that simultaneous trades in actuals and futures could occur for reasons other than risk-reduction. Working has drawn attention especially to hedging which is motivated by the hedger's desire to profit from favourable *changes* in basis.[15] 'The effectiveness of hedging, intelligently used in connection with commodity storage, depends on *inequalities* between the movements of spot and futures prices and on reasonable predictability of such inequalities.'[16] For this type of hedging, which for convenience, and following a lead given by Working, will be called 'arbitrage hedging',[17] stability in the basis is no virtue, because with such stability there can be no opportunity to profit from simultaneous but opposite transactions in the actuals and futures markets. What is a virtue for insurance hedging is a vice for arbitrage hedging.

Arbitrage hedging is partly speculative inasmuch as the eventual outcome of hedging (the combined result of simultaneous but opposite transactions in the spot market and the futures market) cannot be perfectly predictable when the hedge is opened. The degree of difficulty of prediction differs greatly according to circumstances. It is smallest when the hedge is to be carried through until the month in which the particular futures contract matures and delivery of the commodity can be made on it (for example, July for a July futures). In this case predictability is high; in the month of its maturity the price of the futures contract approximates more or less closely to the spot price of the basic contract grade of the commodity, because the commodity can be delivered in settlement of the contract. An element of unpredictability – and hence of uncertainty of outcome – persists even here, because in practice there need not be a fixed or

[15] The existence and nature of hedging induced by the expectation of profit are occasionally referred to in studies of futures markets before Working's articles. Both this type of hedging and also insurance hedging are referred to in an extract from an address in 1928 by a grain trader, J.C.Lyman, quoted in J.B. Baer and O.G.Saxon, *Commodity Exchanges and Futures Trading*, New York, 1949, p. 238. See also G.W.Hoffman, *Future Trading upon Organised Commodity Markets in the United States*, Philadelphia, 1932, chs. xix–xx, *passim*, and esp. pp. 417–8.

[16] Working, 'Hedging Reconsidered', pp. 547–9.

[17] 'Hedging of the sort here considered is not properly comparable with insurance. It is a sort of arbitrage.' Working, 'Futures Trading and Hedging', p. 325.

wholly predictable relationship between the two prices.[18] By the same process of reasoning it follows that, other things being equal, the direction and extent of change in the basis (the difference between the spot price and the futures price) are easier to predict the larger is the basis, positive or negative, when the hedge is opened. This is so because the larger the opening basis, the safer it is to rely on the tendency for the two prices to come together as the futures contract approaches and then reaches its delivery month.

It is at the kernel of the notion of arbitrage hedging that the hedger buys and holds a stock of the commodity because of his expectation of a profit through hedging, a profit large enough to cover the costs of carrying the stock.[19] The expectation of a profit in the associated actuals and futures transactions motivates the stock-holding. If all stock-holding were either of this kind or straight-forward (unhedged) speculative stock-holding, then insurance hedging would be ruled out. But all stock-holding does not fall within the categories of arbitrage and speculation. Stocks are held for reasons other than the prospect of a favourable movement in the

[18] Generally, the mature futures price stands below the spot price of the contract grade. This is so because the seller's delivery options (as to grade, quality, place and date) have a depressing effect on the price of the futures contract; they make the contract relatively less valuable because of the uncertainty created for buyers. If this differential were known and constant, its existence would not matter. But it need not be constant, and can vary within limits. An analysis was made of the relationship between mature futures and spot price for US middling cotton in Liverpool for the period March 1938 to August 1939. Official closing prices were obtained for each Friday where available. The excess of spot price over mature futures price ranged from 0·11 to 0·58 pence per pound in seventy-three observations. The range of the middle half of the observations was from 0·19 to 0·37, and the median 0·32 pence per pound. During this period the spot price rarely fell outside the range 4·50 and 5·50 pence per pound.

The predictability of the relationship between the spot price and the mature futures price is further impaired where the futures contract is so designed that different grades may serve as the *effective* contract grade from time to time. This possibility is present in respect of every futures contract in which the premiums or discounts on the delivery of non-basis grades are fixed in advance and so can get out of line with intergrade price differences in the actuals market. Most futures contracts are of this kind, cotton futures being the main exceptions. (The post-war 'mixed' cotton contract on the Liverpool market was, however, deliberately designed with 'fixed' differences; see below, p. 380–2.)

[19] For convenience, the discussion proceeds in terms of 'short hedging'. It applies also *mutatis mutandis* to 'long hedging'. Working, however, seems to have considered the possibility only of short arbitrage hedging.

spot-futures price relation or in the spot price. Some stocks are held in conjunction with other economic activities such as manufacturing or trading operations, where the availability and continuity of supplies have utility (referred to in the theory of storage as the 'convenience yield'). Those who hold stocks because of their convenience yield may wish to reduce the associated price risks by means of insurance hedging. They may hedge even on occasions when the hedged outcome is expected to be a loss. They would do this when exposure to the risk (or near-certainty) of a hedged loss is considered to be less onerous than exposure to adverse price movements in the actuals market, and the holding of stock is thought to be warranted by considerations of convenience yield.

Thus the undeniable fact that there is some arbitrage hedging does not mean that there cannot be some insurance hedging. It is impossible to measure the relative importance of the two types because the distinction between them depends upon motivation and not form; moreover, in practice an operator may at the same time be motivated in part by arbitrage and in part by insurance considerations.

In some of their publications Working and Gray seem to suggest that in practice insurance or risk-avoiding hedging is unimportant or negligible, at least relatively to arbitrage hedging.[20] Their assessment, if it were correct, would mean that virtually everything which has been said or written about hedging by businessmen or economists would be incorrect. In other (and later) publications, however, both authors have used expressions in connection with hedging practice which, while they are appropriate for references to insurance hedging, are inappropriate for references to arbitrage hedging. Thus Working has referred to 'hedging pressure', a phenomenon which is incompatible with arbitrage hedging. (Such pressure refers to a situation in which futures are sold heavily for cover.) He has also referred to the 'price at which hedged stocks will be carried', and to the rendering of a 'service for which hedgers are willing to pay';[21] and similarly, Gray has written: 'Coffee importers who require a short hedge have paid a price for it, as have short hedgers in Minneapolis wheat futures.'[22] The inappropriateness for arbitrage hedging of such notions as paying a price for a service is obvious. Arbitrage

[20] See articles referred to in footnote 13, above.

[21] H. Working, 'Speculation on Hedging Markets', *Food Research Institute Studies*, May 1960, pp. 203, 207 and 209.

[22] Gray, 'The Importance of Hedging . . .', p. 76.

hedging pertains to action based on the perception of a profitable opportunity. The arbitrage hedger is not under any constraint to act: he operates when he expects relative prices to move in his favour, and refrains when he does not. He does not need a 'service' which has a cost and for which he is prepared to pay. Yet, to take another example, both Working and Gray have written of hedging 'needs' or the 'need' for hedging[23] – expressions which seem to apply more aptly to the practice of insurance hedging by those who want to hold stocks but to reduce the associated risk.

The available evidence, although it is incomplete, makes it clear that the origins of futures trading in various commodities are to be explained in large part by the emergence of an extensive demand for arrangements by which market operators could avoid or reduce risk. It is difficult to see why this demand for insurance hedging should later have ceased to be important, as is claimed by Working.[24] Moreover, the motive of risk avoidance is prominent in the usual explanations by market organisations, brokers and hedgers of the contemporary practice of hedging. While such explanations may be over-simplified, the prominence given to risk avoidance does at least point to the importance of risk avoidance among the motives for hedging. Thus attempts to measure the effectiveness of a particular market in providing for insurance hedging cannot be dismissed on the grounds that they relate to a non-existent or trivial activity in contemporary business practice.[25]

Professor Working appears to have claimed that certain market phenomena cannot be explained satisfactorily in terms of insurance hedging, and that their explanation is helped by an understanding of the nature of arbitrage hedging. One of these phenomena is the

---

[23] Working, 'Speculation on Hedging Markets', pp. 210 and 214; Gray, 'The Importance of Hedging . . .', p. 81; and Gray, 'Why Does Futures Trading Succeed or Fail?' in *Futures Trading Seminar*, vol. 3, 1966, Madison, Wis., pp. 120–3 and 125.

[24] Working has written that 'pure risk-avoidance hedging, though unimportant or virtually non-existent in modern business practice, may have played a significant part in the early history of futures markets'. H. Working, 'New Concepts Concerning Futures Markets', *American Economic Review*, June 1962, p. 442. He does not explain why this alleged decline in risk-avoidance hedging has taken place. The use of the adjective 'pure' in any case is not helpful.

[25] Working, in 'New Concepts Concerning Futures Markets', pp. 436–43, attempts to identify a number of different categories of hedging in practice. Two

size of commodity stocks.[26] Larger stocks of a commodity tend to be held commercially when the (opening) basis (the futures price *less* the spot price) is positive than when it is negative. Expressed in more general terms, there is a tendency for the size of stocks to be positively related to the size of the basis. In terms of arbitrage hedging, this is readily explicable. Opportunities for profitable short hedging of this type are present when there is a positive basis (i.e. a contango); and the bigger the contango, the bigger is the likely profit from the expected convergence of the futures price and the actuals price. Hence this type of hedging is encouraged, and in consequence larger stocks are held. But it would be wrong to suppose that the same phenomenon cannot be explained in terms of insurance hedging. The bigger the opening contango, the smaller the likely 'cost' of insurance for holders of stocks – indeed, the expected cost of insurance may be negative. The disutility of holding stocks by risk-avoiders is reduced, and their willingness to carry larger stocks is thus increased. The relation between the volume of hedged stocks and basis will be the same whether the hedger is looking for a *profit* from the hedging itself or whether he makes his decisions on the basis (in part) of the likely *cost* of hedging the carrying of stocks.[27]

Working claims also that arbitrage hedging, rather than 'any special desire to minimise risks, helps to explain why many dealers

of these seem to be largely indistinguishable from insurance hedging in motivation: 'operational hedging' and 'selective hedging'. The former is not well defined by Working. It is, however, described as reducing risk, and the 'business advantages of operational hedging ... depend on the existence of a high correlation between changes in spot prices and changes in futures prices over short intervals'. The same condition applies generally to insurance hedging. 'Selective' hedging is 'the hedging of commodity stocks under a practice of hedging or not hedging according to price expectations. Because the stocks are hedged when a price decline is expected, the purpose of the hedging is not risk avoidance, in the strict sense, but the avoidance of loss.' This definition begs the question as to how *certain* (in the mind of the hedger) the outcome must be before the hedge can be considered to be *loss*-avoiding rather than *risk*-avoiding.

[26] Working, 'Futures Trading and Hedging', pp. 326–7.

[27] L. G. Telser, in a forthcoming study, 'The Supply of Speculative Services in Wheat, Corn and Soybeans', reports some of his findings in these terms: 'The empirical findings ... support one of the major conclusions ... that short hedgers respond to futures prices so as to increase their returns from hedging (or, equivalently, reduce the cost of hedging).'

and processors sometimes hedge and sometimes do not'.[28] Opportunities for arbitrage hedging clearly vary according to the prevailing basis. Again, however, the same phenomenon would be observable were all hedging to be of the insurance hedging type. Since the (likely) cost of insurance varies according to market circumstances, the extent to which holders of stocks are prepared to hold stocks and to hedge them also varies. There is nothing in the concept of insurance hedging which requires the insurance hedger to hedge his entire stock at all times regardless of spot-futures prices relationships in the market, or to make his own decision as to the size of stock to be held regardless of these price relationships; and there is nothing in the concept which requires him to refrain from exercising judgment as to the choice of hedging instrument (that is, choice from among the available futures contracts which differ in their delivery months) so as to take full advantage of market facilities.[29] To hold otherwise is to imply either that the insurance hedger is indifferent to the likely cost of insurance or that he has no reasonable basis for assessing the likely cost.

Thus the market phenomena considered by Working can be explained as satisfactorily in terms of insurance hedging as in terms of arbitrage hedging.

3. MARKET BIAS AND HEDGING

Assessment of a market in terms of its suitability for arbitrage hedging would seem to call for the generation, as in the studies of insurance hedging, of a series of hypothetical hedge outcomes, and the examination of the distribution of hypothetical profits and losses as seen from the point of view of either a short hedger or a long hedger. A market which tended to produce a preponderance of gains to short hedgers would be attractive to short but not to long arbitrage

[28] Working, 'Futures Trading and Hedging', pp. 325–6. See also Working, 'Futures Markets under Renewed Attack', *Food Research Institute Studies*, February 1963, pp. 16–17.

[29] The statistical studies, on the other hand, may seem to suppose that the insurance hedger holds a constant stock and hedges it fully on a routine pattern. But these assumptions of a routine or programme are made only in order to enable the investigator to generate a series of hedge outcomes on a random basis, and are not intended to represent commercial behaviour. Studies such as mine should perhaps have emphasised this point, and underlined the fact that in practice the decision whether or not to hedge is not one taken only after the decision has been taken as to the quantity of stock to hold.

hedging; while a market which tended to produce a preponderance of perfect or near-perfect hedges (in my terminology) would be attractive to neither short nor long arbitrage hedgers.

Professor Gray has developed a different approach to the assessment or testing of a futures market's effectiveness for arbitrage hedging.[30] His testing procedure does not call for a series of hedged outcomes, but is applied to a series of transactions in futures contracts alone. He develops a statistic which measures what he calls the 'expectational bias' in a market. This is calculated as the average profit or loss for a series or programme of hypothetical trades in futures contracts, in each of which trades a futures contract is bought and subsequently re-sold at the beginning of its month of maturity. Ideally, the series should fall within a period in which the spot price is the same at the beginning as at the end; otherwise, an adjustment for the change in the level of spot prices has to be made.[31] If the average of the profits and losses so calculated is not significantly different from zero, there is said to be no expectational bias. If, on the other hand, there is a significant difference, the market is said to be lop-sided, unbalanced or biased in favour of either the long or the short interest. Gray makes the further point that where the average value of outcomes is zero, the average value of the basis (meaning the opening basis) also is zero.[32]

Gray claims that 'testing the basis for an average value of zero is

[30] 'The Importance of Hedging . . .', pp. 70–81.

[31] Ibid., pp. 71 and 75.

[32] Ibid., p. 78. The equality, in the defined circumstances, is readily established. Let S and F be spot and futures prices, respectively; let $F(i)$ be the price of the futures contract with month of maturity being the ith month; let sub-scripts denote the opening and closing dates (months) of the hedge; and let $(-)$ and plus $(+)$ represent purchases and sales, respectively. In R. H. Snape and B. S. Yamey, 'Tests of the Effectiveness of Hedging', *Journal of Political Economy*, October 1965, pp. 540–4, it is shown that the aggregate (and hence average) outcome of a series of trades in futures as specified by Gray is the same as that for a series of hedges as required for the stability-of-basis test for insurance hedging: that is

$$-F(1)_0+F(1)_1-F(2)_1+F(2)_2 \dots - F(n)_{n-1}+F(n)_n =$$
$$= [S_0-F(1)_0-S_1+F(1)_1]+[S_1-F(2)_1-S_2+F(2)_2] \dots +$$
$$+[S_{n-1}-F(n)_{n-1}-S_n+F(n)_n]$$

If it is assumed, as Gray does (p. 79), that as an approximation the mature futures price is equal to the spot price, i.e. that $S_i = F(i)_i$, then the right-hand side of the equation reduces to:

$$S_0-F(1)_0+S_1-F(2)_1 \dots +S_{n-1}-F(n)_{n-1},$$

a meaningful, severe and discriminating test of the effectiveness of futures markets for hedging'.[33] Moreover, he writes that the expectational bias is a measure of the 'most important dimension of hedging costs, and hedging costs the most important indicator of market effectiveness'.[34]

Considering that Gray is not concerned with insurance hedging, and that he is critical of the stability-of-basis test, it may come as a surprise that, for comparable patterns of hypothetical transactions, Gray's expectational bias has the same value as the *average* of the hedging outcomes derived for the stability-of-basis test for the effectiveness of *insurance* hedging; and that, put differently, the average value of the opening basis is equal to the average value of the change in basis from the opening to the closing of the hedge.[35] Since the stability-of-basis test tests unambiguously for insurance hedging (and as such is rejected by Gray) and since the *average* is one form of expressing its results, one must doubt whether Gray's test, which yields the same statistic, is really applicable to the different concept of arbitrage hedging. Indeed, it is apparent that a market in which the opening basis was persistently zero – so that there was no expectational bias whatever – would be wholly unattractive for arbitrage hedging (if, as Gray seems to require the hedges were to be carried into the future's delivery month). When the Gray test would be most completely satisfied, the pickings for arbitrage hedgers would be non-existent.[36] On the other hand, such a market

which is the sum of the opening basis at each successive transaction date. Thus Gray's 'expectational bias' is the same as the average value of the opening basis.

These two measures would not be the same for a series of trades in which each trade is closed in some month *before* the month of the future's maturity, or where $S_i \neq F(i)_i$. The expectational bias would then be equal to the difference between the average opening basis and the average closing basis.

[33] 'The Importance of Hedging . . .', p. 78.

[34] Ibid., p. 70. It may be repeated here that the idea of the 'cost' of hedging is inappropriate to arbitrage hedging.

[35] See Snape and Yamey, op. cit. The formulation of the equality in the first half of the sentence holds generally; the formulation in the second half is more restricted, and depends upon an average value of zero for the closing basis – which means effectively that the futures are held to their maturity and that $F(i)_i = S_i$. See footnote 32.

[36] It is interesting to note that in Gray's study of the potato futures market, favourable results for short hedgers were said to occur in a market which – on the evidence presented – appears to have been biased: '. . . buyers of futures contracts have characteristically paid too high a price . . .'. R.W.Gray, 'The

would be ideal for insurance hedgers – all hedges would be perfect.[37]

It may be concluded that the test for expectational bias and the test for stability of basis give the same information; that they relate to the same characteristic of the spot–futures price relationship; and, further, that the expectational bias has no direct or distinctive relevance for the suitability of a market for arbitrage hedging.

The expectational bias may seem to have more relevance for arbitrage hedging in a different context. Zero bias means that the cards are not stacked in favour of or against the trader.[38] A random selection of trades within the period would tend to yield a zero net outcome. It is not at all clear, however, that this feature is of any special interest to the arbitrage hedger: he is looking for particular opportunities in which the basis is likely to change, and as such is not concerned whether the *average* value of the opening basis is or is likely to be zero. Indeed, in so far as he can rely on the tendency for spot and futures prices to approximate each other in the delivery month, the arbitrage hedger is in a position to judge the attractiveness of the *individual* situation without his knowing anything of the *average* value of the (opening) basis. Knowledge of the latter gives him no additional information relevant for any particular decision.[39]

In criticising the stability-of-basis type of test, Gray has said that 'the hedger has no right to expect and no reason to want basis

Attack upon Potato Futures Trading in the United States', *Food Research Institute Studies*, vol. IV, 1964.

[37] Gray might have had in mind that with a zero (opening) basis an arbitrage hedger at worst need suffer no loss, since he could hold his position until the futures contract matured when the basis would again be zero (so that he suffered no loss other than the carrying and transaction costs), and that he might during the intervening period be presented with a more favourable opportunity of closing out and taking a profit (see Working, 'Futures Trading and Hedging', p. 323). But if this is what was intended, it would have been necessary to test also for bias at intervening intervals, since without bias at some stage there could be no (statistical) expectation of profit. Moreover, from the short hedger's point of view, the chances of making a profit would be even better if the market were biased *ab initio* in his favour, since he would then be assured of *some* profit simply by holding to maturity even if a more profitable opportunity did not present itself in the interim.

[38] See Snape and Yamey, 'Tests of the Effectiveness of Hedging', p. 544; also Gray, 'The Importance of Hedging . . .', p. 107.

[39] Gray, 'The Importance of Hedging . . .', pp. 106–7, at one point links absence of bias with a hedger's long-run 'opportunity' to 'predict the basis'. It is not clear what Gray had in mind here. But the opportunity for reliable

stability. . . . Logically the basis should vary through time, hence he has no right to *expect* it not to.'[40] This misconceives the nature of insurance hedging. The risk-avoiding hedger, unlike the arbitrage hedger, has every reason to 'want' basis stability. However, as we have seen, even if he cannot have it in practice, he may nevertheless engage in insurance hedging. Even if he should be certain that the basis would change and would change adversely, he might decide to enter into a spot commitment (so as to be able later to supply a customer or keep his production going) and to hedge it, if he prefers to make the more or less certain loss rather than to bear the risk of a possibly larger loss unhedged. Moreover, it is by no means obvious that in all circumstances it is 'logical' to expect the basis to change over the time-period of interest to the hedger. Where the opening basis is zero and the hedge is to be carried through to the future's maturity, it is reasonable to expect that the basis will remain unchanged.[41] In fact, in those markets which Gray examined and characterises as being effective for hedging, *on the average* the basis must have been stable over the trading period; a 'balanced' market without expectational bias is one in which the basis *on the average* remains unchanged between the opening and the closing trades. It would be surprising in these circumstances if a fair proportion of all the individual basis changes did not closely approximate the average basis change. Again, where the futures contract is not held until the month of its maturity, it cannot be assumed that the basis will change, or that it will change in a particular direction or to any particular extent, between the opening of the hedge and its closing.[42]

prediction is greater whenever the degree of bias is known with some certainty, regardless of what is the degree of bias.

Perhaps Gray intended to say little more in his article than that when, say, a market is biased against short hedgers, short hedging will tend to be limited. (This, as was shown earlier, would be true both of arbitrage hedging and of insurance hedging.) And this, as Gray notes (ibid., p. 106), is likely to affect the viability of such a futures market. The experience of the Liverpool cotton futures market after the war when it suffered from a persistent large backwardation – a large expectational bias against short hedging – is a case in point (below, pp. 371–383).

[40] 'The Importance of Hedging . . .', p. 78.

[41] More accurately, this is so where opening basis is the same as the typical difference between the spot price and the price of a matured future; see above, footnote 18.

[42] This statement is consistent with the fact that in many markets there is a clear *tendency* for basis to change over the life of a contract of given maturity,

[Thus of the 416 hypothetical hedges on which my paper is based, just under one-half (190) were cases in which the basis in fact changed little if at all (less than 0·1 pence per pound) over the eight-week period of the hedges.] It is the purpose of the stability-of-basis type of test to provide some information about the volatility of the basis in a particular market.

Stress has been placed on the fact that the Gray test for expectational bias produces the same result as the stability-of-bias test when the latter is expressed in the form of the average profit or loss from a series of hedged transactions. The series of individual hedging outcomes generated for use in the stability-of-basis test can, however, be expressed in ways other than the arithmetic average, as has been done in the paper; and this enables the utility of the particular market as a medium for insurance hedging to be examined from several different angles.

It should be noted that such a series of hedging outcomes may reflect a situation in which the average outcome is significantly different from zero – that is a market with a significant expectational bias or lop-sidedness – but in which the majority of hedges nevertheless improve the position of the insurance hedger in the sense that his loss without hedging would have been greater than his loss with hedging. Insurance hedging may be predominantly of the 'improving' varieties in a market in which changes in basis over the

the change reflecting the 'normal' diminishing effect of the cost of carrying the goods through time. Such movements in the basis do not, however, occur invariably; and in any particular case the movement may be irregular even though it tends to follow the 'normal' pattern.

It may seem as if the stability-of-basis test could be improved by making an adjustment for carrying costs. (Cf. 'It follows that in any test of the effectiveness of hedging ... some allowance should be made as a correction for the relative [i.e. relative to futures price] increase in cash [i.e. actuals] price due to carrying charges.' G. W. Hoffman, *Hedging by Dealing in Grain Futures*, Philadelphia, 1925, p. 81.) However, such a correction, even if desirable, seems impracticable. The relevant carrying charges are neither easy to calculate for any particular set of circumstances nor stable with changes in circumstances (including changes in the size of total stocks carried in the market). Any adjustment would probably have to make use of some sort of average value, the application of which to each of a number of hedges might introduce as much error as it purported to counteract. In any event, the relevant charges would be relatively small where the hedges were open for short periods such as eight weeks. (It may be noted that the test developed by Gray makes no allowance for carrying costs.)

hedge period are large (that is, one in which spot and futures prices do not move closely together). This would be so provided that the fluctuations in spot prices are large enough in relation to the imperfections in the hedging. A market in which all hedges are under-compensating may yet be attractive to some insurance hedgers – to those who are prepared to pay positive insurance premiums so that they need not be exposed to the risk of price fluctuations in the actuals market. The greater the expected variability of prices in the actuals market, the more valuable as hedging medium is a market with a given degree of hedging imperfection. In this sense a market which would fail the Gray test for expectational bias – and hence also perform poorly in the stability-of-basis test in terms of the average outcome – might nevertheless be a worthwhile medium for insurance hedging.[43] Such a market would have been an even better medium, of course, had hedging imperfections been smaller, and the average value of the hedging outcomes consequently nearer to zero.[44]

The point made in the preceding paragraph may be illustrated. The average value and the dispersion of the hedging outcomes in the US 1938–40 cotton sample examined in my paper are such that one would conclude from them that the market in that period was unbalanced or biased (p. 356, above).[45] Yet most of the hedges were

[43] Gray presumably had in mind this kind of consideration when he wrote: 'All futures markets mentioned here [in his article], including those that were so lopsided that they died, easily pass this test of basis variability [viz. "a comparison of basis variability with cash-price variability"]. Indeed, such an ineffective hedging medium as the [heavily lop-sided] coffee-futures market would appear not only effective in such a comparison, but *more* effective than the [balanced] Chicago wheat-futures market.' 'The Importance of Hedging . . .', p. 78; also p. 77.

[44] Note, however, that a market with zero expectational bias (this is, with average outcome of zero on the stability-of-basis test) would in certain unlikely circumstances nevertheless be harmful for insurance hedging. For example, if all hedges were in the aggravating category, insurance hedging would be perverse; yet the average hedged outcome could be zero.

[45] The test for bias for the sample period was made also for the distribution of futures-trading outcomes on a comparable pattern of transactions following Gray's procedure, and including an appropriate adjustment for the change in spot price level between the beginning and the end of the period. The average value of the outcomes for this distribution is naturally the same as that for the change-of-basis (i.e. hedging) outcomes ($-3 \cdot 67$d. per lb). But not surprisingly the standard deviation is several times larger ($108 \cdot 85$ against $16 \cdot 57$). The value of t drops accordingly ($0 \cdot 36$ as against $2 \cdot 25$). Thus, whereas one could infer with a high degree of confidence from the 'Gray' distribution that the average outcome

of the 'improving' varieties (p. 355, above).[46] The performance or characteristics of a market cannot be judged on the basis of one statistic alone.

did not differ significantly from zero – that the market was balanced and unbiased – from the data for the hedging outcomes one would infer that the (same) average probably did differ significantly from zero, and that the market was biased. Generally, the test for bias is likely to be more severe when applied to hedging outcomes than when it is to the corresponding futures-trading outcomes, since the variability of the former is likely to be smaller than that of the latter.

[46] This would be so even if all over-compensating hedges were excluded from the 'improving' category.

16

COTTON FUTURES TRADING
IN LIVERPOOL*

The beginnings of trading in cotton futures in Liverpool go back to the 1860s. The growing need for protection (by hedging) against price changes, opportunities for speculative activity and improvements in international market communications combined to make some form of futures trading both desirable and possible. Over the decades the organisation and practices of the futures market were adapted to changing needs and circumstances, under the control and supervision, since 1882, of the Liverpool Cotton Association.

The cotton futures market, in common with other markets, was suspended during the Second World War. The import and distribution of raw cotton were entrusted to the official Cotton Control which, at an early date, also instituted a cover scheme to provide its spinner-customers with security against price changes to replace the facilities for hedging on an organised futures market. Thus far the raw cotton market had been treated in the same way as other organised commodity markets. But soon after the end of the war, it became clear that the Labour government had a special and unique place for the cotton trade in its programme of nationalisation. It was special in that the trade had not, before the war, exhibited those general characteristics (e.g. labour troubles, tendency towards a high degree of concentration) which were held to make nationalisation imperative; it was unique, in that government policy envisaged the restoration of trading in other commodities to private traders and organised markets as soon as circumstances permitted.

As from the beginning of 1948 the import and distribution of raw cotton were conducted by a statutory monopoly, the Raw Cotton Commission, until the 1952–3 season. In that season spinners were allowed to contract out and make private arrangements for buying cotton, though still enjoying the benefits of the commission's cover scheme. The commission, which was being by-passed on a much

---

* *Three Banks Review*, March 1959, pp. 21–38.

larger scale in the following season, was put into liquidation in 1954, and for all intents and purposes ceased to play a part in the market. The Liverpool futures market was re-opened ceremonially by Lord Derby on 18 May 1954. Other types of raw cotton trading had, of course, started with the 1952–3 season.

1

It is not the purpose of this article to review or to assess the operations of the Raw Cotton Commission[1] or to examine the principle of state trading in cotton. But the experiment in state trading, whatever one's assessment of its results might be, demonstrates that there is an alternative to an organised market which includes futures dealings in its facilities. And the idea of state trading continues to have its political supporters. For these reasons the activities of the re-opened Liverpool market attract more attention, and more influential attention, than similar markets which have not undergone the same treatment in the recent past. Apart, therefore, from the intrinsic interest of the events since 1954, there is the political interest in this particular market.

Members of the Liverpool market do not hide their disappointment at the comparatively small volume of business in futures transacted since 1954. Though no statistics are available of pre-war trading, the post-war level of activity has been much lower. Moreover, the trend has been downwards. During the season August 1954 to July 1955 the average monthly volume was over 5,800 contracts of 100 bales; in 1955–6, it had declined to about 3,200 and in the following season to just under 2,000; and in the last completed season, 1957–8, the volume was just over one-half of that of the previous year. These statistics, and the contrast with pre-war experience, can be illustrated graphically. In the centre of the trading ring in the imposing building of the Liverpool Cotton Association there is a small stand which is linked by telephone to the nearby board on which officials record all transactions as they are made. When trading is brisk and therefore noisy, an official is required to mount the stand to telephone the prices of deals to the operators of the blackboard, who would otherwise be unable to distinguish all the details. Before the war it was often necessary to use the stand.

[1] For an account and assessment of its operations as a monopolist, see pp. 302–41, above.

Since the re-opening of the market, it has not once been necessary for this stand to be occupied.

It would be a mistake, however, to ascribe the limited extent of futures trading operations to deficiencies in the organisation of the market. It would also be a mistake to attempt to explain the reduction in market business mainly or largely in terms of, for example, the reduction in size of the United Kingdom cotton textile industry or the increase in the degree of concentration in that industry (an increase partly the result of official policy). The main reason is the post-war multiplication of government intervention in most of the cotton-producing countries, including the principal ones, the United States, Egypt and the Sudan. These acts of intervention have taken a variety of forms, but basically that of control, or attempted control, of cotton sales and selling prices. These controls have necessarily led to a contraction of futures trading, a type of trading which flourishes in conditions in which neither public nor private market controls are operative.

The matter can be stated simply. Suppose that the government of an important producing country exercises control over the price paid to farmers and over the supplies entering world trade. If it pitches its prices too high, unsold stocks accumulate in government hands. As these stocks build up, external confidence in its ability to hold its selling price will weaken. Stocks in the consuming countries will be run down in the anticipation of a collapse of prices, and there will be a smaller quantity of the commodity to be hedged in the futures market. Moreover, the structure of market prices will reflect the expected break in prices. The price of those futures contracts on which delivery is due or imminent (as also the related price of the commodity in the actuals market) will stand well above the prices of other futures contracts stipulating delivery in months to come. Backwardation, that is to say, will be pronounced.[2] This discourages

[2] The market situation described here is analogous to that which arises whenever, towards the close of a crop year, the market expects that the succeeding crop will be relatively large. The spot price of the commodity tends to exceed the price of futures contracts with delivery months within the next crop year, reflecting the coincidence of relatively tight current supplies and the expectation of relatively easier future supplies. (See above, p. 338, for a short discussion of 'new crop discounts'.) Such a break in the continuity of the structure of prices intertemporally occurs because in practice consumption can be deferred to a limited extent only. In contrast, there need be no corresponding break in the structure

373

the hedging of the (reduced) stocks at a time when the need for hedge cover is keenly felt – holders of stocks fear that prices will fall, but cannot get effective cover because of the backwardation. Finally, speculative traders tend to be chary of operating on any scale because the timing and magnitude of the eventual fall in prices will not depend upon largely impersonal market forces but principally upon the decision of a government.[3] Thus both major sources of business in futures trading – hedging and speculation – tend to be constricted.

But even when there is general confidence that the government in question can go on accumulating stocks, or that it can sell its accumulation in a steady and regular manner, futures trading is affected adversely, though differently. Here the operations of the government are likely to keep prices steady for long periods, creating a situation in which merchants and users have little need for hedging because the price risks are small and are known to be small, and other dealers have little opportunity for speculative trading.

The influence of United States cotton policy on futures trading in Liverpool is examined more closely in the following sections. It will be shown that the Liverpool Cotton Association has tried to ward off the worst results of this policy by introducing changes in its practices; but little has been or could have been achieved in the circumstances. It is undoubtedly discouraging to all concerned that the market, resuscitated after an enforced hibernation of fifteen years, should have had to suffer from government measures in supplying countries, principally those in the United States. It is little

of prices in the converse situation when the market expects greater relative scarcity to succeed greater relative abundance of supplies: supply can be deferred readily to the required extent by the holding of stocks – an adjustment facilitated by the presence of contango in the inter-temporal price structure.

[3] It may be asked why an apparently analogous situation in the market for foreign exchange tends to *encourage* speculation, viz. when it is widely expected that a government will devalue its currency. One material difference concerns the maintenance of the current price of the traded item. If the expected devaluation does not take place, the speculator's maximum loss (in terms of foreign currency) is the difference between the price at which he sold the currency forward and the (maintained) price of the currency. If, in the case of commodity speculation, the ('world') price of the commodity does not fall as expected, the speculator is exposed to the further loss should the 'local' price of the commodity rise (as it might well do in a narrow market in which relatively many speculators have to buy). A further difference is that a government is more likely to intervene to support the forward price of its currency, thereby making speculation more attractive (by reducing its 'cost'), than it is to support forward futures prices.

comfort for them to know that cotton futures trading in the United States has also had to contend with difficulties flowing from the same measures.

A state trading authority would also have been operating in a most unfavourable setting for much of the time since 1954. The winding-up of the Raw Cotton Commission in 1954 spared it from the ordeal of having to cope with a series of most difficult situations affecting its stock-holding and pricing policies. Had it continued in operation, as a monopolist state trading body, the volume of criticism of its decisions and policies would have become greatly amplified. Possibly it would also have lost the support of many adherents to the view that the state should engage in cotton trading and so willy-nilly carry the price risks of a particular branch of manufacturing industry.

2

When the futures market was re-opened in 1954, the market authorities recognised that changes in conditions, both at home and abroad, required some changes in the pre-war arrangements. Three of these changes may be considered by way of illustration. First, it was recognised that it would take time for stocks of cotton in the spot market to be built up; moreover, it was thought that more spinning firms, especially the combines, would buy cotton direct from the producing countries, so that trading stocks in the United Kingdom would be smaller than before. To ensure that those who were forced to make delivery on a futures contract would have access to deliverable grades of cotton, and in this way to remove the possibility of corners and squeezes, the delivery period on contracts was raised to two months as against the pre-war period of one month. Thus a 'March–April' futures contract permits delivery within the two months, though trading in it ceases at the end of the first month. The extra month gives the seller ample opportunity to secure supplies to meet his commitment. The fact that only a very small proportion of all contracts have been settled by actual delivery testifies to the technical adequacy of the contract terms in this respect.

The second change reflected the fact that cotton prices are now much higher than before the war and that government intervention might be expected from time to time to lead to sudden material changes in prices. With the pre-war practice of weekly settlements by members of losses or gains on open contracts, the risk of financial embarrassment would have been greater. Hence a system of daily settlements has been introduced to safeguard the fulfilment of contracts.

The third change has been to admit private limited liability companies to full membership of the futures market. This was designed to attract new capital into a market which had been closed for a long time, and to meet the problems caused by high rates of personal taxation. A number of private companies have joined the market, including in a few cases the wholly-owned trading subsidiaries of large textile manufacturing companies. Some of the pre-war partnership members have formed private companies; yet sometimes they find it expedient, presumably in consideration of trading connections or credit standing, to continue their partnership side-by-side with their company.

Before the war four futures contracts were traded on the Liverpool market: an American contract, an 'Empire and miscellaneous growths' contract (which attracted little support), and two Egyptian contracts. When the market re-opened in 1954, only one contract was introduced, an American cotton contract with basis grade middling $\frac{15}{16}$ inch. This provided a contract in the most important growth; and its specification was such that it was closely connected with the contract traded in the New York market, thus facilitating straddle transactions between the two markets. At the time conditions in the other major producing countries were not such as to encourage the launching of other contracts; in Egypt, for example, government intervention was disruptive of normal trading, and the Alexandria futures market was closed. However, when conditions had improved, further contracts were introduced: one for Egyptian long-staple cotton in September 1955 and another for Sudan cotton in March 1956. But neither has succeeded in attracting any substantial body of dealing, and for long periods trading in them has been dormant. Continuing government controls over the disposal of crops have vitiated the attempt to revive futures dealings in Egyptian-type cotton. Meanwhile, those traders and spinners in the United Kingdom who are obliged to carry stocks of longer-stapled cotton are unable to cover their price risks effectively.

British exchange controls have affected the operations of the cotton market. They have probably had little direct effect on the futures market, thanks to the Bank of England scheme which has granted considerable business freedom to participants; in particular, it does not seem to have affected the volume of speculative trading. Until recently, however, the controls have limited Liverpool's trade in actual dollar cotton (as distinct from cotton futures) with foreign buyers, and this may have kept some business away from the futures market. But this was certainly not a major influence; and their importance could not have been as great as that of exchange controls in some foreign countries which have curtailed foreign participation in the Liverpool market.

3

Trading in the American cotton contract began at a brisk rate and business was growing in the first months. Merchants and spinners had to re-learn how to use the market; spinners, in particular, had had the security of the virtually automatic cover schemes of the Cotton Control and of the Raw Cotton Commission for many years. Moreover, it was possible for spinners to use the rival hedging facilities of the New York market, and the relative narrowness of the Liverpool market made the New York market more attractive for some hedgers. Thus the initial narrowness of the re-opened market to some extent hampered its subsequent growth, a type of circular interaction which has persisted. Straddle operations between New York and Liverpool, on the other hand, helped to broaden the Liverpool market, and to add to its efficiency. These straddle operations, in which in the simplest case the straddler buys (or sells) a New York contract and simultaneously sells (or buys) a correspondingly dated Liverpool contract when their prices get out of line, not only keep the two markets in line, but help each to absorb sudden bursts of hedge-buying or selling with less disturbance to prices – that is, at less cost to the hedgers.

Trouble for the new market was building up as unsold stocks of cotton were accumulating on government account in the United States. The market expected that the United States government would soon have to dispose of its growing stocks and that this would mean lower prices abroad. During the second quarter of 1955 this showed itself in two ways: in Liverpool the prices of futures for forward months were being quoted at substantial, and increasing, discounts below those of the currently maturing futures contracts (that is, a marked backwardation was developing), and stocks of both American and American-type cottons in the United Kingdom were being reduced. The period of very marked backwardation,

377

reflecting the market's expectation of lower prices in the future, persisted throughout most of the 1955-6 season until, after some tentative steps had been taken, it became clear that the United States government had adjusted its policy. It introduced a two-price selling system with export prices lower than domestic prices, and embarked on a steady programme of liquidating its accumulated stocks in world markets at 'competitive' prices. This restored confidence, and for the next two seasons more normal price relationships between futures contracts of different maturities were re-established in the quotations chalked up on the board of the Liverpool market.

In the meantime the Liverpool Cotton Association had tried to minimise the impact of changes in American official policy and of the prevailing uncertainty. The first step was taken after it had been officially announced in the United States that from the beginning of 1956 a large quantity of short-staple cotton would be released for sale abroad at competitive prices. It was feared that this would disrupt the prices of the Liverpool $\frac{15}{16}$ inch basis contract, and arrangements were made for the introduction of a new 1 inch basis contract in place of the original. In fact, it made little difference by the time it came into use, because by then the market expected that all the accumulated stocks, and not only the shorter-staple cotton, would soon be made available for export sales at competitive prices; and, until the decision of this kind was in fact made by the United States government, the backwardation continued in the quotations for the new contract as well as for the old.

In the period during which marked backwardation prevailed it was almost impossibly expensive to hedge stocks of cotton by dealings in Liverpool futures since, in general, the hedge had to be placed by making sales at a relatively low price, and lifted by subsequent purchases at a relatively high price. (Hedging in New York was not to the same extent subject to this disability, because it was not expected that the disposal of the accumulated stocks would be allowed to affect directly the domestic price of cotton, so that backwardation was not present so markedly in New York as in Liverpool. But Lancashire spinners hedging in New York were subject to another risk. This risk was that before they lifted their hedges, export prices might be reduced relatively to domestic prices in the United States, with consequent impairment of their hedge cover.) In general, then, the Liverpool market was not able to serve potential hedgers satisfactorily because of the uncertainty about American cotton policy; many spinners must have regretted that they no longer had recourse to the Raw Cotton Commission's cover scheme. Moreover, the reduction in the level of stocks, also a reflection of the uncertainty, limited the amount of potential hedging.

At the same time straddle operations were severely limited, thus adding to the difficulties of the Liverpool market. The essence of a straddle is that it does not involve a price risk. Provided that the straddler is well-informed and acts expeditiously, the outcome of the operation is a simple matter of the difference between the observed inter-market price discrepancy and the costs of putting through the two transactions in the two markets. But once the link between the two markets is broken, there can be no assurance that their prices will move together. A straddle operation becomes subject to the risk that the two prices will not move closely together, because the same forces of supply and demand no longer obtain in both markets. The expectation of a two-price policy in the United States broke the link; the implementation of the policy has continued to keep the two markets apart right down to the present time. Business in straddles has dwindled.[4]

Thus both hedging and straddle operations were reduced during the period of uncertainty. Speculative trading was also inhibited by the prevailing uncertainty, because most operators were not prepared to take up large open positions exposed to the vagaries of United States policy. It is in point to add here that since the re-opening of the Liverpool market speculation by people outside the cotton trade (broadly defined) has been on an insignificant scale as compared with the situation before the war. This is no doubt largely due to the availability of many attractive opportunities elsewhere for the

---

[4] The trade uses the term 'parity' when referring to the relationship between Liverpool and New York futures prices. Parity is the difference between Liverpool and New York prices for similarly dated contracts, converted at the ruling rate of exchange, and expressed in cent points per lb. In the first half of 1955 the parity of the nearest-month contract on the first trading day of each month ranged between +249 and +297. By March 1956 the parity had fallen to −661 for the old $\frac{15}{16}$ inch Liverpool contract. The parity for the new 1 inch contract then stood at +193. By mid-1956 this had been reduced to −203. During the years 1957 and 1958 the parity was further reduced, with fluctuations, from −346 on 2 January 1957 to −543 on 2 December 1957, and then to between −649 and −701 in May to July 1958. These figures illustrate the breaking of the link between the two markets arising, first, from uncertainty about United States policy, and later, from the two-price system adopted for United States cotton disposals.

employment of short-term capital, and to other factors; but it may be noted, as a contributory factor, that Liverpool brokers are much less willing to advise outside parties on market trends now that the market is subject to governmental intervention on so large a scale.

4

The narrative must now be interrupted to explain the introduction in July 1956 of a new American-type cotton futures contract which has, since then, been traded together with the American middling 1 inch contract. The new contract has come to be called the mixed contract, since its terms allow for the delivery of United States middling cotton as well as other growths (e.g. Mexican) which have the general spinning characteristics of American middling cotton.

This type of contract was first considered at a time when the American government's policy for dealing with its vast accumulation of stocks had not yet crystallised into a definite programme of disposals with a subsidised competitive export price. As other suppliers of American-type cotton did not wish or were not able to withhold supplies from world markets as the American government was doing, the spot prices in Liverpool, and elsewhere, of roughly equivalent types of cotton were often out of alignment, with the prices of United States cotton sometimes well above those of substitute growths. These divergences made it costly to hedge holdings of these outside growths by means of dealings in the only available futures contract, the 1 inch American middling contract; this difficulty was superimposed upon that created for hedgers of all growths of American-type cotton by the wide backwardation in the structure of futures prices, a feature which has been considered in the preceding section.

The new mixed contract was devised to meet this situation, or its recurrence at any time, by means of a novel departure from the traditional type of cotton futures contract. It provides, in short, for a number of alternative basis growths of cotton, instead of the traditional basis of one growth. At any time the value of the mixed contract reflects the value of the cheapest of the deliverable growths, after allowing for the fixed premia or discounts (expressed as a percentage of the contract price) specified for each of the growths. These fixed differences are determined in the light of assessments of relative spinning values. Thus, should the spot price of American cotton be materially higher than that of, say, Mexican cotton, the latter and not the former price would govern the prices of early maturities of the mixed contract; but should the Mexican price be relatively too high, there would be a shift in effective basis to the American. To the extent that the cheapest of the range of deliverable growths would attract current business and also tend to influence yarn prices, the mixed contract with its floating basis could be expected to be more serviceable to hedgers than a contract based on a single growth.

When introduced, the mixed contract allowed for the delivery of American cotton (middling of 1 inch staple), and also of designated qualities (grade and staple) of Mexican, East African, Nigerian and Syrian cotton.[5] American and Nigerian basis cottons were deliverable at contract price (at par), Mexican and Syrian at discounts of 2 and 3 per cent, respectively, and East African at a premium of 3 per cent. The details were altered in June 1958 (for delivery months from July 1959 onwards) to take account of changes in the estimated spinning values of the different growths, and in the suitability of different growths for inclusion in the contract in the light of political and supply conditions in the countries of origin. Thus Syrian cotton was excluded, and Pakistan cotton included; while Mexican cotton was made tenderable at par instead of the earlier 2 per cent discount.

Although the contract refers to a specified basis quality (grade and staple) for each deliverable growth, there is provision within each growth for a deliverable range of qualities.[6] In this respect the mixed contract is similar to the companion American middling contract, and adjustments in the contract price for the delivery of qualities other than the basis quality are, for both contracts, settled by agreement between buyer and seller, or failing this, by arbitration.

[5] Though both the American and the mixed contracts have as basis middling grade 1 inch staple, the precise specifications differ in detail. Thus the former refers to cotton of 'fair character', and the latter to cotton of the superior 'good character', and the former allows delivery of grades down to strict low middling of $\frac{15}{16}$ inch staple, while the latter sets the lower limit at strict low middling of 1 inch staple. These differences explain why it is possible for the mixed contract to command a higher price than the American contract of the same month of delivery. Of course, the price of the mixed contract can fall below that of the American contract, as was indeed intended in its design.

[6] Thus the basis quality of Pakistan cotton is 'choice of 1 inch staple', but delivery, at discount, is allowed down to the 'choice' grade of $\frac{31}{32}$ inch staple, while the buyer has to make premium payments to the seller for cotton delivered up to the grade of 'superchoice' and the staple $1\frac{1}{32}$ inch.

By the time the mixed contract came into operation, the situation which had given rise to its introduction was resolving itself. The American government's decision to sell its stocks at world competitive prices in the 1956–7 season removed the price discrepancy between American and similar growths in export markets, and American cotton, which had been under-sold in these markets, soon regained its strong position. In fact, during the two seasons 1956–7 and 1957–8, American cotton was generally the cheapest of American-type cottons in Liverpool, and its price almost invariably governed that of the mixed contract; on the few occasions when actual delivery has been made, it has involved American cotton. It is only in recent months that Mexican cotton has at times been relatively cheaper and therefore has acted as the price-maker for the mixed contract. In the circumstances the new contract has not attracted as much trade as the established and more traditional American contract. In practice the prices of both the old contract and the new have been based on American cotton, and the established contract has had the attraction to traders of familiarity and a wider market. However, the new mixed contract is now available if the predisposing circumstances for its use should recur. The equipment of the market has been strengthened.

5

The new policy of the United States government to maintain a two-price system from the 1956–7 season and to sell abroad at world prices led to a marked reduction in the Liverpool prices of American cotton. Between August and October 1956, the first months of that season, the spot price of 1 inch American middling ranged between 26 and 28d. per pound, as against a range of 31 and 33d. in April and May of the same year. (It is of interest that during April and May the October–November futures contract was traded at a discount or backwardation of over 4d. per pound, a fairly accurate market forecast of the eventual impact of the introduction of the new American policy.) After this initial adjustment, prices in Liverpool remained remarkably steady during both the 1956–7 and 1957–8 seasons. The large accumulation of American cotton, the release of which was being carefully controlled by a government which was not a weak seller, had this steadying influence; and the government's task was facilitated by the fact that world consumption of cotton was edging upwards, and consuming countries were engaging in re-stocking, encouraged by the stability in prices.[7]

Confidence in the American policy was shown by the re-emergence of a more normal price structure in the Liverpool futures market. Backwardation first shrank to negligible amounts, and soon prices on both contracts showed a contango, that is prices of some forward contracts stood above those of the maturing contracts. But this did not help to boost turnover in the market. The steadiness in prices, and confidence in continued stability, meant that spinners and merchants did not feel any strong need to hedge their stocks, the total amount of which rose markedly; and for the same reasons there was little prospect of profit in speculative trading.

During the most recent months of the current 1958–9 season backwardation has re-appeared, most markedly in respect of the 1959–60 new-crop quotations. A large American crop is expected for the next season, and government stocks in America are again accumulating. The familiar symptoms are here again, though in a much milder form than in 1955 and 1956.[8]

Addendum

The course of prices of American spot cotton in Liverpool from 1954 to 1959 is illustrated in the accompanying diagram. The monthly prices are the official market closing prices on the third Friday of the month. The two longish periods of relatively stable prices are clearly shown: the first after the drastic reduction in the level of spot prices which occurred in the 1955–6 season, and the second after the less drastic reduction during the 1958–9 season. (The reprinted article was written while the process of this second reduction was taking place.) It will also be seen that the two reductions,

[7] The 'visible supply' of American cotton in the United Kingdom (roughly, traders' stocks and stocks afloat) stood at the low figure of 49,000 bales at the end of July 1955, and at the same figure a year later. By the end of the next season the stock had risen to 172,000 bales, and it stood at 188,000 bales at the end of the 1957–8 season. The visible supply of all growths of cotton at the end of the four seasons was 300,000, 182,000, 308,000 and 331,000 bales, respectively. It will be observed that the proportion of American cotton in the total was about one-quarter in July 1956 and had risen to well over one-half two years later.

[8] The original paper included a further section which has been omitted here. That section discussed the effects of the yarn-spinners' selling-price agreement, and of its abandonment, on futures trading.

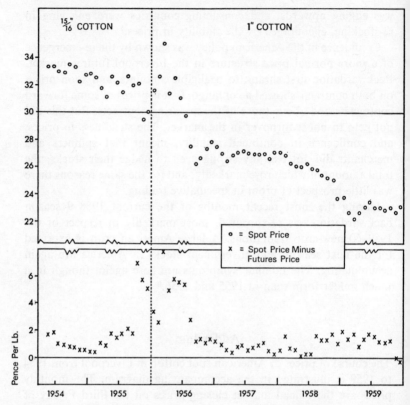

and more especially the first, took place over periods of several months, and that in the process there were sharp fluctuations. Part of this volatility of prices must have been due to the smallness of the stocks held in Liverpool when the market was expecting the price to fall as a result of expected changes in the policy of the United States government.

The diagram also shows the course of the differential between the price of spot cotton and the price of a forward futures contract. Each observation refers again to the third Friday; and the differential is the spot price *less* the price of a selected forward futures contract. For this purpose the futures contract has been selected on the basis that its maturity was not less than two clear months ahead, but not any further ahead than was unavoidably necessary by virtue of the fact that there were only five contract maturities per year (March, May, July, October and December). The differentials therefore do not refer uniformly to a fixed period; but this was unavoidable, and is of little significance for present purposes.[9]

The highest positive values of the differential, i.e. the largest backwardations, occurred shortly before and during the two periods within which the level of spot prices declined from a higher relatively stable level. In each case the backwardations narrowed to more 'normal' levels once the new spot price level had become established after the United States government had implemented the previously anticipated change in cotton price policy.

It will be noted that in the period covered in the diagram the differential was positive (showing backwardation) on every date except the last two, when a zero differential and a contango were registered respectively. It may seem to follow that the market was unbalanced, with a bias operating against short hedgers at all times, requiring them (if they were to hedge) to sell futures relatively cheaply (that is, cheaply relatively to spot prices) to open their hedges, and to buy futures relatively dearly when they closed their hedges. But such an inference would be mistaken to the extent that spot prices tended also to exceed the prices of futures contracts which were closer to their maturity than those selected for use in the preparation of the diagram. In fact, over the period 1956 to 1959, on the average the spot price of (actuals) 1 inch American cotton exceeded the price of the futures contract in its month of maturity by 0·8d. a pound. (There was a considerable variation in the maturity-month basis, the co-efficient of variation, for seventy-five weekly observations, being 61 per cent.) Thus the differentials shown in the diagram are, when seen realistically from the point of view of a hedger, over-stated: they are not adjusted so as to remove that part of the price difference which might be said to have had nothing to do with the fact that the futures contract had some two or three months to run to maturity. If such an adjustment were made crudely by raising the base line in the diagram to the 0·8d. position on the vertical axis, it will be seen that a contango (= negative backwardation) relationship occurred not infrequently within the period. This does not alter the fact that at other times within the period there were large backwardations. Moreover, as is stated in the paper (above, p. 383), contango as it is usually measured (without adjustment) occurred at times in respect of futures contracts closer to their maturity than those used in the preparation of the diagram.

[9] All prices taken from the annual volumes of *Tattersall's Cotton Trade Review*.

17

BIDDING AGREEMENTS AT AUCTIONS*

If the buyers in a market agree not to compete among themselves, the prices at which goods are exchanged in that market will be lower than the competitive prices. The price reductions provide an incentive to the buyers to combine so as to refrain from competition, provided some acceptable formula or arrangement can be arrived at for sharing the gain among the participants.

Organised restraints on the competition of buyers are not peculiar to sales by auction. Nevertheless, certain agreements among buyers at auctions have been singled out for special condemnatory treatment by a statute of 1927, the Auctions (Bidding Agreements) Act.[1] This article traces the development of the law in England leading up to this legislation, considers its contents and effects, and offers some comment on bidding agreements from the point of view of the economist.

1

Agreements to restrain bidding at auctions are said to be widely prevalent at all kinds of auctions. They take a variety of forms to suit the different requirements of different situations. Each prospective buyer may agree to bid only for specified lots, so that only one member of the group bids, on his own account, for the items in which he is most interested. He does not interfere with the bidding of his associates in respect of their chosen lots, and he, in turn, is left alone by them. Alternatively, one member may bid on behalf of all the members of the group. The purchases may be shared subsequently by dividing them in a pre-arranged manner, each member paying the appropriate part of the purchase price. This method of division is practicable where the goods are fungible. Where they are not, a more complicated share-out may be necessary. The 'knockout' or 'settlement' is the common solution adopted by 'rings' at auctions for determining the division of the goods bought and of

---

* *Butterworths South African Law Review*, 1955, pp. 73–80.
[1] 17 & 18 Geo. 5, ch. 12.

the profits secured by the concerted bidding. A knock-out involves a second auction of the ring's purchases among the members of the ring – a recognition, ironically, that competition is the best way for determining the values of the goods in question. Details vary, but, in essence, the profits (the difference between the prices at the public and the subsequent private auctions) are divided in a pre-arranged manner and each lot goes to the highest bidder. Sometimes the second auction proceeds in stages or divisions. In one variant of such proceedings the least important members of the ring are first required by the 'chairman' to bid among themselves for the least valuable items. The profits of this stage are shared out among those members taking part, and they then withdraw. The process continues until the most substantial members are left to compete for the most valuable items. In this way the proceedings can be arranged so that the lion's share of the profits are likely to go to the leaders.[2]

Examples of each of the principal methods are encountered in the reported cases which are reviewed below. It may be noted that participation in bidding agreements and knock-outs need not be confined to dealers; some of the cases involved prospective buyers who did not intend to resell the goods.[3] But in general the problem of auction rings and knock-outs is concerned with the activities of dealers; the indignation which the subject arouses from time to time is focused on them.

2

A review of the case law must start with *Levi* v. *Levi*[4] in 1833. This was an action for slander. In the course of his judgment Gurney, B., dealing with evidence of the holding of knock-outs, observed that 'owners of goods have a right to expect at an auction that there will

[2] An interesting account of other arrangements may be found in Minutes of Evidence and Proceedings of the Select Committee of the House of Lords on the Auctions (Bidding Agreements) Bill, 1926, p. 24. (This report will be referred to as H.L. Select Committee.) See also *Sunday Times*, 8 and 15 November 1964. It appears that 'hangers-on' or 'mouchers' often attend sales without the intention of buying but with the intention of participating in any knock-out that may be going. The knock-out by division tends to reduce their share of the profits.

[3] A witness giving evidence to the 1926 Select Committee said that he once had noticed from his auctioneer's rostrum that the wife of one of His Majesty's Judges and some friends were having a 'little knock-out'. H.L. Select Committee, p. 27.

[4] 6 C. & P. 239.

be an open competition from the public; and if a knot of men go to an auction upon an agreement among themselves of the kind that has been described they are guilty of an indictable offence and may be tried for conspiracy'. This *dictum* expresses very well the source of the common dislike of auction rings. Whether it was sound in law is another matter; in fact, it was not followed in any subsequent decision. Parke, B., in delivering the considered opinion of the Judicial Committee of the Privy Council in a case in 1850, referred to Gurney's views as 'a mere *dictum* in a *nisi prius* case, and cannot, we think, be relied upon'.[5]

A simple bidding agreement had come up for consideration six years earlier in *Galton* v. *Emuss*.[6] Two landowners agreed not to bid against each other at an auction for a property adjoining their own estates, in return for which the purchaser undertook to give his associate the option to buy certain property at a specified price in the event of its being sold. The property was then, in fact, bought by private contract. The terms of the agreement were held to be enforceable, there being 'no authority to show that an arrangement to retire from being a competitor for an estate is illegal'.[7]

This case established that a bidding agreement was binding upon the parties concerned. The other main issue, whether a sale by auction affected by a bidding agreement was binding upon the vendor, was decided in *In re Carew's Estate*[8] and *Heffer* v. *Martyn*[9] in 1858 and 1867 respectively; judgment in both cases was given by Sir John (later Lord) Romilly, M.R. Both cases involved simple bidding agreements, not knock-outs; in the first the property was

---

[5] *Doolubdass Pettamberdass and others* v. *Ramloll Thackoorseydass and others*, 5 Moo. Ind. App. 109. This case concerned a wager agreement based on the price of opium at a forthcoming sale by auction. The price at the auction was raised by the interested party and his agents who bid it up well beyond the critical level. One of the arguments advanced for holding that the contract was unenforceable apparently was that since it was illegal to depress a price at an auction by concerted action to restrain bidding, it was also illegal to raise a price at an auction by a combination to promote bidding.

[6] 13 L.J.Ch. 388.

[7] In a recent case, *Pallant* v. *Morgan*, [1953] 1 Ch. 43, the facts were substantially the same as in *Galton* v. *Emuss*. The enforceability of the agreement was upheld, notwithstanding some uncertainty in the terms of the agreement.

The Auctions (Bidding Agreements) Act, 1927, did not apply to this agreement which was between two non-dealers concerning the purchase of land.

[8] (1858) 26 Beav. 187.

[9] (1867) 36 L.J.Ch. 372.

divided between the two participants, and in the second the purchaser paid a sum of money to his prospective competitor. In the
first case the sale was held to be valid because there was no rule
'that a mere agreement, between two persons, each desirous to buy
a lot that they will not bid against each other, is sufficient to in-
validate a sale to one of them'.[10] In *Heffer* v. *Martyn* this proposition
was extended: 'I think also they may take money for abstaining to
compete as well as arrange to take one lot against another.'

The legal propriety of bidding agreements had now been firmly
settled; neither they nor the consequent sale would be invalidated,
unless the transactions were tainted with an intent to defraud and
deceive.[11]

The enforceability of bidding agreements *inter se* was gone into
thoroughly in *Rawlings* v. *The General Trading Company*[12] in 1921.
Two English dealers travelled to Dublin in 1919 to attend an auction
of surplus tin shell-cases, the property of the Ministry of Munitions.
They agreed not to bid against each other but to divide the purchases between them; they feared each other's competition but not
that of the Irish buyers present. The defendant, who bought the
goods, subsequently repudiated the agreement, and the action was
brought by the other party to enforce it. In the lower court, Shearman,
J. held that, at any rate where the goods sold were the property of
the state, a bidding agreement was against public policy, and hence
unenforceable.[13] On appeal Bankes and Atkin, L.JJ. held that the
agreement was not illegal, Scrutton, L.J. dissenting.

The majority were content to follow the authorities. On the other
hand, Scrutton, L.J., while holding that the agreement was a restraint
of trade which was reasonable between the parties, held that it was
contrary to public policy and hence not enforceable.

---

[10] Reference had been made to the report of an eighteenth-century case which
pointed to such a rule in similar circumstances. The Master of Rolls held, without explanation, that the earlier *dictum* 'did not bear on the proposition' quoted
in the text above.

[11] Where one party to a bidding agreement – the non-buying party – had nevertheless taken part in the bidding to 'show strength' against outside competitors,
it was held that there 'was no evidence that this was done in pursuance of the
agreement between the parties', and that it fell 'far short of an agreement to
defraud' the seller. *Rawlings* v. *The General Trading Co. Infra*, note 12.

[12] [1921] 1 K.B. 635.

[13] [1920] 3 K.B. 30.

The effect on the public or the community was that free competition at auctions, affording a ready market for realising goods, was restrained, and the property of any member of the public selling goods might be sold below its true value. ... The agreement, if carried out or enforced by injunction, would deprive the public of the advantage of free competition at auctions.

This was particularly important when the goods sold 'were those of the public themselves, of the state'. Thus at a time when the courts had already progressively whittled away considerations of public policy as justification for interfering with monopoly and restrictive agreements generally, Scrutton, L.J. was invoking this lapsing principle in the special case of agreements in restraint of buyers' competition at auctions. He also made a different and telling point: 'I cannot believe that, if the parties to an agreement for a knock-out came to the court for an injunction to restrain one of their members from bidding at the auction contrary to his agreement, the court would grant the injunction.' It seems that there has been no case covering this particular point; the members of a knock-out or bidding agreement do not seek publicity, certainly not *before* the auction.

Cohen v. *Roche*[14] in 1927 is important not for its contribution to the development of the case law but for the sequel it had. The defendant, an auctioneer, had knocked down his own property, eight Hepplewhite chairs, to the plaintiff. Shortly after the hammer fell, he heard a loud shout and knew that the plaintiff and others were holding a knock-out on his premises. He refused to deliver the goods, apparently not because he thought that he was entitled to treat the sale as void, but 'in order to get a little publicity on knock-outs'.[15] In the resulting legal action McCardie, J. found for the plaintiff; but the subject of knock-outs received a good deal of publicity and legislation followed.

3

In 1926 Lord Darling introduced a Bill in the House of Lords to outlaw knock-outs and other bidding agreements at auction sales. It was welcomed by the representative bodies of auctioneers. The Bill was sent to a Select Committee, which heard evidence from

[14] [1927] 1 K.B. 169.
[15] H.L. Select Committee, p. 29.

auctioneers, the defendant in *Cohen* v. *Roche*, and dealers. One of the latter had at one time worked with a knock-out, and later against it. Though the undesirability of knock-outs and rings was generally conceded, there were strong doubts about the efficacy of the proposed legislation; even its staunchest supporters claimed no more than some deterrent effect for it. The informality of the agreements and arrangements was thought to be an insurmountable obstacle and it was believed that the law would easily be evaded. The Bill became law, and took effect from the beginning of 1928.

The Auctions (Bidding Agreements) Act is widely drawn to strike at bidding agreements at sales by auction:

> If any dealer agrees to give, or gives, or offers any gift or consideration to any other person as an inducement or reward for abstaining, or for having abstained, from bidding at a sale by auction either generally or for any particular lot, or if any person agrees to accept, or accepts, or attempts to obtain from any dealer any such gift or consideration as aforesaid, he shall be guilty of an offence under this Act.

The prohibition would seem to cover knock-outs and other less elaborate bidding agreements, including an agreement between two dealers not to bid against each other on particular lots. Sales of land are excluded from the scope of the Act, which refers to 'goods' only. Offenders are liable on summary conviction to a fine not exceeding one hundred pounds, or to not more than six months' imprisonment, or to both. In England and Wales no prosecution may be instituted without the consent of the Law Officers of the Crown. The vendor may treat a sale as one induced by fraud if the sale has been subject to a bidding agreement in respect of which a conviction has been secured.

It is however provided that 'where it is proved that a dealer has previously to an auction entered into an agreement in writing with one or more persons to purchase goods at the auction *bona fide* on a joint account and has before the goods were purchased at the auction deposited a copy of the agreement with the auctioneer, such an agreement shall not be treated as an agreement made in contravention' of the Act. In other words, the Act renders illegal *undisclosed* bidding agreements and is not aimed at bidding agreements as such.[16]

[16] Some critics objected to this limitation, as they wished to stimulate competition at auctions. See editorial, *The Estates Gazette*, 14 January 1928, p. 43.

Up to 1950 no prosecutions were instituted under the Act.[17] It was generally agreed that the prevalence of knock-outs and rings had not been affected by the legislation, though some knock-outs may have become more careful and private in their arrangements.[18]

The first action, taken under the Act in 1950, was based on circumstances somewhat reminiscent of those of the *Rawlings* case after the First World War. The Ministry of Supply held sales of scrap metal. The leading dealers were said to operate as a buying ring and to hold a fairly complicated knock-out afterwards. Eight dealers were charged at the Central Criminal Court in London with 'conspiring together to contravene the provisions' of the Act and were found guilty; seven were fined one hundred pounds each, the eighth fifty pounds. They were acquitted of another charge of conspiracy to cheat and defraud the Crown of certain moneys 'by divers and subtle means'.[19] On appeal the convictions were quashed on the ground 'that as the offence under ... the Act of 1927 was created for the first time by [the Act], and a definite procedure for its trial, namely summary trial only, with the consent of one of the Law Officers, was prescribed by the Act, and as the particulars of the conspiracy alleged were in terms or in substance the offence prescribed by the Act, the offence was not triable on indictment, and the indictment should have been quashed at the outset'.[20]

4

In the debates preceding the placing of the Auctions (Bidding Agreements) Act of 1927 on the statute book, the question was asked more than once why agreements in restraint of competition at auctions should be made illegal when other restrictive agreements in industry and trade, though known to be widespread, did not incur the displeasure of Parliament nor the censure of the Courts. The answer may be that there was a strong feeling that auctions should be

---

[17] According to various authoritative statements. But according to a letter in *The Estates Gazette*, 19 January 1929, p. 78, there had been a conviction in Rugby, with a fine of ten pounds.

[18] In 1932 a prominent auctioneer said: 'The futility of this law passes comprehension in that no one with any knowledge, even superficial, of the sale rooms, would have considered it worth while to draft such an enactment'. *The Estates Gazette*, 19 November 1932, p. 757. See also *House of Commons Debates*, 27 November 1930, col. 1479, and 27 October 1932, col. 1136.

[19] *The Times*, 28 November 1950.

[20] *Rex* v. *Barnett and others*, 35 Cr. App. R. 37.

competitive, or a belief that bidding agreements often were tainted with fraud and deception, or that the interests of an important sector of the electorate, the farming community, were adversely affected by auction rings.

Yet the effects of bidding agreements on the interests of the sellers are basically the same as those of any agreement among buyers not to compete. If the agreements are effective (on which more below), they reduce the price below the competitive price in the interests of the buyers.[21] The reduced prices, in turn, may discourage sellers, and, in the case of agricultural produce for example, this is likely to lead to a contraction of supplies. The lower prices paid by the buyers need not be passed on (in the form of lower prices) for the benefit of the final purchasers who buy from the members of the ring; most dealers are not likely to resell cheaply merely because they have bought cheaply.[22] The possibly reduced supplies will naturally be to the disadvantage of the final consumers.

The economic issue concerns the extent to which bidding agreements succeed in depressing the prices received by sellers below those which the highest bidders would be prepared to pay in the absence of the agreements. The magnitude of this difference varies from one market situation to another, but, in the main, it depends on the comprehensiveness of the ring and on the availability and effectiveness of alternative channels of disposal open to the sellers. On the first point it may be noted that at many auctions the knock-out or ring is not alone in the field; outsiders, independent dealers[23] and sometimes rival rings are present with the result that sellers are given the benefit of competitive buying. At well-advertised and well-attended sales rings have less opportunity of affecting prices. A

[21] However, the point of view has been expressed that knock-outs may sometimes be worked as a matter of convenience to dealers without the intent or effect of keeping prices low, or that, by allowing a number of dealers to pool their buying, they permit the more effective representation of the dealers at sales held simultaneously, with the effect of promoting more effective competition at sales. (See evidence of a past president of the Auctioneers' and Estate Agents' Institute, H.L. Select Committee, pp. 9 and 12.) This probably refers to very exceptional circumstances.

[22] It is interesting that the 1927 Act does not render illegal bidding agreements between non-dealers. In such agreements the benefit of the monopoly 'exploitation' of the sellers accrues to members of the public as distinct from dealers.

[23] It is sometimes said that some dealers are forced into the ring unwillingly, fearing that if they remained outside, the prices of the lots they wish to buy would be run up against them by the ring. See H.L. Select Committee, p. 29.

skilful auctioneer, too, may sometimes, if authorised by the seller, use his discretion and run the price up against the ring. Moreover, where sellers such as farmers have a continuing interest in auctions, they tend to avoid the smaller auctions or those where knock-outs or rings are known or believed to operate, and instead make use of larger auction markets.[24]

Although disposal by auction is widely used for the sale of certain commodities (for example agricultural products, land and works of art), it is not the only method of sale open to sellers of these commodities. But the method of sale by auction is often preferred by sellers (and buyers) precisely because the method of sale by private treaty is considered to be unsatisfactory. It may be unsatisfactory because the commodity in question is susceptible to marked price fluctuations or is of a highly unstandardised nature, so that there may be some advantage in submitting it to the test of a public competitive market valuation rather than in relying on the private price bids of individual buyers. The seller, because of the nature of the commodity, may not be able to assess the appropriateness of individual private bids and it may be costly to obtain bids from many possible buyers; he may prefer to use a market where rival bidders are conveniently assembled. It is the technical superiority of auctions in certain circumstances which explains their existence; and, within the limits of this superiority, rings at auctions may deprive sellers of part of the benefits without driving them away.

In some of the cases which have come before the courts the right of the seller to fix a reserved price has been looked upon as the main defence against the activities of rings.[25] But often this defence is of little value. Difficulties arise because the seller does not always have sufficient information to fix an appropriate reserved price. He can set an appropriate reserved price only if he is able to ascertain the approximate market value of the article before the auction sale is held. But, as has been suggested above, the method of sale by auction is often preferred in certain circumstances because it is difficult to ascertain market valuations in any other way. In a sense the fixing of a reserved price tends to be a useful safeguard mainly where the advantage of sale by auction itself is limited.

The task of setting a reserved price which is not likely to be seriously out of line with market values is not equally difficult in all

[24] An instance of this is described in H.L. Select Committee, p. 33.
[25] See the judgments in *In re Carew's Estate* and *Heffer* v. *Martyn*.

cases. Farmers have access to information about immediately past market prices of produce and livestock and this can serve as a guide in their marketing decisions. Its value is reduced to the extent that the goods are not standardised and their price movements are frequent and sharp; lack of standardisation and price fluctuations reduce the relevance of reported market prices. It follows that the sellers of antiques, for example, usually are in a more difficult position than farmers; moreover, they enter the market sporadically and their general knowledge of market values is likely to be limited. Even here a competent auctioneer or dealer may be able to help in arriving at a realistic reserved price.

It may be noted that where goods are bulky or perishable the high cost of moving them or of delaying their sale also reduces the value of the safeguard of reserved prices. In this respect sellers of antiques and land are generally better placed than sellers of agricultural products and used household furniture.

Since auctions serve a useful commercial purpose and are not easily replaceable by other equally satisfactory methods of sale, measures which improve their functioning are to be welcomed. The removal of restraints on bidding competition is therefore a useful objective; even where, as in many agricultural markets, rings are not likely to influence average prices materially, no undesirable consequences are likely to follow from their removal. But, if British experience is a guide, it is very difficult to eliminate these restraints by legislative prohibition. The difficulty lies essentially in the extreme informality and spontaneity of the arrangements; in these respects they differ markedly from many other restrictive practices and agreements, which are more promising subjects for treatment by legislation.

Addendum

The major effect of a successful or effective agreement among buyers at an auction is analogous to that of a successful price agreement among sellers: the former reduces the price paid to the sellers of the goods, while the latter raises the price charged to the buyers of the goods. However, the analogy does not apply in all respects.

Assuming that entry of new firms into the industry or trade is not difficult, a sellers' price agreement tends to break down if the sellers attempt to maintain their prices materially above the competitive level. New firms will be attracted into the trade by the above-normal profits being made in it and by the possibility of gaining business readily by selling at prices just below those set by the agreement. Such sellers' agreements, where entry is easy, therefore tend to be unstable when they attempt to raise prices (and profit margins) materially. The entry of new firms, or the potentiality of such entry, serves as a restraint on sellers' agreements and as a protection for buyers.

The role of new entry is similar in the case of buyers' agreements in which the maximum price to be paid to sellers is laid down collectively. Here entry, actual or potential, protects the interests of sellers. If the agreement prices are too low, new firms will become established as buyers by offering higher prices to sellers than those fixed in the agreement. The agreement will collapse or the agreed prices raised to preserve the members' business.

An agreement among buyers not to bid competitively at an auction does not operate in the same way. A potential new entrant to the ranks of the buyers' trade does not know in advance how high the ring will be prepared to bid in order to secure the goods: the freedom of action of the ring (as distinct from that of its members) is not shackled in advance. Confronted by the competition of a new entrant at the auction, the ring will realise that it cannot dictate the prices, and it has every incentive to bid against the outsider up to the level of estimated market values (or even higher if it is thought expedient to deny business to the newcomer). The fact that the ring's maximum price bids are not known in advance – in contrast to the known buying prices of a buyers' cartel or selling prices of a sellers' cartel – robs the new entrant (or any independent competitor) of the certainty or opportunity of gaining business cheaply by acting competitively.

Thus a dealers' ring at auctions may be highly profitable and yet stable in the sense that it does not attract competition from new-comers even where entry into their trade may not require a high degree of special knowledge or skill or large initial investment of capital. Indeed, ease of entry is likely to have a different effect. The higher profit margins in the trade – secured by the suppression of competition at the auctions – make it attractive for new firms to attend auctions as potential bidders with the intent of being invited to join the ring and share in the gains so as to forestall price-raising activity on their part. (See footnote 2, above.) This type of entry would not, however, serve as a protection to the sellers, since prices would not be affected (except to the extent that an increase in the number of participants in the ring might make for instability in the longer run). It would merely divide the gains of collective monopsony action among a larger number of firms. The gains would be distributed differently as a result of new entry: but the sellers would be no better off.

This is not to imply that it will be in the interests of all dealers present at an auction to join a bidding agreement. Some, including new entrants, may prefer independent action and reasonably calculate that this is in their particular interests even though it involves an intensification of competition and reduction of profit margins in the trade generally. The point which has been made is that the activities of a ring and the resultant high profits would not by themselves provoke the entry of independent *competing* firms which would make their profits by undermining the ring.

18

AGGREGATED REBATE SCHEMES
AND INDEPENDENT COMPETITION*

1

Aggregated rebate schemes operated by groups of sellers have been examined by the Monopolies Commission both in general terms[1] and also in more detail in the context of a number of particular industries.[2] One of the conclusions reached by the commission is that 'the principal objection to the use of an aggregated rebate ... is that it impedes competition from independent producers, because of its strong economic incentive to buyers to confine their purchases to members of the group [operating the scheme]'.[3] It is not the purpose of these notes to challenge this general conclusion. Instead, the purpose is to analyse the special conditions necessary for the achievement through aggregated rebate schemes of an inhibiting effect on independent competition, and the still more special conditions in which the same sort of effect cannot be achieved by alternative group pricing arrangements which do not involve discrimination among buyers according to the amount of their total requirements or purchases from the group.[4] On the first point, the commission's reports are uninformative; the second point lay outside the scope of the commission's discussions, but is none the less of some interest for public policy.[5] The present discussion of the

---

* *Oxford Economic Papers*, February 1960, pp. 41–51.

[1] Monopolies Commission, *Collective Discrimination*, 1955, chap. 7.

[2] Monopolies Commission: *Report on the Supply of Electric Lamps*, 1951, para. 292; *Report on the Supply of Insulated Electric Wires and Cables*, 1952, para. 313; *Report on the Supply and Export of certain Semi-Manufactures of Copper and Copper-Based Alloys*, 1955, paras. 317–19; *Report on the Supply and Export of Pneumatic Tyres*, 1955, para. 532; *Report on the Supply of Hard Fibre Cordage*, 1956, para. 293; *Report on the Supply of Linoleum*, 1956, paras. 213–15.

[3] *Collective Discrimination*, para. 210.

[4] Because they involve such discrimination, tying devices such as exclusive dealing arrangements, full-line forcing, or two-part tariffs are not considered in this paper; they may well be effective substitutes for an aggregated rebate scheme.

[5] Aggregated rebate schemes are since 1957 subject to registration under the

economics of aggregated rebate schemes is not meant to be complete; in particular, no attention is given here to the effects of the sellers' discrimination among buyers on competition among the buyers, though in some situations these may well be the most material consequences of an aggregated rebate scheme.

It will be shown that an aggregated rebate scheme can achieve a tying effect on customers – and hence impede independent competition – only in situations where the supplies coming from the two sources, group and independent, differ in a way which is significant to customers. It will be shown, further, that in some situations, but not in others, the asymmetry in supply can be used by the group to obstruct independent competition without the employment of price discrimination among customers on the basis of total purchases (but with the employment of another form of price discrimination).

It is assumed in what follows that a number of otherwise independent suppliers have an agreement to sell their products at agreed minimum prices, subject to the deferred repayment of aggregated rebates to buyers. (This combination will be referred to as an aggregated rebate scheme.) The rebate provisions are of the kind which the Monopolies Commission found to be most usual in practice:[6] the amount of rebate earned by any buyer is calculated from his total purchases from members of the group during a given period, the rebate period. A sliding scale with several rates of rebate is employed, the rate rising step by step with the buyer's total purchases. The rebate, at the highest rate on the scale reached by the buyer, is applied to all his purchases from the group. It is assumed further – and this appears to be the case in practice – that differences in the rates of rebate allowed on different aggregates of purchases exceed any corresponding differential savings in cost to the individual sellers in the group. It is also assumed that there is a competing independent seller (or number of sellers) outside

Restrictive Trade Practices Act, 1956, and are adjudicated by the Restrictive Practices Court. An aggregated rebate scheme operated by a dominant supplier is much the same in its effects as a scheme operated by a group of suppliers; it is likely to be more effective in that there is no need to reconcile different interests. The analysis in this paper applies *mutatis mutandis* to a dominant firm's aggregated rebate scheme. The activities of dominant firms are subject to investigation by the Monopolies Commission on reference by the Board of Trade.

[6] *Collective Discrimination*, para. 192. The report discusses variants, which are not considered in this paper.

the group, and that members of the group do not have cost advantages in respect of the production and sale of those comparable products supplied both by themselves and by their independent competitor(s).

2

Two aspects of aggregated rebate schemes call for preliminary consideration; neither is specifically discussed in relation to independent competition in the reports of the Monopolies Commission, though both have some bearing on independent competition.

First, sales by members of the group to buyers earning different rates of rebate yield different rates of profit per unit. Sales to the smaller buyers (smaller in the total of their purchases from the group) are more profitable than those to the larger. This differential profitability may weaken the cohesion of the group, and tempt members into deviations from the agreed prices, particularly when capacity is not fully used. When capacity is strained, on the other hand, sellers may give special preference to the more profitable sales to the smaller buyers unless the agreed prices are raised sufficiently to avoid the rationing of supplies, or larger buyers may have to offer additions to the agreement prices. It is more important for present purposes, however, that, other things being equal, the smaller buyers, who are discriminated against in the aggregated rebate scheme of the group, are likely to be willing customers of independent suppliers as well as being the relatively more profitable customers. To this extent an aggregated rebate scheme has a weakness, as a device for restraining the activities of independent competitors.

The second point concerns the bargaining power of large buyers. It is sometimes said that an aggregated rebate scheme (with larger rebates for larger aggregated purchases) is a necessary concession given under pressure to the large buyers. This explanation was noted by the Monopolies Commission in three reports;[7] the commission did not, however, pronounce on its validity or explain why the concessions had been considered necessary. Two types of situation may be distinguished. First, without concessions to the large buyers, they might individually use the offer of large and regular orders to cause individual sellers in the group to subvert the structure of agreed prices; the concession of specially favourable rebates is then

[7] *Pneumatic Tyres*, para. 532; *Hard Fibre Cordage*, para. 293; *Linoleum*, para. 213.

the sacrifice made to secure the cohesion of the group of sellers. It is not likely, however, that the net prices (i.e. agreed prices less rebates) charged to the big buyers would be lower than those which would obtain in the absence of any effective agreement among the group. Hence, in so far as a particular aggregated rebate scheme merely represents an organised concession to large buyers, the scheme cannot be considered as an obstacle to independent competitors.

The second type of situation is where the large buyers enjoy a strong bargaining position because they are (or are believed to be) in a position to become their own suppliers of the product(s) in question, and thus also possibly to become rival suppliers to other buyers as well. An aggregated rebate scheme can have the effect of forestalling the establishment of new capacity by the backward integration of former buyers; but it can do this only if the net prices charged to these buyers are lower than they would be otherwise. This could come about where, in the absence of any agreement, individual sellers would not take into account the effect of their prices on the long-term possibility that large buyers might be provoked into backward integration, and where, also, a high degree of oligopolistic interdependence among *all* sellers would set a floor to prices above the long-run average costs of production even with the presence in the market of some large buyers. The aggregated rebate scheme then permits the group of sellers to make a collective sacrifice of short-term profits on their sales to large buyers in order to obtain greater long-term benefits. To the extent that this strategy succeeds, it works to the advantage of independent competitors as well as to that of the group. In short, in both types of situation the recognition of the bargaining power of certain buyers does not react adversely on independent competitors.

Assuming that the sole purpose of the group arrangements is to allow for the varying bargaining strength of different categories of buyer, it should be apparent that generally the only effective substitute for an aggregated rebate scheme would be some other equally and obviously discriminatory system of pricing. But in those situations in which the specific requirements of the larger buyers (as to products or grades) differ significantly in composition from those of the smaller buyers, appropriate adjustment in product or grade price differentials may be a way of bestowing favours in the desired direction (e.g. special prices for special brands). In practice, however, the aggregated rebate scheme has greater flexibility and adaptability in such situations.

3

We begin now with the analysis of the restraining effect of aggregated rebate schemes on competition by taking a simple case, to which complicating features will be added subsequently. The simple situation is that of the supply of a standardised product (or group of standardised products) produced by all suppliers, group members as well as outsiders, where all sellers have equal access to all buyers at all times. It is assumed, further, that at the beginning of each rebate period all sellers and buyers have full knowledge of prices and rebate rates and conditions, and of the quantities to be bought by each buyer. Each independent seller can vary his prices as between different buyers, and can operate his own aggregated (or other) rebate system, with rates graded, if necessary, according to the total requirements (from all sources) of each buyer.

At the beginning of a rebate period a buyer will decide to be wholly loyal to the group if there is some advantage (or at least no disadvantage) in terms of his total outlay. Such loyalty is certain only where the buyer's total outlay (or average net price) is lower than it would be with alternative purchasing arrangements involving varying degrees of disloyalty, including complete disloyalty. And there is nothing in the assumed situation which precludes an independent supplier from matching the group's terms to any buyer. The complete exclusion of independent competitors from the entire market could be achieved only if the group were to quote net prices lower than those of the independents to all (size-) categories of buyers. Such price-and-rebate terms would in their effects be similar to a simple price agreement with fixed prices lower than those which the independent sellers are prepared to meet. The material difference is the discrimination in *net* prices among buyers; but since the independent sellers could practise the same kind of discrimination, the issue for public policy concerns the price discrimination *per se*, and not the effect of the scheme on independent competition. As the costs of the members of the group and the independents are assumed to be the same, the group could not undersell independents in respect of all categories of buyer except where it deliberately reduced its net prices to unremunerative levels to drive out the independents. But then it would be the temporary predatory price-cutting and not the rebate scheme as such which has the monopolising effect.

In principle the situation is not altered when we drop the assumption of perfect knowledge by those in the market. Sellers may not know what the total purchases of a particular buyer will be; and buyers themselves may be uncertain. Again, changes in prices during the rebate period may not be foreseeable. There is no reason, however, why such uncertainty should necessarily bias buyers in favour of greater loyalty to the group; this is so irrespective of the methods of pricing used by the independent seller(s).

4

The position is materially different when a rebate period is already under way and a buyer has been placing his orders solely (or predominantly) with members of the group. If he now should buy from an independent seller, to that extent he sacrifices the chance of earning a higher rate of rebate on *all* his purchases from the group; and to that extent the incentive to loyalty is strengthened. Expressed differently, the independent supplier has to quote a net price to the partly committed buyer which is lower than the net price quoted by the group.

Suppose the group's basic price for the product is £1 per ton, with a discount rate (applicable to all purchases) of 4 per cent on purchases up to 1,000 tons, and of 5 per cent on purchases over 1,000 tons in a rebate period. A particular buyer has already bought 1,000 tons from the group, and needs a further 100 tons for the rest of the period. Should he place the order with a member of the group, he qualifies for the higher rate of rebate. His total outlay increases from £960 (i.e. £1,000−£40) to £1,045 (i.e. £1,100−£55); the 'marginal price' to him of the 100 tons is £85. To induce him to be disloyal, an independent competitor has to quote a price no higher than £85. If this price is unremunerative to him, he is excluded. But is there any reason why it should be unremunerative to him, considering that the sale of the 100 tons by the member of the group adds only £85 to the total revenue of the members of the group? If the group is able to sell at this 'price', then, on our assumptions, should not the independent supplier also be able to do so without impairing his competitive position? The answer is, in principle, in the negative where the 'marginal' net prices charged by the group are below (avoidable) cost. Provided the average net price (here £95 per 100 tons) is remunerative, the aggregated rebate scheme, stipulating in effect both the price as well as the quantity to be bought, may have a pre-emptive effect in respect of the orders of the favoured and already partly committed buyers, adverse to the interests of independent competitors, without, however, involving the group in losses.[8]

There is nothing in the foregoing, however, to prevent the independent supplier from making similar or equivalent bargains with buyers at the beginning of each period. It is only within a rebate period that initial loyalty can be made to breed further loyalty. But in the situation postulated at the beginning of this section there is no inherent bias in the operation of this effect as between the group on the one hand, and the independent competitor(s) on the other.

It may be noted, in passing, that the intra-period tying effect of an aggregated rebate scheme cannot be achieved by a straightforward price agreement. It would obviously not do for the group deliberately to quote relatively high prices at the beginning of the period and then to reduce them progressively; neither will the reverse procedure do the job – in both cases the link between price and quantity is absent.

5

The effect considered in the preceding section is a short-run (intra-period) feature of all aggregated rebate schemes of the class discussed

[8] The strength of the intra-period tie depends partly on the details of the scheme itself and partly on the requirements of buyers. (This also applies to the possible longer-term tying effects in the situations which are considered in Section 6 et seq.) Thus in the particular example used in Section 4, a buyer with requirements of less than 1,000 tons a period is not in any way affected even when he has made his initial purchases from the group; in sales to him the gap between 'marginal price' and 'average price' never opens. Again, for a buyer with requirements in excess of 1,000 tons a period, the gap opens only once, at the 1,000 tons mark; once he has bought more than 1,000 tons from members of the group (having placed his initial orders with the group), there is no further incentive to loyalty. (Uncertainty as to whether a buyer will reach the 1,000 tons level may stimulate loyalty.) In other words, within the range of any rebate bracket, the scheme operates merely as a flat discount off the relevant purchases. It is not the level of the rebate, but changes in the level of the rebate, which have the special tying effect. The most pervasive tying effect is therefore achieved where the rebate rate rises continuously with the amount of aggregated purchases; in practice this means a scheme with numerous rebate brackets or steps, each covering a small range of purchase aggregates.

in this paper; but as has been shown, it does not necessarily operate adversely to independent competition either in the short run or in the long run. An aggregated rebate scheme serves as a *long-run* restraint on independent competition only in those situations in which, by virtue of existing limitations on the quantity and range of output of the independent sellers, buyers are obliged to buy part of their total requirements in each rebate period from members of the group. In such cases the buyers in question are already partly committed to the group before the rebate period begins. In effect, so long as the limitations are present, these buyers are always part of the way inside a rebate period; their initial loyalty to the group is compulsory; and a rebate scheme can be used, as before, to give the group an advantage over the independent firms in the competition for the uncommitted business of the buyers. Expressed differently, the group can offer to reduce prices on those purchases which will have to be made from its members, but on condition that other purchases are also made from them. The disability of the independent sellers can be overcome only by an extension of their capacity in quantity or range; the disability may itself render this extension more difficult.

It is apparent, then, that an aggregated rebate scheme can restrain or impede independent competition only when there is, from the point of view of buyers, a significant difference between the position of the group of suppliers and that of the independent suppliers, an asymmetrical situation which enables the former to have some hold over customers. The force of this restraint will differ from one situation to another. It will depend in part on the detailed provisions of the aggregated rebate scheme itself (see footnote 8). It will also depend on the nature and extent of differences in the requirements of the various buyers in the market for the product(s): what is a significant asymmetry for one particular buyer may not be the same for another. (This will be illustrated below.) Moreover, the duration of the restraint depends ultimately on the ease or difficulty with which the independent competitors are able so to extend their output as to remove the asymmetry.

In what follows no attempt is made to list all conceivable types of asymmetry. Instead, two pairs of situations are considered, the first pair concerning the supply of a standardised product, the second the supply of a range of products including non-standardised products.

405

6

Consider again the supply of a standardised product. The independent supplier(s) cannot, it is now assumed, supply the product regularly at all times during the rebate period, and storage costs are particularly high. Sporadic imports of a relatively perishable or bulky low-value product may provide an example. Here the independent supplier cannot supply a regular user's requirements for the whole rebate period, whereas the members of the group can do so. The buyer who requires regular supplies is therefore partly committed to the group. (A somewhat analogous situation is where the costs of transporting the commodity are relatively high, where the individual's requirements are spread over a large area, and where the supply outlets of the independent supplier(s) are geographically more concentrated than those of the group.)

In principle, the asymmetry which gives rise to the tying effect of an aggregated rebate scheme in the postulated circumstances can also be used in a simple price agreement with similar effect.[9] When the irregular supplier is absent, the group can raise its price; the monopoly profits can be used to 'subsidise' the price when irregular supplies become available, so that these supplies are discouraged.

Consider, once more, the supply of a standardised product. The output of the independent supplier(s) is now assumed to be too small to meet the full periodic requirements of large buyers. Such buyers are necessarily partly committed to the group, and the tying effects of an aggregated rebate scheme follow in respect of these buyers.[10] In this case, however, the asymmetry is such that it cannot be exploited to like effect by a simple pricing agreement without a rebate scheme. Moreover, even special discounts to the large buyers, not linked to quantities bought from the group, would not serve the purpose.[11]

[9] The two methods are likely to have different effects on the revenues of the various members of the group. This aspect is considered more fully in another but analogous context, below.

[10] In this case small buyers, whose total requirements could be supplied by the independent supplier(s), would not recognise the asymmetry in the two sources of supply, and would not be tied.

[11] The group could, of course, require such buyers to make lump sum payments for the privilege of buying from the group (the amount of such payments depending upon the amount of a buyer's necessary purchases from the group) and use the proceeds to reduce the firm price (i.e. not subject to rebate) of the product.

7

We turn now to a situation where the members of the group supply a wider range of products than the independent competitor(s) and where there are no good substitutes for some of the products supplied by the group. The simplest case for exposition is where all sellers can supply standard lines but where some or all of the members of the group supply patented or otherwise exclusive products as well. Buyers are thus obliged to buy the particular exclusive lines they require from members of the group, whereas they can also patronise the independent suppliers for the standard lines.

The asymmetry is obvious, and an aggregated rebate scheme operated by the group can have an adverse effect on the independent competitors. Differences in the requirements of the two categories of lines by different buyers again weaken the tying effect, and in the limiting case, a buyer in the market for standard lines alone is not tied at all. But it is also obvious that the tying effect of the rebate scheme derives from the group's monopoly of the exclusive lines, and persists only so long as the monopoly persists. It follows that the group could, in principle, erect obstacles to the advance of independent competitors without a rebate scheme. It could price the exclusive lines to yield the highest monopoly profits, and use the proceeds to set the prices of the standard lines at levels low enough to deter independent competition. It is the element of monopoly, and not the particular practice, which provides the leverage in the postulated situation.

The members of the group will not necessarily be indifferent as between an aggregated rebate scheme and a pricing system as outlined in the preceding paragraph. The total revenue accruing to the group may be affected by the method adopted, applied so as to achieve a given degree of deterrent effect. (It seems impossible to say *a priori* whether an aggregated rebate scheme is more or less 'economical' to its practitioners than an alternative method.) Moreover, even where the total revenue is not affected, its division among the members of the group may well differ. Prima facie, in one respect at least, the aggregated rebate scheme gives greater flexibility in arranging the division of the total profits.[12] This is so because,

---

[12] There is always an arbitrary element in the distribution of profits among members of a group operating an aggregated rebate scheme, since the individual member's revenues depend upon the categories of buyer to whom he sells – and he cannot be sure in what rebate-category a particular buyer will fall.

within limits, the prices of individual lines within the range can be varied without altering the deterrent effect; the buyer is interested in the total outlay on a range of lines, and not in the itemised composition of the outlay. Thus the base prices of standard lines could, for example, be set rather high if the group wished to ensure the adherence of members producing only (or mainly) the standard lines. The limits to this flexibility are set by differences in the composition of the requirements of different buyers.

With the alternative method of straight prices this flexibility is lost, because then the particular prices of individual lines matter to the buyer, and have to be set by the group in the light of the absence or presence of competition. Assistance can be given to the members who concentrate on standard lines only by having, in addition, some sort of profit-sharing arrangement within the group.

The second situation with a range of heterogeneous products is more complicated (and more far-fetched) than the first considered in this section. A certain product is produced in a variety of designs. New designs are prepared and offered annually to retailer-buyers, each of whom wants a certain number of new designs to sell in his shop. The final demand for the various designs is largely unpredictable. The manufacturers announce the prices of their designs at the beginning of the year. Each manufacturer sets the same price on all his designs, since the costs of production are the same and there is no reason to believe that one particular design will sell better or worse than the others. The members of the group agree on this uniform price and on the rates of rebate. The prices of designs are not altered during the year. A buyer who does not place an introductory order for a particular design at the beginning of the year is not supplied with that design later in the year.

Assume now that there are three suppliers, *A*, *B*, and *C*, each producing six designs a year. A certain retailer requires ten new designs a year. In the circumstances he must buy at least four designs from *A* and *B* to make up a full range. If *A* and *B* organise an aggregated rebate scheme, the necessary asymmetry is present to produce some tying effect on the retailer, and *C*'s competitive disadvantage is apparent. As before, however, the tying effects of the scheme are weakened by differences in the requirements of buyers; for example, *C*'s disadvantage as against *A* and *B* is reduced in respect of buyers who need fewer designs.

The present situation differs from that previously discussed in that the deterrent effect of the rebate scheme cannot be duplicated in a simple price agreement with different prices for different lines. *Ex hypothesi* the sellers have no means of picking the winners, and hence of pricing the successes so as to produce profits with which to subsidise the prices of the less successful. The aggregated rebate scheme, on the other hand, achieves this result. This case is therefore similar to the second case of a standardised product considered in Section 6; the similarity lies in the fact that in both cases it is not possible to identify *ex ante* those particular sales in respect of which the group has a valuable 'monopoly' power.[13]

8

We return, in conclusion, to the reports of the Monopolies Commission. The discussions of aggregated rebate schemes may be criticised not for the conclusions on the restraining effects of such schemes, though an aggregated rebate scheme need not necessarily have these effects, but for the absence of explanation of the asymmetry (between the positions of the group and the independents vis-à-vis buyers) which made it possible for the mechanism to be employed in a particular situation. The reports on particular industries do not contain sufficient data to enable the reader to infer the nature of the operative asymmetry, nor to assess the strength of the restraint which, as has been shown, depends in part on differences in the situations of different buyers.

Addendum

Until the end of 1956 the Monopolies Commission was the body which investigated whether collective restrictive agreements in industry and trade were or were not against the public interest. In six of its investigations into restrictive agreements in individual industries it encountered collective aggregated rebate schemes. (For list and references, see footnote 2, above.) In all these cases, except *Pneumatic Tyres*, the commission reported that the rebate scheme was against the public interest. In each of the relevant reports the adverse effect on independent competitors was mentioned as a reason why the scheme was against the public interest. (In *Electric Lamps* the scheme was criticised additionally because of the waste of manpower involved

[13] Again, the group could take advantage of the width of the range of its products by requiring lump-sum payments from buyers who must have recourse to it.

409

in the working of the elaborate statistical and accounting 'machinery'; and in *Linoleum* the points were made also that the scheme unduly restricted competition among the member-firms in the association working the scheme and that it discriminated without cost-justification among customers.)

Pneumatic Tyres provides the exception in that the commission did not condemn the aggregate rebate scheme for the supply by firms in the industry of giant tyres to nine large commercial-vehicle manufacturers. The commission reported, *inter alia*: 'No question arises of these rebates having a tendency to defeat outside competition since there are no United Kingdom tyre manufacturers outside the TMC [Tyre Manufacturers' Conference Ltd]. These arrangements . . . appear to be largely the result of pressure from the vehicle manufacturers concerned.' The report does not refer to the possible effects of the scheme on potential entrants into the United Kingdom market or on foreign suppliers. This apparent omission was not repeated in the *Hard Fibre Cordage* report published a few months later: 'This consideration [that the scheme hampers an independent manufacturer in the marketing of his goods] is not weakened by the circumstance that there are at present no independent manufacturers in this industry; we do not see why a newcomer, if there were one, should be forced to join the federation or existing members be deterred from leaving it.'

The commission has not encountered aggregated rebate systems practised independently by single firms in dominant market positions – a category of cases which since 1957 forms a large part of its activities.

Since 1957, as has been noted above, the Restrictive Practices Court has been entrusted with the task of adjudicating collective agreements in restraint of competition. No collective aggregated rebate scheme has yet been declared by the court to be not against the public interest. In three cases in which the main (horizontal) price agreement was held to be not against the public interest, the associated aggregated rebate scheme was struck down. In *Black Bolts and Nuts* the court said of the scheme: 'This is really no more than a sop to the large buyer and an inducement to him to restrict his purchases to members of the association.'[14]

In *Cement* the court found that the scheme created 'a privileged

<hr>

[14] *Re Black Bolt and Nut Association's Agreement* (1960), L.R. 2 R.P. 50, at p. 97.

class of purchaser', had no 'economic justification' in terms of differences in the costs of supply, and that it had 'the positive disadvantage of discouraging the purchasers from buying cement from non-members of the federation, thus making it more difficult for a member to resign from the federation or for a new manufacturer to enter the industry without joining the federation.'[15] In *Permanent Magnets* the court had to assess an aggregated rebate scheme which had had little publicity among buyers until the hearings. It had been introduced by the sellers because of the saving in costs consequent upon large orders, 'and it took its present form because some large buyers prefer to put in a number of repeat orders and most prefer to obtain their supplies from more than one manufacturer . . .'. The court decided, however, that 'as the result of the publicity attaching to this case' the rebate scheme 'now has some of the objectionable features of such a [loyalty] rebate'. As it was not reasonably required in connection with the main price agreement, the court declared the scheme to be against the public interest.[16]

[15] *Re Cement Makers' Federation* (1961), L.R. 2 R.P. 241, at p. 289. The treatment of the scheme in the judgment is analysed in R. B. Stevens and B. S. Yamey, *The Restrictive Practices Court*, 1965, pp. 208–11.

[16] *Re Permanent Magnet Association's Agreement* (1962), L.R. 3 R.P. 119, at p. 172.

Index

INDEX

417